Corporate Human Rights Obligations: in Search of Accountability

Nicola M.C.P. Jägers

INTERSENTIA
Antwerpen – Oxford – New York

This Volume is an adapted version of a dissertation defended at Utrecht University on 2 October 2002.

Nicola M.C.P. Jägers
Corporate Human Rights Obligations: in Search of Accountability

CRC prepared by: G.J. Wiarda Institute, Utrecht University Institute for Legal Studies, Boothstraat 6, 3512 BW Utrecht

ISBN 90-5095-240-2
D/2002/7849/35
NUR 828

Corporate Human Rights Obligations: in Search of Accountability

To my parents Maryon and Theo Jägers

School of Human Rights Research Series, Volume 17

The titles published in this series are listed at the end of this volume.

ACKNOWLEDGEMENTS

'Business needs human rights and human rights need business.' This was put forward by Mary Robinson, the High Commissioner for Human Rights in 1998 and the idea seems to be gaining ground. The topic of corporate responsibility for human rights has received mounting attention from many different sides, including the business community, since I started my research four years ago. It would seem that a process has started that cannot be reversed. I hope that this book will contribute to the ongoing debate in this evolving field of international law.

During the course of my research I have met many interesting people that were willing to give me their time and share their thoughts with me. I have greatly benefited from their insights in the subject. Several people I would like to mention specifically, as they have been indispensable for this project. Foremost, my supervisor Professor Fried van Hoof to who I owe a great deal. His ever lucid comments and support were of fundamental importance for this dissertation. I am indebted also to Professor Willem van Genugten for his willingness to become involved in the project. His suggested improvements were invaluable. My appreciation furthermore goes to Professor Peter Baehr, Professor Andrew Clapham, Professor Adriaan Dorrestijn, Professor Cees Flinterman, and Dr. Ian Seiderman for their willingness to read and comment on the final manuscript. In the preparation of the book for publication I was assisted by Peter Morris, who scrupulously corrected my English, and by Irnsje Veerman and Willemien Vreekamp who most efficiently generated the layout of the book. I thank them for their contributions. I am particularly pleased that I was able to conduct this research at the Netherlands Institute of Human Rights (SIM) which has proven to be a friendly and stimulating environment. My colleagues have been indispensable during the often solitary work. My thanks especially goes to Saskia Bal for her help in tracking down books and for the invaluable information in the SIM databases. I am also indebted to Maeycken Hoeneveld for taking care of the paperwork and removing other potential obstacles. Special thanks go to Yvonne Donders and Manon van Dooren and not only for agreeing to be my *paranymfs.*

I owe a particular debt of gratitude to three people who have patiently stood by me through the trials and tribulations of writing this dissertation. First and foremost, Conrad who has unconditionally supported me in this endeavor and has made sure that I never lost sight of more important things in life. And, finally, my parents who time and time again have been able to induce me to believe that nothing is impossible and for that I would like to dedicate this book to them.

TABLE OF CONTENTS

PART B
AVENUES FOR ENFORCEMENT AND IMPLEMENTATION

Abbreviations and Acronyms

AC	Appeal Cases (Law Reports, UK)
ACHPR	African Charter on Human and Peoples' Rights
ACHR	American Convention on Human Rights
All ER	All England Law Reports
ATCA	Alien Tort Claims Act
CEDAW	Convention on the Elimination of All Forms of Discrimination Against Women
CERD	Convention on the Elimination of All Forms of Racial Discrimination
CIME	Committee on Investment and Multinational Enterprises (OECD)
CLC	Commercial Law Cases
ECHR	European Convention on Human Rights
ECrtHR	European Court of Human Rights
EcomHR	European Commission on Human Rights
ESC	European Social Charter
EU	European Union
F. 2d	Federal Reporter (second series) (USA, Courts of Appeals)
F. 3d	Federal Reporter (third series) (USA, Courts of Appeals)
FDI	Foreign Direct Investment
F. Supp.	Federal Supplement (USA, Federal District Courts)
GA	General Assembly (UN)
GAOR	General Assembly Official Records
GATT	General Agreement on Tariffs and Trade
HRC	Human Rights Committee
IACHR	Inter-American Court of Human Rights
IAComHR	Inter-American Commission on Human Rights
ICC	International Criminal Court
ICCPR	International Covenant on Civil and Political Rights
ICESCR	International Covenant on Economic, Social and Cultural Rights
ICSID	International Centre for the Settlement of Investment Disputes
ICJ	International Court of Justice
ICJ Rep.	International Court of Justice Reports
IcomJ	International Commission of Jurists
ICSID	International Centre for the Settlement of Investment Disputes

ICTR	International Criminal Tribunal for Rwanda
ICTY	International Criminal Tribunal for the former Yugoslavia
ILC	International Law Commission
ILM	International Legal Materials
ILO	International Labour Organisation
IMT	International Military Tribunal
Lloyds Rep.	Lloyd's Law Reports (UK)
MAI	Multilateral Agreement on Investments
MNCs	Multinational Corporations
MNEs	Multinational Enterprises
NAALC	North American Agreement on Labor Cooperation
NAFTA	North American Free Trade Agreement
NIEO	New International Economic Order
NGO	Non Governmental Organisation
OAS	Organisation of American States
OAU	Organisation of African Unity
OECD	Organisation for Economic Cooperation and Development
PCIJ	Permanent Court of International Justice
TLR	Times Law Reports (UK)
TNCs	Transnational Enterprises
UDHR	Universal Declaration of Human Rights
UN	United Nations
UNCC	United Nations Compensation Commission
UNCLOS	United Nations Convention on the Law of the Sea
UNCTAD	United Nations Conference on Trade and Development
UNCTC	United Nations Commission on Transnational Corporations
UNRIAA	United Nations, Reports of International Arbitrary Awards
UNTS	United Nations Treaty Series
UK	United Kingdom
USA	United States of America
US	United States
U.S.	United States Supreme Court Reports
VCLT	Vienna Convention on the Law of Treaties
V.R.	Victorian Reports
WHO	World Health Organisation
WIR	World Investment Report
WLR	Weekly Law Reports (UK)
WTO	World Trade Organisation
YBILC	Yearbook of the International Law Commission

CHAPTER I
GENERAL INTRODUCTION

1 INTRODUCTION

Present-day international relations have undergone far-reaching changes since the Universal Declaration of Human Rights (UDHR) was adopted over fifty years ago. As a result of scientific, economic, political and cultural developments new actors have gained a considerable influence on the international plane. Non-governmental organisations, international financial institutions and (multinational) corporations now play a substantial role in various areas previously considered to fall within the exclusive domain of thc State. The often used but rather opaque term 'globalisation' refers to these developments. This term encompasses many different processes. It refers primarily to the progressive elimination of barriers facilitating the free flow of capital, information, labour and goods and increasing interdependence between States.

A study of the obligations and the accountability of corporations for human rights violations presupposes that these entities have an impact on the enjoyment of human rights. As will be described in the following section, globalisation has contributed to the increased influence of corporations in general, and to their effect on human rights in particular. In section 2 of this introduction I will attempt to set the stage for this study by discussing those developments labelled as globalisation. Some introductory remarks will be made on what is actually meant by this rather fashionable term. The consequences of the globalisation processes for the protection and promotion of human rights will be discussed. The role of the main actors in the processes will be examined. It is concluded that globalisation presents a challenge to international human rights law to respond to new powerful actors on the international scene. The objective of this study is to answer the questions that arise in this respect with regard to corporations. Sections 3, 4 and 5 will set out the aim and structure of the present research.

2 GLOBALISATION

After World War II an international system aimed at the protection and promotion of human rights started to develop. Based on the realisation that atrocities such as those committed during this war should never be allowed to occur again, a whole series of treaties, conventions and declarations were drawn up in the international and regional context. The first step taken was the adoption by the United Nations General Assembly of the Universal Declaration of Human Rights (UDHR) in 1948.[1] This was followed by the adoption of two legally binding documents in 1966: the International Covenant on Civil and Political Rights (ICCPR) and the International Covenant on Economic, Social and Cultural Rights (ICESCR).[2] This proved to be the impetus for the drafting of numerous human rights conventions within the United Nations. To name but a few: the Convention on the Elimination of All Forms of Discrimination against Women,[3] the Convention against Torture and Other Cruel, Inhuman or Degrading Treatment or Punishment[4] and the Convention on the Rights of the Child.[5] Human rights instruments were also developed at the regional level, such as: the European Convention for the Protection of Human Rights and Fundamental Freedoms,[6] the American Convention on Human Rights[7] and the African Charter on Human Rights and Peoples' Rights.[8]

The international machinery aimed at enhancing the observance and protection of human rights has continued to rapidly expand and has obtained increasing authority. Human rights have become a permanent part of the international political agenda. The decision to establish the post of United Nations High Commissioner for Human Rights in 1993 can be seen as evidence of the increased importance given to human rights issues.[9]

The attention to the promotion and protection of human rights in the post World War II era was paralleled by a number of other developments. These developments, taken together, are currently often referred to as globalisation. This phrase is widely used and is the subject of a great deal of confusion.[10] It is mostly associated with the

---

1 Adopted and proclaimed by General Assembly resolution 217 A (III) of 10 December 1948.

2 Adopted and opened for signature, ratification and accession by General Assembly resolution 2200 A (XXI) of 16 December 1966.

3 Adopted and opened for signature, ratification and accession by General Assembly resolution 34/180 of 18 December 1979.

4 Adopted and opened for signature, ratification and accession by General Assembly resolution 39/46 of 10 December 1984.

5 Adopted and opened for signature, ratification and accession by General Assembly resolution 44/25 of 20 November 1989.

6 Signed in Rome on 4 November 1950; entered into force on 3 September 1953.

7 Signed in San Jose on 22 November 1969; entered into force on 18 July 1978.

8 Adopted by the 18th Assembly of the Heads of State and Government of the OAU on 27 June 1981 in Nairobi.

9 The creation of this post was recommended in the Vienna Declaration and Programme of Action. UN Doc. A/Conf.157/23. It was adopted by General Assembly resolution 48/141 on 20 December 1993.

10 Many scholars have addressed the issue of globalisation. There is an abundant amount of literature on the topic. For literature regarding globalisation and human rights see, *inter alia*,: Robert McCorquodale and Richard Fairbrother, 'Globalization and Human Rights', in: *Human Rights Quarterly*, Vol. 21, 1999, pp. 735-766, Jeffrey L. Dunoff, 'Does globalisation advance human rights?', in: *Brooklyn Journal of International Law*, Vol. XXV, No. 1, 1999, pp. 125-139, Jack Donnelly, 'Human Rights, Globalisation, and the State', in: *The Role of the Nation-State in the 21st Century: human rights, international organisations and foreign policy: essays in honour of Peter Baehr*, Monique Castermans, Fried van Hoof and Jacqueline Smith [eds.], 1998, pp. 401-410, Kamal Hossain, 'Globalisation

rapid expansion of trade and capital across national boundaries in the period after World War II. But globalisation has a multifaceted nature. It entails much wider and more complex processes involving virtually every aspect of life. The term globalisation not only refers to the tremendous expansion of international flows of trade and finance as a result of the liberalisation and deregulation of national and international markets, but also to the global expansion of communication flowing from technological innovations. These innovations, such as communication satellites and the creation of the information highway, facilitate the global exchange of information. Together with technological advances in transportation, these developments have turned the world into what is often called a 'global village'. Besides the economic and technological dimensions of globalisation, a third political dimension can be distinguished. This refers to the growing institutional framework of international organisations such as, for example, the World Trade Organisation (WTO). The co-operation between States and large corporations in such institutions has been referred to as 'globalisation from above'. This is countered by 'globalisation from below' which refers to the building of a critical civil society.[11] Finally, as has been described above, there has been a vast expansion of human rights instruments and institutions aimed at the promotion and protection of human rights around the globe. This can be seen as another dimension of globalisation; the globalisation of justice.

The processes of globalisation have accelerated with the end of the Cold War. Several developments contributed to the economic dimension of globalisation. The collapse of communism in 1989 provided immense opportunities for corporations from the Western States to expand their trade and increase their profits. The market mechanism has been embraced on a worldwide scale. Another significant development further propelling the processes of globalisation is the trend that can be detected at the national level during the last two decades of the twentieth century towards deregulation and less restrictive measures governing foreign direct investment.[12] This has led to a significant increase in foreign direct investment surpassing 1.3 trillion dollars in 2001.[13] Moreover, there has been a proliferation of bilateral investment treaties and

and the Promotion of Human Rights', in: *Reflections on International Law from the Low Countries,* Erik Denters and Nico Schrijver [eds.], Martinus Nijhoff, The Hague, 1998, pp. 101-115.

11 UN Doc. E/CN.4/Sub.2/2000/13, 15 June 2000, paras. 8-9 and McCorquodale and Fairbrother, *supra* n. 10, pp. 735-766 at p. 739 (quoting Richard Falk).

12 John M. Kline, 'International regulation of transnational business: providing the missing leg of global investment standards', *Transnational corporations*, Vol. 2, no. 1, February, 1993, pp. 153-164. The United Nations Conference on Trade and Development (UNCTAD) defines foreign direct investment as 'an investment involving management control of a resident entity in an economy by an enterprise resident in another country. Foreign direct investment involves a long-term relationship reflecting an investor's lasting interest in a foreign entity'.

13 In 1982 foreign direct investment amounted to $ 57 billion. UNCTAD, *World Investment Report 2001: Promoting Linkages*, United Nations, New York and Geneva, 2001. Available at: http://www.unctad.org/wir/contents/wir01content.en.htm (accessed on 8 January 2002).

multilateral treaties intending to remove trade barriers. There is a growing clamour for international regulation to facilitate trade. In the context of the General Agreement on Tariffs and Trade (GATT), the WTO and the Organisation for Economic Co-operation and Development (OECD), States have concluded, or are in the process of concluding, several multilateral treaties to assure further economic liberalisation. An example is the (so far unsuccessful) attempt to attain a Multilateral Agreement on Investment (MAI) within the framework of the OECD. The aim of this agreement is to ensure a level playing field for foreign direct investment by removing trade barriers and by demanding national treatment for foreign investors.[14] Furthermore, several regional free trade organisations have been created such as the European Union (EU), the North American Free Trade Agreement (NAFTA) and the Association of South East Asian Nations (ASEAN). These organisations are creating a so-called 'layered governance' in the global economy. These multilateral institutions indicate the trend away from State dominance.

It should be pointed out that globalisation is not a new phenomenon. International trading has existed for centuries. It can be argued that the current developments differ in scope and speed, however. Globalisation involves new and more markets, international rules, tools of communication and new actors.[15] Several entities have emerged as major forces in the processes of globalisation.

Firstly, States play a large role in the process of globalisation. Their endeavours (motivated for the large part by the fact that governments are often active partners of multinational corporations) to remove trade barriers and promote free trade, contribute to this ongoing process. At the same time, the processes of globalisation are also restricting the regulatory power of States. Functions of the State are being taken over by international organisations, such as the United Nations. Moreover, due to increasing privatisation, the traditional functions of the State are now also being conducted by private entities. However, the fear that States will lose international regulatory control must not be exaggerated. Corporations remain dependent on national and international regulation that can only be effectively drawn up by States.[16]

---

14 The MAI was intended to be finalised in the course of 1996. However, in 1998 the efforts within the OECD were abandoned partly as a result of concerns raised regarding the possible negative social consequences of this treaty. It was argued that the draft MAI fundamentally conflicted with the goals and objectives of current international human rights law and environmental law. The fear was that the emphasis in the MAI on national treatment would seriously restrict a State's ability to draw up national legislation aimed at protecting vulnerable individuals and the environment as the draft MAI provided for a dispute settlement procedure granting jurisdiction to investors to challenge national laws.

15 United Nations Development Programme, *Human Development Report 1999, Globalization with a Human Face*, Oxford University Press, Oxford/New York, 1999, Box 1.1.

16 Peter Malanczuk, 'Globalization and the future role of sovereign states', in: *International Economic Law with a Human Face*, Friedl Weiss, Erik Denters and Paul de Waart [eds.], Kluwer Law International, The Hague etc., 1998, pp. 45-65.

Secondly, the international financial institutions, such as the International Monetary Fund (IMF) and the World Bank, have been called the 'institutional mechanisms of globalisation'.[17] Both institutions were established at the Bretton Woods Conference in the United States in 1944. The World Bank was given the task of assisting in the reconstruction of Europe and, subsequently, to encourage production in less-developed countries. The IMF was established in order to assist in solving balance of payment problems. The importance of both institutions has considerably grown during the last few decades. The IMF has acquired an additional role as the guarantor of the private international financial system. It can be stated that the IMF and the World Bank have played a dominant role in shaping the essential characteristics of the global economy.[18]

Thirdly, Non-Governmental Organisations (NGOs) play an important role in the processes of globalisation. An increasing number of these groups are organised across national borders. The total number of NGOs rose from 23,600 in 1991 to almost 44,000 in 1999.[19] A survey has identified at least 325 organisations that can be considered international human rights NGOs.[20] Most of these NGOs have been established within the last few decades. Especially the great advances made in the field of global communication have increased the power of NGOs. The tasks and the possibilities for NGOs to act as investigative and warning systems for the protection of human rights have been greatly enhanced with, for example, the development of the Internet. NGOs are often established to mitigate the negative effects of the globalisation process.

Finally, the subjects of this research, corporations involved in international trading, are major actors in the processes of globalisation. The transnational activities of privately organised companies are not a twentieth century phenomenon, however. In the seventeenth century the Dutch East India Company, for example, operated on a transnational scale. However, this corporation limited its operations to trade between Europe and Asia. Today's corporations differ from those of the seventeenth century regarding the complexity of their businesses and the internationalisation of their production. The number of multinational corporations in the world has jumped from 7,000 in 1970 to more than 60,000 with over 800,000 foreign affiliates in 2001. In 1999 the top 100 corporations, ranked by foreign assets, had sales totalling $ 4

17 UN Doc. E/CN.4/Sub.2/2000/13, 15 June 2000, para. 24.

18 UN Doc. E/CN.4/Sub.2/2000/13, 15 June 2000, para. 20.

19 United Nations Development Programme, *Human Rights Development Report 2000: Human Rights and Human Development*, Oxford University Press, Oxford/New York, 2000, pp. 79-80.

20 This survey only looks at the NGOs that operate across national borders. Most of these NGOs are based in Western Europe and North America. The Middle East and Eastern Europe are the least represented regions. Jackie Smith and Ron Pagnucco with George A. Lopez, 'Globalizing Human Rights: The Work of Transnational Human Rights NGOs in the 1990s', in: *Human Rights Quarterly*, Vol. 20, 1998, pp. 379-412 at p. 383.

trillion.[21] Ninety percent of the top 100 corporations are based in the so-called Triad countries (European Union, Japan and United States), while only three corporations on this list are from developing States.[22] Of the 100 largest concentrations of wealth in the world, 51 per cent are owned by global corporations and only 49 per cent by States. *Mitsubishi's* trade volume is greater that the gross national product of Indonesia, *Ford's* trade totals more that South Africa's gross national product and *Royal Dutch Shell's* income is more than Norway's.[23] These figures illustrate the immense power which multinational corporations have acquired.

3 Globalisation and Human Rights

The effect of globalisation on the enjoyment of human rights has come under increased scrutiny. On the one hand, it is argued that the processes of globalisation can have many positive effects on human rights. Globalisation can be considered as the framework of economic growth and social progress. The enhancement of free trade, on the whole, can be beneficial to all the countries involved. Economic growth may increase the resources available for the realisation of human rights. Based on quantitative, empirical research into the relationship between levels of foreign direct investment and human rights, Meyer comes to the conclusion that the main actors in the processes of globalisation – multinational corporations – have a positive impact on the enjoyment of economic and social rights and an indirect positive influence on civil and political rights.[24] Moreover, it can be argued that political and legal globalisation processes have many positive effects on the protection and the promotion of human rights.

On the other hand, as can be deduced from the Human Development Reports of the United Nations Development Program (UNDP), globalisation also has many adverse effects on the enjoyment of human rights. It has become clear that economic growth does not automatically lead to a better protection and promotion of human rights. The

21 UNCTAD, *World Investment Report: Promoting Linkages*, United Nations, New York and Geneva, 2001. Available at: http://www.unctad.org/wir/contents/wir01content.en.htm (accessed on 8 January 2002) and UNCTAD, *World Investment Report 2000 Cross-border Mergers and Acquisitions and Development*, United Nations, New York and Geneva, 2000. Available at: http://www.unctad.org/wir/contents/wir00content.en.htm (accessed on 8 January 2002).

22 These three corporations are *Hutchison Whampoa, Petróleos de Venezuela* and *Cemex*, UNCTAD, *World Investment Report 2001: Promoting Linkages*, United Nations, New York and Geneva, 2001. Available at: http://www.unctad.org/wir/contents/wir01content.en.htm (accessed on 8 January 2002).

23 UN Doc. E/CN.4/Sub.2/1998/6, 10 June 1998, para. 7.

24 Meyer compares the so-called Engines of Development Theory, according to which multinational corporations have a positive influence on human rights, with the Hymer Thesis, which claims that multinational corporations directly contribute to violations of human rights. William H. Meyer, 'Human Rights and MNCs: Theory Versus Quantative Analysis', in: *Human Rights Quarterly*, Vol. 2, 1996, pp. 368-397 and William Meyer, *Human Rights and International Political Economy in Third World Nations: Multinational Corporations, Foreign Aid, and Repression*, Westport, Connecticut, 1998. Several scholars have rejected the conclusions drawn by Meyer, however. They claim that the

Human Development Report of 1999 entitled *Globalization with a Human Face* brings the tremendous inequities generated by (in particular economic) globalisation to light.[25] According to the UNDP the economic gains have greatly benefited a few countries at the expense of many others. Globalisation is increasing the gap between the North and the South as most of the major actors in the process originate from the North. The Human Development Report 2000 noted that, in 1998, the least developed countries, with 10 per cent of the world population, accounted for only 0.4 per cent of global exports, representing a consistent descent from 0.6 per cent in 1980 and 0.5 per cent in 1990.[26] The processes of globalisation have also reinforced inequalities within the North, in the countries that are supposed to be the main beneficiaries of globalisation. The countries in the North increasingly depend on migrant workers to sustain their economies yet this has not always produced benefits for these migrant workers. For example, in the European Union the drive towards one single market has increased the mobility of the workers of its member States which has resulted in increasing restrictions for migrant workers.[27]

Besides the UNDP, other organs of the United Nations are increasingly paying attention to the issue of the negative consequences of globalisation on human rights.[28] The Secretary-General of the United Nations, Kofi Annan, has repeatedly articulated the need to recognise the fact that, besides the possibilities of globalisation to improve human life, the process also threatens human security.[29]

Several elements can be distinguished that contribute to the adverse consequences of globalisation on human rights. The activities of the international financial institutions

quantitative analysis based solely on the relationship between direct foreign investment and human rights is too simplistic and additional evidence points in the direction of a less favourable relationship between the presence of multinational corporations and human rights. See, Jackie Smith, Melissa Bolyard and Anna Ippolito, 'Human Rights and the Global Economy: A Response to Meyer', in: *Human Rights Quarterly,* Vol. 21, 1999, pp. 201-219 and the reaction by Meyer on pp. 220-228. See also the reviews of Meyer's book *Human Rights and International Political Economy in Third World Nations*, 1998 by Sigrun I. Skogly, in: *American Political Science Review*, Vol. 93, No.3, 1999, p. 761 and by Morton E. Winston, in: *Human Rights Quarterly*, Vol. 21, 1999, pp. 824-249.

25 United Nations Development Programme, *Human Development Report 1999: Globalization with a Human Face*, Oxford University Press, Oxford/New York, 1999.

26 United Nations Development Programme *Human Development Report 2000: Human Rights and Human Development*, Oxford University Press, Oxford/New York, 2000, p. 82.

27 UN Doc. E/CN.4/Sub.2/2000/13, 15 June 2000, paras. 28-29.

28 See, *inter alia*, the reports of the Special Rapporteur on the realisation of economic, social and cultural rights of the Sub-Commission on the Promotion and Protection of Human Rights: UN Doc.E/CN.4/Sub.2/1990/19, 6 July 1990 and UN Doc.E/CN.4/Sub.2/1991/17, 18 July 1991 and the reports by Mr. Joseph Oloka-Onyango and Ms. Deepika Udagama of the Sub-Commission: UN Doc. E/CN.4/Sub.2/2000/13, 15 June 2000 and UN Doc. E/CN.4/Sub.2/2001/10, 2 July 2001. See also resolution 1999/59, 28 April 1999 of the Commission on Human Rights and General Assembly resolution 54/165, 24 February 2000.

29 See the preliminary report of the Secretary-General, *Globalization and its impact on the full enjoyment of all human rights*, UN Doc.A/55/342, 31 August 2000.

have raised concern with regard to their adverse effect on human rights. During the 1980s the IMF and the World Bank introduced 'structural adjustment lending' which implies that in order to receive loans, certain economic, but also political conditions need to be met. The main features of these programmes are budgetary and monetary measures of austerity combined with economic deregulation. The aim is to encourage economic growth. However, the experience with these structural adjustment programmes is that they have negative impacts on human rights and have impeded sustainable development.[30] The special rapporteur of the Working group on structural adjustment programmes established by the Economic and Social Council has recognised that such programmes might be necessary and beneficial for economic growth, but their design has generally been motivated by the objective of ensuring the repayment of interest on debts owed and not on the promotion and protection of human rights.[31] The protests concerning the social implications of these structural adjustment programmes have prompted the IMF and the World Bank to modify them. The role and possible human rights obligations of the international financial institutions will not be further discussed in the present study.[32]

In the second place, the policies of the organisations aimed at enhancing trade liberalisation, such as the WTO and the NAFTA, can have a detrimental effect on the effective enjoyment of human rights. As will be discussed in chapter VIII, the obligations that States have under international trade agreements can be in conflict with their human rights obligations.

Finally, the impact of corporations on the enjoyment and the effective protection and promotion of human rights is considerable. As will become clear in the present study, corporations can influence human rights in several ways. In the first place, the impact of corporate activities on human rights can be considerable, as a result of the pressure which corporations exert on States to lower national standards of protection. As was stated in a United Nations working paper on this topic: '[corporations] have a presence in the vital sectors and are thus in a position to block any moves towards the respect for and protection of human rights.'[33]

The competition between corporations is leading to lower social and environmental standards, a process that has been called 'a race to the bottom'. Because of the economic power of these entities and their ability to invest in other countries they can

30 See, *inter alia*, Sigrun I. Skogly, *The Human Rights Obligations of the World Bank and the International Monetary Fund*, Cavendish Publishing, London, 2001, pp. 20-26, Hossain *supra* n. 10, p. 106 and Henry J. Steiner and Philip Alston [eds.] *International Human Rights Law in Context. Law, Politics, Morals. Text and Materials,* Clarendon Press, Oxford, 1996, p. 1140.

31 See: UN Doc. E/CN.4/1999/47, 11 January 1999.

32 For a study on the question of the possible human rights obligations of the IMF and the World Bank see, Skogly, *supra* n. 30.

33 UN Doc. E/CN.4/Sub2/1998/6, 10 June 1998, para. 7.

force a country, competing for foreign direct investment, to lower its standards. An illustration of the tendency of host countries to lower standards, are the so-called export processing zones. In these enclaves, corporations can benefit from a certain number of fiscal and financial incentives. It is primarily in these export processing zones that workers' rights to join a national union for collective bargaining and/or industrial action are largely restricted by governments, based on the belief that strong unions will discourage foreign direct investment. Independent trade unions are therefore only present to a limited extent or are completely absent.[34] In general, it can be argued that the conditions for workers in these zones are generally poor and hazardous to health. Serious pollution and the early burn out of employees are also associated with these zones.[35]

Besides the pressure from corporations on States to lower standards, corporations can themselves be involved in human rights violations, either directly or in collusion with others, such as States. There are various examples of human rights violations that reveal the apparent involvement of corporations. Highly publicized cases in the 1990s were the controversial activities of *Shell* in Nigeria,[36] *British Petroleum* in Colombia[37] and *Nike* in, *inter alia*, Indonesia.[38] Examples of corporate involvement in human rights violations will be used as illustrations throughout this study.

Finally, several corporations are increasingly recognising that they have responsibilities in the field of human rights and are actively promoting human rights.

The reality of the increased importance of corporations and their impact on human rights lays the foundations for the present study. In recent years the negative impact of corporations on the effective enjoyment of human rights has received increasing attention.[39] It should be noted that attention to the social impact of corporate activities

34 UN Doc. E/CN.4/Sub.2/1995/11, 24 July 1995, para. 64.

35 UN Doc. E/CN.4/Sub.2/1995/11, 24 July 1995, paras. 61-67.

36 See, *inter alia:* Human Rights Watch, *The Price of Oil: Corporate Responsibility and Human Rights Violations in Nigeria's Oil Producing Communities*, New York, 1999; Human Rights Watch, *Nigeria, the Ogoni crisis: a case study of military repression in South East Nigeria*, New York, 1995; Heike Fabig, 'The Body Shop and the Ogoni', in: *Human Rights Standards and the Responsibility of Transnational Corporations*, Michael Addo [ed.], Kluwer Law International, The Hague etc., 1999, pp. 309-321, and Sigrun I. Skogly, 'Complexities in Human Rights Protection: Actors and Rights Involved in the Ogoni Conflict in Nigeria', in: *Netherlands Quarterly of Human Rights*, Vol. 15, No. 1, 1997.

37 See, *inter alia*, Human Rights Watch, *Colombia: Human Rights Concerns raised by the Security Arrangements of Transnational Oil* Companies, 1998. This document is available at: http://www.hrw.-org/advocacy/corporations/colombia/ (accessed on 11 January 2002).

38 See, *inter alia*, Christopher L. Avery, *Business and Human Rights in a Time of Change,* Amnesty International UK Section, 2000, pp. 65-68.

39 See *supra* note 28 with regard to the increasing concern within the United Nations. Scholars are also devoting increased attention to the link between corporate activities and human rights. See, *inter alia*, Michael Addo [ed.], *Human Rights Standards and the Responsibility of Transnational Corporations,* Kluwer

is not new, however. For example, the role of corporations in this respect was already heavily debated as regards their involvement with the Nazi regime during World War II and with the apartheid regime in South Africa.

In sum, it can be concluded that corporations, the main actors in the processes of globalisation, in various ways have a significant impact on the enjoyment of human rights. It was pointed out above that corporate activities can also have a positive effect on human rights. This will not be the focus of the present study, however. The frequently negative influence of corporations on the promotion and protection of human rights justifies the emphasis placed in this study on the human rights obligations of corporations.

4 Research Objective

From a historical perspective, the human rights doctrine was developed as a means of ensuring protection for individuals from abuses of State power. However, as was mentioned previously, the process of globalisation has transformed international society from a collection of sovereign States to one that also includes influential private bodies. Consequently, the capability of States to regulate their affairs has diminished. Despite the diminished capability of States to effectively protect human rights, they remain the cornerstones of the human rights system. In the light of the influence of corporations on human rights, however, this conventional approach is inadequate. It is argued that the current developments point to a void in international law, a deficiency in legal accountability.

In the new context there is an urgent need to rethink many traditional issues of international law. To some extent, international law has responded to the changed international relations in the post-war period. International law has and still is expanding. For example, the number of entities that can be considered to be subjects of international law has increased. Nevertheless, a great deal of debate remains concerning the extent to which international law is applicable to non-state entities. This study is based on the presumption that, given the considerable influence that corporations have on the effective enjoyment of human rights, it is necessary to clarify the legal issues surrounding the topic of human rights obligations and corporations.

Law International, The Hague etc., 1999, and Menno T. Kamminga and Saman Zia-Zarifi [eds.], *Liability of Multinational Corporations under International Law,* Kluwer Law International, The Hague etc, 2000.

The overall aim of the present study is therefore:

To identify if and to what extent corporations have obligations under international law with regard to human rights. If obligations can be discerned, how can they be enforced?

On the basis of this analysis some recommendations will be made for a framework for enforcement.

5 Defining Corporations

The aim of this research is to examine whether human rights obligations pertaining to corporations actually exist and how corporations can be held accountable for violations of possible human rights obligations. A first, necessary step is to clarify what is meant in the present study by the term 'corporations'.

First and foremost, the subject of this study will be the multinational corporation, which basically refers to 'a legal person that owns or controls production, distribution or service facilities outside the country in which it is based'.[40] Many different terms and definitions are used for such an entity: transnational[41] corporation, transnational enterprise, multinational corporation and multinational enterprise.[42] The common feature of these large and often rather opaque corporations is that they operate across national borders. Operating in many different countries places these corporations outside the effective supervision of domestic and international law, which can result in a deficiency in legal accountability. Multinational corporations can operate with a considerable degree of autonomy and can shift their operations from one State to another. Moreover, the impact of large corporations on the effective enjoyment of human rights will, given their influence, generally be greater than is the case with smaller business entities. These characteristics of multinational corporations give rise to many of the issues that will be dealt with in this study.

---

40 Menno T. Kamminga, 'Holding Multinational Corporations Accountable for Human Rights Abuses: A Challenge for the EC', in: *The EU and Human Rights*, Philip Alston [ed.], Oxford University Press, Oxford, 1999, p. 553. This definition resembles the definition used in the International Labour Organisation's Tripartite Declaration of Principles concerning Multinational Enterprises and Social Policy: 'Multinational Enterprises include enterprises, whether they are of a public, mixed or private ownership, which own or control production, distribution, services or other facilities outside the country in which they are based'.

41 The term transnational enterprise is linked with the United Nations which consistently use this term. Moreover, the term 'transnational' is closely associated with the movement in the 1970s for a New International Economic Order (NIEO).

42 For an elaboration on the question of definition see: P.T. Muchlinski, *Multinational Enterprises and the Law*, Blackwell, Oxford, 1995, pp. 12-15.

However, it is important to note that the findings of this study are not restricted to large multinational corporations. *Grosso modo* the findings apply to *all* business entities. Besides the large multinational corporations, smaller businesses can also have a significant impact on the enjoyment of human rights. For example, a corporation that lacks foreign subsidiaries can nevertheless come into contact with international commerce by means of its supply chains.[43]

In this study, preference is given to the term corporation. Besides this term, the words 'business' and 'company' will also be used. The term corporation has been chosen instead of enterprise because the latter is sometimes associated with the concept of a public State enterprise. The impact of these entities on the protection and promotion of human rights can also be significant and will also be addressed in this study. However, the main focus is on the private, non-State corporation which is an independent legal person. The scope of this study is intentionally broad. I do not deem it necessary to come to a precise definition of the term corporation as any definition will necessarily exclude certain entities. With regard to basic human rights obligations I do not deem it appropriate to differentiate between corporations and, in principle, this study will therefore concern *all* business entities. Nevertheless, the findings will be particularly relevant to the activities of large, multinational corporations.

6 Structure of the Study

This study is divided into three parts. In Part A, I will apply international (human rights) law to corporations. The answer to the question whether international human rights obligations exist for corporations, requires a re-examination of several traditional doctrines in the light of the changed circumstances. Part A therefore first addresses particular theoretical issues arising from human rights doctrine. This part also aims to further clarify the role which corporations play with regard to the enjoyment of human rights.

In chapter II, the issue of international legal personality will be addressed. According to the traditional view, States have full legal personality under international law; they are the bearers of rights and duties. However, in line with the changed present-day reality, the number of entities with international legal personality has grown. It will be examined whether corporations can be considered to have international legal personality. This is a necessary first step, as the rights and obligations of corporations may depend on their position under international law.

In the second section of chapter II, the concept of the horizontal effect, or *Drittwirkung*, of human rights is examined. Traditionally, human rights are considered to be solely applicable in a vertical relationship, between the State and the individual. Considering the changed circumstances described above, the notion that human rights

43 Example given in UN Doc. E/CN.4/Sub.2/2001/WG.2/WP.1, 31 May 2001, para. 22.

violations committed by private persons against other private persons cannot be placed outside the ambit of human rights law if that law is to be effective, is gaining acceptance.

In chapter III, I will examine the provisions contained in the International Bill of Rights[44] on a case-by-case basis. A preliminary list of norms will be presented which can be applied in the legal relations between private parties, notably with respect to corporations. Subsequently, in chapter IV a discussion will be included on the possibly ensuing human rights obligations for corporations. The aim is to clarify the content of possible corporate human rights obligations. An analogy will be drawn with the different levels of State obligations that have been discerned in scholarly writing on the international law of human rights.

After having addressed the theoretical questions surrounding the applicability of international human rights law to corporations, the next issue that will be discussed is how the possible human rights obligations on the part of corporations can be enforced. In the final analysis the identification of possible human rights obligations for corporations will not be of much use if these obligations cannot be enforced. Therefore, in part B, I will discuss the existing avenues for addressing human rights violations by corporations. The structure of Part B is both logical and chronological, starting with an analysis of the existing mechanisms (*de lege lata*) and working towards discussing possible future enforcement mechanisms (*de lege ferenda)*. Supervision at the international and national level will be discussed.

In chapter V, the non-judicial supervision of corporations at the international level will be dealt with. Several international non-binding standards, some of which date back to the 1970s, make it clear that the concept of social responsibility for corporations is not new. In this chapter these guidelines and codes of conduct will be analysed from the perspective of their effectiveness regarding the enforcement of possible corporate human rights obligations. The focus of the present study is to determine whether corporations have legally binding obligations under international law. Nevertheless, in chapter V some observations will be made regarding the issue of self-regulation. The lack of clarity surrounding the issue of the responsibility of corpora tions and human rights has given rise to an explosive growth of corporate codes of conduct. The growing number of private codes indicates the growing acceptance by corporations of the role that they play with regard to social issues. In this study the advantages and disadvantages of self-regulation will be discussed.

The focus of this book on the obligations of corporations gives rise to the question of whether the fulfilment of basic human rights should be the responsibility of these non-democratically controlled entities or whether efforts should be undertaken to

44 The International Bill of Rights consists of the Universal Declaration of Human Rights, the International Covenant on Civil and Political Rights and the International Covenant on Economic, Social and Cultural Rights.

improve and strengthen the role of States. Or should both entities play a role in this respect? Widening the scope of those entities responsible for human rights by including non-State actors may give rise to the fear that this will undermine the present system of human rights protection as this will provide States with a possibility to evade their human rights obligations. However, it will be argued that the examination of the obligations and accountability of corporations does not, in any way, diminish the obligations incumbent upon States. The aim of this study is to examine the human rights obligations of corporations that exist *alongside* the obligations of States. In the light of the impact of non-state entities such as corporations on the effective enjoyment of human rights, this fear is not a sufficient reason not to re-examine the traditional dichotomy in the human rights doctrine of the individual versus the State. Nevertheless, the human rights system is a State-based system. States are the entities that are primarily responsible for upholding human rights. Therefore, in chapter VI, I will turn my attention to the responsibility of States for violations of human rights by non-state actors in general and corporations in particular.

It can be argued that with the rise of other powerful entities like corporations on the international plane the capability of States to effectively protect human rights has been seriously weakened. Moreover, it may prove difficult to determine which State is responsible given the problems that may arise when attempting to establish the nationality of corporations. Due to complex business structures these entities are often considered to be 'Stateless'. Besides, corporations often have the means and the possibility of evading national legislation. The fact that corporations operate in several countries under various legal systems provides these entities with the possibility of 'forum shopping' for the legal system that best suits their economic goals. Hence, the most effective way to secure the effective protection and promotion of human rights is to address companies directly. In chapters VII and VIII, I will deal with the possibilities for directly enforcing human rights obligations on corporations.

In chapter VII, an analysis is presented of the possibilities for enforcing human rights obligations on corporations at the national level. Civil litigation against corporations has most notably emerged in the domestic courts of the United States and the United Kingdom, where a degree of direct corporate responsibility for human rights violations seems to be recognised.

Finally, in chapter VIII, the possibilities for holding corporations directly accountable for human rights violations before judicial bodies at the international level will be discussed. A brief excursion will be made into the field of international criminal law and the area of international trade agreements.

Based on the analysis in Parts A & B, in the final part, which consists of chapter IX, conclusions will be drawn as regards the question whether corporations have human rights obligations and I will also make some recommendations regarding the issue of enforcement.

This study has been conducted by means of an analysis of relevant literature and the case-law of international, regional and national bodies. Moreover, documents of international and regional organisations have been examined. The study was concluded in March 2002.

PART A

HUMAN RIGHTS OBLIGATIONS FOR CORPORATIONS: A THEORETICAL FRAMEWORK

CHAPTER II
ISSUES OF DOCTRINE

1 INTRODUCTION

The question whether corporations have human rights obligations and, if so, how these obligations can be enforced, challenges traditional concepts of international law. Before embarking upon an analysis of this question, two concepts in particular need to be addressed.

Firstly, in order to determine the obligations of corporations for human rights violations under international law, the status of corporations under international law must be examined. This requires elaborating on the concept of international legal personality since this concept is frequently conceived as a prerequisite for bearing international rights and duties. This doctrine will be addressed in section 2.

Secondly, the concept of human rights obligations for corporations deviates from the traditional concept that human rights apply only in a vertical relationship, *i.e.* the State has obligations towards individuals. The idea that human rights law might also entail obligations for non-State entities, *viz.* has horizontal effect, is gaining acceptance as a result of increased attention to infringements on human dignity by non-State entities. Any discussion of obligations for corporations must therefore first deal with the concept of the horizontal application of human rights, also known as *Drittwirkung*. The doctrine of *Drittwirkung* will be discussed in section 3.

2 THE LEGAL STATUS OF CORPORATIONS UNDER INTERNATIONAL LAW

As mentioned, international legal personality is considered a prerequisite for operating on the international plane. According to some authors corporations do not have international legal personality as no binding international agreement that directly addresses corporations exists. Corporations are not recognised as independent international legal persons. Corporations are therefore said to be mere objects of international law and can bear no obligations towards the international community.[1] This section

1 See for example: Ian Brownlie, *Principles of Public International Law*, 5th ed., Clarendon Press, Oxford, 1998, p. 66, Francois Rigaux, 'Transnational Corporations', in: *International Law: Achievements and Prospects,* M. Bedjaoui [ed.], UNESCO, 1991, p. 129, Antonio Cassese, *International Law in a Divided World*, Oxford University Press, Oxford, 1986, p.103, Hans W. Baade, 'The legal effects of codes of conduct for multinational enterprises', in: *Legal Problems of Codes of Conduct for Multi-*

addresses the question of whether the concept of legal personality indeed constitutes an obstacle to holding corporations accountable for human rights violations. It will be argued that this is not the case. The conclusion that corporations are international legal persons in itself does not say anything about which rights and obligations corporations have. This question will be dealt with in the subsequent chapters.

2.1 Subjects of International Law

To be a subject under international law is usually taken to imply that an entity has rights and duties and the capacity to maintain its rights.[2] Under international law the primary subjects are States. States have full and original international personality, meaning that personality does not need to be conferred on these entities. It is interesting to observe that before the rise of the positivistic doctrine in the 19th century, there was no insistence that States were the only subjects of international law. For example, the large corporations of the 17th century such as the English East India Company (EIC) and the Dutch United East India Company (VOC) clearly operated at the international level. These companies could occupy land, wage wars and conclude treaties.[3] However, in the 19th century legal scholars from the positivistic school defended the assumption that only sovereign States could be considered as subjects of international law. All other entities were labelled objects of international law meaning that they had no direct rights or duties and, logically, no means of invoking any rights. This followed from the idea that international law by its nature only addressed sovereign States. At that time, international law was concerned mainly with State issues, such as the delimitation of the jurisdiction of States, the immunities of States, their diplomatic representatives and their property and the law of war.[4]

In the 20th century this strict subject-object dichotomy came under pressure. The types of entities with legal personality have diversified. Several practical developments demonstrated the need to enlarge the number of subjects of international law and prompted States to endow other entities with legal personality.

---

national Enterprises, Norbert Horn [ed.], Studies in Transnational Economic Law. Vol. I, Kluwer, The Hague etc., 1980, p.8.

2 This definition derives from the: *Reparations for Injuries Suffered in the Service of the United Nations* case, I.C.J. Rep.1949, 179. The definition of legal personality will be discussed in greater detail in section 2.3.

3 Koen de Feyter, *World Development Law. Sharing Responsibility for Development*, Intersentia, Antwerp etc., 2001, paras. 243 - 246. For the development of the subject-based definition of international law, see: M.W. Janis, 'Individuals as Subjects of International Law', in: *Cornell International Law Journal*, 1984, Vol. 17, Nr. 1, pp. 61-78.

4 H. Lauterpacht, *The International Protection of Human Rights, Recueil des Cours*, 1947, p. 8.

The first example was the creation of *The Free City of Danzig*. This protectorate[5] was created to solve conflicting interests between Poland and Germany. The territory was placed under the protection of the League of Nations. The Permanent Court of International Justice (PCIJ) recognised that *The Free City of Danzig* had international personality, except in so far as treaty obligations created special relations in regard to the League and to Poland.[6] In the case concerning the *Jurisdiction of the Courts of Danzig*, the PCIJ affirmed that practical needs can override theoretical considerations in regard to international legal personality. States can grant entities certain rights and duties making them subjects of international law, if they feel the practical need to do so.[7] The traditional dichotomy between subjects and objects of international law was further weakened with the recognition that international organisations can posses international legal personality. The treaty establishing an international organisation can contain provisions explicitly granting international legal personality to the organisation. If this is not the case the existence of *de facto* legal personality can be deduced from the powers and operations of the organisation.[8] This occurred in the *Reparations for Injuries Suffered in the Service of the United Nations* case.[9] The International Court of Justice (ICJ) concluded that, *in casu* the United Nations, had legal personality as:

> '(…) the Organisation was intended to exercise and enjoy, and is in fact exercising and enjoying, functions and rights which can only be explained on the basis of the possession of a large measure of international personality and the capacity to operate upon an international plane.'[10]

Individuals are also recognised as subjects of international law. This was first acknowledged in the *Jurisdiction of the Courts of Danzig* case.[11] Since the Second World War, the position of the individual as a subject of international law has been firmly established. In 1945 the United Nations Charter expressly recognised that the individual has

---

5 The Free City of Danzig was created in Articles 100-108 of the Treaty of Versailles. Besides protectorates, under certain circumstances 'State-like' entities such as condominiums and internationalised territories are also considered to be legal subjects. See Brownlie,*supra* n. 1, pp. 59-62.

6 Brownlie, *supra* n. 1, pp. 60-61.

7 This case concerned the question whether an agreement between Poland and Danzig, regulating the conditions of employment of Danzig railway officials who had passed into the service of the Polish Administration, created rights and obligations for individuals or merely for States. The Permanent Court held that 'it can not be disputed that the very object of an international agreement, according to the intention of the contracting parties, may be the adoption by the parties of some definitive rules creating individuals rights and obligations enforceable by the national courts'. PCIL, Advisory opinion No. 15, Ser. B, 1928.

8 Sigrun I. Skogly, *The Human Rights Obligations of the World Bank and the International Monetary Fund*, Cavendish Publishing, London, 2001, p. 65.

9 *Reparations for Injuries* case, *supra* n. 2, p. 179.

10 *Reparations for Injuries case*, *supra* n. 2, p. 179.

11 PCIL, Advisory opinion No. 15, Ser.B, 1928. *Supra* note 7.

fundamental rights. Moreover, the fact that international law imposes duties and liabilities upon individuals as upon States was acknowledged during the trials before the criminal war tribunals in Nuremberg and Tokyo. With the establishment of the ad-hoc tribunals for the former Yugoslavia (ICTY) and Rwanda (ICTR) and the permanent International Criminal Court (ICC), the obligations of the individual under international criminal law have become irrefutable. With the rise of the human rights doctrine in the postwar era, the attention to the rights of the individual increased. The acknowledgement of the fact that individuals have rights was taken to imply that they should have the means of effectuating these rights. For this reason, supervisory organs, among which is the European Court of Human Rights (ECrtHR) in Strasbourg, were created where individuals can bring claims against States to effectuate their rights. As a result of these developments, individuals increasingly participate in the international legal system and, in today's theory of international law, are considered as subjects of international law.

Finally, it has been recognised that, under humanitarian law, insurgent or rebel groups in a civil war have certain rights and obligations because they control some territory and might become the effective new government of the State.[12]

To sum up, practical developments have led to the expansion of the number of subjects on the international plane. Besides States, individuals, international organisations and insurgent or rebel groups, are considered to be legal subjects under international law. They derive their legal status from States. They can therefore be called derivative subjects, as opposed to the original subjects: States.

2.2 Rejection of the Subject-Object Dichotomy

As described in the previous section, with the expansion of the number of entities that are considered to be international legal persons, the traditional dichotomy between subjects and objects of international law has come under pressure.

The question arises whether the subject-object dichotomy serves any real purpose. Higgins has called the concept of legal personality 'an intellectual prison' and 'the whole notion of subjects and objects has no credible reality and (…) no functional purpose.'[13] And as Van Hoof states: '[the term 'personality'] may even be considered an empty shell because it does not give a clue as to what rights and/or duties the entity

12 In the Geneva Conventions of 1949 and the two additional protocols of 1977, insurgent forces as well as State armies are obliged to protect prisoners and to respect prohibitions such as those on attacking civilians, taking hostages, carrying out terrorist acts, or using starvation as a method of combat. See also: article 8 of the Rome Statute of the International Criminal Court UN Doc. A/Conf/183/9, 17 July 1998.

13 Rosalyn Higgins, *Problems and Process. International Law and How We Use It*, Clarendon Press, New York, 1994, pp. 49-50.

concerned has in the concrete case at hand.'[14] It might prove useful to use a more realistic and dynamic approach to the topic at hand: the concept of 'participants'. The concept was first introduced by Wolfgang Friedmann, as far back as 1964[15] and has recently been defended by Rosalyn Higgins.[16] According to Higgins: 'individuals are participants, along with states, international organizations (…), *multinational corporations*, and indeed private non-governmental groups' (emphasis added).[17] According to Higgins, international law is formed by the needs of the international community. This community is composed of different participants all pursuing the maximisation of different values by making different claims.[18] Recognising the role played by all the different actors on the international plane, *i.e.* to refer to participants instead of subjects, would bring international law into conformity with present-day reality.

Notwithstanding this observation, I will demonstrate in the following paragraphs that even when one insists on the concept of international legal personality, the concept does not pose an obstacle with regard to holding corporations accountable for human rights violations.

2.3 Defining International Legal Personality

From legal literature on the topic of international legal personality it appears that a great deal of conceptual confusion exists. Hence, before addressing the issue whether corporations can be considered legal persons, the concept of legal personality requires further examination.

Whether a particular entity can be considered an international person depends on the definition that is applied. The prevalent definitions used in the literature on international legal personality emphasise the fact that the entity has certain rights and possibilities for enforcing these rights as the decisive elements of international legal personality. For example, according to Brownlie, a subject of international law is 'an entity capable of possessing international rights and duties and having the capacity to maintain its rights by bringing international claims'.[19]

---

14 Fried van Hoof, 'International Human Rights Obligations for Companies and Domestic Courts: An Unlikely Combination?', in: *The Role of the Nation-State in the 21st Century: human rights, international organisations and foreign policy: essays in honour of Peter Baehr*, Monique Castermans-Holleman, Fried van Hoof and Jacqueline Smith [eds.], Kluwer Law International, The Hague etc., 1998, pp. 47-59, at p. 53.

15 Friedmann states that international law needs to be reordered from five different perspectives, one of which is 'the inclusion, as participants and subjects of international law, of public international organisations and to a less definite extent, of private corporations and individuals', Wolfgang Friedmann, *The Changing Structure of International Law,* Stevens & sons, London, 1964, pp. 70-71.

16 Higgins, *supra* n. 13, p. 50. See also: Van Hoof, *supra* n. 14.

17 Higgins, *supra* n. 13, p. 50.

18 Higgins, *supra* n. 13, p. 50.

19 Brownlie, *supra* n. 1, p. 57.

This definition is based on the one formulated in the *Reparations for Injuries* case, where the ICJ held that the United Nations (UN) is a 'subject of international law and capable of possessing international rights and duties, and that it has the capacity to maintain its rights by bringing international claims'.[20] In other words, according to the ICJ, international personality consists of three elements: international legal subjectivity, international legal capacity and international *jus standi*.[21]

The definition of legal personality as formulated by the ICJ raises many questions however. The distinction between 'a subject of international law' and 'the capacity to possess international rights and duties' is not clear. After all, rights and duties can only be conferred upon an entity that is capable of bearing rights and duties. It would therefore seem that legal capacity and legal subjectivity are the same.[22] Consequently, several authors have come to the conclusion that the difference is not important.[23] In a study on the legal personality of minorities and indigenous peoples, Meijknecht disagrees with the assumption that the difference between legal capacity and legal subjectivity is insignificant. She argues that the difference is relevant, as the mere fact that an entity has the *capacity* to bear rights and duties does not have to mean that the entity in fact *has* rights and duties.[24] In the context of this study, I do not see the need to differentiate between the element of capability and subjectivity. In the following paragraphs it will be demonstrated that the international legal order has in fact bestowed corporations with rights and duties in the international realm and, therefore, the question relating to capacity is redundant.

Furthermore, in its definition the ICJ identifies *jus standi* as one of the constitutive elements of international legal personality. This is a source of controversy in legal literature. Scholars disagree whether *jus standi* is a necessary element for legal personality.[25]

Notwithstanding the question whether procedural capacity is indeed an essential element, it should be observed that in its definition the ICJ places emphasis on the capacity of an entity to maintain its *rights* by bringing an international claim. It does

20 *Reparations for injuries* case, *supra* n. 2, p. 179.

21 See for an elaborate survey of the ICJ's definition of 'international personality': Anne Meijknecht, *Towards International Personality: The Position of Minorities and Indigenous Peoples in International Law*, Intersentia, Antwerp etc., 2001, pp. 23-63.

22 Brownlie refers to the definition of the ICJ as follows: 'the indicia referred to depend on the existence of a legal person. All that can be said is that an entity of a type recognized by customary law as capable of possessing rights and duties and of bringing international claims, and having these capacities conferred upon it is a legal person'. Brownlie, *supra* n. 1, p. 57.

23 See, *inter alia,* Peter Malanczuk, *Akehurst's Modern Introduction to International Law,* 7th rev., Routledge, London, 1997, p. 91.

24 Meijknecht, *supra* n. 21, p. 49.

25 For a survey of the views that exist in international legal doctrine see: Meijknecht, *supra* n. 21, pp. 58-61. According to Meijknecht, an international subject becomes an international person when it has procedural capacity. See also, Carl Aage Nørgaard, *The Position of the Individual in International Law*, Munksgaard, Copenhagen, 1962, pp. 34-76.

not mention the aspect of being held responsible in case of a failure to live up to an obligation. This is understandable given the background of the case. In the *Reparations for Injuries* case the UN General Assembly sought the advice of the ICJ after the killing of Count Bernadotte, an employee of the UN, in Palestine. The question was whether the UN had the legal capacity to instigate an international claim against a State in the event of an agent suffering injury in the performance of his duties. The ICJ therefore focussed on the existence of rights and their enforceability on the international plane.

As the ICJ did not explain the exact meaning of, nor the relationship between the three constitutive elements of the concept of legal personality as formulated in the *Reparations for Injuries* case, the definition has remained a source of confusion.

The conceptual analysis of the position of the individual under international law which was undertaken by Nørgaard as far back as 1962, offers appropriate tools for clarifying the concept of legal personality. The terminology developed by Nørgaard makes a clear distinction between the constitutive elements of legal personality and, as opposed to the ICJ definition, includes the duty-element of legal personality. Consequently, I consider his terminology more appropriate in the context of this study.

Nørgaard unfolded his ideas in his book *The Position of the Individual in International Law.* Building on the analysis of Alf Ross,[26] Nørgaard distinguishes two constituent elements of the concept of legal personality. According to the definition by Nørgaard a legal person is the subject of rights & proceedings and/or duties & responsibility/examinations. He subdivides the subject of rights into two categories. The first category is the subject of rights, or what Ross calls the subject of interests. This is a

> 'person who has a substantive right under the legal rule notwithstanding the problem of whether the person himself has any legal capacity to take any action by which to enforce his substantive right or whether such action can only be taken by another, in international law normally his state.'[27]

Here such a right will be referred to as a 'material right'. Secondly, Nørgaard distinguishes the subject of proceedings, which refers to 'a person that can bring a claim as a case before a tribunal'.[28] By using this terminology Nørgaard clarifies that one entity can be the bearer of a material right while another entity is the subject of proceedings. The other constituent element of the concept of legal personality, according to Nørgaard, is the subject of duties. Again, he subdivides this category into two groups. The

---

26 Alf Ross, *A Textbook of International Law. General Part*, Longman, Green and Co., London, 1947.

27 Nørgaard, *supra* n. 25, p. 33.

28 Nørgaard, *supra* n. 25, p. 33. Nørgaard distinguishes a third category which he calls the 'subject of petitions', *i.e.* a person who, according to a certain procedure, can petition an international organ, which must then deal with the petition, although, unlike a tribunal, it has no power to deliver binding judgments. For the sake of clarity, I will group these last two categories together; both are subjects of proceedings.

first category is the subject of duties, or what Ross calls the subject of conduct. This is a

> 'person of whom a legal rule requests a certain conduct; in other words, a person who has a substantive duty under the legal rule irrespective of the problem of whether he personally can be held responsible for violating it or whether only another, in international law normally his state can be held responsible for his act or omission.'[29]

Here the term 'material duties' will be used. The second category discerned by Nørgaard is the 'subject of responsibility'. This refers to a

> 'person who can be sued and held responsible before a tribunal'.[30] On the duty-side Nørgaard also adds a third category, which he calls 'subject of examinations'. This refers to 'a person that, in the case of an alleged non-observance of a duty, is under an obligation to have the question of whether or not a rule laying down the duty has been violated examined by an international organ, which is not a tribunal and which cannot deliver binding judgments'.[31]

Here these two categories will be grouped together. Again, Nørgaard makes it clear that the subject of duties does not by necessity have to be the subject of responsibility and examinations.
In sum, the definition of a legal person is:

Subject of rights:	- subject of (material) rights
	- subject of proceedings
and/or	
Subject of duties:	- subject of (material) duties
	- subject of responsibility/examinations

The terminology applied by Nørgaard helps to clarify the discussion on legal personality. Whether an entity can be considered a legal person mainly depends on which aspect of the definition is applied *i.e.* which element is considered to be the central and decisive quality of the concept of legal personality.

Returning to the definition of legal personality as it was developed by the ICJ in the *Reparations for Injuries* case, it can be observed that the three composing elements of legal personality discerned by the ICJ are also present in the analysis by Nørgaard. The

29 Nørgaard, *supra* n. 25, p. 33.
30 Nørgaard, *supra* n. 25, p. 33.
31 Nørgaard, *supra* n. 25, p. 33.

only difference is that Nørgaard's theoretical framework pays more attention to the element of duties and the enforcement of duties.

As stated above, in the literature and in case-law emphasis is frequently placed on the element of rights and especially the enforceability of rights as the most central and important aspect. In this study the duty-side is the prime focus. The following chapters will consist of an empirical research into the question of which human rights obligations can be discerned for corporations and how they can be enforced. In the light of this, Nørgaard's analytical approach to the issue of legal personality is functional.

This chapter merely aims to set the stage by addressing the issue of legal personality as such. In the subsequent sections I will demonstrate that, to use the words of Nørgaard, corporations 'have been brought into contact with international law'[32] and that the doctrine of legal personality does not constitute a conceptual obstacle as regards the human rights obligations of corporations.

2.4 Do Corporations have Legal Personality?

Traditional international law does not recognise corporations as legal subjects. According to this view, corporations on the international plane are dependent on States to exercise diplomatic protection on behalf of them.[33] This view is rather outdated, however. Firstly, most corporations today act very much independently from any State. Secondly, nowadays corporations are less in need of protection compared to the 1960s when large-scale expropriation and nationalisation by developing countries took place.[34]

For the analysis of whether corporations are legal persons, Nørgaard's terminology will be used. The two constituent elements of legal personality, material rights & proceedings, material duties & responsibility, will be addressed.

2.4.1 Material Rights

Firstly, do corporations have material rights? International law has displayed the tendency to emphasise the rights of corporations. It has been concerned with protecting investment rather than regulating the duties of corporations. Before the Second World

32 Nørgaard, *supra* n. 25, p. 304.

33 In the *Barcelona Traction Case* the ICJ decided that diplomatic protection on behalf of a corporation might be exercised by the home State. The Court recognised that identifying the home State could prove to be problematic as no absolute test of the 'genuine connection' required between the corporation and the home State had found general acceptance. *Case Concerning the Barcelona Traction Light and Power Company, Limited (Second Phase) (Belgium* v. *Spain)*, 1970, I.C.J. Rep., para. 70.

34 For example, the nationalisation measures of Iran with regard to the Anglo-Iranian Oil Company, of Indonesia with regard to the Dutch tobacco plantations and of Cuba with regard to American-owned sugar refineries.

War and in the decade after the War the international community was preoccupied with protecting investors. Emphasis was put on issues such as protection against expropriation and compensation. During the 1970s this emphasis shifted, due to pressure from the recently decolonialised States and as a result of several sensational cases of abuse of corporate power[35], towards the duties of corporations, which resulted in various, non-binding, international codes of conduct for corporations. Examples are the codes negotiated in the context of the International Labour Organisation (ILO) and the Organisation for Economic Co-operation and Development (OECD).[36] However, during the 1980s and the 1990s a return to the emphasis on the rights of corporations can be detected as part of the efforts to promote free trade. The emphasis on rights for corporations came to the fore in organisations such as the North American Free Trade Agreement (NAFTA) established in 1988. Under NAFTA corporations have access to a panel for dispute settlement.[37] This emphasis on the rights of corporations rather than on their duties culminated in the draft Multilateral Agreement on Investments (MAI), which was drawn up within the OECD. In the draft strong emphasis was put on the rights of corporations at the expense of the rights of States. Corporations would be able to instigate a claim against a State that violated the rules of the MAI. States would not be able to bring a claim against a corporation, however. Partly as a result of strong public criticism the negotiations within the OECD failed and the MAI was not adopted.[38]

In the context of possible rights for corporations the so-called international agreement doctrine should be briefly discussed.[39] According to this doctrine, 'internationalised contracts' – contracts concluded between a host-State and a corporation particularly in the field of oil concessions or development agreements – confer rights on corporations. These contracts frequently contain an 'applicable law clause' stating that the contract is to be governed by 'general principles of law', 'general principles of the law of nations' or 'principles of the law of the concessionary State not inconsistent

---

35 Most well-known is the case of the involvement of the American corporation ITT in the coup d'état in Chile, which brought Pinochet to power.

36 *OECD-Declaration on International Investments and Multinational Enterprises* adopted in 1976 and the *ILO Tripartite Declaration of Principles Concerning Multinational Enterprises and Social Policy* of 1977. See chapter V.

37 NAFTA will be dealt with in more detail in chapter VIII.

38 See chapter I, note 14.

39 This matter will be discussed only briefly in this section as nowadays the issue of the proper qualification of internationalised contracts has lost much of its previous significance because most contracts are now placed under the national legal system of the host State. See: Peter Malanczuk, 'Multinational Enterprises and Treaty-Making. A Contribution to the Discussion on Non-State Actors and the 'Subjects' of International law', in: *Multilateral Treaty-Making. The Current Status of Challenges to and Reforms Needed in the International Legislative Process*, Vera Gowlland-Debbas [ed.], Proceedings of the American Society of International Law/ Graduate Institute of International Studies, Forum Geneva, May 16 1998, Geneva, Switzerland, Martinus Nijhoff Publishers, The Hague etc., 2000, pp. 45-72.

with international law'.[40] Moreover, these contracts often impose the obligation that in case of a dispute use will be made of international arbitration. According to some authors these clauses in 'internationalised' contracts place these contracts on the international plane, making corporations the bearers of specific rights under international law.[41]

Other authors, however, disagree with the international agreement doctrine.[42] The main argument against the elevation of corporations to subjects of international law by means of an internationalised contract is put forward by Malanczuk.[43] He observes that the international agreement doctrine relies on an analogy drawn from the derivative international legal personality of international organisations. However, this analogy is flawed because the personality of an international organisation is the result of agreements amongst the member States of that organisation as reflected in the constituent instrument. Recognition of the personality of a corporation by one single State is not enough to elevate the corporation to a subject of international law.[44] Moreover, the point of view that a single State can grant international personality to a corporation implies that this State can also unilaterally withdraw such legal personality. According to Malanczuk, 'this is incompatible with the principle of *pacta sunt servanda*.[45] Consequently, it cannot be stated that international contracts between a State and a corporation bestow the corporation with international rights.

As far as human rights are concerned it may be concluded that corporations enjoy certain of these rights. This issue is controversial however, as corporations are not the intended beneficiaries of human rights. They are organisations and therefore have no inherent ability to suffer the harmful consequences associated with human rights deprivation. Nevertheless, it is clear that corporations do enjoy the benefits of a number of human rights such as, for example, the right to own property, the right to freedom of expression and the right to a fair trial. Authors have argued, however, that the fact that corporations enjoy the *benefits* of certain human rights does not necessarily mean

---

40 Malanczuk, *supra* n. 39, p. 62.

41 See: Higgins, *supra* n. 13, pp. 54-55, Peter Fischer, 'Transnational Enterprises', in: *Encyclopaedia of Public International Law*, 8, North-Holland, Amsterdam *etc*., 1985, pp. 518, Matthias Herdengen, *Internationales Wirtschaftsrecht*, C.H. Beck'sche Verlagsbuchhandlung, Munchen, 1995, p.58, Friedmann, *supra* n. 15, p. 221-224. This line of reasoning was applied in the case of *Texaco v. Libya,* where it was decided that the contracts between the Libyan State and the Texaco corporation were internationalised contracts as a result of 'their nature as economic development agreements and [the] recourse to international arbitration for the settlement of disputes'. The applicable law was therefore international law. *Texaco Overseas Petroleum Company/California Asiatic Oil Company* v. *Government of the Libyan Arab Republic*, Arbitral Award of 19 January 1977, I.L.M. (1978) p. 3 para. 40. It should be noted that this line of reasoning has not been continued in later arbitration.

42 See, *inter alia*, Brownlie, *supra* n. 1, pp. 66, 549-551, Malanczuk, *supra* n. 39, p. 58-62.

43 Malanczuk, *supra* n. 39, p. 60.

44 Malanczuk, *supra* n. 39, p. 60.

45 Malanczuk, *supra* n. 39, p. 60.

that the pertinent rules create *rights* for companies.[46] One way of proving that companies are the bearers of rights is to show that the treaty conferring the rights also provides a possibility of enforcement.[47] Under the European Convention on Human Right (ECHR) corporations can file a complaint under article 34 of the ECHR which reads:

> '[t]he Court may receive applications from any person, non-governmental organisation or group of individuals claiming to be the victim of a violation by one of the High Contracting Parties of the rights set forth in the Convention or the protocols thereto (...).'

Complaints from corporations have been accepted by the Court under the broad heading of non-governmental organisations. For example, in the case *Autronic v. Switzerland* the Court held that ' (...) Article [10] applies to 'everyone', whether natural or legal persons'.[48] The same language can be found in Article 1 of Protocol 1, which states: 'Every natural or legal person is entitled to the peaceful enjoyment of his possessions'.[49] The case-law of the ECHR provides the best example of the applicability of human rights standards to corporations as a victim. Under the ECHR corporations have rights and possibilities for enforcing these rights. It must be noted that not all rights can be conferred upon a legal person. An example of this is the right to life.

In sum, it can be concluded that corporations are the subject of material rights at the international level.

2.4.2 Proceedings

The element of enforceability is often considered to be the decisive quality of legal personality. According to Verzijl

> 'the true test of "personality" in a given legal order would seem to be not whether an individual or composite entity derives rights from that order, but whether he or it is in a position to pursue or/and enforce them within it.'[50]

46 Malanczuk, *supra* n. 23, p. 100. Malanczuk makes the comparison with animals. Rules prohibiting cruelty to animals do not confer rights on animals.

47 Malanczuk, *supra* n. 23, p. 101.

48 22 May 1990, *Autronic AG* v. Switzerland, A.178, para. 47. For a more detailed description of the various case law regarding corporations under the ECHR see Michael K. Addo, 'The Corporation as a Victim of Human Rights Violations', in: *Human Rights Standards and the Responsibility of Transnational Corporations*, Kluwer Law International, The Hague etc., 1999, pp. 187- 196, at pp.194-196.

49 Protocol to the Convention for the Protection of Human Rights and Fundamental Freedoms, as amended by Protocol No. 11, Paris, 20.III.1952.

50 J.H.W. Verzijl, *International Law in Historical Perspective*, Part II International Persons, A.W. Sijthoff-Leyden, Leyden, 1969, p.3.

It can be observed that corporations are frequently the subjects of proceedings. Especially in the area of arbitration, corporations are provided with the possibility of enforcing their rights. Various international instruments can be discerned where corporations are considered to be the subject of proceedings, *i.e.* corporations can bring a claim to enforce their substantive rights. In 1981, the Iran-United States Claims Tribunal was created as part of the settlement of the Teheran hostage crisis. Before this Tribunal corporations have legal standing under certain conditions.[51] Another example is the United Nations Compensation Commission (UNCC) set up after the defeat of Iraq in 1991. In the procedure before the UNCC corporations can bring claims for compensation against Iraq.[52] Under the United Nations Convention on the Law of the Sea (UNCLOS) the 'Seabed Disputes Chamber' was set up.[53] This Chamber has jurisdiction relating to disputes between parties to a contract. This can be States but also natural or legal persons, such as corporations.[54] Under the Convention establishing the International Centre for the Settlement of Investment Disputes (ICSID), drawn up under the auspices of the World Bank, corporations are also recognised as subjects of international law. Art. 25 (1) of this Convention states: 'the jurisdiction of the Centre shall extend to any legal dispute arising directly out of an investment between a Contracting State (...) and a national'.[55] And, as mentioned earlier, private parties also have access to an arbitration-panel under NAFTA. Also under the draft-MAI, corporations would be able to bring claims before an international tribunal against a State that treats them less favourably than other investors.[56] Reference should also be made to the 1995 Energy Charter Treaty as this treaty also provides for the direct (without a previously negotiated arbitral agreement) access of private investors to international arbitration against States for breaches of obligations in the treaty. Under the treaty there is no corresponding right of the host State against the corporation.[57] Finally, as men-

51 Set up under the Declaration of the Government of the Democratic and Popular Republic of Algeria Concerning the Settlement of Claims by the Government of the United States of America and the Government of the Islamic Republic of Iran, 19 Jan. 1981, reprinted in (1981) I.L.M. 230.

52 Set up under Security Council Resolution 692 (1991) of 20 May 1991.

53 Set up under Annex VI of the UN Convention on the Law of the Sea, 10 December 1982, 21 I.L.M. (1982) 1261.

54 Article 187, Part XI, section 5 UNCLOS.

55 Either a natural or a legal person, which has the nationality of a Contracting State other than the State to the dispute (article 25 para. 2 sub. a and b).

56 See Part V of the MAI negotiating text as of 24 April 1998. See also chapter I, note 14.

57 Art. 26 of the Energy Charter Treaty. Malanczuk mentions this Treaty as an example of the increasingly independent role of corporations *vis-à-vis* States. He argues that corporations are in this limited sense attaining international legal personality. Malanczuk, *supra* n. 39, p. 70. For more on the Energy Charter Treaty see: Thomas W. Waelde, 'Sustainable Development and the 1994 Energy Charter Treaty: Between Pseudo-Action and the management of Environmental Investment Risk', in: *International Economic Law with a Human face*, Friedl Weiss, Erik Denters and Paul de Waart [eds.], Kluwer Law International, The Hague, 1998, pp. 223-270.

tioned earlier, under the ECHR corporations can instigate a claim against a State party for a violation of human rights under the Convention.

It can be concluded that corporations are the subjects of material rights and proceedings at the international level.

2.4.3 Material Duties

Do corporations have material duties, *i.e.* do international legal rules exist which require certain conduct from corporations irrespective of the question of whether the corporation can be held responsible for violating the rules? International law occasionally directly addresses corporations. In the field of environmental protection several treaties contain binding material duties for corporations. Several treaties in the field of maritime issues directly place obligations on corporations. For example, under the International Convention on Civil Liability for Oil Pollution Damage, direct liability for oil pollution is placed on the owner of a ship.[58] The same kind of direct obligations for legal persons can be found in the Council of Europe's Convention on Civil Liability for Damage Resulting from Activities Dangerous to the Environment.[59]

Direct duties for corporations are also found in the codes of conduct drafted by the ILO and the OECD during the 1970s. UN resolutions on South Africa, adopted by the General Assembly during the 1980s, also mentioned corporations as the addressees of international duties.[60] More recently the UN Sub-Commission on the Promotion and Protection of Human Rights has been dealing with corporations as the bearers of obligations.[61] As has been said, the examples mentioned here are all of a non-binding nature. Nevertheless, these codes and resolutions are an indication of the willingness of States to assume that corporations are the addressees of obligations under international law.[62]

In the field of human rights binding international duties on the part of corporations have to be deduced from instruments that are originally directed at States. This touches upon the doctrine of horizontal effect or *Drittwirkung*. According to this doctrine certain rights do not only apply to the vertical relationship between governments and individuals but also in horizontal relationships, for example between an individual and a corporation. The concept of *Drittwirkung* will be dealt with in more detail in section 3.

---

58 Article 4 of the Protocol of 1992 to Amend the International Convention on Civil Liability for Oil Pollution Damage 1969, International Maritime Organisation, 1992.

59 Adopted in June 1993. At the time of writing this Convention had not yet come into force.

60 Example cited in Kokkini-Iantrou and De Waart, 'Foreign Investments in developing countries -legal personality of multinationals in international law', in: 14, *Netherlands Yearbook of International Law*, Martinus Nijhoff, Dordrecht, 1983, pp. 87-131 in note 45.

61 See for more on the codes of conduct and recent developments within the UN, chapter V.

62 Kokkini-Iatridou and De Waart, *supra* n. 60, p. 114.

2.4.4 *Responsibility and Examinations*

By differentiating between responsibility and examinations, Nørgaard makes it clear that the notion of enforcement should be given a broad interpretation. Enforcement can take place at different levels.

To be a subject of responsibility refers to the possibility to sue the duty holder before a tribunal. Even though corporations have obligations at the international level, the subjects of responsibility remain predominantly States. For example, the treaties in the field of corruption that place obligations on corporations identify States as the subjects of responsibility. Treaties against corruption in the Council of Europe,[63] the Organisation of American States[64] and the OECD[65] require State Parties to criminalise the bribery of and by individuals and businesses. For example, article 2 of the OECD Convention on Combating Bribery of Foreign Public Officials in International Business Transactions states that 'Each Party shall take such measures (…) to establish the liability of legal persons for the bribery of a foreign public official'.[66] Other examples can be found in the field environmental protection. The Global Convention on the Control of Transboundary Movements of Hazardous Wastes[67] requires State Parties to outlaw such 'illegal traffic' by legal persons in its national laws.[68]

However, according to the analytical model by Nørgaard, enforcement should be given a wider interpretation. Obligations can also be enforced through 'examinations'. This is the case where a subject is examined by an international organ not being a tribunal.[69] Corporations are subject to examinations at the international level. For

63 See article 18 of the Council of Europe Criminal Convention on Corruption, adopted on 27 January 1997, which states: 'Each Party shall adopt such legislative and other measures as may be necessary to ensure that legal persons can be held liable for the criminal offences of active bribery, trading in influence and money laundering (…)'.

64 See article VIII of the OAS Inter-American Convention against Corruption, adopted on 29 March 1996 which reads: ' each State Party shall prohibit and punish the offering or granting, indirectly or directly, by its nationals, persons having their habitual residence in its territory, and businesses domiciled there, to a government official of another State (…).

65 OECD Convention on Combating Bribery of Foreign Public Officials in International Business Transactions, adopted 23 May 1997.

66 OECD Convention on Combating Bribery of Foreign Public Officials in International Business Transactions, adopted 23 May 1997.

67 Adopted in Basel in 1989.

68 See, articles 2(14), 4(3) and 9(5).

69 This is the case under European Community law. Under Articles 81 and 82 (*ex* Articles 85 and 86) of the Treaty corporations are prohibited from engaging in activities which prevent, restrict, or distort competition within the common market or to exploit, in an improper manner, a dominant market position. The European Commission has extensive authority to enforce these provisions *vis-à-vis* corporations. Strictly speaking, however, European Community law, which has a *sui generis* character can not be compared to international law. See, for a discussion of Articles 81and 82 of the Treaty: Menno T. Kamminga, 'Holding Multinational Corporations Accountable for Human Rights Abuses:

example, under the codes of the ILO and the OECD, mentioned earlier,[70] complaints regarding corporations can be examined.[71] The question of the enforceability of obligations for corporations in the field of human rights will be more elaborately dealt with in part B of this book.

2.5 Concluding Remarks

In section 2.1 it was pointed out that the number of entities that can be considered legal persons is growing and that the subject-object dichotomy is under increasing pressure. Nevertheless, even when examining the status of corporations on the basis of the traditional concept of legal personality, it becomes clear that the position that these entities are not subjects of international law is no longer tenable. Corporations are subjects of international rights and proceedings and/or international duties and responsibility/examinations. In sum, corporations are bestowed with legal personality.

It must, however, be observed that the above discussion of legal personality with reference to corporations demonstrates a rather fragmentary picture. Corporations seem to enjoy limited legal personality confined to particular instances. This leads some authors to conclude that corporations have a limited degree of legal personality.[72] However, this observation may cause confusion. It is true however, that having legal personality does not mean the same thing in all cases. The rights and duties can differ depending on the subject. Or as was pointed out by the ICJ in the *Reparations for injuries* case: 'The subjects of law in any legal system are not necessarily identical in their nature or in the extent of their rights, and the nature depends on the needs of the community.'[73]

The fact that international legal personality does not imply the same thing in all cases is also important in the light of countering what seems to be the main argument against the recognition of corporations as subjects of international law: the fear that corporations would be able to interfere in the affairs of States.[74] Just as is the case with international organisations, the international legal personality of corporations differs from that of States. Recognising the legal personality of corporations does not pose a threat to the status of States as the prime bearers of duties on the international plane. Kamminga and Zia-Zarifi have formulated it as follows:

A Challenge for the EC', in: *The EU and Human Rights,* Philip Alston [ed.], Oxford University Press, Oxford, 1999, pp. 553-569, at. p.565.

70 See p. 28.

71 As will be discussed in chapter V, the supervisory mechanisms of these codes are not very effective. Nevertheless, that does not detract from the point that corporations can be the subject of examinations.

72 Akehurst, 6th ed., 1991, p. 70, Kokkini-Iatridou and De Waart,*supra*, n. 60, pp. 117-124

73 *Reparations for Injuries* case, *supra* n. 2, p. 179.

74 Menno T. Kamminga and Saman Zia-Zarifi [eds.], *Liability of Multinational Corporations under International Law,* Kluwer Law International, The Hague etc, 2000, p. 6.

> 'international law is not a zero-sum game in which conferring legal subjecthood on one entity denies it to all others. (…) [I]nternational legal personality of corporations points toward growth of a complementary system of law that fills the penumbra of existing State-centered international law and facilitates, as well as regulates, activity by, through, and with sovereign States and their citizens.'[75]

It may be concluded that the doctrine of legal personality does not constitute a conceptual obstacle to recognising human rights obligations for corporations. It has been demonstrated that corporations have, under international law, certain material rights, possibilities of enforcing these rights, and material duties, while in certain cases, claims can be brought against corporations. In the words of Nørgaard, corporations 'have been brought into contact with international law'.[76] Corporations have international legal personality and are therefore capable of possessing international human rights obligations

At this point, I find it useful to return to the definition formulated by the ICJ in the *Reparations* case. It was pointed out above, that in this definition legal personality consists of three elements: legal subjectivity, legal capacity and *jus standi*. It has been demonstrated that all three constitutive elements of international legal personality are present in the case of corporations.

The conclusion that corporations are international legal persons is important as it implies that no inherent conceptual reason exists why corporations could not be bestowed with international human rights obligations.

The observation that corporations have rights and duties in the international realm is not as such very helpful as it does not help us to settle the question whether companies have obligations under international law in the field of human rights, let alone what these obligations might be. This study will try to identify human rights obligations for corporations. As mentioned earlier,[77] the rights and obligations of international organisations are not equal to those of States. Identifying the obligations which corporations should observe will clarify this point. In Part B the possibilities for enforcement will be discussed. The concept of human rights obligations for corporations deviates from the traditional concept that human rights apply in a vertical relationship, *i.e.* the individual has rights *vis-à-vis* the State. Any discussion of obligations for corporations must therefore first deal with the concept of the horizontal application of human rights, also known as *Drittwirkung*.

75 Kamminga and Zia-Zarifi, *supra* n. 74, p. 6.
76 Nørgaard, *supra* n. 25, p. 304.
77 See p. 34.

3 *Drittwirkung*

3.1 Introduction

In the previous sections it has been demonstrated that the doctrine of legal personality does not constitute an obstacle to recognising human rights obligations on the part of corporations; corporations can be the bearers of international obligations. The conclusion that corporations have obligations and can violate human rights implies that international human rights law is applicable between non-State entities, *e.g.* it has horizontal effect. This notion constitutes a departure from the traditional approach that human rights are held by the individual exclusively against the State. In this section the concept of horizontal effect will be discussed. In the next chapter a tentative list will be drawn up of rights which *prima facie* seem to be applicable in legal relations between an individual and a corporation.

3.2 The Concept of *Drittwirkung*

The notion that entities other than States threaten human rights is not new. Especially in the context of the national legal order the idea has been developed that fundamental rights not only create subjective rights against interference by public authorities but also contain values that permeate the entire legal order.[78] In other words, fundamental rights can have a horizontal effect. The term *Drittwirkung (der Grundrechte)*, which basically means 'third-party effect', originates from a doctrinal debate in Germany. The 'third party' refers to the party outside the classical relationship between the individual versus the State. The term *Drittwirkung* is also commonly used with reference to the horizontal effect of international norms. The present analysis deals with obligations in the international sphere. Therefore, the doctrine of *Drittwirkung* will only be examined in relation to international legal norms.[79]

---

78 E.A. Alkema, 'The third-party applicability or "*Drittwirkung*" of the European Convention on Human Rights', in: Franz Matscher, Herbert Petzold, Gérard J. Wiarda, *Protecting Human Rights: The European Dimension*, Carl Heymanns Verlag, Cologne etc., 1988, p. 34, Andrew Clapham, 'The "*Drittwirkung*" of the Convention', in: *The European System for the Protection of Human Rights*, R.St.J. Macdonald *et al.* [eds.], 1993, Kluwer Academic Publishers, The Hague etc., pp. 163-206, at p. 165.

79 For a discussion of the doctrine in the national context in the Netherlands, see *e.g.* M.B.W. Biesheuvel, 'Horizontale werking van grondrechten' (I) [third-party applicability of fundamental rights (I)], in: *NJCM-Bulletin* 6-3, 1981, pp. 147-169, M.B.W. Biesheuvel, 'Horizontale werking van grondrechten' (II) [third-party applicability of fundamental rights (II)], in: *NJCM-Bulletin* 6-4, 1981, pp. 205-225, J. Boesjes, 'De horizontale werking van grondrechten' [The third-party applicability of fundamental rights], in *Nederlands Juristen Blad*, 8 September 1973, Vol. 29, pp. 905-916, L.F.M. Verhey, *Horizontale werking van grondrechten, in het bijzonder van het recht op privacy [The third party applicability of fundamental rights ('Drittwirkung'), especially of the right to privacy,* W.E.J. Tjeenk Willink, Zwolle, 1992.

The doctrine of *Drittwirkung* is a much discussed but rather vague concept. Especially in relation to the ECHR, *Drittwirkung* is a heavily debated topic.[80] But the concept is also discussed with regard to other treaties.[81] Many different interpretations and distinctions exist. Scholarly opinions vary from a complete denial to the recognition of the existence of *Drittwirkung*. The arguments in favour or against *Drittwirkung* are frequently based on an implicit definition of the concept. It is therefore important to clarify what is precisely meant by the concept of *Drittwirkung*.

The distinction made by Van Dijk and Van Hoof between applicability and enforceability helps us to clarify the discussion. Firstly, *Drittwirkung* is taken to mean that provisions apply not only between the State and the individual but also in the legal relations between private parties. Secondly, *Drittwirkung* is defined as the possibility for the individual to bring a claim against another private party.[82] In the latter approach the element of enforceability is considered of paramount importance. As far as this second approach is concerned, two forms of *Drittwirkung* can be discerned. Firstly, there is the form known as *direct Drittwirkung*. This means that the individual can lodge a complaint directly against a private party by invoking a human right, before an international court or supervisory body. According to some authors there can be no such horizontal effect at the international level as no enforcement mechanism against non-state entities is provided for.[83] Two observations should be made regarding this point. Firstly, the enforcement of international law does not merely take place at the international level. National courts play an important role in this respect too. In States where treaties are self-executing, the individual can invoke the rights in a treaty against another individual before a national court.[84] In these situations it can be argued that the international norm has horizontal effect, albeit at the national level. Moreover, it should be observed that the fact that procedural obstacles exist does not mean that there are no obligations for non-State entities.[85] This position is based upon the idea that, due to

80 See, for example, A. Drzemczewski, 'The European Human Rights Convention and Relations between Private Parties', NILR, Vol. XXVI, 1979, pp. 163-181; Clapham, *supra* n. 78, P. van Dijk and G.J.H. van Hoof, *Theory and Practice of the European Convention*, 3rd ed., Kluwer Law International, The Hague etc., 1998, pp. 22-26 and Andrew Clapham, *Human Rights in the Private Sphere*, Clarendon Press, Oxford, 1993.

81 For the *Drittwirkung* of the International Covenant of Civil and Political Rights (ICCPR), see *inter alia*, Manfred Nowak, *U.N. Covenant on Civil and Political Rights: CCPR Commentary*, Engel, Kehl am Rhein 1993, especially pp. 37-38.

82 Van Dijk and Van Hoof, *supra* n. 80, pp. 22-26.

83 D.J. Harris, M. O'Boyle and C. Warbrick, *Law of the European Convention on Human Rights*, London, 1995, p.21.

84 In those States where treaties are not self-executing, the State will have the obligation to secure these rights under national law. If the State does not comply with this obligation, it can be held responsible before an international court or committee. In such a situation the horizontal effect of a treaty is of a very indirect nature. See, with reference to the ECHR, Van Dijk and Van Hoof, *supra* n. 80, p. 23.

85 M.A. Eissen, 'The European Convention on Human Rights and the Duties of the Individual', *Nordisk Tidsskrift for International Ret,* Vol. 32, 1962, p. 233.

their nature, human rights permeate the whole legal system. This will be further explored in section 3.3.1.

The absence of direct enforcement for private parties at the international level does not necessarily bar horizontal effect; it merely means that the enforcement of the obligations for non-State entities is indirect, *i.e.* through the obligations that States have under the provisions concerned. This approach constitutes the second form of *Drittwirkung*, that of *indirect Drittwirkung.* According to this view, complaints concerning the activities of a private party can only be lodged if responsibility can be traced back to the State authorities. This is the case when a violation is the result of an act or omission on the part of the domestic legislator, of the courts or of the administrative authorities.

3.3 Arguments in Favour of *Drittwirkung*

The question whether or not human rights have horizontal effect is frequently answered by weighing arguments in favour or against the existence of the horizontal effect of a human rights treaty. In the remainder of this chapter, I will discuss whether arguments in favour or against *Drittwirkung* can be inferred from the nature of human rights and from the general provisions in the core human rights documents which together make up the International Bill of Rights: the Universal Declaration of Human Rights (UDHR), the International Covenant on Economic, Social and Cultural Rights(ICE SCR) and the International Covenant of Civil and Political Rights (ICCPR). In chapter III, I will analyse, on a rights-by-rights basis, the horizontal effect of each separate right within the International Bill of Rights.

Before addressing the question whether *Drittwirkung* exists with regard to international human rights law, it should be mentioned that international humanitarian law is clear regarding the applicability of its provisions to non-State entities. Responsibilities for persons can be found in the Convention on the Prevention and Punishment of the Crime of Genocide. Article 6 reads:

> '*Persons* charged with genocide or any other of the acts enumerated in article III shall be tried by a competent tribunal of the State in the territory of which the act was committed, or by such international penal tribunal as may have jurisdiction with respect to those Contracting Parties which shall have accepted its jurisdiction.' [Emphasis added][86]

86 Convention on the Prevention and Punishment of the Crime of Genocide, 78 U.N.T.S. 277, which entered into force on 12 January 1951.

Furthermore the Nuremberg Rules provide that,

> 'The following acts, or any of them, are crimes coming within the Jurisdiction of the Tribunal for which there shall be *individual responsibility* (a) Crimes against Peace... (b) War Crimes...(c) Crimes against Humanity.' [Emphasis added][87]

Finally, the Rome Statute of the ICC provides that individual criminal responsibility shall arise for the crimes enumerated in the Statute.[88]

3.3.1 Nature of Human Rights

As was pointed out in section 3.2, it has been argued that the fact that international human rights law poses procedural obstacles to enforcing human rights obligations on the part of non-State entities, does not mean that there are no obligations for such non-State entities.[89] Such arguments often refer to the idea of natural law. If human rights are considered to derive from nature their horizontal effect is not really controversial. Human rights are considered to be fundamental for the dignity of the individual. Therefore, the realisation of these rights should not be confined to protection against the State. The individual should be protected against all violations of human rights, and not only when the violator can be directly identified as an agent of the State. Alkema has observed:

> 'These rights (...) were derived from man's 'inherent' dignity and founded in the law of nature rather than in one single belief or religion. The rights (...) are therefore less closely connected with the polarity of the citizen versus the State than the fundamental rights laid down in national constitutions.'[90]

In this line of reasoning *Drittwirkung* is eminently relevant for human rights in general. Moreover, arguments in favour of *Drittwirkung* can also be derived from the specific content or nature of a particular right.[91]

An argument put forward by many scholars who deny the existence of *Drittwirkung* is the fact that States are the addressees under international human rights law. Nevertheless, in the words of Van Hoof:

---

87 Nuremberg Rules of the International Military Tribunal, in: Agreement for the Prosecution and Punishment of the Major War Criminals of the European Axis, 82 U.N.T.S. 279, which entered into force on 8 August 1945.

88 Article 25 of the Rome Statute for the International Criminal Court, UN Doc. A/Conf.183/9, 17 July 1998.

89 Eissen, *supra* n. 85, p. 233.

90 Alkema, *supra* n. 78, p. 35.

91 See chapter III.

> 'it should be observed from the outset that (...) *Drittwirkung* cannot be denied on the basis of the argument that norms belonging to the international law of human rights are primarily couched in terms of State obligations. The fact that the drafters of international human rights instruments intended to provide protection against State entities does not preclude extension of that protection vis-à-vis other entities in view of changed circumstances.'[92]

In sum, arguments in favour of the horizontal effect of human rights emanate from the very nature of human rights themselves. Moreover, the fact that States are the original and primary addressees of obligations under international human rights law does not preclude the existence of *Drittwirkung*. Law should be interpreted in a 'contextual and evolutive manner'.[93] This is in line with the principal rule of treaty interpretation, as is laid down in article 31 of the Vienna Convention on the Law of Treaties (VCLT), which reads: 'a treaty shall be interpreted in good faith in accordance with the ordinary meaning to be given to the terms of the treaty in their context and in the light of its object and purpose'.[94] Moreover, in its advisory opinion on *the Legal Consequences for States of the Continued Presence of South Africa in Namibia*, the ICJ stated that 'an international instrument has to be interpreted and applied within the framework of the entire legal system prevailing at the time of the interpretation'.[95]

3.3.2 General Provisions in the International Bill of Rights

It has been put forward that arguments in favour of *Drittwirkung* can be inferred from some of the general provisions of the International Bill of Rights.[96]
The Preamble of the UDHR provides that:

> 'The General Assembly proclaims this Universal Declaration of Human Rights as a common standard of achievement for all peoples of all nations, to the end that every *individual* and *every organ of society*, keeping this Declaration constantly in mind, shall strive by teaching and education to promote respect for these rights and freedoms and

---

92 Van Hoof, *supra* n. 80, p. 55.
93 Clapham, *supra* n. 80, p. 93-94.
94 Signed in Vienna on 23 May 1969, entry into force: 27 January 1980.
95 Advisory opinion of the ICJ on *The Legal Consequences for States of the Continued Presence of South Africa in Namibia (South West Africa)*, I.C.J. Rep. 1971, p.31, para. 53.
96 This section will mainly focus on the International Bill of Rights, which consists of the UDHR, the ICCPR and the ICESCR as these documents have universal application. At the time of writing, the ICCPR has been ratified by 147 States and the ICESCR by 143 States. Nevertheless, when relevant, other human rights treaties will also be discussed. It is noteworthy that two regional treaties are much more explicit regarding the duties of non-state entities. In the African Charter on Human and Peoples' Rights a comprehensive list of duties of the individual is provided for in chapter II. The American Declaration on the Rights and Duties of Man contains clear language in chapter II as to both the rights and the duties of individuals.

by progressive measures, national and international, to secure their universal and effective recognition and observance.' [Emphasis added]

Hence, according to the preamble, besides States, individuals and other organs of society have duties under the UDHR. Commenting on this part of the preamble, Henkin stresses:

'Every individual includes juridical persons. Every individual and every organ of society excludes no one, no company, no market, and no cyberspace. The Universal Declaration applies to them all.'[97]

Article 29, para.1 of the UDHR refers to *everyone's* duties to the community. Furthermore, article 30 of the UDHR asserts that no State, *group* or person may interpret the Declaration in any way that is aimed at the destruction of these rights. From the formulation of these provisions it may arguably be inferred that the UDHR was intended to apply also to non-State entities.

Both the 1966 Covenants are legally binding documents. Can general provisions be discerned in the Covenants, which create obligations for non-State entities? The fifth preambular paragraphs of both the ICCPR and the ICESCR state that the individual has 'duties to other individuals and the community [and] is under a responsibility to strive for the promotion and observance of the rights recognised in the present Covenant'. Such provisions in a preamble are not without legal significance. The preamble is especially important as an aid to interpretation.

Consequently the formulation of several general provisions in the International Bill of Rights provides arguments to support *Drittwirkung*. Nevertheless, the exact nature of the obligations that can be derived from these general provisions remains to be determined.

Several other general provisions of a more procedural nature in the ICCPR, the ICESCR and, notably, the ECHR have given rise to a discussion as to whether or not these provisions can be seen as evidence of the existence of indirect *Drittwirkung*. As explained above,[98] in the case of indirect *Drittwirkung* the focus is on the element of enforceability. Under current international law it is – as a general rule – not possible to enforce human rights obligations on private parties directly at the international level. Therefore, violations of human rights by private parties must be redressed on the basis of an act or omission on the part of the State.

Article 1 ECHR has been put forward as evidence of *Drittwirkung*. According to article 1 ECHR States 'shall *secure* to everyone within their jurisdiction the rights and freedoms (...) of this Convention'. [Emphasis added]. According to some this article

97 Louis Henkin, 'The Universal Declaration at 50 and the Challenge of Global Markets', in: *Brooklyn Journal of International Law*, Vol. XXV, No.1, 1999, pp. 17-25, at p. 25.

98 See p. 38.

implies (indirect) *Drittwirkung* as States are obliged to take measures that are necessary to enable individuals to enjoy their rights, including the removal of some private obstacles to the enjoyment of these rights.[99] However, scholars who reject the possibility of indirect *Drittwirkung* use this article as an argument against *Drittwirkung* itself.[100] Van Dijk and Van Hoof correctly observe that this provision cannot be used as an argument *pro* or *contra* possible *Drittwirkung* as

> 'one cannot deduce from [article 1 of the ECHR] whether the Contracting States are obliged to secure the rights and freedoms only in relation to the public authorities or also in relation to other individuals.'[101]

Therefore, Van Dijk and Van Hoof conclude that for possible *Drittwirkung* other arguments have to be advanced.[102] It can be concluded that this provision in the ECHR does not independently provide a conclusive answer to the question whether the human rights in the ECHR are applicable in the legal relations of non-State entities. According to some scholars the corresponding article in the ICCPR is somewhat clearer.[103] Article 2 ICCPR requires States not only to 'respect' but also to 'ensure' the rights provided for in the Covenant.[104] As was observed by one commentator:

> 'the ability to enjoy most ICCPR human rights would be totally undermined if States had no duties to control human rights abuse in the private sector. It is therefore likely that the general duty in article 2(1) [ICCPR] on States to 'ensure' ICCPR rights entails a duty, of perhaps varying degrees of strictness, to protect individuals from abuses of all ICCPR rights by others.'[105]

Buergenthal concurs with this interpretation of the word 'ensure'. He upholds that 'as regards some rights in some circumstances, [the word ensure] may perhaps require the

---

99 Dzremczeski, *supra* n. 80, p. 176.

100 See, for example, Harris, O'Boyle and Warbrick, *supra* n. 83, pp. 21-22.

101 Van Dijk and Van Hoof, *supra* n. 80, p. 24.

102 Van Dijk and Van Hoof, *supra* n. 80, p. 24.

103 Sarah Joseph, Jenny Schultz and Melissa Castan, *The International Covenant on Civil and Political Rights. Cases, Materials, and Commentary*, Oxford University Press, Oxford, 2000, p. 24 See also: T. Buergenthal, 'To Respect and to Ensure: State Obligations and Permissible Derogations', in: *The International Bill of Rights, The Covenant of Civil and Political Rights*, Louis Henkin [ed.], Colombia University Press, New York, 1981, pp. 72-91, p. 77. David Weissbrodt, 'Non-State Entities and Human Rights within the Context of the Nation-State in the 21st Century', in: *The Role of the Nation-State in the 21st Century: human rights, international organisations and foreign policy: essays in honour of Peter Baehr*, Monique Castermans, Fried van Hoof and Jacqueline Smith [eds.], 1998, pp. 175-195, and Nowak, *supra* n. 81, p. 503.

104 Article 2 (1) ICCPR reads: '[e]ach State Party to the present Covenant undertakes *to respect and to ensure* to all individuals within its territory and subject to its jurisdiction the rights recognised in the present Covenant (…)'. [Emphasis added].

105 Joseph, *supra* n. 103,, p. 24

state to adopt laws and other measures against private interference with the enjoyment of the rights (...)'.[106] Besides the duty to refrain from violating a right, to which the word 'respect' refers, the State also has the duty 'to ensure that individuals and non-State entities do not abuse human rights'.[107] The corresponding provision in the ICESCR also uses the term 'ensure'.[108] It may, therefore, be concluded that the word 'ensure' provides support for the horizontal effect of the ICCPR and the ICESCR.

Article 2 (3)(a) ICCPR and the analogous article 13 ECHR have also been interpreted as an argument in favour of *Drittwirkung*. According to these articles State Parties are obliged to ensure that 'any person whose rights or freedoms (...) are violated shall have an effective remedy, *notwithstanding* that the violation has been committed by persons acting in an official capacity' [emphasis added].

According to some commentators the term 'notwithstanding' would seem to indicate that a remedy is also required for violations by persons *not* acting in an official capacity.[109] Other authors, however, disagree, arguing that the word 'notwithstanding' merely indicates that the State is responsible for violations committed by its officials.[110] It should be concluded that these articles do not offer a conclusive argument in favour of, or against *Drittwirkung*. On the other hand, article 2 (3)(a) ICCPR and article 13 ECHR are so-called ancillary provisions. They can only be invoked in conjunction with other articles. Therefore, it may be assumed that these articles, read together with articles that have a certain measure of horizontal effect, can strengthen this effect.[111]

Finally, article 5 (1) ICCPR (which corresponds to article 5(1) ICESCR and article 17 ECHR) has been put forward as evidence of *Drittwirkung*. The article reads:

> 'nothing in the present Covenant may be interpreted as implying for any State, group or person any right to engage in any activity or perform any act aimed at the destruction of any of the rights and freedoms recognised herein (...).'

On the basis of this article, some authors conclude in favour of the horizontal effect of the provisions in the instruments concerned. Eissen deduces from this article that not only States, but also individuals have the obligation to respect the norms in the

---

106 Buergenthal, *supra* n. 103, p. 77.

107 Weissbrodt, *supra* n. 103, p. 181.

108 Article 3 ICESCR reads: '[t]he States Parties to the present Covenant undertake *to ensure* the equal right of men and women to the enjoyment of all economic, social and cultural rights set forth in the present Covenant'.[Emphasis added].

109 Eissen , *supra* n. 85, p. 178, Jerome B. Elkind and Anthony Shaw, *A Standard for Justice. A Critical Commentary on the Proposed Bill of Rights for New Zealand*, Oxford University Press, Oxford *etc.*, 1986, pp. 27-30. See also, Clapham, *supra* n. 78, p. 200.

110 See, *e.g.*, D.H.M. Meuwissen, *De Europese Conventie en het Nederlandse Recht* [The European Convention and Dutch Law], Sijthoff, Leiden, 1968.

111 Nowak, *supra* n. 81, p. 38.

treaties.[112] However, even though private actors are mentioned explicitly, some doubt exists whether Article 5 (1) ICCPR (and the corresponding articles in the ICESCR and ECHR) can be put forward as evidence of *Drittwirkung*. This article is intended to protect against the abuse of the right to complain.[113] Prohibiting any abuse, however, cannot be equated with the general obligation for individuals to respect the rights of others in their private legal relations.[114]

3.4 Concluding Remarks

Summarising, it can be concluded that support for the hypothesis of the *Drittwirkung* of international human rights law can be inferred from the nature of human rights and from the general provisions of the human rights treaties. However, these general provisions do not independently provide strong enough evidence for the conclusion that norms of international human rights law can be applied horizontally.[115] From the discussion in the literature it becomes clear that several of the general provisions mentioned above are susceptible to different interpretations. Referring to the ECHR, Van Dijk and Van Hoof argue:

> '(…) one may conclude that *Drittwirkung* does not ensue imperatively from the Convention. On the other hand, nothing in the Convention prevents states form conferring *Drittwirkung* upon fundamental rights and freedoms.'[116]

Consequently, the general provisions do not 'stand in the way' of horizontal effect; they provide for the possibility of *Drittwirkung.* However, it would be too far-fetched to conclude that *Drittwirkung* exists when such a conclusion is based merely on these general provisions. It is therefore necessary to examine each right in the International Bill of Rights separately in order to establish whether the right in question is applicable to non-State actors, *i.e.* has horizontal effect.

---

112 Eissen, *supra* n. 85, p. 236.
113 See, with reference to article 17 ECHR: Van Dijk and Van Hoof, *supra* n. 80, p. 750.
114 See, with reference to article 17 ECHR: Van Dijk and Van Hoof, *supra* n. 80, p.25.
115 With reference to the ECHR: Van Dijk and Van Hoof, *supra* n. 80, p. 25.
116 Van Dijk and Van Hoof, *supra* n. 80, p. 25.

CHAPTER III
APPLICABLE NORMS

1 INTRODUCTION

In the previous chapter it was concluded that the nature of human rights and the general provisions in the International Bill of Rights support the conclusion that human rights can be applicable in horizontal relations. However, recognising the possibility of *Drittwirkung* does not mean that all provisions can be applied in the legal relations between private parties. A sound analysis necessitates an examination of each provision on a case-by-case basis. This analysis will be conducted in section 2 of this chapter. The focus will be on the core human rights documents which together make up the International Bill of Rights: the UDHR, the ICESCR and the ICCPR. Other documents will only be taken into account when they provide relevant arguments for the discussion on *Drittwirkung*. A tentative list of articles will be presented, which may have effect in private legal relations and are notably relevant for the activities of corporations.

Identifying provisions that may be applicable to corporations is of little use without addressing which obligations can ensue from these provisions. This question will be addressed in chapter IV. The issue is approached from the assumption that various layers of obligations can be derived from each separate human right.

2 APPLICABLE NORMS

In order to answer the question whether or not the provisions in the International Bill of Rights can be applicable in the legal relations of corporations, the provisions will be analysed on a case-by-case basis. In this analysis two different approaches to *Drittwirkung* come to the fore. In some interpretative statements, such as several General Comments by the supervisory bodies[1], explicit reference is made to direct

---

1 Several of the international human rights treaties, such as the ICCPR, the ICESCR, the CAT and the CERD, provide for the possibility for the supervisory bodies to adopt so-called General Comments. These are interpretative statements of the provisions in the international human rights treaties. The General Comments are not binding but they have practical authority as they reflect the experience with the particular provision and are the result of debate among the members of the supervisory bodies. See, for example, art. 40 [4] ICCPR and Ineke Boerefijn, *The Reporting Procedure under the Covenant on Civil and Political Rights. Practice and Procedures of the Human Rights Committee*, Intersentia, Antwerp etc., 1999, pp. 294-297.

human rights responsibilities of corporations. In these cases the applicability of the provision in question to these entities is clear. Mostly, however, the supervisory organs are compelled to have recourse to the indirect type of *Drittwirkung*.[2] In other words, the work of the committees is couched in terms of State obligations. The State is held accountable, not the private entity. It should be reiterated that the fact that, under the current system, the State is ultimately held accountable, does not imply that the norm in question is devoid of horizontal effect. It merely means that *enforcement* of the norm is currently only possible against the State. The question arises what common factor connects the private act and the responsibility of the State. The common factor is the existence of an alleged infringement of a right, since without the original infringement by a non-state-actor there would be no responsibility on the part of the State. The fact that States are explicitly obliged to prevent and punish private interference should be interpreted as a recognition of the horizontal effect of the norm as it makes apparent that this particular provision applies beyond mere protection against public authorities. In sum, aspects of procedure do not hinder the horizontal effect of a provision. In the following analysis indirect *Drittwirkung* will therefore also be taken into account.

2.1 Peremptory Norms

Before embarking upon an analysis of each separate provision in the International Bill of Rights in order to determine whether the provision may be applicable in the legal relations of corporations, an observation needs to be made regarding certain categories of rights. Some commentators come to the conclusion that certain human rights provisions can or should be applicable in horizontal relations because of their special status in international law.[3] Several of the provisions that will be dealt with in the subsequent analysis are considered to protect peremptory norms and therefore to have a special status. For example, several human rights provisions belong to the category of customary international law. These provisions are applicable to all States regardless of whether they have adopted the documents in the International Bill of Rights. In the light of indirect *Drittwirkung* this implies that all States are obliged to protect these norms against private violations. According to the Human Rights Committee, the following rights in the ICCPR belong to customary international law: prohibition of slavery; prohibition of torture or cruel, inhuman or degrading treatment or punishment;

---

2 See chapter II, p. 38.

3 See Menno T. Kamminga and Saman Zia Zarifi [eds.], *Liability of Multinational Corporations under International Law,* Kluwer law International, The Hague etc, 2000, p.8, where they argue that corporations 'are bound by those few rules applicable to all international actors' and they are therefore 'prohibited from engaging directly or indirectly in violations of *jus cogens* principles'. See also, Meron who states that 'the prohibition of slavery and genocide apply, of course, also to private persons and groups', Theodor Meron, *Human Rights and Humanitarian Norms as Customary Law*, Clarendon Press, Oxford, 1989, p.165.

prohibition of arbitrary deprivation of life; freedom of thought, conscience and religion; prohibition of advocating national, racial or religious hatred; marriage and minority enjoyment of their own culture.[4] Some of the human rights provisions enumerated in the analysis below can even be considered to belong to the *jus cogens* category. Even though international consensus on what exactly belongs to this category is lacking, the following of the human rights provisions that will be discussed below, are frequently considered to belong to this category: right to life; prohibition of torture or other cruel and inhuman or degrading treatment or punishment; prohibition of racial or other forms of discrimination; prohibition of slavery and the slave trade.[5] These peremptory norms have a special status in international law in that they are, in the words of Brownlie, relatively indelible.[6] These norms can only be set aside by other rules of *jus cogens*. This special character has led to the following observation with regard to the applicability of *jus cogens* norms to corporations,

> '[I]f the exhortation in the Universal Declaration that all organs of society should respect human rights is to have meaning, it must mean – at the very least – that businesses should not violate these fundamental rights.'[7]

One commentator applies the same kind of reasoning regarding non-derogable rights – rights from which no derogation is possible, not even in times of emergency[8] – by stating that these rights can be considered to be directly applicable to corporations because of their special character.[9] However, as pointed out by Seiderman, non-derogable rights are not necessarily superior norms. The non-derogable quality of these rights may be for the reason that no emergency situation would reasonably serve as a

---

4 UN Doc.A/50/40, General comment No. 24 [52], Vol. I (1995), Annex V (p. 119-125); UN Doc. CCPR/C/21/Rev.1/Add.6, 2 November 1994, para. 8.

5 This enumeration is derived from Ian D. Seiderman, *Hierarchy in International Law,* Intersentia, Antwerp etc., 2001, chapter III 'Jus Cogens', p. 121. According to Seiderman a minimum core of *jus cogens* can be derived from non-derogable treaty rights, international criminal law and judicial and scholarly pronouncements. Besides the rights referred to here, Seiderman also identifies the following human rights of a *jus cogens* character: the prohibitions against genocide, summary and extra-judicial executions, the application of the death penalty to juveniles, arbitrary detention, disappearances and criminal violations of humanitarian law, including crimes against humanity and some war crimes. See also, Ian Brownlie, *Principles of Public International Law*, 5th ed., 1998, p. 515 and the *Third Restatement of Foreign Relations Law*, 1987, Section 702 (n).

6 Brownlie, *supra* n. 5, p. 515.

7 International Council on Human Rights Policy, *Beyond Voluntarism. Human rights and the developing international legal obligations of companies*, February 2002, p. 63.

8 See, for example, article 4 (2) ICCPR.

9 Laurence Dubin, 'The Direct Application of Human Rights Standards to, and by, Transnational Corporations', in: *Globalisation, Human Rights and the Rule of Law. The Review*, International Commission of Jurists, Adama Dieng [ed.], 1999, No. 61, pp. 35-66, at p. 39-40. For the relationship between non-derogable rights and *jus cogens*, see Seiderman, *supra* n. 5, pp. 84-89.

basis for their suspension.[10] Therefore, the mere fact that a right is classified as non-derogable is not sufficient to support the proposition that the right is directly applicable to corporations.

In sum, the fact that certain rights are considered to protect fundamental norms, as is the case with the rights belonging to the *jus cogens* category, should be considered as an additional argument supporting the assumption that these provisions may have horizontal effect. Nevertheless, in order to reach a conclusion as to whether a particular provision has horizontal effect, each provision needs to be examined individually.

2.2 Analysis of Specific Provisions

The following analysis of each specific human rights provision in the International Bill of Rights will be conducted on the basis of articles 31 and 32 of the Vienna Convention on the Law of Treaties (VCLT) that provide the general and supplementary rules by which to interpret treaties. According to article 31 'a treaty shall be interpreted in good faith in accordance with the ordinary meaning to be given to the terms of the treaty in their context and in the light of its object and purpose'. First, the object and purpose of the UDHR and the Covenants in general will be discussed. Subsequently, the wording and the context of the substantive articles will be examined.

Article 31(2) provides for the definition of context:

> 'The context for the purpose of the interpretation of a treaty shall comprise, in addition to the text, including its preamble and annexes:
> (a) any agreement relating to the treaty which was made between all the parties in connection with the conclusion of the treaty;
> (b) any instrument which was made by one or more parties in connection with the conclusion of the treaty and accepted by the other parties as an instrument related to the treaty.
> Moreover, there shall be taken into account, together with the context:
> (a) any subsequent agreement between the parties regarding the interpretation of the treaty or the application of its provisions;
> (b) any subsequent practice in the application of the treaty which establishes the agreement of the parties regarding its interpretation;
> (c) any relevant rules of international law applicable in the relations between the parties.

10 Seiderman, *supra* n. 5, p. 85. See also General Comment No. 29, UN Doc. CCPR/C/21/Rev.1/Add.11, 27 July 2001, para 11 where the HRC argues that ' [t]he proclamation of certain provisions of the Covenant as being of a non-derogable nature [can] partly [be seen] as recognition of the peremptory nature of some fundamental rights (...). However, it is apparent that some other provisions of the Covenant were included in the list of non-derogable provisions because it can never become necessary to derogate from these rights during a state of emergency (...). The HRC mentions the articles 11 (imprisoned merely on the ground of inability to fulfil a contractual obligation) and 18 (Freedom of thought, conscience and religion) as examples.

4. A special meaning shall be given to a term if it is established that the parties so intended.'

According to article 32 VCLT recourse may furthermore be had to supplementary means of interpretation including the preparatory work of the treaty and the circumstances of its conclusion.[11] The *travaux préparatoires* may be of use to further clarify the meaning of a provision. Consequently, when necessary, these supplementary means of interpretation will also be addressed in order to answer the question whether a particular provision has horizontal effect.

Other important sources of interpretation will also be addressed. These sources include the interpretations by the treaties' supervisory bodies, the ICESCR's UN Committee on Economic, Social and Cultural Rights and the ICCPR's UN Human Rights Committee (HRC).[12] These supervisory bodies have on several occasions dealt with the issue of violations of human rights by private entities in the so-called General Comments which contain interpretative statements on the provisions of the Covenants. The statements in these General Comments regarding the applicability of certain human rights provisions to non-State entities have, to my knowledge not been contested by States. According to the HRC these General Comments can be considered to constitute a 'jurisprudential commitment'.[13] It is submitted that the General Comments can serve as an indication of a development towards recognition of the principle of horizontal effect under the ICCPR and the ICESCR. Case-law can also be of assistance when interpreting a treaty provision. Hence, the case-law under the Optional Protocol of the ICCPR will be examined to see whether the HRC has recognised the horizontal effect of ICCPR provisions.

When relevant, interpretations by other supervisory bodies will also be taken into account. It is particularly interesting to examine the case-law under the European Convention on Human Rigths (ECHR) as the concept of *Drittwirkung* has been most explicitly recognised by the European Court of Human Rights and the – now defunct – European Commission on Human Rights.[14] This is not surprising in view of the fact that the Court and the Commission have applied a particular contextual and evolutive

11 Recourse may be had to these supplementary means of interpretation in order to confirm the meaning resulting from the application of article 31 or to determine the meaning when the interpretation according to article 31(a) leaves the meaning ambiguous or obscure; or (b) leads to a result which is manifestly absurd or unreasonable.

12 The applicability of the general rule of interpretation as laid down in article 31 VCLT in the interpretation of the ICCPR, has been confirmed by the HRC. In the case *Van Duzen* v. *Canada*, submitted under the Optional Protocol to the ICCPR, the HRC clearly stated that when interpreting the provisions of the ICCPR regard should be had, *inter alia,* to its object and purpose. UN Doc. A/36/40, p. 150, para. 10.2.

13 UN Doc. CCPR/C/133, 22 December 1997, para. 57.

14 For an elaborate survey of these cases, see Andrew Clapham, *Human Rights in the Private Sphere*, Clarendon Press, Oxford, 1993, pp. 178-245.

approach when interpreting the Convention.[15] Other treaties and agreements on human rights adopted after the realisation of the International Bill of Rights can also provide assistance in finding subsequent practice in interpretation and will therefore, when relevant, be taken into account

In sum, to answer the question whether a human rights provision in the International Bill of Rights lends itself for application in the legal relations of a corporation, the provision will be interpreted by examining its general wording, the context (in the light of the object and purpose of the treaty/declaration) and, if necessary, the preparatory work and the circumstances of its conclusion. In this analysis, particular attention will be paid to the interest that a specific provision aims to protect, as it is the nature of the provision and not so much its formulation that entails horizontal effect.

The analysis will be conducted following the order of the provisions in the UDHR and the corresponding provisions in the ICCPR and the ICESCR. For the sake of clarity the conclusions of the analysis which provisions are or which provisions are not applicable to the legal relations of corporations will be presented in a table on page 73. The UDHR will be the point of departure but the emphasis will be placed on the corresponding provisions in the Covenants, as the aim is to find applicable norms of a legally binding nature.

2.2.1 Object and Purpose of the International Bill of Rights

Clearly an article cannot be interpreted independently from the whole text of the treaty. The general rules for interpretation in the VCLT provide that a treaty shall be interpreted within its context, which includes the preamble of the treaty. The preamble can assist in elucidating the object and the purpose of the agreement.[16] At this point it is therefore important to reiterate that the preamble of the UDHR provides 'that every individual and every organ of society (…) shall strive (…) to promote respect for these rights'. It was observed in the previous chapter that the two Covenants contain similar provisions directly addressing non-State actors.[17] It is therefore argued that the Parties that adopted the UDHR and ratified the Covenants had the shared expectation that the International Bill of Rights would also address non-State entities. However, as concluded in the preceding chapter, on their own, these provisions do not offer sufficient

15 *Tyrer* v. *United Kingdom*, Judgment of 25 April 1978, series A, Vol.26, p. 15: 'The Court must also recall that the Convention is a living instrument which (…) must be interpreted in the light of the present day conditions'. This position was repeated in later case-law such as *Marckx* v. *Belgium*, Judgment of 13 June 1979, Series A, Vol. 31, p.19 and *Dudgeon v. UK*, 1981, Judgment of 22 October 1981, Series A, Vol. 45, p. 24. For more on the interpretation of the Convention, see: P. van Dijk and G.J.H. van Hoof, *Theory and Practice of the European Convention on Human Rights*, 3rd ed., Kluwer Law International, The Hague etc., 1998, pp. 72-82, regarding evolutive interpretation see, pp. 77-80.

16 Ian McTaggart Sinclair, *Vienna Convention on the Law of Treaties*, 2nd. rev. and enlarged ed., Manchester University Press, Manchester, 1984, pp. 127-128.

17 See p. 41-44.

evidence for the *Drittwirkung* of each separate provision in the International Bill of Rights. Nonetheless, they do constitute the background against which each provision in the UDHR, the ICCPR and the ICESCR should be interpreted.

It is concluded that, in general, the object and purpose of the International Bill of Rights is to promote the observance of and respect for human rights not only by States but also by non-State entities such as corporations. In the light of this general object and purpose I will now examine each substantive provision in the International Bill of Rights in order to answer the question as to whether the particular provision can be applicable to the legal relations of corporations.

2.2.2 Tentative List of Norms Applicable to Corporations

Equality and the *Prohibition of Discrimination*

The UDHR contains an explicit reference to the concept of equality in a separate provision.[18] In the ICESCR and the ICCPR the most important articles regarding the promotion of equality are the provisions on the prohibition of discrimination.[19] They do not explicitly refer to discrimination between private individuals as such, but the wording of the general articles on discrimination, article 2 (2) ICESCR and article 3 ICCPR, is sometimes taken to imply that the prohibition of discrimination is not restricted to public bodies. The fact that States should 'guarantee' the exercise of rights without discrimination suggests that the obligation extends beyond public bodies, in other words: that it has indirect horizontal effect. Such a conclusion cannot, however, be drawn based merely on the wording of these provisions as it is not clear whether the provisions also oblige State Parties to guarantee these rights against private interference. In General Comment 18 [37] that deals with the prohibition of discrimination as laid down in articles 2(1), 3 and 26 of the ICCPR, the HRC affirms the assumption that these articles have indirect horizontal effect. The HRC states that it wishes to be informed 'if there remain any problems of discrimination in fact, which may be practised either by public authorities, by the communities, or by private persons or bodies.'[20]

This implies that the general prohibition of discrimination extends beyond public bodies. The concept of equality and non-discrimination can also be found in various other substantive articles of the Covenants. For example, the principle of non-discrimination is set forth in article 20 (2) ICCPR which deals with war propaganda and in article 7 ICESCR on the enjoyment of just and favourable conditions of work. The

18 Article 1 UDHR.

19 Articles 2[1], 3, 4[1], 20[2], 24[1] and 26 ICCPR and articles 2 [2-3], 3 and 7 ICESCR. In the UDHR the prohibition of discrimination can be found in article 2.

20 UN Doc.CPR/C/21/Rev.1/Add.1 (pp. 1-4), 9 November 1989, para. 9.

work of the supervisory bodies on these substantive articles confirms that equality and the prohibition of discrimination also cover private activities.[21]

Non-discrimination provisions in human rights instruments drawn up after the adoption of the two Covenants of 1966 are more explicit as regards the indirect horizontal effect. Article 2 (e) of the Convention on the Elimination of All Forms of Discrimination Against Women (CEDAW)[22] obliges States to take measures against private entities to eliminate discrimination.[23] A similar obligation can be found in the Convention on the Elimination of All Forms of Racial Discrimination (CERD).[24] The applicability of the prohibition of discrimination to corporations has been affirmed in various legally non-binding documents. For example, the Copenhagen Declaration on Social Development and Programme of Action[25] sets forth in paragraph 45:

> 'Particular efforts by the public and private sectors are required in all spheres of employment policy to ensure gender equality, equal opportunity and non-discrimination on the basis of race/ethnic group, religion, age, health and disability, and with full respect for applicable international instruments.'

Even though the Copenhagen Declaration is not legally binding it does provide assistance for the purpose of interpretation as it may indicate the subsequent practice of the States that have adopted the International Bill of Rights. The significant Declaration was adopted by the vast majority of States and can be taken to reflect the majority stance.

Finally, the Tripartite Declaration of Principles Concerning Multinational Enterprises and Social Policies of the International Labour Organisation (ILO)[26] should be mentioned. According to article 22, multinational enterprises should be guided by the principle of non-discrimination throughout their operations.[27] Again, this document is

---

21 See also p. 65-66, 70.

22 GA Res. 34/180, 34 UN GAOR Supp. (No.46), at p. 193, UN Doc. A/34/46, which entered into force on 3 September 1981.

23 See also, articles 2 (b), 11 [1] and 13 ICEDAW.

24 Article 2 (d) ICERD states: 'Each State Party shall prohibit and bring to an end, by all appropriate means, including legislation as required by circumstances, racial discrimination by any persons, group or organization'. Article 5 (f) states: '(...) States Parties undertake to prohibit and eliminate racial discrimination (...), notably in the enjoyment of the following rights: (...) the right of access to any place or service intended for use by the general public, such as transport, hotels, restaurants, cafes, theatres and parks'.

25 Adopted at the World Summit for Social Development, Copenhagen, 12 March 1995, UN Doc. A/CONF.166/9 (1995).

26 Adopted by the Governing Body of the International Labour Office at its 204th Session (Geneva, November 1977 as amended at its 279th Session (Geneva, November 2000). The ILO Tripartite Declaration will be discussed in detail in chapter V, p. 109 *ff.*

27 As a general principle it is stated in article 8 of the ILO Tripartite Declaration that 'All Parties concerned by this Declaration should respect (...) the Universal Declaration of Human Rights and the cor-

not legally binding but the Declaration is a high-level statement representing the vast majority of States.

We may conclude that, besides the indirect *Drittwirkung* of the provisions on equality and the prohibition of discrimination, these norms are also directly applicable to horizontal relations.

The Right to Life[28]

From the wording of the article in the ICCPR dealing with the right to life it does not appear, *prima facie*, that protection extends beyond a public violation of this right. Article 6 [1] ICCPR requires that State Parties protect the right to life 'by law'.[29] However, given the fundamental importance of this right it is suggested that the article should be interpreted as also covering private relations. Nowak argues that this vital article can be considered to have an 'all-round effect' *i.e.* to ensure solemnly proclaimed fundamental rights against encroachment by private parties and governmental organs alike.[30] The *travaux préparatoires* confirm this conclusion. The majority of delegates spoke out in favour of the indirect horizontal effect of the norm by obliging States to protect life against unwarranted actions by public authorities as well as by private persons.[31] The HRC has frequently referred to the threat to the right to life posed by private actors when commenting on State reports.[32] Even though the State is held ultimately accountable, the fact that the Committee explicitly makes the connection between the right to life and private actors, can be taken to mean that the right to life is indeed applicable between private actors

The way in which corporations infringe the right to life will often be indirect by means of support rendered to governments that violate the right to life. But corporations can also be more directly involved. For example, corporations can directly infringe the right to life by employing private security forces that violate human rights[33], by causing extensive environmental damage or as a result of inadequate safety measures. An example of the latter is the accident in Bhopal, India, in 1984 when toxic gas leaked from a Union Carbide plant killing over 2,000 people and injuring over 200,000. In the light of the object and purpose of the right to life it can be submitted that this provision is applicable in the legal relations of corporations.

---

responding International Covenants (...). As all Parties includes employers this is a confirmation of the horizontal effect of human rights in general.

28 Article 3 UDHR and Article 6[1-6] ICCPR.

29 This clause is not included in article 3 UDHR.

30 Manfred Nowak, *U.N. Covenant on Civil and Political Rights: CCPR Commentary,* Engel, Kehl am Rhein 1993, p. 106 note 12.

31 Marc J. Bossuyt, *Guide to the 'Travaux Préparatoires of the ICCPR*, Martinus Nijhoff Publishers, Dordrecht, 1987, p. 120.

32 See, for example, UN Doc.CCPR/C/79/Add.14, 28 December 1992, para. 6.

33 See, for example, the report by Human Rights Watch, *The Price of Oil. Corporate Responsibility and Human Rights Violations in Nigeria's Oil Producing Communities,* January 1999.

The Prohibition of Slavery, Slave Trade, Servitude and Forced or Compulsory Labour[34]

From the absolute formulation of this article it can be deduced that it covers slavery and comparable practices, whether of a public or private nature. The prohibition of slavery and comparable practices is notably threatened by economic actors. For this provision to be effective it clearly should apply to private entities. As Nowak observes regarding the prohibition of slavery in the ICCPR:

> '(…) slavery functions as a means of economic oppression exclusively for the benefit of *private interests*. (…) The true eradication of slavery and comparable practices is therefore opposed not by the State's national interests but rather by deeply ingrained socio-cultural traditions (…) and by unscrupulous *business interests*.'[35] [Emphasis added]

This observation leads Nowak to conclude that the prohibition of slavery has indirect horizontal effect.[36] This conclusion can be drawn based on the fact that the prohibition of slavery is a norm of a *jus cogens* character. Given the fundamental character it should be concluded that the State should protect against a violation of the prohibition of slavery irrespective of whether the violation is of a public or a private nature. Whereas in the past slavery was defined narrowly, nowadays the definition is broader including forced labour. In a report on forced labour in Myanmar, the ILO comes to the conclusion, after a thorough analysis of existing instruments at the international level,

> 'that there exists now in international law a peremptory norm prohibiting any recourse to forced labour and that the right not to be compelled to perform forced or compulsory labour is one of the basic human rights'.[37]

It may therefore be concluded that, given their peremptory character, both the prohibition of slavery ànd of forced labour have horizontal effect.

It is worth mentioning two related lawsuits filed in a federal court in the United States.[38] These class action suits were brought against *inter alia*, the American corporation *Unocal* regarding its joint venture activities in the Tenasserim region in Myanmar (formally known as Burma). Myanmar's military regime, the State Law and Order

---

34 Article 4 UDHR and Article 8 ICCPR.

35 Nowak, *supra* n. 30, p.145.

36 Nowak, *supra* n. 30, p.145.

37 *Forced labour in Myanmar (Burma)*, Report of the Commission of Inquiry Appointed Under Article 26 of the Constitution of the International Labour Organisation to Examine the Observance by Myanmar of the Forced Labour Convention, 1930 (No. 29), ILO, Part IV, Geneva, 2 July 1998, para. 203.

38 *John Doe I* v. *Unocal Corp.*, 963 F. Supp. 880 (C.D. Cal. 1997) (Unocal 1) and *National Coalition Government of the Union of Burma* v. *Unocal*, Inc., 1997 U.S. Dist. Lexis 2097 (Unocal II). These cases will be addressed in detail in chapter VII.

Restoration Council (SLORC), seized power in the Southeast Asian country in 1988 and has since been strongly criticised by the international community for its widespread political repression and other human rights abuses. *Unocal* signed an agreement with the State-controlled company 'Myanmar Oil & Gas Enterprises' (MOGE) to develop an oil pipeline (the *Yadana* pipeline) for the transportation of natural gas and oil from the Andaman Sea to Thailand via the Tenasserim region of Myanmar. In the complaint the plaintiffs alleged, *inter alia*, that the corporation, in conjunction with the government, used forced labour to clear the area for the project. The court held,

> 'Although there is no allegation that SLORC is physically selling Burmese citizens to the private defendants, plaintiffs alleged that, despite their knowledge of SLORC's practice of forced labor, both in general and with respect to the pipeline project, the private defendents have paid and continue to pay SLORC to provide labor and security for the pipeline, essentially treating SLORC as an overseer, accepting the benefit of and approving the use of forced labor.'[39]

The court, equating forced labour to slave trading, held that, as such, the claim was 'included in that "handful of crimes" to which the law of nations attributes individual responsibility'.[40]

It may be concluded that, in the light of the fundamental nature of the prohibition of slavery and forced labour, these provisions should be interpreted as having effect in the legal relations of corporations.

The Prohibition of Torture, Cruel, Inhuman and Degrading Treatment[41]

In General Comment 22 [44] the HRC concludes that the aim of article 7 ICCPR is 'to protect both the dignity and the physical and mental integrity of the individual'.[42] Moreover, article 7 ICCPR prohibits not only inhuman treatment but also degrading treatment. A dynamic interpretation of these provisions requires that the word 'degrading' should be interpreted as also covering degrading situations, which might be the result of unjust corporate practices. Corporate activities can pose a serious threat to the dignity and the physical and mental integrity of the individual. First and foremost this will arise from direct or indirect support for government policies. The right not to be tortured is frequently violated by public authorities, such as the police. Corporations may become involved due to the fact that they, for example, pay or otherwise support State security forces that commit these violations. But corporations can also be more directly involved. This can arise, for example, in the case of privatised prisons.

39 Unocal I, 963 F. Supp. at 891.
40 Unocal I, 963 F. Supp. at 891. This case will be further discussed in chapter VII.
41 Article 5 UDHR; article 7 ICCPR.
42 UN Doc.A/47/40 (1992), Annex VI (pp. 193-195), 3 April 1992, para. 2.

The horizontal applicability of the prohibition of torture, cruel and inhuman treatment further becomes clear from the broad interpretation of the HRC. In its view 'article 7 protects in particular, children, pupils and patients in teaching and medical institutions'.[43] This implies indirect horizontal effect: the State must ensure that these individuals are not subjected to torture, cruel or inhuman behaviour. The indirect horizontal effect of the prohibition of torture and cruel or inhuman treatment has been recognised in General Comment 7 [16] that also deals with article 7 ICCPR. Here the HRC argues: 'it is also the duty of public authorities to ensure protection by the law against such treatment even when committed by persons acting outside or without any official authority'.[44] In General Comment 20 [44] the HRC explicitly states:

> 'it is the duty of the State party to afford everyone protection through legislative and other measures as may be necessary against the acts prohibited by article 7, whether inflicted by people acting in their official capacity, outside their official capacity or in a private capacity.'[45]

The indirect horizontal effect of the prohibition of torture has been expressly enunciated in article 4, paragraph 1 of the Convention against Torture, which reads: '[e]ach State Party shall ensure that *all* acts of torture are offences under its criminal law. (...). [emphasis added]'[46] The European Court of Human Rights and the (former) Commission on Human Rights have also recognised the indirect horizontal effect of the provision in the ECHR prohibiting torture or cruel, inhuman or degrading treatment. This issue has emerged in the case-law on corporal punishment in private schools in the United Kingdom.[47]

It may be concluded that the prohibition of torture, cruel and inhuman treatment is applicable in the legal relations between non-State actors.

The Right to Liberty and Security of Person and the Prohibition of Arbitrary Arrest[48]
The reasoning in the previous section on the prohibition of torture, cruel, inhuman and degrading treatment, can also be applied to the first paragraph of article 10 in the ICCPR, which provides for the right to liberty and security of person. In practice, the

---

43 UN Doc.A/47/40 (1992), Annex VI (pp. 193-195), 3 April 1992, para 5.

44 UN Doc.A/37/40, 27 July 1982, para.2.

45 UN Doc. A/47/40, (1992), Annex VI (pp. 193-195), 3 April 1992, para.2.

46 Convention against Torture and Other Cruel, Inhuman or Degrading Treatment or Punishment, Adopted and opened for signature, ratification and accession by General Assembly resolution 39/46 of 10 December 1984, entry into force 26 June 1987.

47 See, inter alia, *Y* v. *United Kingdom,* report of 8 October 1991, Application no. 13134/87, *Wendy and Jeremy Costello-Roberts* v. *United Kingdom*, report of 8 October 1991, Application 14229/88. For a detailed discussion of these cases and other case-law, Andrew Clapham, *Human Rights in the Private Sphere*, Clarendon Press, Oxford, 1993, pp. 189-203.

48 Article 9, 10 ICCPR.

HRC frequently deals with article 10 in conjunction with the prohibition of torture, cruel, inhuman treatment, as set out in article 7 ICCPR.[49] Paragraphs 2-5 of article 9 ICCPR, which deal with procedural requirements regarding arrest and detention, cannot not be considered to have horizontal effect, however, as they require institutional measures in the field of law, such as procedural guarantees.

The Recognition of a Person Before the Law and Equality Before the Law,[50] *the Right to an Effective Remedy,*[51] *the Prohibition of Arbitrary Arrest,*[52] *the Right to a Fair Trial,*[53] *the Right to Presumption of Innocence*[54]

These rights are grouped together because the reasoning with regard to their possible horizontal effect is the same. From the wording of these rights it is clear that they are primarily directed at the State. These provisions call for institutional protection by providing procedural guarantees and creating specific legal institutions. This is the responsibility of State-organs. It is difficult to imagine how a non-state entity, such as a corporation, could violate these rights. Consequently it must be concluded that these rights do not have horizontal effect.

The Right to Privacy[55]

Clearly, both States and non-State entities can pose a threat to the enjoyment of the right to privacy. Nowadays, corporations especially pose a threat by disregarding personal data in their data banks or by spying on their employees.[56] In the light of the interest that the right to privacy aims to protect, it is submitted that this provision should be interpreted as being applicable at the horizontal level. The private threat to article 17 ICCPR has been recognised in General Comment No. 16 [32] where the HRC argues: 'in [our] view (…) this right is required to be guaranteed against all such interference and attacks whether they emanate from State authorities or from natural or legal persons.'[57]

49 See, UN Doc. A/47/40 (1992), General Comment No. 20 [44], Annex VI (pp. 193-195), 3 April 1992, para. 2 and the General Comment on article 10, No. 9 [16], UN Doc. A/37/40 (1982) Annex V (pp. 96-97); UN Doc.CCPR/C/21/Rev.1, (pp. 8-9), 28 July 1992, para 2.

50 Articles 6, 7 UDHR; articles 14, 16 and 26 ICCPR.

51 Article 8 UDHR.

52 Article 9 UDHR.

53 Article 10 UDHR and article 14 [3] ICCPR.

54 Article 11 UDHR and article 14 [2] ICCPR.

55 Article 12 UDHR and article 17 ICCPR.

56 *The Economist*, 'Don't pry Companies', 6 October 1990. This article describes the routine practiced by some corporations in that they regularly search cars, lockers, handbags, desks and so forth, claiming that economic risks necessitate such actions to guard against possible alcoholics and drug abusers.

57 UN Doc. A/43/40 (1988) Annex (pp. 181-183); UN Doc.CCPR/C/21/Rev.1, (pp. 19-21), 23 March 1988, para.1.

The *travaux préparatoires* confirm the conclusion that the right to privacy has indirect horizontal effect. During the drafting of article 17 ICCPR there was express recognition of the horizontal effect of this provision as it was mentioned that the State must guarantee the protection of this right against interference by private parties.[58] The indirect horizontal effect of the right to privacy under the ICCPR has thus been recognised.

The European supervisory bodies have also confirmed the indirect horizontal effect of the right to privacy on several occasions even though article 8 ECHR, the provision that deals with the right to privacy, does not explicitly provide for protection against private interference. The leading case is *X and Y* v. *The Netherlands*.[59] In this case the European Court stated:

> 'there may be positive obligations inherent in an effective respect for private or family life. These obligations may involve the adoption of measures designed to secure respect for private life *even in the sphere of the relations of individuals between themselves*.'[60] [Emphasis added]

It can be concluded that the provision on the right to privacy can be applicable in the legal relations of corporations.

The Right to Freedom of Movement[61]

Article 12 paragraph 3 provides States with the possibility to restrict the freedom of movement on specific public policy grounds.[62] This might suggest that article 12 ICCPR is exclusively applicable to States. However, these possibilities for restrictions on the part of the State should not detract from the object and purpose of the provision, which is to provide everybody with the right to liberty of movement and freedom to choose his residence. Article 12 ICCPR does not refer to any particular addressee as regards this responsibility. It is submitted that, in the light of the object and purpose of this provision, it can be considered to be applicable to corporations. This is especially so in the case of corporations which, due to the nature of their activities, have a significant impact on their environment, such as mining companies and oil companies,

58 Bossuyt, *supra* n. 31, p. 341 and pp. 346 f. and Nowak, *supra* n. 30, p. 289.

59 Series A no. 91 (1985). Other cases where the indirect horizontal effect of article 8 ECHR has been recognised are, *inter alia*, *Airey* v. *Ireland*, Judgement of 9 October 1979, Series A no. 32 and *Powell and Rayner* v. *United Kingdom*, Judgment of 21 February 1990, Series A no. 172. See also chapter VI, pp. 150-155.

60 At paragraph 23 of the judgment.

61 Article 13 UDHR and article 12 ICCPR.

62 Paragraph 3 reads: 'The above-mentioned rights shall not be subject to any restrictions except those which are provided by law, are necessary to protect national security, public order (ordre public), public health or morals or the rights and freedoms of others, and are consistent with the other rights recognized in the present Covenant'.

and which can severely hamper the enjoyment of the right to freedom of movement and residence.

The effect on the right to freedom of movement will often be indirect. For example, in the above mentioned federal lawsuit against *Unocal* due to their joint venture activities in Myanmar, one claim was that of the forced and violent relocation of entire villages in the Tenasserim region in order to clear and level the ground for the purposes of the project. It is clear that limiting obligations concerning the freedom of movement to States can in practice defeat the interest that the right to freedom of movement purports to protect. Finally, in General Comment 27 [67] the HRC has acknowledged the indirect horizontal effect of the right to freedom of movement by stating that 'the State party must ensure that the rights guaranteed in article 12 are protected not only from public but also from private interference'.[63]

It can be concluded that the right to freedom of movement can be applicable in the legal relations of corporations.

The Right to seek and enjoy Asylum[64] and *the Right to Nationality*[65]

These provisions are only found in the UDHR, not in the two Covenants. It is clear that these provisions do not have horizontal effect. They require the State to take institutional measures to guarantee these rights. It is difficult to imagine a corporation having a great deal of influence on the right to seek and enjoy asylum or the right to a nationality.

The Right to Family Life and the Right to Marry,[66] *Protection of Children*[67]

The general wording of the right to marry does not provide any arguments in favour of horizontal effect. This provision requires the State to provide for the necessary institutions to enable its fulfilment. The articles in the ICCPR and in the ICESCR, however, also protect family life in general. In General Comment 19 [39] the HRC clearly recognised the horizontal effect of this provision by observing that: 'State Parties often fail to give enough information on how the State *and society* are discharging their obligation to provide protection to the family and the persons composing it. [emphasis added]'[68]

Article 10 ICESCR protects more than just the right to marry and family life in general. Paragraphs 2 and 3 of this article read as follows:

---

63 UN Doc. CCPR/C/21/Rev.1/Add.9, UN Doc.A/55/40, Vol. I (2000), Annex VI A (p. 128-132), 18 October 1999, para.6.

64 Article 14 UDHR.

65 Article 15 UDHR.

66 Article 16 UDHR, article 23 ICCPR and article 10 ICESCR.

67 Article 10 [3] ICESCR and article 24 ICCPR.

68 UN Doc. A/45/40 Vol. I (1990) Annex VI sub B (pp. 175-177), 24 July 1990, para.1.

'(2) special protection should be accorded to mothers during a reasonable period before and after childbirth. During such period working mothers should be accorded paid leave or leave with adequate social security benefits.

(3) Special measures of protection and assistance should be taken on behalf of all children and young persons without any discrimination for reasons of parentage or other conditions. Children and young persons should be protected from economic and social exploitation. Their employment in work harmful to their morals or health or dangerous to life or likely to hamper their normal development should be punishable by law. States should also set age limits below which the paid employment of child labour should be prohibited and punishable by law.'

The protection of children is also provided for in article 24 ICCPR. This provision is of particular importance in the light of the widespread use of child labour. The provisions protecting the rights of children can also be considered to have horizontal effect. The State must prevent interference by its own agents but also by private parties.[69] Regarding the provision in the ICESCR, Craven observes: 'there is a clear recognition here that the responsibility of the State goes beyond the actions of itself or its agents, to positive protection of the individual from third party violations.'[70]

The relevance of the provisions protecting the rights of children for corporations is manifest. Corporations, especially in the fashion and apparel industries, frequently work with manufacturers and sub-contractors in so-called low-labour-cost countries. In these countries the use of children in the production process is rather common. Finally, article 3 of the International Convention on the Rights of the Child (ICRC) should be mentioned. This article reads:

'In all actions concerning children, whether undertaken by public or *private social welfare institutions*, courts of law, administrative authorities or legislative bodies, the best interests of the child shall be a primary consideration.'[71] [Emphasis added]

Concluding, it can be stated that the right to protection of children and family life can be applicable to the legal relations of corporations.

69 Nowak *supra* n. 30, p. 424.

70 Matthew Craven, *The International Covenant on Economic, Social and Cultural Rights. A Perspective on its Development*, Clarendon press, Oxford, 1995, p. 112.

71 The indirect horizontal effect is also reflected in articles 2[2], 3[3], 19[1] and 32 of the ICRC.

The Right to Property[72]

The UDHR is the only document of the International Bill of Rights that explicitly deals with the right to property in its article 17. The two Covenants do not contain provisions protecting the right to property. In scholarly writings two different aspects of the right to property have been discerned.[73] Firstly, the right has a classical aspect, *i.e.* the negative obligation of the State not to interfere with the right to property. Secondly, the right contains a social aspect that refers to the role of society with regard to the individual's right to property. Even though the ICESCR and the ICCPR do not contain an explicit provision on the right to property, the social aspects of property are implicitly referred to in the articles dealing with self-determination (1 [2] ICESCR and 1 [2] ICCPR).

Strictly speaking, article 17 UDHR does not create a 'right' to property as such but merely addresses restrictions on property ownership.[74] While it is not clear who bears the responsibility, the language of this provision is broad and comprehensive. However, the right is not an absolute one as persons can be deprived of their property under certain circumstances, although this may not be done arbitrarily. The *travaux préparatoires* indicate that the term 'arbitrarily' prohibits unreasonable interference by States.[75] However, in practice corporations are often the violators of the right to property in collusion with the State. Künneman describes several examples of large-scale deprivation of property by corporations in the 1990s.[76]

If the social aspects of the right to property are stressed, then it is clear that corporations do play a role. Howard and Donnelly have interpreted the right to property in terms of subsistence. According to them the right to property entails that,

> 'no individual or family should be deprived, either by private citizens, corporate entities, or the State, of the property that he or she, or the household unit may own or control in order to produce food or an individual or household income.'[77]

---

72 Article 17 UDHR.

73 Th.R.G. van Banning, *The Human Right to Property*, Intersentia, Antwerp 2002, *forthcoming* (pp. 14-16 of the manuscript) one file with the author.

74 Asbjørn Eide, Catarina Krause and Allan Rosas [eds.], *Economic, Social and Cultural Rights*, Martinus Nijhoff Publishers, Dordrecht etc. 1995, p. 146.

75 Catarina Krause & Gudmundur Alfredsson, 'Article 17', in *The Universal Declaration of Human Rights: a common standard of achievement*, Gudmundur Alfredsson and Asbjørn Eide [eds.], Martinus Nijhoff, The Hague, 1999, pp. 359-378, p. 364.

76 Fons Coomans and Fried van Hoof, *The Right to Complain About Economic, Social and Cultural Rights*, SIM Special No. 18 (Utrecht, 1995), pp. 134-135. The impact of the right to property on other human rights and notably the role of corporations has also been addressed within the UN. See, *inter alia*, the resolutions of the UN General Assembly and the UN Human Rights Commission: GA resolution 42/115, 7 December 1987 and UN Human Rights Commission resolutions UN Doc.E/CN.4/RES/1987/18, UN Doc.E/CN.4/RES/1988/19.

77 Jack Donnelly and Rhoda E. Howard, 'Assessing National Human Rights Performance: A Theoretical Framework', in: *Human Rights Quarterly*, Vol. 10, 1998, pp. 214-248, at p. 247.

If the provision is interpreted in the light of a subsistence right, it can arguably be concluded that article 17 UDHR, in certain circumstances, can be applicable to corporations. A corporation that deprives an individual of his or her means of existence by taking away property violates the interest that the provision on the right to property aims to protect.

The Right to Freedom of Thought, Conscience and Religion[78]

In the ICCPR these freedoms can be restricted on specifically enumerated grounds. However, as was discussed with reference to the freedom of movement[79], this clause on restrictions should not detract from the object and purpose of the provision which *in casu* is to provide everybody with the right to freedom of thought, conscience and religion.

General Comment 22 [48] does not shed much light on whether other entities besides the State bear responsibility for the right to freedom of thought, conscience and religion. The General Comment does however reflect the absolute nature of certain aspects of this right by stating,

> '[Article 18] does not permit any limitations whatsoever on the freedom of thought and conscience or on the freedom to have or adopt a religion or belief of one's choice. These freedoms are protected unconditionally, as is the right of everyone to hold opinions without interference in article 19.1.'[80]

The HRC continues by observing that the freedom to manifest religion or belief can consist of a broad range of acts including, *inter alia*, the observance of holidays and days of rest.[81] It is clear that corporations can profoundly affect this right. It is therefore submitted that, in the light of its object and purpose, the provisions on the right to freedom of thought, conscience and religion can be applicable in the legal relations of a corporation.

The Right to Freedom of Opinion, Expression and Information[82]

The absolute wording of the right to freedom of opinion, expression and information indicates that the articles extend beyond protection against interference by public authorities. Unlike the ECHR, article 17 ICCPR does not contain the phrase 'without government interference'. The *travaux préparatoires* confirm the horizontal effect of

78 Article 18 UDHR and article 18 ICCPR.

79 See p. 58.

80 UN Doc.A/48/40, Part I, (1983), Annex VI (p. 208-211); UN Doc.CCPR/C/21/Rev.1/Add.4, 20 July 1993, para. 3.

81 UN Doc.A/48/40, Part I, (1983), Annex VI (p. 208-211); UN Doc.CCPR/C/21/Rev.1/Add.4, 20 July 1993, para. 4.

82 Article 19 UDHR and article 19 ICCPR.

this provision.[83] This can be deduced from the decision taken during the drafting process not to add to the phrase 'the right to hold opinions without interference' the qualification 'by governmental action'. It was concluded that the right to freedom of expression was not only threatened by censorship measures by governments, but equally by private financial interests and media monopolies.[84]

However, even with respect to the provisions where the phrase 'without interference by a public authority' is included, private activities are not automatically excluded. For example, in article 10 ECHR, which contains the right to freedom of expression, the phrase 'without interference by a public authority' is included. Nevertheless, Clapham argues that it cannot be concluded that the drafters of the ECHR chose to limit the ambit of article 10 to the public sphere through the insertion of this phrase.[85] According to Clapham the

> 'inclusion of the phrase "interference by a public authority" was intended only to reinforce the State's willingness to hold public officials accountable rather than grant them immunity as state agents. (...).'[86]

The recognition that the freedom of expression is especially threatened by private entities is reflected in article 19 paragraph 3 ICCPR, which reads: '[t]he exercise of the rights provided for in paragraph 2 of this article carries with it special duties and responsibilities'. The inclusion of this paragraph and especially the reference to special duties and responsibilities was decided upon on the basis of the consideration that freedom of expression needs to be protected from the powerful influence of the modern media.[87] The HRC has rarely had to address the issue of indirect horizontal effect in the case-law on the optional protocol of the ICCPR. The indirect horizontal effect of the freedom of expression has, however, been recognised in a few cases.[88]

It can be concluded that, in the light of their general object and purpose, the provisions protecting the freedom of thought, expression and information may be applicable in horizontal relations.

---

83 Bossuyt, *supra* n. 31, p. 385.

84 Nowak, *supra* n. 30, p. 344.

85 Clapham, *supra* n. 14, pp. 229-231

86 Clapham, *supra* n. 14, p. 231.

87 Erica-Irene A.Daes, *Freedom of the Individual under Law. A Study on the Individual's Duties to the Community and the Limitations on Human Rights and Freedoms under Article 29 of the Universal Declaration of Human* Rights, United Nations, New York, 1990, p. 58. The ECHR includes a similar clause that sets limits on the freedom of expression.

88 See, *inter alia*, *Hertzberg* v. *Finland* (61/79), *B.d.B.* v. The Netherlands (273/88) and *Lindgren et al.* v. *Sweden* (298-9/88), para. 10.4.

The Right to Take Part in Government[89]
From the language of article 25 ICCPR it can be concluded that this provision is directed exclusively towards the State. The provisions require, *inter alia*, access to public service and elections. This requires institutional measures on the part of States.

The Right to Social Security[90]
The right to social security is mentioned in two articles in the UDHR. In article 22 UDHR the right to social security is connected to the right of everyone to the realisation of economic, social and cultural rights. This is one of the rare occasions where the UDHR explicitly mentions that the obligation rests upon the State.[91] States are called upon to co-operate in the creation of a world order that will make the enjoyment of the social, economic and cultural rights a reality. This resembles article 28 UDHR which sets forth the *right to a just social and international order*. This general obligation on States to co-operate clearly cannot have any horizontal effect. The right to social security will, however, mostly be associated with a list of social security benefits, which have become standard in Western liberal and socialist democracies. This list is provided in article 25 (1) UDHR. In addition to the right to an adequate standard of living this article reads as follows: '[e]veryone has (…) the right to security in the event of unemployment, sickness, disability, widowhood, old age or other lack of livelihood in circumstances beyond his control'.

Such an enumeration is lacking in the ICESCR article on social security that simply provides that States 'recognise the right of everyone to social security, including social insurance'.[92] So far there have been no General Comments on the interpretation of article 9. The *travaux préparatoires* provide evidence of the ideological debate that took place during the drafting of the articles on social security. Contrary to the Western States, the communist States advocated a great deal of State involvement.[93] It is clear that the provision on the right to social security calls for some form of State action. It can therefore be concluded that this provision is not applicable in the legal relations of corporations.

---

89 Article 21 UDHR and article 25 ICCPR.

90 Article 22, 25 [1] UDHR and article 9 ICESCR.

91 The only other provision where the State is explicitly mentioned is article 16 [3] UDHR which deals with the protection of the family.

92 Article 9 ICESCR.

93 Johannes Morsink, *The Universal Declaration on Human Rights: origins, drafting and intent*, PENN, Philadelphia, 1999, p. 200.

The Right to Freedom of Assembly[94] *and the Right to Form a Trade Union*[95]
The indirect horizontal effect of these provisions has been affirmed during the drafting of the provision on the right to freedom of association in the ICCPR (the right to form a trade union can be seen as a special case of freedom of association). The United States was unsuccessful in its efforts to limit the protection of the freedom of association to protection against 'governmental interference'.[96] In various non-legally binding documents adopted after the Covenants came into force, the direct applicability to corporations of the provisions on the right to freedom of assembly and the right to form a trade union has been confirmed. Naturally, the ILO plays an important role in this respect. The Tripartite Declaration mentioned earlier[97] contains elaborate provisions directed at corporations regarding the freedom of association and the right to organise.[98] It is concluded that these provisions are applicable in the legal relations of corporations.

The Right to Work, Conditions of Work and the Right to Rest and Leisure[99]
It hardly needs explaining that these provisions can be seriously threatened by corporations. Corporations are the violators *par excellence*. This, however, does not hold true for the right to work. This provision is exclusively directed towards the State, as becomes clear from the language of article 6 paragraph 2 ICESCR which reads,

> 'The steps to be taken by a State Party to the present Covenant to achieve the full realization of this right shall include technical and vocational guidance and training programmes, policies and techniques to achieve steady economic, social and cultural development and full and productive employment under conditions safeguarding fundamental political and economic freedoms to the individual.'

The right to just conditions of work and rest and leisure are clearly relevant to corporate conduct. It appears that these provisions are explicitly designed for horizontal relations. As Craven argues,

> 'In the context of article 7 [ICESCR] (...), if State obligations were limited to ensuring that public employees enjoyed fair conditions of work, the right would largely be deprived of effect (especially in the case of 'mixed' or 'market' economies). (...) It must be assumed that where the State is not in a position to ensure the rights itself, it must

94 Article 20 UDHR and article 21 ICCPR.
95 Article 23 [4] UDHR, article 8 ICESCR and article 22 ICCPR.
96 Nowak, *supra* n. 30 , p. 387.
97 See p. 52.
98 Articles 41-55.
99 Articles 23, 24 UDHR, articles 6 and 7 ICESCR .

> regulate private interactions to ensure that individuals are not arbitrarily deprived of the enjoyment of their rights by other individuals.'[100]

The indirect horizontal effect of the guarantees surrounding work also comes to the fore in a recent case that has arisen under the complaint procedure of the European Social Charter.[101] In the very first case brought under the complaint procedure, the International Commission of Jurists and the European Trade Union Confederation alleged that Portugal had failed to monitor labour conditions in private enterprises adequately. The European Committee of Social Rights found that Portugal was indeed responsible.[102]

The direct applicability of these provisions to corporations has also been affirmed in the ILO Tripartite Declaration which provides for detailed provisions on the conditions of work and life, wages, benefits and safety and health.[103]

The Right to an Adequate Standard of Living (Food, Housing, Clothing)[104]

In General Comment No. 12 on the right to adequate food the Committee on Economic, Social and Cultural Rights states that 'violations of the right to food can occur through the direct action of States or other entities insufficiently regulated by States'[105] and,

> '[w]hile only States are parties to the Covenant and thus ultimately accountable for compliance with it, all members of society – individuals, families, local communities, non-governmental organizations, *as well as the private business sector* – have responsibilities in the realization of the right to adequate food (...). The private business sector – national and transnational – should pursue its activities within the framework of a code of conduct conducive to respect of the right to adequate food (...).' [Emphasis added][106]

100 Craven, *supra* n. 70, p. 112.

101 The European Social Charter was adopted at Turin, Italy, in October 1961. The complaint procedure This Protocol was opened for signature on 9 November 1995 and entered into force on 1 July 1998.

102 This case concerned the employment of minors under the age of 15 being employed in several economic sectors where working conditions posed a threat to their health. The decision of the European Committee of Social Rights was reported to the Committee of Ministers. In resolution ChS (99) 4, adopted on 15 December 1999, the Committee of Ministers decided the case by referring to an earlier recommendation according to which Portugal was requested to provide information in its next report on the measures it had taken regarding the same subject of the complaint. *International Commission of Jurists* v. *Portugal*, Case 1/1998, http://www.humanrights.coe.int/cseweb/GB/GB3/GB32.htm, (accessed on 1 March 2002.)

103 Articles 33 - 40 ILO Tripartite Declaration.

104 Article 25 UDHR and article 11 ICESCR.

105 UN Doc. E/C.12/1999/5, 12 May 1999, para. 19.

106 UN Doc. E/C.12/1999/5, 12 May 1999, para. 20.

The Committee thus explicitly recognises the direct horizontal application of the provision on the right to food. With regard to the right to housing, the Committee has acknowledged the indirect horizontal effect of this provision by stating that,

> 'in view of the increasing trend in some States towards the Government greatly reducing its responsibilities in the housing sector, States parties must ensure that legislative and other measures are adequate to prevent and, if appropriate, punish forced evictions carried out, without appropriate safeguards, by private persons or bodies.'[107]

Right to Education[108]

From the language of the provisions on the right to education it is clear that the primary responsibility for the fulfilment of this right rests with the State. This is especially clear in article 14 ICESCR according to which State Parties should draw up a plan of action for the fulfilment of the right to education. The ensuing obligations for States are elaborated upon in the accompanying General Comment No. 11.[109] The Committee on Economic, Social and Cultural rights has, however, recognised that the provision on the right to education can entail obligations for non-State entities. In General Comment No. 13 the Committee, under the heading 'obligations of actors other than States parties', argues as follows,

> '[c]oordinated efforts for the realization of the right to education should be maintained to improve coherence and interaction among all the actors concerned, including the various components of civil society.'[110]

In this General Comment the Committee notably refers to various bodies within the UN system and the international financial institutions. It is submitted that the Committee has herewith recognised that the provision on the right to education is applicable to non-State entities and that this provision may therefore also entail responsibility for corporations.

The Right to Participate in the Cultural Life of the Community, Protection of Minorities[111]

Corporations can pose a very serious threat to minorities. A restrictive interpretation of the right to protection for minorities, an exclusively State-oriented interpretation, would deprive this provision of its object and purpose. The impact of corporations on the right to protection of minorities is recognised by the Committee on Economic,

107 UN Doc. E/C.12/1999/5, 12 May 1999, para. 20; UN Doc. E/C.12/1997/4, 20 May 1997, para. 9.
108 Article 26 UDHR and article 13, 14 ICESCR.
109 UN Doc. E/C.12/1999/4, 10 May 1999.
110 UN Doc. E/C.12/1999/10, 8 December 1999, para. 60.
111 Article 27 UDHR, article 27 ICCPR and article 15 ICESCR.

Social and Cultural Rights.[112] Even though the State is held accountable, the fact that the Committee makes explicit reference to the relationship between corporations and this right can be interpreted as an acknowledgement of the effect of this provision between private parties. Again, the activities of mining companies are particularly relevant. For example, the cases brought by indigenous tribes against oil corporations in Nigeria, the Amazon region and in Papua New Guinea demonstrate the impact of corporate activities on the right to freely dispose of natural wealth and the protection of minorities.[113]

Finally, several provisions will be analysed that are included in the two Covenants but not in the UDHR.

The Right to Self-Determination and the Right to Freely Dispose of Natural Wealth and Resources[114]

The right to self-determination was formulated against the background of de-colonialisation and was intended to provide protection against oppressive States. In the meantime world politics has changed, while new circumstances require a wider interpretation. Two dimensions can be distinguished in the right to self-determination as provided for in the first article of both the ICESCR and the ICCPR: paragraph 1 deals with the political content of the right to self-determination while paragraph 2 affirms the economic content of this right. According to paragraph 2 'all peoples may, for their own ends, freely dispose of their natural wealth and resources' and 'in no case may a people be deprived of its own means of subsistence'. In present-day circumstances this economic aspect of the right to self-determination is particularly threatened by the activities of corporations. Notably, mining and mineral corporations pose a severe threat to the ability of (indigenous) peoples to freely use their resources. The wider applicability of article 1 paragraph 2 has been confirmed by the HRC in General Comment 12 [21] by stating that '[t]his Right entails corresponding duties for all States *and the international community.'* [Emphasis added].[115] In view of the threat posed by corporations this should be interpreted as including these entities. The indirect horizontal effect of the provision on the right to self-determination has also been confirmed by the HRC.[116] Especially in the context of apartheid the question has regularly been asked whether States should prohibit corporations to do business in and with the South

112 See, *inter alia*, UN Doc. E/C.12/1/Add.23, 13 May 1998, para. 29.

113 This case-law will be discussed in more detail in chapter VII.

114 Article 1 ICESCR and article 1 ICCPR.

115 UN Doc.A/39/40 (1984) Annex VI (pp. 142-143); CCPR/C/21/Rev.1 (pp. 10-12), 12 April 1984, para. 5.

116 This issue arises especially with regard to the third paragraph of article 1 [3] ICCPR which reads: '[t]he State Parties to the present Covenant (...) shall promote the realization of the right to self-determination, and shall respect that right in conformity with the provisions of the Charter of the United Nations'.

African regime.[117] Finally, the fundamental nature of the right to self-determination should be taken into consideration when interpreting this right. As was stressed by the HRC,

> 'The right of self-determination is of particular importance because its realization is an essential condition for the effective guarantee and observance of individual human rights and for the promotion and strengthening of those rights. It is for that reason that States set forth the right of self-determination in a provision of positive law in both Covenants and placed this provision as article 1 apart from and before all of the other rights in the two Covenants.'[118]

If the object and purpose of this provision is to be fulfilled and in the light of the fundamental importance that should be attached to the right to self-determination, a dynamic interpretation of these articles should lead to the conclusion that the economic aspect of this provision applies horizontally.

The Right to the Highest Attainable Standard of Physical and Mental Health[119]

In its General Comment No.14, the Committee on Economic, Social and Cultural Rights has clearly recognised that the provision on the right to health is directly applicable to the private business sector. The Committee uses the same wording as in General Comment No. 12 on the right to adequate food:

> 'While only States are parties to the Covenant and thus ultimately accountable for compliance with it, all members of society – individuals, including health professionals, families, local communities, intergovernmental and non-governmental organizations, civil society organizations, *as well as the private business sector* – have responsibilities regarding the realization of the right to health. (…).'[120] [Emphasis added]

It can be concluded that the right to health can be applicable in the legal relations of corporations.

---

117 Dominic McGoldrick, *The Human Rights Committee. Its Role in the Development of the International Covenant on Civil and Political Rights*, 1994, Clarendon, Oxford, p. 252.

118 UN Doc. A/39/40 (1984) Annex VI (pp. 142-143); CCPR/C/21/Rev.1 (pp. 10-12), 12 April 1984, para. 1.

119 Article 12 ICESCR.

120 UN Doc. E/C.12/2000/4, 4 July 2000, para. 42.

The Prohibition of Imprisonment due to an Inability to fulfil a Contractual Obligation,[121] *Expulsion must be based on Law,*[122] *The Prohibition of Conviction for an Offence that was not an Offence at the Time it was committed*[123]
From the wording of these provisions it should be concluded that they are only applicable to States. The realisation of these rights requires institutional measures. Therefore, these provisions cannot be considered to have horizontal effect.

The Prohibition of War Propaganda[124]
Article 20 ICCPR requires States to prohibit, by law, any propaganda for war, and the advocacy of national, racial, or religious hatred. As a result of the inclusion of the phrase 'by law', this provision could be interpreted as only constituting an obligation for States. However, the provision can also be interpreted as being indirectly applicable to private entities. The State is obliged to prohibit not only official State propaganda but also war propaganda by private persons.

2.3 Concluding Remarks

The provisions in the International Bill of Rights were drafted with primarily States in mind. When the Declaration and the Covenants were drafted the main aim was to protect the individual from assaults on human dignity by the State as occurred in the Second World War. Nevertheless, it has been demonstrated that the general provisions do show that duties for non-State entities were considered important. Moreover, many of the rights enunciated in these instruments do not clearly identify who bears responsibility for respecting and protecting these rights. At this point it should be recalled that the object and purpose of the International Bill of Rights is to protect human dignity by promoting respect for human rights. If the interpretation of its provisions, in the light of its object and purpose, is geared to the changing circumstances, the horizontal effect of many of the provisions cannot be denied. In other words, if the interest that is to be protected is taken as the point of departure it is clear that many provisions in the International Bill are applicable in the legal relations of corporations. In the words of Meron: 'broad interpretations of rights are necessary for the effective protection of human dignity, which is the goal of human rights law'.[125]

It has been observed that the object and purpose of the provisions in the core human rights documents increasingly require that the obligations apply – directly or indirectly, at the horizontal level – to private entities. Such interpretations have been rendered by national courts and by the treaty bodies. Reference to the direct responsibilities of non-

121 Article 11 ICCPR.
122 Article 13 ICCPR.
123 Article 15 ICCPR.
124 Article 20 ICCPR.
125 Meron, *supra* n. 3, p. 170.

State entities is most explicit in the interpretative documents regarding social, economic and cultural rights. It appears that this evolution has advanced furthest with regard to these rights. This is confirmed in the *Quito-Declaration on the Enforcement and Realisation of Economic, Social and Cultural Rights.*[126] In principle 17 of this Declaration it is set forth that while States have the primary obligation to respect these rights, 'other actors such as multinational corporations and multinational organizations also have the duty to respect these rights and are accountable to them'. Furthermore, as discussed in the previous section, several provisions on civil and political rights can also be applicable to the legal relations of corporations. However, in most cases, it is only the indirect kind of *Drittwirkung* of the particular provision that has been recognised.

This has led some commentators to the conclusion that these provisions with indirect horizontal effect need to be reformulated in order to apply directly to corporations.[127] However, as stated earlier, the fact that the State is ultimately held accountable does not imply that the particular norm is not applicable at the horizontal level. It merely means that direct enforceability against the non-State actor at the international level is not yet possible. It has been demonstrated here that certain provisions can be applicable to corporations without the need for any reformulation.

To sum up, in the process of interpretation a trend towards increasing horizontal application of certain human rights provisions can be discerned. The adoption of the *Declaration on the Right and Responsibility of Individuals, Groups and Organs of Society to Promote and Protect Universally Recognized Human Rights and Fundamental Freedoms*, by the UN General Assembly in March 1999[128], affirms this development towards the horizontal application of human rights provisions. The third paragraph of the Preamble of this Declaration reads: 'all members of the international community shall fulfil, jointly and separately, their solemn obligation to promote and encourage respect for human rights and fundamental freedoms'. Article 18 provides,

> '1. Everyone has duties towards and within the community, in which alone the free and full development of his or her personality is possible.
>
> 2. Individuals, groups, institutions and non-governmental organizations have an important role to play and a responsibility in safeguarding democracy, promoting human rights and fundamental freedoms and contributing to the promotion and advancement of democratic societies, institutions and processes.
>
> 3. Individuals, groups, institutions and non-governmental organizations also have an important role and a responsibility in contributing, as appropriate, to the promotion of

---

126 Adopted in Quito, Ecuador in July 1998 by five regional non-governmental networks and more than 50 non-governmental organisations working on economic, social and cultural rights.

127 See, Dubin, *supra* n. 9, p. 41.

128 UN Doc. A/Res/53/144, adopted on 8 March 1998.

> the right of everyone to a social and international order in which the rights and freedoms set forth in the Universal Declaration of Human Rights and other human rights instruments can be fully realized.'

In the same vein article 16 sets forth:

> 'Individuals, non-governmental organizations and relevant institutions have an important role to play in contributing to making the public more aware of questions relating to all human rights and fundamental freedoms through activities such as education, training and research in these areas to strengthen further, *inter alia*, understanding, tolerance, peace and friendly relations among nations and among all racial and religious groups, bearing in mind the various backgrounds of the societies and communities in which they carry out their activities.'

This Declaration is a clear recognition of the direct human rights responsibilities of non-State entities such as corporations.

On the basis of the foregoing analysis it may be concluded that certain human rights provisions in the International Bill of Rights are applicable to the legal relations of corporations (in some cases pre-eminently so), while others are clearly not. Moreover, in my view an argument can be made that, within the group of applicable norms, certain provisions are also applicable on grounds of principle. It has been demonstrated in the above analysis, that certain provisions are interpreted as being directly applicable to non-State entities due to the fact that they aim to protect interests of a fundamental nature. The fact that these provisions belong to the category of *jus cogens* can be considered to support the assumption that these provisions are in principle applicable to corporations. Furthermore, it has been demonstrated that certain provisions are applicable to corporations in practice.

The conclusions following from the preceding analysis may be summarised as follows:

APPLICABLE NORMS		NORMS NOT APPLICABLE
In practice and on grounds of principle	***In practice***	
Equality	Right to freedom of thought, conscience and religion	Right to recognition as a person before the law and equality before the law
Prohibition of discrimination	Right to privacy	Right to an effective remedy
Right to life	Freedom of movement	Right to a fair trial
Prohibition of slavery, slave trade and forced labour	Right to family life	Right to presumption of innocence
Prohibition of torture, cruel or inhuman and degrading treatment	Prohibition of exploitation of children	Right to seek and enjoy asylum
	Right to property	Right to a nationality
	Freedom of opinion, expression and information	Right to take part in government
	Right to participate in the cultural life of the community and the protection of minorities	Prohibition of arbitrary arrest and unlawful detention.
	Prohibition of war propaganda	Prohibition of imprisonment due to inability to fulfil a contractual obligation
	Right to form a trade union (right to assembly)	Prohibition of retroactive penal laws.
	Right to favourable conditions of work, rest and leisure	Prohibition of conviction for offence that was not an offence at the time it was committed
	Right to liberty and security of person	Expulsion must be based on law
	Right to an adequate standard of living (in particular, the right to food)	Right to social security
	The right to freely dispose of natural wealth and resources	Right to marry
	Right to health	Right to work
	Right to education	

In the above analysis, several examples of the potential impact of corporations on the rights concerned have been added in order to illustrate the potential relevance of the particular human rights provisions to corporate conduct. In some cases, it can be argued that, in the light of present-day circumstances, particular provisions would largely be deprived of effect if protection were only offered against the activities of State agents.

In the next chapter an attempt will be made to identify more precisely the exact implications for corporations. Based on the norms enumerated in this section, the next section will demonstrate, by means of examples, that corporations do indeed have human rights obligations.

CHAPTER IV
HUMAN RIGHTS OBLIGATIONS OF CORPORATIONS

1 INTRODUCTION

In the previous chapter it has been concluded that certain human rights provisions in the International Bill of Rights can be applicable to the legal relations of corporations. In this chapter an attempt will be made to clarify the implications of that conclusion on the basis of an identification of correlative obligations. This analysis will be conducted on the basis of a typology of obligations that can be derived from each separate human right.

In scholarly writings different types of obligations have been distinguished in an attempt to clarify the concept of human rights obligations.[1] The types of obligations are distinguished and described in order to provide insight into the various types of State obligations in the human rights field.

One distinction which is often made is that between obligations of conduct and obligations of result. An obligation of conduct refers to behaviour (active or passive) which the bearer of an obligation should follow or abstain from. An obligation of result points to the results which the bearer of an obligation should achieve or avoid.[2] This distinction is related to the distinction between positive and negative obligations. Negative obligations require the bearer of an obligation to refrain from doing anything that can impair a right. Positive obligations require positive action on the part of the bearer of an obligation. It has been suggested that the distinction between negative and positive obligations coincides with the distinction between civil and political rights on the one hand, and economic, social and cultural rights on the other. According to this view, civil and political rights oblige the bearer of an obligation to abstain from a particular action and are therefore of a negative nature as opposed to economic, social and cultural rights, which are of a positive nature as they require positive action. This point of view, however, cannot be maintained. Scholarly writings[3] and the United Nations human rights mechanisms have demonstrated that every human right can

1 Several authors have addressed the theory of rights and obligations: Henry Shue, *Basic Rights. Subsistence, Affluence, and U.S. Foreign Policy*, Princeton University Press, Princeton, 1980; Asbjørn Eide, *The Right to Food*, UN Doc. E/CN.4/Sub.2/1987/23, 7 July 1987; G.J.H. van Hoof, 'The Legal Nature of Economic, Social and Cultural Rights: a Rebutal of Some Traditional Views', in: *The Right To Food,* P. Alston and K. Tomaševski [eds.], Stichting Studie- en Informatiecentrum Mensenrechten – SIM/Martinus Nijhoff Publishers, Utrecht/Dordrecht, 1984.

2 See, with reference to the right to food, Eide, UN Doc. E/CN.4/Sub.2/1987/23, 7 July 1987, para. 71.

3 See, *inter alia*, Jack Donnelly, *Universal Human Rights in Theory and in Practice*, Cornell University Press, New York 1989, p. 33.

contain both negative and positive aspects. For example, with regard to article 6 ICCPR, which contains the right to life, the HRC has upheld that this right does not merely require the State to refrain from interfering, it also requires States to take positive action *e.g.* to reduce infant mortality, to increase life expectancy and to take measures to eliminate malnutrition and epidemics.[4]

Likewise, whether an obligation of conduct or an obligation of result will be applicable depends on the concrete circumstances. From the corporate side it is often maintained that only negative obligations can apply to the activities of corporations. However, from the analysis presented below, it can be concluded that, in certain circumstances, obligations of a positive character can also be discerned for corporations.

2 Tripartite Typology

The abstract categories of negative/positive obligations or obligations of conduct/result are not very useful to clarify the nature and scope of human rights obligations for corporations. A more sophisticated, and therefore more useful, analytical tool is the tripartite typology as developed by Shue and Eide. This tripartite typology discerns several levels of obligations. Every human right, whether civil, political, economic, social or cultural, may include several or all of the obligations discerned in the typology.

The tripartite typology of obligations was first developed by Henry Shue in his book *Basic Rights -Subsistence, Affluence and U.S. Foreign Policy*.[5] In this work Shue rejects the dichotomy between economic rights and political rights.[6] He claims that both categories of rights contain certain basic rights, which are fundamental to every human being. Distinctions exist, according to Shue, between duties, not between rights. According to Shue, the complete fulfilment of each right involves the performance of multiple kinds of obligations.[7] The three types of duties Shue distinguishes are:

> 'I. Duties to *avoid* depriving
> II. Duties to *protect* from deprivation
> III. Duties to *aid* the deprived'[8]

4 UN Doc. A/37/40 (1982) Annex V (pp. 93-94); CCPR/C/21/Rev.1, (pp. 4-6), 27 July 1982, para. 5.
5 Shue, *supra* n. 1.
6 Shue, *supra* n. 1, p. 7.
7 Shue, *supra* n. 1, p. 52.
8 Shue, *supra* n. 1, p.52.

Shue's tripartite typology has been applied by a number of human rights scholars and within several human rights forums, especially with regard to the right to food.[9] In 1987, the tripartite typology was reintroduced by Eide, at that time the Special Rapporteur on the Right to Food, in several UN-reports on the right to food.[10] Eide, slightly altering the terms used by Shue, distinguishes State responsibility for human rights at the following three levels:

'I. the obligation to *respect* human rights
II. the obligation to *protect* human rights
III. the obligation to *fulfil* human rights'[11]

According to Eide, the obligation to respect requires States to abstain from doing anything that violates the recognised right. The second obligation, to protect, requires States to take the necessary steps to prevent individuals from violating the recognised rights. Finally, the obligation to fulfil requires the State to take measures to ensure the attainment of the recognised needs.[12] The first level of obligation, the obligation to respect, corresponds with the notion of negative obligations. The second and third level of obligation, the obligation to protect and the obligation to fulfil, relate to the concept of positive obligations. All three levels of obligations can entail elements of both obligations of conduct and obligations of result.[13]

The typology by Eide has gained considerable acceptance and has been applied by numerous scholars and also in non-academic work. It offers a functional tool by which to clarify obligations inherent in human rights.

The tripartite typology was developed by Eide with the responsibility of States in mind. The three types of obligations discerned are State obligations. This is in line with traditional international human rights theory. The fact, however, that traditionally the

9 In 1984 this concept was further elaborated in the book: *Food as a Human Right*, A. Eide [*et al.*] [eds.], Tokyo: UN University, 1984. This book contains the results of a research project regarding the right to food concluded by the Regional and Global Studies Division of the United Nations University in Tokyo, Japan. See also: P. Alston and K. Tomaševski, *The Right to Food: From Soft to Hard Law*, SIM/Martinus Nijhoff, Dordrecht/Utrecht, 1984. This book contained the results of a conference organised by the Netherlands Institute for Human Rights (SIM, in Utrecht, The Netherlands).

10 In 1983, the Economic and Social Council of the United Nations authorised the Sub-Commission for the Prevention of Discrimination and Protection of Minorities to carry out research into the right to food, ECOSOC res. 1983/140 of 20 May 1983. One of the members of the Sub-Commission, Asbjørn Eide, was appointed Special Rapporteur on the Right to Food. He published two interim reports (UN Docs E/CN.4/Sub.2/1983/25 and E/CN.4/Sub.2/1984/22). In 1987 he submitted his final report: UN Doc. E/CN.4/Sub.2/1987/23, 7 July 1987.

11 Eide, UN Doc. E/CN.4/Sub.2/1987/23, 7 July 1987, para. 66.

12 Eide, UN Doc. E/CN.4/Sub.2/1987/23, 7 July 1987, paras. 67-69.

13 This was also stated in the Maastricht Guidelines, which discuss State obligations. See paragraph 7 of the *Maastricht Guidelines on Violations of Economic, Social and Cultural Rights*, adopted in Maastricht, January 1997, reprinted in International Commission of Jurists, *Economic, Social and Cultural Rights: A Compilation of Essential Documents*, November 1997.

State is the bearer of obligations regarding human rights does not imply that it is only the State which has such obligations. It was demonstrated in the previous chapter that international human rights law applies to more entities than only the State. Eide also pointed this out in his report on the right to food where he argues that 'it should be kept in mind, however, that all members of society share a responsibility for the realisation of human rights'.[14] The realisation of a right may require more entities than just the State to undertake, or to abstain from, certain action. As Shue observes:

> '(...) for every basic right – and many other rights as well – there are three types of duties, all of which must be performed if the basic right is to be fully honoured *but not all of which must necessarily be performed by the same individuals or institutions.*'[15] [Emphasis added]

I therefore maintain that the tripartite typology can also be used as an analytical tool to identify obligation(s) that may be derived from a human right for non-State entities such as corporations.

For an analysis of the human rights obligations of corporations, it is useful to distinguish another level of obligations, *i.e.* the obligation *not to co-operate*. The involvement of corporations in human rights violations is often of an indirect nature, *i.e.* corporations become involved in human rights violations by supporting regimes that violate human rights. Complicity in human rights violations, which may occur in such situations, differs from the complicity that can occur in relation to subcontractors. Therefore, a distinction should be made between the obligations that may come into play in these two situations. With regard to business partners and subcontractors an obligation to protect may exist. Regarding corporate activities in/with repressive regimes the obligation not to co-operate may play a role in some circumstances. An excursion into such an additional type of obligations for corporations will be made in section 4 of this chapter.

Until now the tripartite typology has mainly been applied by scholars to one single human right in order to identify the different State obligations that result from this particular right.[16] Here the typology will be applied to a number of the rights that have been identified in the previous chapter as being applicable to the legal relations of corporations. I will not deal with those rights that are clearly relevant for corporations, such as the right to collective bargaining or the right to just and favourable conditions

---

14 Eide, UN Doc. E/CN.4/Sub.2/1987/23, 7 July 1987, para. 65.

15 Shue, *supra* n. 1, p. 52.

16 See Eide on the right to food, UN Doc. E/CN.4/Sub.2/1987/23, 7 July 1987; on the right to education, see A.P.M. Coomans, *De Internationale Bescherming van het Recht op Onderwijs [The International Protection of the Right to Education]*, NJCM, Leiden, 1992; on the right to health: Brigit C.A. Toebes, *The Right to Health as a Human Right in International Law*, Intersentia, Antwerp etc. 1998 and on the right to property: Th.R.G. van Banning, *The Human Right to Property*, Intersentia, Antwerp etc. 2002, *forthcoming*.

of work. It is more interesting to analyse the rights that, at first sight, might not seem to directly concern corporations. For this analysis two rights from the category of economic, social and cultural rights have been selected: the right to food and the right to health. From the category of civil and political rights the following rights will be analysed: the right to life and the prohibition of slavery and forced labour. The ensuing – tentative – enumeration of obligations is not meant to be exhaustive. The main purpose of this chapter is to demonstrate, how human rights obligations for corporations may be identified in practice.

First, the different categories of obligations which, in accordance with the tripartite typology can be derived from each single human right, will be discussed in general. Subsequently, an attempt is made to identify the various obligations for corporations to respect, to protect, and to fulfil following from the right to food, health, life and the prohibition of slavery and forced labour.

A preliminary remark should be made regarding the different character of the human rights obligations of States and those of corporations. The human rights obligations of States are ultimately based on the notion of sovereignty. This implies that the human rights obligations of States are of a broader character than corporate human rights obligations, as the scope of the latter will depend on the leverage of the corporation. The situations in which corporate human rights can be identified will be discussed in the following sections.

2.1 Obligation to Respect

According to Eide, the first obligation, *i.e.* the obligation to respect,

> 'requires the State, and thereby all its organs and agents, to abstain from doing anything that violates the integrity of the individual or infringes on his or her freedom, including the freedom to use the material resources available to that individual in the ways she or he finds best to satisfy basic needs.'[17]

The obligation to respect is in essence a negative obligation not to interfere and is applicable to more entities than just the State. This category of obligations can be considered the least controversial in the light of its applicability to corporations. This is also apparent in various corporate codes of conduct where corporations recognise the obligation to respect.[18]

17 Eide, UN Doc. E/CN.4/Sub.2/1987/23, 7 July 1987, para. 67.

18 See, for instance, *British Petroleum's* policy guide on human rights, which states: 'We are committed to respect the rule of law, conduct our business with integrity, and show respect for human dignity and the rights of the individual wherever we do business'. This policy guide is available at http://www.bp.com. (accessed on 27 June 2001).

For a corporation the obligation to respect may arise at several levels. In the first place a corporation has the obligation to abstain from direct interference with the rights of its employees. The very close relationship between the corporation and its employees creates a clear responsibility. However, the obligation to respect also applies beyond the circle of employees. This obligation calls for non-interference with the means with which individuals or groups take care of their own needs. This implies that a corporation is under the obligation to respect the rights of people residing on the land where the corporation operates. In addition to the obligations of corporations towards those people residing on their land, obligations to respect the rights of the wider community where the corporation operates also exist. A corporation must abstain from activities that impair the human rights of other people such as is the case when corporate activities result in severe environmental damage.

Violations of the duty to respect by corporations often take place in partnership. Numerous examples exist where corporations consciously assist States in the forcible transfer of a population from land which the corporation needs for its operations. In doing so the corporation becomes an accomplice in the violation of the human rights of these people. For example, the Canadian corporation *Talisman Energy* has been accused of supporting the forceful displacement of peoples in Sudan by the government, actions which are related to oil extraction.[19]

In the light of the fact that human rights violations by corporations frequently take place in partnership it is relevant to examine the notion of complicity under international criminal law. As pointed out by Clapham and Jerbi,[20] complicity under international law has been defined in the context of international crimes. In the *Akayesu* case the UN Rwanda Tribunal, looking at the notion of complicity in national civil and criminal systems, concluded that an individual can be an accomplice to a crime even where the principal perpetrator has not been identified or where guilt could not be proven.[21] Moreover, the accomplice need not even have desired that the crime be committed. According to the Court: '(…) anyone who knowing of another's criminal purpose, voluntary aids him or her in it, can be convicted of complicity even though he regretted the outcome of the offence.'[22]

19 See for a detailed account: Georgette Gagnon and John Ryle, *Report on an Investigation into Oil Development, Conflict and Displacement in Western Upper Nile Sudan*, October 2001. The report can be found at: http://www.worldvision.ca/ (accessed on 14 November 2001).

20 Andrew Clapham and Scott Jerbi, *Towards a common understanding of business complicity in human rights abuses*, Background paper for the Global Compact dialogue on the role of the private sector in zones of conflict, New York, 21-22 March 2001, http://www.globaldimensions.net/articles/cr/complicity.html (accessed on 1 March 2002). The Global Compact is discussed in chapter V, pp. 128-130.

21 *The Prosecutor* v. *Jean-Paul Akayesu*, Case No. ICTR-96-4-T, 2 September 1998, para. 531 *Annotated Leading Cases of International Criminal Tribunals. The International Criminal Tribunal of Rwanda 1994-1999*, André Klip and Göran Sluiter [eds.], Intersentia, Antwerp etc., 2001, p. 502.

22 *The Prosecutor* v. *Jean-Paul Akayesu*, para. 539, Klip and Sluiter, *supra* n. 21, 2001, p. 504.

On the basis of this definition of complicity, in the specific context of individual criminal responsibility, Clapham draws the conclusion that 'it seems safe to assert that international law considers that intentional participation in an internationally wrongful act constitutes complicity in the breach of international law.'[23]

The joint venture activities of the American multinational corporation *Unocal* in Burma provide an example of a violation of the duty to respect in partnership. A claim has been brought against *Unocal* with regard to their operations in Burma before the US District Court of California.[24] In this case a group of farmers brought a class action suit against *Unocal*, a number of its executives, the French corporation *Total S.A.*, the State-owned *Myanmar Oil and Gas Enterprise (MOGE)* and the military government in Burma (the State Law and Order Restoration Council (SLORC). The plaintiffs claimed that the business partner of *Unocal*, the State-owned corporation *MOGE,* made use of forced labour in the process of constructing the so-called Yadana pipeline in Burma. Furthermore, according to the plaintiffs, entire villages were forcefully relocated. As a result of the forced relocation the villagers were deprived of their crops and livestock. In addition to these violations of the right to food and the prohibition of forced labour, the complaint stated that several other human rights violations occurred in the area, including crimes against humanity, torture, violence against women, arbitrary arrest and detention and cruel and degrading treatment. Even though *Unocal* did not carry out these violations itself, it was decided by the district court that the corporation's conduct could be sufficient to amount to participation in slavery. According to the court:

> 'Although there is no allegation that SLORC is physically selling Burmese citizens to the private defendants, plaintiffs alleged that, despite their knowledge of SLORC's practice of forced labor, both in general and with respect to the pipeline project, the private defendants have paid and continue to pay SLORC to provide labor and security for the pipeline, essentially treating SLORC as an overseer, accepting the benefit of and approving the use of forced labor.[25]

This case shows that proceedings can be brought against a corporation for intentionally participating in human rights violations carried out by State authorities. In this case by continuing to pay the violator despite knowledge of the fact that forced labour was being used. Besides the intentional participation in human rights violations committed

---

23 Clapham and Jerbi, *supra* n. 20, conclusion.

24 *John Doe* v. *Unocal Corp.*, 963 F. Supp. 880 (C.D. Cal. 1997). This case is referred to as Unocal I because a related lawsuit was filed against Unocal in the same year by the National Coalition Government of the Union of Burma (NCGUB), the Federation of Trade Unions of Burma (FTUB) and an individual plaintiff. This case is referred to as Unocal II. Both cases will be discussed in detail in chapter VII.

25 Unocal I, 963, F. Supp at 892.

by States, which constitutes a violation of the corporate duty to respect, corporations may also inadvertently become involved in human rights violations when operating in States that violate human rights. In such a situation the possibility of corporations to influence the State may be limited. In section 4 of this chapter an excursion will be made into the so-called obligation not to co-operate which pertains to such situations.

It may be concluded that a corporation should abstain from acts independently or through participation, that result in violations of the human rights of individuals.

2.2 Obligation to Protect

The second obligation according to Eide is the obligation to protect, which,

> 'requires from the State the measures necessary to prevent other individuals or groups from violating the integrity, freedom of action, or other human rights of the individual – including the prevention of infringements of his or her material resources.'[26]

The applicability of the obligation to protect, which is positive in character, to corporations is somewhat less clear than in the case of the obligation to respect. It is submitted here that the human rights obligations of corporations, however, extend further than merely the negative obligation to respect. Interesting in this respect are the so-called allocative principles which Shue describes. He argues that the obligation to respect and the obligation to protect are closely interdependent. The guiding principle is 'the responsibility to take due care':

> 'One may not have intended to cause anyone any harm at all, but once one knows that serious harm is resulting from the ongoing operation of some institution, the benefits of which one continues to accept, one can no longer claim to be ignorant of the harm to be done: "in such situations, knowledge is not only power but also responsibility, because it places us in a position to act".'[27]

With regard to the State the obligation to protect has frequently been interpreted as the obligation to adopt legislation.[28] Corporations are not in the position to do this. How

---

26 Eide, UN Doc.E/CN.4/Sub.2/1987/23, 1987, 7 July 1987, para. 68.

27 Henry Shue, 'The Interdependence of Duties', in: *The Right to Food*, P. Alston and K. Tomaševski [eds.], International Studies in Human Rights, Netherlands Institute of Human Rights, Martinus Nijhoff Publishers, 1984, p. 91, quoting from his earlier work: Henry Shue, ' Exporting hazards', in: *Boundaries: National Authonomy and Its Limits*, Peter G. Brown and Henry Shue [eds.], Maryland Studies in Public Philosophy (Totowa, N.J.: Rowman and Allenheld), 1981, p. 136.

28 See, for example, the matrix developed by Eide. The obligation to protect the right to food consists, for a great part, of developing national legislation. Eide, UN Doc. E/CN.4/Sub.2/1987/23, 7 July 1987, p. 29. In Coomans's matrix regarding the right to education, the focus is also on the development of legislation, Coomans, *supra* n. 16, p. 234. See also the matrix presented by Toebes regarding the right

ever, this does not imply that corporations cannot realise the obligation to protect by other means. This may be deduced from Van Hoof's definition of the obligation to protect:

> 'the obligation to protect (…) forces the State to take steps – through legislation *or otherwise* – which prevent or prohibit others (third persons) from violating recognized rights and freedoms.'[29] [Emphasis added].

The obligation to protect comes into play in the relationship of a corporation with third parties. The opportunity for a corporation to take measures aimed at preventing human rights violations by third persons is likely to differ considerably depending on who these third persons are. The influence of a corporation on a State or State enterprise is of a different nature than is the case with private subcontractors and other business partners. Where a corporation operates in a State that is engaged in egregious human rights violations, the corporation will often not be in a position to take measures to prevent these violations. As will be explored in section 4 in such situations an obligation not to co-operate may exist. For a corporation the obligation to protect, *e.g.* the obligation to actively protect individuals from the harmful acts of a third party, will in particular enter into play in relation to (sub)contractors, joint venture partners, suppliers, licensees and other business partners. In many countries the major sources of human rights problems lie with these business partners. Corporations have a positive obligation to take measures, through contracts or otherwise, to ensure that their partners do not violate human rights.

Several multinational corporations have recognised the obligation to protect certain human rights in their codes of conduct. For example, *Levi Strauss* in its 'Global Sourcing & Operating Guidelines' says that the company will only do business with partners that adopt certain employment, health and safety standards. These standards cover child labour, forced labour, non-discrimination, working hours, wages and benefits, freedom of association and a healthy and safe workplace.[30] Similar provisions concerning business partners can be found in the corporate codes of conduct of, *inter alia*, *The Bodyshop*,[31] *Reebok*[32] and *British Petroleum*.[33]

---

to health. The obligation to protect mostly consists of the adoption of legislation. Toebes, *supra* n. 16, pp. 314-315.

29 Van Hoof, *supra* n. 1, p. 106.

30 Levi Strauss & Co., *Global Sourcing and Operating Guidelines: Business Partner Terms of Engagement*, adopted in 1991, http://www.levistrauss.com/about/code.html (accessed on 1 March 2002).

31 The Body Shop, *Trading Charter*, adopted in 1994, http://www.the-body-shop.com/usa/aboutus/charter.html (accessed on 20 November 2001).

32 Reebok, *Human Rights production standards*, adopted in 1992, http://www.reebok.com/about_reebok/human_rights/default.asp (accessed on 17 July 2001).

33 British Petroleum, *BP and Human Rights - Policy Statement*, http://www.bp.com. See the section on policies, expectations and guidelines which can be found under the heading corporate reporting. (Accessed on 17 July 2001).

It is possible that a corporation takes measures to prevent other individuals or groups from violating human rights but that, despite good intentions, these human rights violations still occur. It is important to realise that the obligation to protect, like the obligation to respect and fulfil, contains both elements of conduct and of result.[34] It will, therefore, not be sufficient when the action undertaken by the corporation consists merely of drafting guidelines. The obligation of result requires that the measures taken by the corporation include a continuous evaluation of these measures.

2.3 Obligation to Fulfil

The third obligation, according to Eide, is the obligation to fulfil, which

> 'requires that the State takes the measures necessary to ensure for each person within its jurisdiction opportunities to obtain satisfaction of those needs, recognised in the human rights instruments, which can not be secured by personal efforts.'[35]

Van Hoof has refined the obligation to fulfil by dividing it into the obligation to 'ensure' and the obligation to 'promote':

> 'The obligation to ensure requires more far-reaching measures on the part of the government in that it has to actively create conditions aimed at the achievement of a certain result in the form of a (more) effective realization of recognised rights and freedoms. The obligation to promote is also designed to achieve a certain result, but in this case it concerns more or less vaguely formulated goals, which can only be achieved progressively or in the long term.'[36]

Obligations to fulfil are mainly of a programmatic nature and require positive action. Imposing this type of obligation on corporations is usually considered the most controversial. States are and should be primarily responsible for the obligation to fulfil. It is contended, however, that besides the State's obligation to fulfil, a corporation may have a certain degree of responsibility towards society that goes beyond the obligation to respect and protect human rights.

Here I would like to make the tentative proposition that corporations might have an obligation to fulfil human rights in cases where employees are, as a result of their employment, devoid of the means to obtain satisfaction of their needs. This will occur when a corporation operates in a territory where the State is unable to fulfil the rights of the people living there. Such a situation may arise where a corporation operates in a remote, isolated part of the country or in a so-called 'failed State'. Moreover, the obligation to fulfil may come into play in situations where a corporation in fact acts as a State, *e.g.* if a corporation exercises traditional government functions. As will be

34 *Maastricht Guidelines*, *supra* n. 13, para. 7.

35 Eide, UN Doc.E/CN.4/Sub.2/1987/23, 7 July 1987, para. 69.

36 Van Hoof, *supra* n. 1, p.106.

demonstrated below,[37] such obligations will mostly consist of ensuring that an individual has access to those resources needed for survival.

With regard to the obligation to fulfil, the size and the resources of a corporation will play a more prominent role than is the case with the obligation to respect and protect.[38] It is clear that the opportunities for larger corporations to ensure the realisation of certain rights may be significantly greater than for smaller corporations.

3 Corporate Human Rights Obligations following from the Right to Food, Health, Life and the Prohibition of Slavery and Forced Labour

In the following sections an attempt is made to identify the various obligations for corporations to respect, to protect and to fulfil that can be derived from the right to food, health, life and the prohibition of slavery and forced labour.

3.1 Right to Food

3.1.1 Respect

For a State the duty to respect the right to food implies, *inter alia*, that the State may not expropriate land from people for whom control over that land constitutes the only possibility to satisfy their food needs.[39] For a corporation the duty to respect the right to food in general will imply that its corporate activities may not interfere with the ability of people to satisfy their food needs. This obligation is notably relevant for the extraction industry. Oil and mining companies can have a significant impact on the right to food of indigenous people residing on the land where the corporate activities take place.[40] The activities of oil companies in the Niger Delta in Nigeria provide an example. A report by Human Rights Watch entitled *The Price of Oil* demonstrates the profound effect which oil production can have on the environment and thereby on the right to food. Oil production results in damage to the environment as a result of oil-spills and hydrocarbon pollution. But the infrastructure set up to support oil exploration and production may also negatively affect the right to food. According to the report, oil companies have constructed roads or dredged canals, thereby disturbing delicate hydrological systems. As a result, fishing grounds were destroyed and a large percen-

37 See p. 90.

38 This is also recognised with regard to the State's obligation to fulfil. See, *inter alia*, article 2 [1] ICESCR according to which State Parties may implement the obligation to fulfil 'progressively' and 'to the maximum of their available resources'.

39 Van Hoof, *supra* n. 1, p. 107.

40 For more information on the impact of oil-corporations on human rights in general, see *Human Rights and the Oil Industry*, Asbjørn Eide, Helge Ole Bergesen and Pia Rudolfson Goyer [eds.], Intersentia, Antwerp etc., 2000.

tage of the local communities were deprived of their livelihood.[41] This constitutes a violation of the duty to respect the right to food.

3.1.2 Protect

For States the duty to protect the right to food implies the responsibility to prevent or counteract activities and processes which negatively affect the obtaining of food by adopting legislative measures that, for example, prevent local fishing or hunting grounds from being taken over and destroyed by stronger interests.[42] The duty of corporations to protect the right to food implies that the corporation takes measures to prevent its business partners from violating others' right to food. As the Committee on Economic, Social and Cultural Rights has pointed out in General Comment No. 12 regarding the right to adequate food, these measures can consist of a code of conduct as a guide for corporate activities. According to the Committee:

> 'The private business sector – national and transnational – should pursue its activities within the framework of a code of conduct conducive to respect of the right to adequate food, agreed upon jointly with the Government and civil society.'[43]

Adopting a code of conduct in which a company states its policy towards subcontractors and other business partners does naturally not only satisfy the duty to protect the right to food but can also ensure the duty to protect other rights.

3.1.3 Fulfil

The State is under a duty to fulfil the right to food either through assistance or by the direct provision of food or resources that can be used for food.[44] Eide, in his report on the right to food, mentions the provision of food to prisoners as an example of this duty for States. If prisons are run by corporations, such as is often the case in the United States, this obligation to fulfil (obligation to ensure) the right to food will also apply to the corporation.

---

41 Human Rights Watch, *The Price of Oil*, New York, 1999, pp. 53 - 90, specifically pp. 68-72.

42 Example mentioned by Eide in the report on the right to food, UN Doc. E/CN.4/Sub.2/1987/23, 7 July 1987, paras. 175-179.

43 UN Doc.E/C.12/1999/5, 12 April 1999, para. 20.

44 Eide, UN Doc. E/CN.4/Sub.2/1987/23, 7 July 1987, paras. 180-181.

3.2 Right to Health

3.2.1 Respect

With regard to the right to health the obligation to respect implies that States refrain from interfering directly or indirectly with the enjoyment of the right to health. For example, a State must not impede individuals in their access to the available health care services.[45] For a corporation the duty to respect the right to health may require that the corporation abstains from operations that may cause environmental problems that are detrimental to the health of employees and the people residing on the land where the corporation operates. Moreover, where corporations knowingly market unhealthy products, a violation of the obligation to respect the right to health will occur. An example of the latter is the aggressive marketing of powdered milk by multinationals in developing States. Due to a lack of clean water the use of powdered milk leads to an increase in infant mortality. In 1981 the World Health Organisation (WHO) set up a code for the manufacturers of powdered milk, insisting that they must not provide free samples of their product.[46]

3.2.2 Protect

The obligation to protect the right to health first and foremost requires States to take legislative measures to ensure that third parties provide health care services adequately and on an equal footing. This implies, *inter alia*, that the State adopts legislation in order to protect its citizens against those health threats posed by environmental pollution.[47] For corporations the duty to protect the right to health will come into play especially with regard to the 'underlying determinants'[48] of the right to health, such as food and nutrition, housing, access to safe and potable water and adequate sanitation, safe and healthy working conditions, and a healthy environment. The duty to protect may require a corporation to adopt guidelines in order to ensure that the activities of business partners will not lead to violations of other individuals' right to health. For example, a corporation should ensure that their subcontractors promote healthy working conditions.

---

45 Toebes, *supra* n. 16, pp. 316-320 and UN Doc. E/C.12/2000, 11 May 2000, para. 34.

46 The International Code of Marketing of Breast-milk Substitutes, WHO Resolution 34.22. For further information on the Code and alleged violations by corporations see the website of The International Baby Food Action Network (IBFAN): www. ibfan.org (accessed on 31 July 2001).

47 Toebes, *supra* n. 16, pp. 326 - 332.

48 UN Doc. E/C.12/2000/4, 4 July 2000, para.4.

3.2.3 Fulfil

The obligation to fulfil the right to health requires that the State provides access to health care services and informs the public on matters related to health care and/or provides or promotes that others provide family planning and pregnancy-related services.[49] It is conceivable that the obligation to fulfil comes into play when a corporation operates in a remote part where the State is not capable of providing for health facilities. In such a case a corporation may be under the obligation to fulfil the right of its employees to health by providing for health care services and hospitals.

3.3 Right to Life

3.3.1 Respect

The duty to respect the right to life implies that a corporation refrains from activities that lead to loss of life. There is a clear link between the right to life and a clean environment. Therefore, a corporation is under the duty to abstain from activities that cause such damage to the environment that it results in the loss of life. Furthermore, a blatant example of a violation of the duty to respect the right to life occurs when corporations hire death squads. A complaint has been filed in the United States District Court of the Southern District of Florida against the *Coca Cola Company* for allegedly hiring or otherwise directing paramilitary security forces that used extreme violence and murdered, tortured, unlawfully detained or otherwise silenced trade union leaders of the union representing workers at the defendant's facilities in Colombia.[50] The trade union that has filed the complaint, claims that the corporation maintains open relations with murderous death squads as part of a programme to intimidate trade union leaders. The *Coca Cola Company* denies any responsibility, claiming that the company does not own the bottling plants in Colombia that have been accused of complicity in the activities of the death squads. At the time of writing, the complaint has merely been filed. It remains to be seen whether the case will be allowed to proceed and will be heard on the merits. If it is found that the corporation indeed intentionally made use of death squads, this is a clear violation of the obligation to respect the right to life.

---

49 Toebes, *supra* n. 16, pp. 332-336.

50 *SinalTrainal et. al* v. *The Coca Cola Company*, complaint filed on 20 July 2001. The complaint can be found at: http://www.laborrights.org/. (accessed on 10 March 2002). The compliant is based, *inter alia*, on the Alien Tort Claims Act (ATCA). See, for more information about the ATCA: chapter VII, pp. 179-203.

3.3.2 Protect

A corporation is obliged to take measures to ensure that other people within its ambit of influence, such as subcontractors and other business partners, do not violate the right to life of others. An example of a violation in this regard is the security arrangements taken by oil companies to protect their personnel against violence and their property against sabotage. In the report *The Price of Oil*, Human Rights Watch demonstrates that private security forces employed by corporations are frequently responsible for committing large-scale human rights violations.[51] Corporations must formulate rules of engagement with security forces to prevent human rights violations. Corporations should establish screening policies to ensure that individuals or units of security forces that are known to have been responsible for human rights abuses will not be hired. Furthermore, companies should include human rights provisions in contracts with security forces and provide training in relevant human rights standards to guards in their employ. The obligation to protect does not only cover the hiring of security forces but also the aiding of these forces by supplying equipment.[52] In the past, *Shell* has admitted importing guns for the Nigerian police for use by the so-called 'supernumerary police', a group assigned to guard *Shell's* facilities. This group is notorious for human rights violations.[53] By providing this groups with guns the corporation runs the risk of violating their duty to protect the right to life. A complaint against *Chevron* oil company for, *inter alia*, violating the right to life is now under consideration in the United States District Court of California.[54] The plaintiffs in this lawsuit against *Chevron* claim that the corporation was an accomplice in violating the right to life by placing helicopters at the disposal of the Nigerian security forces, resulting in several people being shot. The killings occurred on 25 May 1998 when Nigerian activists took over an offshore oil platform. The Nigerian security forces, notorious for human rights violations, were brought to the platform in *Chevron* helicopters and ended the situation by killing two activists. In such cases, corporations must develop rules to ensure that the weapons or other equipment supplied, are not used to commit human rights violations while guarding their facilities.[55]

51 Human Rights Watch, *supra* n. 41.

52 See, for similar suggestions, Amnesty International, *Human Rights Guidelines For Companies*, Available at: http://www.amnesty.org.uk/business/pubs/hrgc.shtml#5 (accessed on 20 July 2001).

53 Human Rights Watch, *supra* n. 41, pp.174-175.

54 *Larry Bowoto et al.* v, *Chevron Corporation*, Case No. C99-2506 CAL (N.D. Cal 1999). On May 12, 2001 the court ruled that this case could proceed in the United States courts. See further chapter VII, pp. 194-195.

55 Both *Amnesty International* and *Human Rights Watch* have recommended that corporations take such measures. See, Human Rights Watch, *supra* n. 41, pp. 21-23 and Amnesty International, *Nigeria. Time to end contempt for human rights*, 6 November 1996, AI Index: AFR 44/14/96, DISTR: SC/PO/CC/CO/GR and *Sudan-The Human Price of Oil*, 3 May 2000, AI Index AFR: 54/01/00 ERR, DISTR: SC/CC/PG/PO.

3.3.3 *Fulfil*

The obligations that can be derived from the right to life mainly consist of obligations to respect and protect. However, as was explained by the HRC in General Comment 6 [16], the right to life is often interpreted too narrowly. The 'inherent' right to life also requires positive measures from the State.[56] The right to life should be interpreted as extending beyond protection against arbitrary deprivation of life to a duty to ensure access for the individual to the means of survival.[57] In this sense, it can be argued that a corporation may also have an obligation to fulfil the right to life. Given the fact that the protection of the right to life is so closely connected to other human rights, this implies a general obligation to contribute to the promotion and protection of human rights. It may be argued that 'the establishment of an environment conducive to respect for human rights in general will diminish the risks of excesses being committed against the lives of individuals'.[58] As explained above, Van Hoof introduced a refinement of the obligation to fulfil by dividing the obligation into an obligation to 'ensure' and an obligation to 'promote'. Where it concerns access to means of survival, a corporation may have the obligation to ensure. Several human rights are closely connected to the right to life, such as the right to food and the right to a clean environment. Regarding these rights a corporation may have the obligation to ensure. The obligation to promote consists of the more general obligation that can be derived from the right to life, the obligation to contribute to an environment which is conducive to respect for human rights.

3.4 Prohibition of Slavery and Forced Labour

3.4.1 *Respect*

The obligation to respect the prohibition of slavery and forced labour implies for a State that it does not make use of forced labour or slavery. The same obligation applies to corporations: they must not make use of forced labour or slavery in their operations. Certain industries are more likely to violate this obligation than others. Well known are the often slave-like conditions in the apparel industry. Allegations of the widespread use of child-slaves on Ivory Coast cocoa plantations have also emerged in relation to

---

56 UN Doc.A/37/40 (1982) Annex V (pp. 93-94): CCPR/C/21/Rev.1, (pp. 4-6), 27 July 1982, para. 5.

57 B.G. Ramcharan, 'The Concept and Dimensions of the Right to Life', in *The Right to Life in International Law*, B.G. Ramcharan [ed.] Martinus Nijhoff Publishers, Dordrecht etc., 1985, p.6.

58 Ramcharan, *supra* n. 57, p. 7.

the chocolate industry.[59] On 1 October 2001 the chocolate industry accepted responsibility for the poor labour practices on cocoa farms.[60]

3.4.2 Protect

The obligation to protect implies that a corporation takes measures to prevent third parties from violating the prohibition of slavery and forced labour. In relation to the example of slave labour on cocoa plantations in the Ivory Coast, the obligation to protect implies that a corporation ensures that the plantations that supply cocoa implement core international labour standards banning slave labour. Because the chocolate industry purchases its cocoa via the international cocoa exchange or other middlemen, it is impossible to ensure that slave or other forms of illegal exploitation have not been used in the production process. Therefore, the obligation to protect implies that the corporation should directly buy from the plantation instead of buying from third parties.[61] As mentioned previously[62], the chocolate industry has accepted responsibility for the damaging labour practices on the cocoa farms and has announced plans to work together with child labour experts, legislators, growers and unions to eliminate child slavery and other forms of exploitation.

3.4.3 Fulfil

The privatisation of the prison industry can again provide an example where the obligation to fulfil is violated by a corporation. Inmates in the privately owned prisons in the US are often employed in prison industries. Officially this work is voluntary. However, according to some observers, the work in fact amounts to forced labour as prisoners who refuse to work run the risk of solitary confinement and loss of privileges. Moreover, the prisoners are often paid much less than the average wage.[63] In such a

---

59 The use of child-slaves on Ivory Coast cacoa plantations has been documented by Unicef in 1998, www.unicef.org (accessed on 31 July 2001). According to a BBC documentary entitled: *The bitter taste of slavery*, up to 90% of the cocoa farms use slave labour. See the website of Anti Slavery, www.antislavery.org (accessed on 31 July 2001).

60 On this date the so-called 'Harkin-Engel' Protocol (named after U.S. Senator Tom Harkin and Representative Elliott Engel) was signed in which the industry accepts responsibility and announces measures to combat the use of child-slaves. It has been signed by leading members and companies of the cocoa and chocolate industry, the International programme for the Elimination of Child labour (IPEC programme) of the ILO, International Union of Food and Allied Workers, Child Labor Coalition, National Consumers League and the Anti-Slavery group 'Free the Slaves'.

61 Anti Slavery, *Statement on Slavery and Chocolate Production*, available at: www. antislavery.org. (accessed on 31 July 2001).

62 See p. 90 and note 59.

63 See the special feature *The Prison Industry: Human Rights Violations in the U.S.A.* on the website of Corporate Watch, available at: www.corpwatch.org (accessed on 31 July 2001).

case where a corporation in fact takes on a typical State duty, it must ensure that the prohibition of forced labour and slavery is ensured.

4 An Excursion into an Additional Type of Corporate Obligations: The Duty not to Co-Operate

In the foregoing sections corporate duties to respect, protect and fulfil human rights have been identified. In this section an excursion will be made into an additional type of corporate obligations as it is observed that the obligations discerned in the tripartite typology do not fit certain situations in which corporations are involved. Corporations that operate in States that are engaged in egregious human rights violations may unintentionally be brought into a position where they become involved in human rights violations. Besides the risk of becoming complicit in the human rights violations, the operations of the corporation might indirectly support the oppressive regime. In such cases it is not the duty to respect that comes into play seeing that the particular corporation does not in fact 'do' anything that violates the integrity of the individual. Moreover, the duty to protect will not come into play in such a situation, as the corporation may not be in a position to influence the State that commits the human rights violations. In light of this, it is necessary to refine the typology by adding another level of obligations: the duty not to co-operate. It is submitted that an obligation not to co-operate may arise for corporations operating in such States. The duty not to co-operate is placed between the duty to respect and the duty to protect as it has both negative and positive elements.

When does the obligation not to co-operate occur? The answer to this question depends very much on the specific circumstances of each case.[64] This obligation will most clearly arise in cases where the international community has spoken out about the illegality of a regime because of widespread and systematic human rights violations, for example by imposing international sanctions. Co-operation with such regimes may be a violation of the obligation not to co-operate. As put forward by Jungk:

> 'Companies operating in states adopting sanctions, whether unilaterally or as members of a regional organisation of the United Nations (UN), should not, as responsible members of their political community, undermine those sanctions by instituting commercial relations with the isolated government.'[65]

---

64 See: Margaret Jungk, *Deciding Whether to do Business in States with Bad Governments*, The Confederation of Danish Industries, The Danish Centre for Human Rights, The Danish Industrialization Fund for Developing Countries, 2001, p. 5. In this brochure Jungk has developed criteria that corporations should consider when planning to undertake or withdraw operations in States with a poor human rights record.

65 Jungk, *supra* n. 64, p. 5.

For example, during the apartheid regime in South Africa the United Nations adopted numerous resolutions stating the illegality of the regime in South Africa. These resolutions were outspoken regarding the role of corporations. Corporations were requested to disinvest.[66] The Truth and Reconciliation Commission has concluded that the business community was co-responsible for apartheid.[67] In such a situation, where the corporation itself is not directly violating human rights but where its conduct can nevertheless amount to participation, the obligation not to co-operate may come into play.

This obligation does not necessarily imply that a company should completely cease its business operations in such a State. It may also imply that a corporation must take measures to ensure that its operations do not result in violations of the human rights of its workers. A rather unique example of measures taken by corporations in order not to co-operate with a repressive regime is the 'Statement of Principles for US Corporations Operating in South Africa' (the so-called Sullivan Principles). This code of conduct was formulated in 1977 by the Reverend Leon Sullivan, a director of the US corporation *General Motors* which had operated in South Africa since 1926. The Sullivan Principles provided, among other things, that all workers should receive equal pay and there should be no segregation in workers' facilities. Moreover, corporations are required to 'secure rights of black workers to the freedom of association and assure protection against victimisation while pursuing and after attaining these rights'.[68]

More recently, the situation in Myanmar provides an example of a situation where the obligation not to co-operate may come into play. In this case, the international community has been very outspoken regarding the widespread human rights violations by the military government. The United Nations General Assembly and the UN Commission on Human Rights[69] have repeatedly condemned the practice of forced labour in Myanmar. The International Labour Organisation (ILO) has condemned forced labour in Myanmar since the early 1960s. A Commission of Inquiry established by the ILO in 1998 found abundant evidence that the use of forced labour was widespread and

66 See, *inter alia*, Economic and Social Council Resolution 1982/69, 27 October 1982, 1983/74, 29 July 1983 and 1984/53, 25 July 1984.

67 The Final Report of the Truth and Reconciliation Commission, Volume 4, chapter 2, 'Business and Labour'.

68 At their height, the Sullivan Principles involved 178 subsidiaries of signatory firms, which employed 62,400 workers. For more on the Sullivan Principles, see: *Economic Imperatives and Ethical Values in Global Business. The South African Experience and International Codes Today*, S. Prakash Sethi and Oliver F. Williams [eds.], 2000, Kluwer Academic Publishers, Boston etc. See also: Jill Murray, Corporate Codes Of Conduct and Labour Standards, ILO, available at: http://www.itcilo.it/english/actrav/telearn/global/ilo/guide/jill.htm (accessed on 13 November 2000). In 1997 new principles were drawn up – the so-called – *Global Sullivan Principles*, which aim to provide a model for the ethical behaviour of corporations, see: http://www.globalsullivanprinciples.org (accessed on 1 January 2002).

69 See, *inter alia,* UN Doc. E/CN.4/RES/1994/85, 9 March 1994.

systematic.[70] Its report was followed by an unprecedented resolution under the never previously invoked article 33[71] of the ILO Constitution. The resolution, *inter alia*, calls on the organisation's constituents as a whole – governments, employers and workers – to review, in the light of the conclusions by the Commission of Inquiry, the relations that they may have with Myanmar and to take appropriate measures to ensure that Myanmar cannot take advantage of such relations to perpetuate or extend the system of forced or compulsory labour. The resolution also calls on all UN and other multilateral agencies to do the same.[72] According to the International Confederation of Free Trade Unions (ICFTU)

> 'it is impossible to conduct any business relationship in Burma without directly or indirectly supporting the Burmese military dictatorship which is responsible for the extensive use of forced labour, as well as other serious human and trade union rights violations.'[73]

In such cases where the international community clearly speaks out, the obligation not to co-operate will come into play.

The obligation not to co-operate is defined as follows:

> the obligation not to co-operate requires from the corporation operating in States where widespread and systematic human rights violations occur, to either abstain from operations or to take measure to ensure that its operations do not amount to complicity in these human rights violations.

As mentioned earlier,[74] the duty not to co-operate has both negative and positive elements. On the one hand, this duty may require a corporation to withdraw from a State with a poor human rights record. On the other hand, the duty not to co-operate may

---

70 *Forced labour in Myanmar (Burma)*, Report of the Commission of Inquiry Appointed Under Article 26 of the Constitution of the International Labour Organisation to Examine the Observance by Myanmar of the Forced Labour Convention, 1930 (No. 29), ILO, Part IV, Geneva, 2 July 1998.

71 Article 33 of the ILO Constitution provides that: 'In the event of any Member failing to carry out within the time specified the recommendations, if any, contained in the report of the Commission of Inquiry, or in the decision of the International Court of Justice, as the case may be, the Governing Body may recommend to the Conference such action as it may deem wise and expedient to secure compliance therewith'.

72 Under (b), http://www.ilo.org/public/english/standards/relm/ilc/ilc88/com-seld.htm, (accessed on 30 July 2001). An ILO mission visited the country in September and October 2001 and came to the conclusion that, despite new legislation adopted by the junta, the use of forced labour remained widespread. The mission recommended that an Ombudsman be appointed and/or that a permanent ILO presence be established in Myanmar in order to monitor the forced labour situation and to help the authorities to tackle the problem. See the ILO press release of Wednesday 7 November 2001, (ILO/01/48), http://www.ilo.org/public/english/bureau/inf/pr/2001/48.htm (accessed on 16 November 2001).

73 Press Release ICFTU, Brussels November 15, 2001, http://www.icftu.org/ (accessed on 16 November 2001).

74 See p. 92.

require the corporation to take positive measures to ensure that it does not unintentionally participate in human rights violations. The latter element of the duty not to co-operate closely resembles the duty to protect that was discussed in section 2.2. Whereas the duty not to co-operate concerns situations where the perpetrator of the human rights violations is a State, the duty to protect will enter into play with regard to other actors, that can be considered to be within the corporation's ambit of influence.

PART B

AVENUES FOR ENFORCEMENT AND IMPLEMENTATION

CHAPTER V
NON-JUDICIAL SUPERVISION

1 INTRODUCTION

Part B of this book deals with the enforcement and supervision of the human rights obligations identified in part A. How can alleged violations by corporations be addressed? International human rights law first and foremost considers the State to be the bearer of human rights obligations. However, international guidelines on the social policies of corporations do exist at the international level and these directly address corporations. In this chapter these codes of conduct will be analysed. The codes are dealt with under the heading of non-judicial supervision *i.e.* regulation which, in the last resort, is supervised by politically representative bodies or organs.[1] This is the case with the codes discussed here. Moreover, several developments regarding the supervision of the social policy of corporations within the United Nations (UN) and the European Union (EU) will also be discussed. Finally, in section 9 the question will be discussed whether self-regulation, by means of corporate codes of conduct, can function as a tool for the effective enforcement of human rights obligations.

2 INTERNATIONAL CODES DIRECTLY REGULATING CORPORATE CONDUCT

A multitude of codes exists at the international and regional level dealing with (multinational) corporations.[2] The codes discussed in this chapter have been selected because they have been drawn up by major international organisations involving many States and are widely considered to be the most authoritative internationally agreed upon standards for corporate conduct. The following codes will be dealt with: the Guidelines for Multinational Enterprises adopted in 1976 by the Organisation for Economic Cooperation and Development (OECD) and the Tripartite Declaration of Principles Concerning Multinational Enterprises adopted in 1977 by the International Labour Organisation (ILO). The analysis will concentrate on the question of what possibilities the codes offer with regard to regulating corporate conduct as far as human rights obligations are concerned. The first issue that must be addressed is the content of the codes. Do the codes refer to human rights obligations for corporations? This discus-

1 G.J.H. van Hoof, *Rethinking the Sources of International Law*, Deventer, Kluwer, 1983, p. 266.
2 See the overview presented in K.P. Sauvant and V. Aranda, 'The International Legal Framework for Transnational Corporations', in: *Transnational Corporations: The International Legal Framework*, A.A. Fatouros [ed.], Routledge, London, 1994, pp. 83-115, at pp. 86-87.

sion will be brief as the emphasis will be on the enforcement-possibilities under these codes.

The codes concerned are all of a non-binding legal nature. The term 'enforcement' does not seem to be appropriate with regard to formally non-binding rules. In the case of these non-binding codes it is better to use the terms supervision or follow-up.[3] For the analysis of the supervisory mechanisms of the codes the three different functions of supervision distinguished by Van Hoof and De Vey Mestdagh will be used. The first function is the review function, which, in general, consists of evaluating certain behaviour as to its conformity with a particular norm.[4] The second function is the correction function that deals with ensuring compliance by correcting infringements.[5] The third function is the creative function that refers to the elaboration and adaptation of abstract and vague norms that are not sufficiently specific to serve as a basis for effective supervision.[6] On the basis of this typology the effectiveness of the codes' implementation, *i.e.* of the supervisory mechanisms, will be assessed. Moreover, the complexities of the legal status of the codes will be addressed in section 6. For this analysis of the legal character the assessment of the supervisory mechanisms is also important. As Van Hoof points out:

> 'supervision (…) may indeed add to the normative status of a given instrument or rule. It must therefore be taken into account when one tries to determine the legally binding or non-binding character of an instrument or rule.'[7]

3 Background

For a better understanding of the codes a brief analysis of the context in which they were drawn up is presented here. The two codes discussed in the following sections were drawn up during the 1970s. During this decade the activities of corporations became a topic of discussion in international organisations. The activities of corporations encountered growing opposition especially from the developing countries. Many of these countries had recently obtained their political independence. The operations of corporations, mainly concentrated in these developing States, were seen as a perpetuation of their (economic) dependence. Several incidents, such as the well-known example of the involvement of the American corporation *ITT* in the overthrow

---

3 Van Hoof, *supra* n. 1, p.270.
4 Van Hoof, *supra* n. 1, p. 258.
5 Van Hoof, *supra* n. 1, pp. 258-261. As explained by Van Hoof, at the international level a variety of measures can be discerned to correct undesirable behaviour. This can range from the instrument of sanctions on the one hand to 'mobilisation of shame', on the other.
6 Van Hoof, *supra* n. 1, pp. 261-263.
7 Van Hoof, *supra* n. 1, p. 274.

of the democratically elected government of Salvador Allende in Chile,[8] demonstrated the impact of corporations on the internal politics of host countries. Foreign corporations were also seen as supporting apartheid in South Africa. Several other events further prompted the discussion on the regulation of corporations, for example, the corruption scandal in the West regarding the Lockheed affair.[9] International guidelines regulating corporate behaviour were, therefore, called for. The demands of the developing countries received more attention due to the change in the balance of power within the UN. As a result of the process of decolonization the developing countries gradually obtained a numerical majority in the UN.[10] Moreover, the bargaining position of the developing countries had improved as a result of the oil crisis.[11] The 1970s also witnessed large-scale nationalisations of key industries. The industrialised countries, therefore, defended the position that corporations needed to be protected and that the international framework had to focus on the protection of international investment.

The debates within international organisations, such as the UN, the ILO and the OECD, resulted in the drawing up of the various codes that are discussed in the following sections. The context in which the codes were formulated makes it clear that these codes were drafted as a result of a highly politicised debate. Protection of human rights was not the main aim. The key objectives of these codes were

> 'to contribute to improving the climate for foreign investment and to optimize contributions of international investors and [multinational enterprises] to international and national economic objectives while minimizing and helping resolve difficulties which may arise from their operations.'[12]

4 The OECD Guidelines for Multinational Enterprises

Under pressure from the prevailing concerns during the 1970s as described above, the OECD undertook to formulate a set of standards to regulate corporate behaviour. On 21 June 1976 the governments of the OECD member countries, with the exception of the Turkish government, adopted a 'package deal', which consisted of the 'Declaration

---

8 The incident with *ITT* was the immediate cause underlying the decision within the UN to draft a code of conduct. This code will be dealt with in more detail in section 7.1.

9 Johan Kaufmann and Nico Schrijver, *Changing Global Needs: Expanding Roles for the United Nations System*, the Academic Council on the United Nations System, Reports and Papers 1990-5, p. 26.

10 Within the UN this resulted in the call for a New International Economic Order in General Assembly Resolution 3201(S-VI), 1 May 1974. The developments within the UN will be dealt with in more detail in section 7.

11 Sauvant and Aranda, *supra* n. 2, p. 89.

12 Don L. Guertin, 'A Business View on the Implementation of Codes of Conduct', in: *Legal Problems of Codes of Conduct for Multinational Enterprises*, Norbert Horn [ed.], Kluwer, Deventer, Vol.1, 1980, p. 296. At the time when the codes were drafted Guertin was senior adviser on international Issues for the *Exxon* corporation.

on International Investment and Multinational Enterprises' along with four instruments relating to the Declaration.[13] The main aim of the Declaration is to facilitate international trade among OECD members as can be deduced from three of the included instruments which lay down the requirement for the Parties to adopt the principle of national treatment,[14] to improve co-operation on international investment incentives and disincentives, and to minimise conflicting requirements imposed on multinational enterprises by different governments. Annexed to the Declaration are the 'Guidelines for Multinational Enterprises' (hereafter: 'The Guidelines').[15] The Guidelines are recommendations by the Governments of the OECD member countries (and the following four non-members: Argentina, Brazil, Chile and the Slovak Republic) directed at corporations. The Guidelines originally only applied to corporations operating within the OECD countries. This has been changed during the latest review.[16] The Guidelines now apply to corporations operating in or from OECD Member States.

The Guidelines are voluntary and are consequently not legally enforceable.[17] Therefore, each chapter starts with the words 'enterprises should'. The voluntary character also becomes clear from the fact that in the Declaration itself the OECD member countries 'jointly recommend to multinational enterprises to observe the Guidelines'. The OECD Member States clearly did not intend to create binding rules for corporations.

4.1 Content

The Guidelines have been reviewed several times: in 1979, 1982, 1984, 1991 and most recently in 2000.[18] During the 1991 review a chapter on environmental protection was added despite strong opposition from the business world.[19] The latest review, con-

13 For a detailed study on the OECD instruments and their effectiveness see: S.C. van Eyk, *The OECD Declaration and Decisions Concerning Multinational Enterprises. An Attempt to Tame the Shrew*, Ars Aequi Libri, Nijmegen, 1995.

14 The principle of 'national treatment' implies that a country treats enterprises operating on its territory, but controlled by the nationals of another country, no less favourably than domestic enterprises in like situations.

15 The Guidelines can be found on the OECD's website at: www.oecd.org (accessed on 23 November 2001).

16 See p. 109.

17 Para. 1 Concepts and Principles, OECD Guidelines.

18 The revised text of the Guidelines was adopted by the governments of the 29 member countries of the OECD and Argentina, Brazil, Chile and the Slovak Republic at the OECD Ministerial Meeting on 27 June 2000. For a discussion of the 2000 review of the OECD Guidlines, see: Joris Oldenziel, *The 2000 Review of the OECD Guidelines for Multinational Enterprises: A New Code of Conduct?*, SOMO, Amsterdam, September 2000.

19 Jan Huner, 'The Multilateral Agreement on Investment and the Review of the OECD Guidelines for Multinational Enterprises', in: *Liability of Multinational Corporations Under International Law,* Menno T. Kamminga and Saman Zia-Zarifi [eds.] Kluwer Law International, The Hague etc, 2000.

cluded at the Ministerial Meeting of 27 June 2000, formally began in November 1998. In general the 'old' Guidelines were considered to have become quite seriously outdated. The main incentive to review the Guidelines was the opposition against the Multilateral Agreement on Investments (MAI).[20] It was suggested that the Guidelines should be annexed to the MAI in order to acquire a better balance concerning the rights that investors would have been granted under the MAI. Despite the fact that the negotiations on the MAI in the context of the OECD collapsed, the review of the Guidelines continued.

Unlike previous reviews the latest review has brought about significant changes especially regarding the chapters on Environmental Protection and on Employment and Industrial Relations. Besides revisions of the existing text, new chapters dealing with combating bribery and protecting consumers have been adopted. Proposals to enhance the implementation of the Guidelines have also been added. The latter will be dealt with *infra*.[21] The revised Guidelines consist of ten chapters addressing a wide range of corporate activities: concepts and principles, general policies; disclosure; employment and industrial relations; environment; combating bribery; consumers' interests; science and technology; competition and taxation. Given the fact that the OECD is an organisation of industrialised countries it is not surprising that most of these provisions are essentially of a commercial nature. Before analysing the current Guidelines, I consider it relevant to briefly discuss the content of the previous Guidelines, as the differences between the old and the new Guidelines reflect the changing attitude towards the role which businesses should play with regard to human rights.

Before the revision of June 2000 the Guidelines did not explicitly provide that corporations should observe human rights. Certain provisions, especially those in the chapters on Employment and Industrial Relations and Environmental Protection, did deal with human rights, however. The 'old' Guidelines contained provisions prohibiting discrimination. For example, it set forth that 'enterprises should when filling responsible posts in each country of operation, take due account of individual qualifications without discrimination as to nationality (...)'.[22] Furthermore, according to the Guidelines 'enterprises should implement their employment policies including hiring, pay, promotion and training without discrimination'.[23] In the chapter on Employment and Industrial Relations it was laid down that corporations should 'respect the right of their employees to be represented by trade unions (...).'[24] The chapter on Environmental Protection contained several provisions related to human rights. For instance, according to paragraph 1 corporations must assess and take into account in decision making the impact on indigenous natural resources. Other provisions in the Guidelines

20 See chapter I, note 14.
21 See p. 108.
22 Para. 6, chapter on General Policies, OECD Guidelines before the 2000 revision.
23 Para. 7, chapter on Employment and Industrial Relations, OECD Guidelines before the 2000 revision.
24 Para. 1, chapter on Employment and Industrial Relations, OECD Guidelines before the 2000 revision.

related indirectly to human rights by stressing the importance and the impact of the activities of corporations on the well-being of the countries in which they operate. The responsibility of corporations to contribute to increasing prosperity in the host-countries was underlined.[25] In the Guidelines strong emphasis was put on non-interference by corporations in the policies of the countries in which they operate. For example, in the chapter on General Policies it was laid down that corporations should respect the objectives of the countries in which they operate and should not engage in improper behaviour.[26] This clearly reflects the concerns at the time when the Guidelines were drafted. It can be concluded that the provisions in the previous Guidelines, without explicitly referring to major human rights instruments, did contain some provisions that directly or indirectly dealt with human rights.

In the revised Guidelines the role of business regarding human rights is more prominent. Although no reference is made to specific human rights instruments, the Guidelines do explicitly refer to human rights. Paragraph 2 of the chapter on General Policies reads:

> 'enterprises should take fully into account established policies in the countries in which they operate, and consider the views of other stakeholders. In this regard enterprises should: (…) respect the human rights of those affected by their activities consistent with the host government's international obligations and commitments.'[27]

This provision is of a more general nature than the provision as it was formulated in the draft text of 15 March 2000, which provided that enterprises should 'respect the human rights of their employees, as well as encourage the respect of human rights by business partners and in the societies in which they operate'. In the explanatory commentary on the OECD Guidelines it is stated:

> '(…) while promoting and upholding human rights is primarily the responsibility of governments, where corporate conduct and human rights intersect enterprises do play a role, and thus [multinational enterprises] are encouraged to respect human rights, not only in their

25 For example, in the chapter on Employment and Industrial Relations, paragraph 5 read as follows: 'enterprises should, within the framework of law, regulations and prevailing labour relations and employment practices, in each of the countries in which they operate in their operations, to the greatest extent practicable, utilise, train and prepare for upgrading members of the local labour force in co-operation with representatives of their employees and, where appropriate, the relevant governmental authorities'. According to paragraph 1 of the chapter on Science and Technology: 'Enterprises should endeavour to ensure that their activities fit satisfactorily into the scientific and technological policies and plans of the countries in which they operate, and contribute to the development of national scientific and technological capacities, including as far as appropriate the establishment and improvement in host countries of their capacity to innovate'.

26 For example, enterprises should not offer any bribe to any public servant. See paras. 7-9 of the chapter on General Policies.

27 Para. 2 chapter II General Policies, OECD Guidelines.

dealings with employees, but also with respect to others affected by their activities, in a manner consistent with host governments' international obligations and commitments. The Universal Declaration of Human Rights and other human rights obligations of the government concerned are of particular relevance in this regard.'[28]

The paragraph on human rights is clearly a compromise between the Business and Industry Advisory Committee (BIAC), the representative organisation of private business, on the one hand, and NGOs on the other. During the negotiations BIAC reacted negatively, arguing that 'reference to human rights texts may result in an inappropriate shift of governmental responsibility and accountability to companies, creating unclear priorities and potentially conflicting responsibilities.'[29] BIAC initially preferred a reference to human rights in the chapter on labour in order to emphasise that the responsibility of corporations does not extend beyond the circle of their employees. It was, however, decided that a reference to human rights would be made in the chapter General Policies, as it had become apparent that the human rights of persons other than only employees also can be affected by corporate activities.[30] Furthermore, despite pressure from NGOs, it was decided not to refer to the UDHR but merely to require that the activities of corporations respect human rights in conformity with the 'host government's international obligations and commitments'. NGOs feared that this would imply that corporations are merely bound by national laws.[31]

Besides the explicit reference to human rights in paragraph 2 of the chapter on General Policies, the revised Guidelines overall contain more human rights responsibilities for corporations than the old Guidelines. In the chapter on Employment and Industrial Relations provisions have been added to echo all four fundamental principles and rights at work, which are contained in the ILO's Declaration on Fundamental Principles at Work.[32] These are: 'the freedom of association and the right to collective bargaining; the effective abolition of child labour; the elimination of all forms of forced or compulsory labour; and non-discrimination in employment and occupation.'[33] For example, according to the explanatory commentary, corporations are recommended to contribute to the effective abolition of child labour especially by raising the standards of children's education and labour management practices as well as the creation of

28 OECD Guidelines for Multinational Enterprises: Review 2000 Commentaries, 27 June 2000. The commentaries are available at the website of the OECD: www.oecd.org (accessed on 27 November 2001). The commentaries are of an explanatory nature and are not part of the Guidelines.

29 'Contribution on the employment and industrial relations chapter of the OECD Guidelines for Multinational Enterprises, paper compiled by the BIAC ELSA Committee, chapter 8 in *Multinational Enterprises and the Social Challenges of the XXIst century,* R. Blanpain [ed.], Kluwer Law International, 2000, pp. 99-106, p. 100,

30 Oldenziel, *supra* n. 18, pp. 14-15.

31 Oldenziel, *supra* n. 18, p. 15.

32 Adopted at the 86th session, June 1998.

33 Para. 21, Commentary on Employment and Industrial Relations, Commentaries, OECD Guidelines.

high-quality, well paid jobs and contributing to economic growth.[34] In paragraph 2 of the chapter on Disclosure it is set forth that 'enterprises are (...) encouraged to apply high quality standards for disclosure of non-financial information including environmental and social reporting where they exist'. Moreover, in paragraph 5 enterprises are encouraged to communicate additional information that could include 'value statements of business conduct intended for public disclosure including information on the social, ethical and environmental policies of the enterprises and other codes of conduct to which the company subscribes.' These provisions are inspired by the growing number of corporations that have issued voluntary codes of corporate conduct.[35]

From the above survey of the old and the newly revised Guidelines it becomes clear that the emphasis has shifted from non-interference by corporations in the countries in which they operate to requiring corporations to take a more active stance regarding labour rights and human rights. The explicit reference to human rights makes it clear that the concept of corporate responsibility in the area of human rights is gaining acceptance. The language of the revised Guidelines remains, however, of a voluntary nature and stresses the primary responsibility of the State. The question whether the identified responsibilities for corporations can be enforced will now be addressed by analysing the supervisory mechanism of the Guidelines.

4.2 Supervision

All three functions of supervision distinguished by Van Hoof and De Vey Mestdagh –the review function, correction function and the creative function– can be discerned in the supervisory mechanism of the Guidelines. The institutional set-up of the Guidelines consists of three elements: the National Contact Points (NCPs), the OECD's Committee on International Investment and Multinational Enterprises comprising representatives of the OECD Member States (CIME) and the advisory Committees of business and labour federations (BIAC and TUAC).

The OECD Member States are required to establish NCPs whose prime responsibility is to ensure the follow-up of the Guidelines at the national level. The NCPs serve to gather information on experiences with the Guidelines, to promote them, to deal with enquiries, to discuss matters related to the Guidelines and to assist in solving problems that may arise in matters covered by the Guidelines. The NCPs in different countries are required to work together in finding solutions to problems that arise.[36] By gathering information the NCPs perform the review function. The correction function comes to the fore when a NCP comes to the (legally non-binding) conclusion that the

34 Para. 22, Commentary on Employment and Industrial Relations, Commentaries, OECD Guidelines.
35 Para. 15, Commentaries, Commentary on Disclosure, Commentaries, OECD Guidelines.
36 OECD, *Procedural Guidance,* 2001.

Guidelines have been infringed.[37] The NCP can suggest possible solutions aimed at correcting the behaviour that is the subject of discussion. In her study on the OECD Declaration, completed in 1995, Van Eyk examined, by means of a questionnaire sent to the NCPs, the actual functioning of the NCP in daily practice. She concluded that, on the whole, the review and corrective functions of the NCPs do not operate as intended. The effectiveness of the Guidelines has decreased because, mainly due to a lack of interest on the part of the parties concerned, the NCPs have failed as a supervisory mechanism.[38] As will be discussed below, the review carried out in 2000 aims to revive the role of the NCPs.

If necessary an OECD member country, BIAC or TUAC can decide to transmit a problem that has arisen on the national level to the CIME for a clarification of the Guidelines. In the clarification procedure the review, correction and creative function are present. The idea behind the clarification is that the diversity of the legal systems of the various OECD countries might necessitate a clarification of the text of the Guidelines in individual cases. The CIME, which consists of representatives of the governments of the OECD Member States, will provide a clarification after consulting with BIAC and TUAC. The clarification is directed at both the member country and at corporations. However, in its clarification the CIME does not have the authority to refer to an individual corporation that has or has not respected the Guidelines by name.[39] In the case of non-observance no sanction can be imposed upon a member country or a corporation. The fact that the CIME does not have the authority to refer to specific corporations weakens the corrective function of the supervisory mechanism of the Guidelines.[40] This weakness of the supervisory mechanism may explain the fact that, to date, little use has been made of the system. Relatively few requests have been placed before the CIME. Since 1976 thirty cases have been brought before the CIME for clarification, of which eighteen cases were submitted during the first two years. This makes it clear that the parties have lost interest in the Guidelines. Most of the requests for clarification concerned the chapter on Employment and Industrial Relations.[41]

Besides the process of clarification the CIME has the task of conducting periodic reviews of the experiences with the provisions of the Guidelines. Regarding the

37 A complaint can be brought before the NCP by the business community, employees' organisations, and since the 2000 review, by other interested parties such as NGOs.

38 Van Eyk, *supra* n. 13, p. 199. The results of the questionnaire are dealt with on pp. 168-199.

39 CIME 'shall not reach conclusions on the conduct of individual enterprises'. Article 6 of the Decision of the Council on the Guidelines for Multinational Enterprises.

40 Van Eyk, *supra* n. 13, p. 212.

41 For more information on the case-law and the issues raised see the numerous writings by R. Blanpain. For example, Blanpain, in: *Legal Problems of Codes of Conduct for Multinational Enterprises*, Vol. 1, Norbert Horn [ed.], Kluwer, Deventer, 1980, pp. 145-155 and Blanpain, in: 'Multinational Enterprises and the Social Challenges of the XXIst Century', *Bulletin of Comparative Labour Relations*, Vol. 37, Blanpain [ed.], pp. 29-67.

effectiveness of the supervisory mechanism Van Eyk, in 1995, came to the conclusion that:

> 'the parties concerned [have] lost interest in the OECD Guidelines. The trade unions do not seem willing to invest their time and effort in the functioning of legally non-binding instruments. Most of the existing NCPs have also reduced their activities to a minimum and Member countries have lost interest to the point of limiting their efforts to the participation in review discussions within CIME. The [multinational enterprises] if aware of the existence of the "OECD Guidelines" at all, pay little or no attention to them.'[42]

The conclusion that the Guidelines lead a 'silent, if not languishing, existence'[43] still holds true. The Guidelines continue to receive little attention from the parties concerned. A survey conducted by the OECD in 1999 shows that in the voluntary corporate codes of conduct, the adoption of which grew explosively during the 1980s and 1990s, only very few corporations refer to the Guidelines.[44]

Clearly, the experience with the Guidelines described above refers to the old Guidelines. The lack of effectiveness as regards the implementation of the Guidelines was acknowledged at the conference on the OECD Guidelines for Multinational Enterprises held in Budapest in November 1998.[45] This conference was the start of the review process and efforts have been undertaken to breathe new life into the implementation mechanism. The revisions mostly consist of a more detailed restatement of the functions of the NCPs and the CIME and of providing procedural guidance.[46] Moreover, some adjustments have been made to the complaint procedure. Besides the business community and employee's organisations, other interested parties such as NGOs are now also allowed to file a complaint with a NCP.[47] If the parties involved

42 Van Eyk, *supra* n. 13, p. 243.

43 Van Eyk, *supra* n. 13, p. 243.

44 This inventory comprised 233 codes of conduct. Only one code used the OECD Guidelines as a reference. See paragraph 43 of *Codes of Corporate Conduct: An Inventory*, Working Party of the Trade Committee, TD/TC/WP(98)74/FINAL, 29-Apr-1999.

45 This conference was held in Budapest from 16-18 November 1998. The summary of the proceedings (DAFFE.IME (98)18) can be found at the website of the OECD: www.oecd.org (accessed on 27 June 2000).

46 See the OECD Guidelines for Multinational Enterprises, Decision of the Council, June 2000. The decision can be found at the website of the OECD: www.oecd.org (accessed on 27 November 2001).

47 In the Netherlands, at the time of writing, four complaints have been filed with the NCP by NGOs. Two complaints concern the activities of several Dutch corporations that import footballs that have been produced in India. The NGO that has submitted the complaint, *Het Landelijk India Netwerk [National India Network]*, claims that child labour is involved in the production of the footballs. This is in violation of the OECD Guidelines. These complaints have been declared admissible. The other complaints have been submitted by a trade union. One complaint concerns the plan of a Finnish corporation to close down a subsidiary without previous consultation with the workers' organisation, which -according to the trade union- is a violation of the OECD Guidelines. In the other complaint,

do not reach an agreement with regard to the dispute, the NCP is required to issue a statement. This is also an alteration of the old system where the NCP could merely refer a case to the CIME for clarification if no solution was found. In its statement the NCP can decide to make the results of the proceedings public, unless 'preserving confidentiality would be in the best interests of effective implementation of the Guidelines'.[48] Consequently, at the national level the naming of specific corporations might occur. An important revision concerns the changes with regard to the geographical scope of the Guidelines. The reviewed Guidelines are now applicable not only to corporate operations in OECD Member States but also to the activities that take place within non-Member States.

The review efforts and the revisions to the implementation procedure seem to indicate a renewed interest in the Guidelines. Nevertheless, the weaknesses discerned above, the lack of sanctions or possibilities to identify specific corporations (at the international level), remain under the revised mechanism. At the time of writing it is too early to arrive at any conclusions regarding the future effectiveness of the revised Guidelines.

4.3 Concluding Remarks on the OECD Guidelines

The main purpose of the OECD Guidelines is to facilitate international trade. However, since the 2000 review notably more attention is now being paid to the human rights obligations of corporations. All three elements of supervision –review, correction and creative– are present in the supervisory mechanism. Nevertheless, it should be concluded that the supervision under the OECD Guidelines is not very effective as a result of the arrangements with regard to confidentiality and the lack of sanctions. It remains to be seen whether the adjustments to the supervisory system carried out under the 2000 review will improve its effectiveness.

5 ILO 'Tripartite Declaration of Principles Concerning Multinational Enterprises and Social Policy'

The ILO plays an important role with regard to the regulation of corporate activities in the light of human rights, that is to say: labour rights. The ILO has adopted over 180 Conventions dealing with many of the issues identified in the previous chapters. The system of monitoring compliance with these Conventions focuses on the State as the bearer of the obligations.[49] Under the auspices of the ILO, however, a declaration has

---

the trade union claims that a Dutch multinational corporation has violated the OECD Guidelines resulting from its operations in Burma. The complaints with regard to the import of footballs are available (in Dutch) at: www.indianet.nl/ncpbr.html (accessed on 23 November 2001).

48 OECD review June 2000, *Procedural Guidance*, C 4.(b).

49 See chapter VI, pp. 161-164.

been formulated that directly addresses corporations: the 'Tripartite Declaration of Principles concerning Multinational Enterprises and Social Policy' (hereinafter: the Tripartite Declaration).[50] The Tripartite Declaration can be seen as an elaboration of the principles contained in the OECD Guidelines.[51] This section will assess the meaning of the Tripartite Declaration in the light of corporations' human rights obligations by analysing the content of the Tripartite Declaration and its supervisory mechanism.

The regulation of corporate behaviour within the ILO first received attention with the convening of a tripartite meeting of experts on corporations and social policy in 1972. This resulted in the adoption of the Tripartite Declaration at the 204th session on 16 November 1977. The Tripartite Declaration jointly addresses governments, employers' as well as employees' organisations and corporations (in both home and in host States).[52] The aim of the Tripartite Declaration is to:

> 'encourage the positive contribution which multinational enterprises can make to economic and social progress and to minimize and resolve the difficulties to which their various operations may give rise, taking into account the United Nations resolutions advocating the establishment of a New International Economic Order.'[53]

This last clause clearly reflects the political context in which the Tripartite Declaration was drawn up. The Tripartite Declaration has a non-mandatory character. Governments, employers' and workers' organisations and corporations are 'recommended to observe [the principles] on a voluntary basis'.[54] As Gunter points out, 'the non-mandatory character of the Declaration reflects a major condition under which consensus amongst the tripartite parties negotiating the Declaration could be reached'.[55]

---

50 The text of the ILO Tripartite Declaration can be found on the ILO website: http://www.ilo.org/public/-english/standards/norm/sources/mne.htm (accessed on 23 November 2001)

51 OECD Guidelines, Commentaries, Commentary on Employment and Industrial Relations, paragraph 20: 'The International Labour Organisation (ILO) is the competent Body to set and deal with international labour standards (...). The Tripartite Declaration sets out principles in the fields of employment, training, working conditions, and industrial relations, while the OECD Guidelines cover all major aspects of corporate behaviour. The OECD Guidelines and the ILO Tripartite Declaration refer to the behaviour expected from enterprises and are intended to parallel and not conflict with each other. The ILO Tripartite Declaration can therefore be of use in understanding the Guidelines to the extent that it is of a greater degree of elaboration'.

52 Preamble of the Tripartite Declaration under 4.

53 Preamble of the Tripartite Declaration under 2.

54 Preamble of the Tripartite Declaration under 7.

55 Hans Günter, 'The Tripartite Declaration of Principles (ILO): Standards and Follow-Up', in: *Legal Problems of Codes of Conduct for Multinational Enterprises*, Vol. 1, Norbert Horn [ed.], Kluwer, Deventer, 1980, p. 157.

5.1 Content

In comparison to the other codes dealt with in this chapter the Tripartite Declaration refers most explicitly to human rights. The Tripartite Declaration consists of 58 paragraphs, grouped under a preamble and five major sections: General Policies; Employment (employment promotion, equality of opportunity and treatment, security of employment); Training; Conditions of Work and Life (wages, benefits and conditions of work, safety and health); and Industrial Relations (freedom of association and the right to organise, collective bargaining, consultation, examination of grievances, settlement of industrial disputes). In each of these sections emphasis is placed upon the need for all parties to respect the development priorities, social aims and structures of the host countries and the need for corporations to adhere to the best possible practices.

A general reference to human rights is provided in paragraph 1 of the preamble of the Tripartite Declaration: 'Multinational enterprises (…) can (…) make an important contribution (…) to the enjoyment of basic human rights, including freedom of association, throughout the world'. Paragraph 8 of the section on General Policies is more explicit:

> 'All the Parties concerned by this Declaration should respect (…) the Universal Declaration of Human Rights and the corresponding International Covenants adopted by the General Assembly of the United Nations as well as the Constitution of the International Labour Organisation and its principles according to which freedom of expression and association are essential to sustained progress.'

The Tripartite Declaration contains several other specific references to human rights. For example, paragraphs 41-47 of the section on Industrial Relations emphasise the principles of freedom of association and the right to organise.[56] In paragraphs 33-34 it is stated that corporations should provide for fair and equal remuneration.[57] Moreover, in the Tripartite Declaration reference is made to specific ILO Conventions and recommendations that deal with human rights. At the time of its adoption the Tripartite Declaration referred to 15 Conventions and 19 Recommendations.[58] An Addendum was adopted by the Governing Body at its 238th session (November 1987) and 264th

56 Reference is made to ILO Convention Nos. 87 Article 2 and 98 Articles 1 [1], 2 [1]. The right to form trade unions can also be found in Article 23 [4] UDHR and Article 8 ICESCR.

57 The right to fair remuneration can also be found in Article 23, [3] UDHR.

58 To name a few examples: the Tripartite Declaration refers to the Conventions concerning Forced or Compulsory Labour (No. 29), Freedom of Association and Protection of the Right to Organize (No.87) and Discrimination in respect of Employment and Occupation (No. 111). A few examples of the recommendations referred to are the following: Indirect Compulsion to Labour (No. 35), Workers Housing (No.115), Termination of Employment at the Initiative of the Employer (No. 119). For the complete list see the annex to the Tripartite Declaration which can be found on the website of the ILO: www.ilo.org.

session (November 1995) adding new Conventions and Recommendations with provisions relevant to the Tripartite Declaration that have been adopted since 1977. In this Addendum 13 Conventions were added together with 14 Recommendations.[59] Finally, in March 2001 the text of the Tripartite Declaration was revised by a decision of the Governing Body to fully incorporate the fundamental principles and rights at work as these have been laid down in the ILO Declaration on Fundamental Principles and Rights at Work and its Follow-up.[60]

5.2 Supervision

As mentioned above the Tripartite Declaration is non-mandatory. Nevertheless, according to the ILO, 'the fact that the Tripartite Declaration was adopted by a consensus of the ILO's Governing Body creates a political and moral obligation for Member States to follow its recommendations'.[61] The supervisory procedures of the Tripartite Declaration were decided upon in early 1978 and were endorsed by the International Labour Conference at its 1979 session. The supervisory mechanism under the Tripartite Declaration is partly similar to the procedure under the OECD Guidelines. All three elements of supervision –the review, correction and creative function– can be detected. However, the procedure is more limited than the OECD supervisory procedure as no national contact-points exist to monitor compliance with the Tripartite Declaration at the national level.

The review function is carried out by the Governing body by means of a quadrennial survey. The Governing Body requests governments to report, after consultation with employers' and workers' organisations, on the effect given to the principles laid down in the Declaration.[62] The Governing Body expressly stated that consideration of these reports would 'not be designed to determine compliance with what is recognised to be a non-mandatory instrument nor to pass judgement on measures adopted within the Member States.'[63]

59 A couple of examples of the new Conventions referred to are: Promotion of Collective bargaining (No. 154) and Prevention of Major Industrial Accidents (No. 174). Examples of recommendations added are: Employment Promotion and Protection against Unemployment (No.176) and Safety and Health in Mines (No. 183). For the complete list see the Addendum which can be found on the website of the ILO: www.ilo.org.

60 ILO Doc. GB.279/12, see para. 8 of the Tripartite Declaration.

61 See: http://www.ilo.org/public/english.../norm/enforced/ad_hoc/mne_pro.htm (accessed on 26 July 2000).

62 To date, there have been five surveys. The last questionnaire was no. VI covering the years 1992, 1993, 1994 and 1995. In 1997 the analysis of the follow-up and the promotion of the Tripartite Declaration were presented.

63 As quoted by Hans W. Baade, 'Codes of Conduct for Multinational Enterprises: An Introductory Survey', in: *Legal Problems of Codes of Conduct for Multinational Enterprises*, Vol. 1, Norbert Horn [ed.], Kluwer, Deventer, 1980, p. 422, from the ILO documents: ILO, Governing body, 205th Session, Doc. GB.205/10/2/, para.11 (19 January 1978), Doc. GB. 208/6/1/. Para. 5 (25 September 1978).

The responses received are analysed and examined by the Governing Body and recommendations for action based on the findings are adopted by a decision of the Governing Body.

Besides the reporting system, the supervisory mechanism consists of a procedure for the examination of disputes concerning the application of the Tripartite Declaration by means of an interpretation of its provisions.[64] This supervisory procedure was adopted by the Governing Body in November 1980 and revised in 1986.[65] In the interpretation procedure the review, correction and creative functions of supervision are present. Governments of Member States can direct a request for interpretation to the International Labour Office. Workers' or employers' organisations are required to submit a request for interpretation to the State. If the State declines to submit such a request to the International Labour Office, or fails to indicate its intention within three months, the workers' or employers' organisations can submit the request themselves.[66] After informing the relevant organisations and government,[67] the Office brings the request before the Officers of the Subcommittee on Multinational Enterprises, a subcommittee of the ILO Governing Body's Committee on Legal Issues and International Labour Standards. The Officers of the Subcommittee, three persons reflecting the tripartite character of the ILO, decide whether the request may be received. These three Officers can only decide on admissibility after consulting with their group, respectively the workers', employers' or State group. The decision has to be unanimous.[68] If this is not possible the decision with regard to receivability should be made by the entire Subcommittee with an absolute majority.[69] If the request is considered to be receivable, the International Labour Office, in consultation with the Officers of the Subcommittee, prepares a reply to the request for interpretation.[70] The Subcommittee as a whole votes on the reply. The interpretation has to be approved by the Governing Body and is then forwarded to the parties concerned and published in the official bulletin of the ILO.[71] The review body does not name specific individual corporations within the framework of the procedure.

64 The procedure cannot be invoked in respect of national law and practice; in respect of international labour Conventions and Recommendations and in respect of matters falling under the freedom of association procedure.

65 Procedure for the Examination of Disputes (Multinational Enterprises: Tripartite Declaration of Principles), adopted by the ILO Governing body at its 232nd Session (March 1986), Official Bulletin, Vol. LXIX, 1986, Series A, No. 3. See for an explanation the website of the ILO: http://www.ilo.org/public/english/employment/multi/inter/index.htm#todate (accessed on 23 November 2001).

66 Procedure for the Examination of Disputes, *supra* n. 65, paras. 5 and 6.

67 Procedure for the Examination of Disputes, *supra* n. 65, paras. 2 and 3.

68 Procedure for the Examination of Disputes, *supra* n. 65, para. 4.

69 Procedure for the Examination of Disputes, *supra* n. 65, para. 4.

70 Procedure for the Examination of Disputes, *supra* n. 65, para. 7.

71 Procedure for the Examination of Disputes, *supra* n. 65, para. 9.

Over 23 requests have been received so far, but only four have passed the receivability test and reached the interpretation stage.[72] In merely two of these cases did the Officers of the Subcommittee reach the unanimous decision that the request for interpretation was receivable.[73] This demonstrates how difficult it is for the three officers representing the three different parties within the ILO to reach an agreement. The two other cases were declared receivable by majority decisions.[74] All but one of the cases discussed by the Office concerned job losses without prior notification.

The exception is the so-called *ICEF* case.[75] At issue in this case was, *inter alia*, the question whether multinational corporations are obliged to disclose information with regard to health and safety standards, policies and practices applied in subsidiaries, to workers' organisations. As pointed out by Scott, the proceedings in this case are a clear example of the manner in which the tripartite structure of the ILO can hamper an effective supervisory mechanism.[76] The three officers were not able to reach a unanimous decision in the *ICEF* case. Consequently, the case was referred to the Subcommittee. Within the Subcommittee six workers' representatives and one government representative were in favour of an interpretation of the Tripartite Declaration that would require multinational corporations to disclose the standards that are applied throughout the corporate family. Opposing this interpretation were six employers' organisations and three government members. However, no solution was reached as two government representatives abstained. From the perspective of human rights, an interpretation according to which corporations would be obliged to reveal the health and safety standards they apply in their subsidiaries would have been a ground-breaking decision. However, the strongly opposing opinions of the three ILO partners made it impossible to attain that result.

72 Information from the website of the ILO, http://www.ilo.org/public/english/employment/multi/inter/index.htm#todate (accessed on 1 March 2002).

73 Request for Interpretation by the Banking, Insurance and Finance Union (BIFU) of London, 2 May 1984, ILO Doc.GB.229/13/13 and a Request for Interpretation from the Belgian Government, 27 January 1987, ILO Doc.GB.239/14/24 See: http://www.ilo.org/public/english/employ ment/multi/inter/index.htm (accessed on 23 November 2001). See also: Craig Scott, 'Multinational Enterprises and Emergent Jurisprudence on Violations of Economic, Social and Cultural Rights', *Economic, Social and Cultural Rights*, 2nd ed., Asbjørn Eide, Catarina Krause and Allan Rosas, [eds.], Martinus Nijhoff Publishers, Dordrecht, etc., 2001, pp. 563-59, at pp. 572-574 and notes 20 and 21.

74 Request for Interpretation from the Belgian Government, 22 May 1997 ILO Doc.GB.272/6 and the preceding documents on which the discussion is based and Request for Interpretation from the International Federation of Chemical, Energy and General Workers' Unions, 6 March 1995, ILO Doc.GB.264/MNE/2. See: http://www.ilo.org/public/english/employment/multi/inter/index.htm (accessed on 23 November 2001). See also: Scott, *supra* n. 73, pp. 572-574 and notes 20 and 21.

75 Request for Interpretation from the International Federation of Chemical, Energy and General Workers' Unions, 6 March 1995, ILO Doc.GB.264/MNE/2.

76 Scott, *supra* n. 73, pp. 573-574.

5.3 Concluding Remarks on the ILO Tripartite Declaration

As is the case with the OECD Guidelines, the use made of the Tripartite Declaration is limited in practice. As stated by one observer: '(...) so far, the Declaration has not had the impact on international corporate behaviour hoped for by many of those present at its creation.'[77] The voluntary nature of the Tripartite Declaration implies that its effectiveness relies on the commitment of corporations to use the Declaration as a point of reference. However, during the 1980s the emphasis shifted towards deregulation and liberalisation and the Tripartite Declaration fell into disuse. Moreover, as occurred in the *ICEF*-case described in the previous section, the tripartite structure of the ILO, which is reflected in the supervisory mechanism, can hamper the effectiveness of the supervision.[78]

6 The Legal Status of the International Codes

Having discussed the content and the supervisory mechanisms of the OECD Guidelines and the ILO Tripartite Declaration, the question arises what the legal consequences of these codes are in order to assess whether they can be considered an effective enforcement mechanism of the human rights obligations of corporations.

The codes concerned have potential in view of enforcing human rights obligations. As pointed out above, the codes, especially the ILO Tripartite Declaration, deal with human rights issues. Moreover, the codes are the only international instruments that directly address corporations. Nevertheless, it was concluded in the previous sections that the codes have several drawbacks limiting their effectiveness. Should it therefore be concluded that these international instruments are not very useful from the perspective of enforcing human rights obligations on corporations?

One of the drawbacks concerns the non-mandatory character of the international codes. The fact that the codes are of a non-binding nature does not deprive them of every effect, however. Non-binding rules may have normative force. This implies that the addressee of a norm is willing to accept it as a guideline for its behaviour. The general acceptance of the codes by States, corporations and workers' organisations implies that the codes constitute standards which society, as a whole requires to be upheld. Van Eyk has pointed out four criteria by which to assess the possible normative force of such standards.[79]

---

77 Stephan Pursey, *Multinational Enterprises and the World of Work: Globalisation with a Human Face. Article on the 20th Anniversary of the ILO Declaration on Multinational Enterprises and Social Policy.* Document can be found at: http://www.icftu.org/english/tncs/tncs98ilo.html (accessed on 2 September 1998). Stephan Pursey was a member of the tripartite group that drafted the Declaration in 1977.

78 See, Scott, *supra* n. 73, pp. 569-574.

79 Van Eyk, *supra* n. 13, p. 229.

Firstly, the precision of the formulation of the expected behaviour may increase the normative force. Concerning the OECD Guidelines, the references to human rights, even after the revision, remain rather vague and of a general nature. The references to human rights in the ILO Tripartite Declaration are more precise.

Secondly, the normative force of the codes can be enhanced by the insertion of similar norms in other codes because it demonstrates the importance of such norms. It has been demonstrated that reference to the OECD Guidelines and the ILO Tripartite Declarations is in practice, however, somewhat limited.[80]

The last two criteria regarding normative force refer to supervision. The normative force of a behavioural norm is enhanced by the existence of an effective supervisory mechanism and, finally, the fear of possible sanctions when there is non-compliance with the norm, may have a positive effect on its normative force. Both in the case of the OECD Guidelines and the ILO Tripartite Declaration the supervisory mechanism is weak and sanctions are not available. It seems, therefore, safe to conclude that, to date, the OECD Guidelines and the ILO Tripartite Declaration lack significant normative force.

Besides the normative force, non-binding codes can play a role with regard to the accountability of corporations for human rights violations in another manner. The voluntary codes or the provisions thereof may over time evolve into legal rules, for example by transformation into customary international law. For rules to transform into customary international law several elements need to be fulfilled, namely there should be general, uniform and consistent State practice, and the recognition of certain practice as obligatory: *opinio juris sive necessitates.*[81]

The fact that the codes are expressly self-described as non-binding does not stand in the way of the transformation of certain provisions into customary law. As has been argued by Baade with regard to the OECD Guidelines:

> 'Since the OECD Committee which has jurisdiction over these actions is itself composed of delegates of the Member states (regularly including the representative of the home

80 However, this conclusion might be considered rather premature with regard to the OECD Guidelines. Possibly, the adjustments by the 2000 review will revive attention as far as the Guidelines are concerned. At the time of writing this has not yet become clear.

81 See, Ian Brownlie, *Principles of Public International Law*, 5th ed., Clarendon Press, Oxford, 1998, pp. 4-11. See also the *Case of S.S. Lotus (France* v. *Turkey)*, P.C.I.J. Ser. A, No.10), the *Case of Nicaragua* v. *United States* (Merits), I.C.J. Rep. 1986 p.14 and the *North Sea Continental Shelf Cases*, I.C.J. Rep. 1969, p.4. Here the ICJ stated that, for customary international law to be taken to exist, ' State practice (…) should have been extensive and virtually uniform in the sense of the provision invoked; - and should have occurred in such a way as to show a general recognition that a rule of law or legal obligation is involved'.

> country concerned), the follow-up process is manifestly not inherently incapable of giving rise to customary international law.'[82]

At the time of drafting, some expressed the hope that the codes would evolve into customary international law. For example, with regard to the non-binding nature of the OECD Guidelines, Theo Vogelaar –Special Consultant to the OECD Director General on International Investment and Multinational Enterprises, at the time when the Guidelines were drafted– advanced the following:

> 'in the course of time –and when they have been frequently applied– [the OECD Guidelines can] pass into the general corpus of customary international law. Although they do not prescribe legally enforceable rules, they nevertheless constitute a source of law in domains not covered thus far by positive rules of law. As a source of law they may have a wider impact on the solution of problems arising from the activities of [multinational enterprises] than their voluntary nature at first view seems to indicate. (...) The OECD governments have initiated a classic process of lawmaking. Starting from recognized principles and a common concept of what is just and fair behaviour, the law has gradually evolved in every country, resulting in the end in the definition and settlement of legal relations, between States and private bodies, and between private bodies. The guidelines therefore constitute a source of law that means a method to detect and determine rules of law as a positive factor in the process of law creation. (...) In order to qualify as a source of law, the Guidelines must enjoy general acceptance. A last requirement (...) is that continuous use will be made of them in the daily practice. (...) Whether this will materialize depends in great part on the effectiveness of the follow-up procedures.'[83]

It has been concluded that, to date, the follow-up procedures are not very effective. The possibilities of directly imposing obligations on corporations are hindered by the fact that the clarification procedures under the OECD and the ILO do not identify specific corporations. If a corporation does not abide by the conclusions there are no sanctions available. Moreover, it has been concluded that these procedures have fallen into disuse. It may be concluded that there is no general, uniform and consistent practice and therefore the requirements for transformation of rules into customary law are not fulfilled.[84]

Certain provisions in the international codes might have a different status, however. The codes are what has been called 'Zebra codes', *i.e.* instruments that are composed

82 Hans W. Baade, 'Legal Effects of Codes of Conduct for Multinational Enterprises', in: *Legal Problems for Codes of Conduct for Multinational Enterprises*, Vol. 1, Norbert Horn [ed.], Kluwer, Deventer, 1980, p. 12.

83 Theo W. Vogelaar, 'The OECD Guidelines: Their Philosophy, History, Negotiation, Form, Legal Nature, Follow-up Procedures and Review', in: *Legal Problems for Codes of Conduct for Multinational Enterprises*, Vol. 1, Norbert Horn [ed.], Kluwer, Deventer, 1980, pp. 127-139, pp. 135-136.

84 Van Eyk, *supra* n. 13, p. 146.

of binding as well as non-binding provisions.[85] Even though the codes as a whole are of a voluntary nature, individual provisions can have a legally binding character because the provisions either belong to customary international law or because the same provisions are laid down in other documents that are legally binding. Certain provisions in the OECD Guidelines and the ILO Tripartite Declaration referring to human rights have been codified in international human rights treaties. Some commentators submit that the provisions in the codes referring to human rights are provisions that already belong to customary international law.[86]

Finally, it should be pointed out that the codes may play an important role with regard to national legislation regulating corporate behaviour. The implementation of the (human rights) obligations provided for in the various codes is left to the national level. Interesting in this respect is the so-called 'legitimising' or 'legitimisation' function of codes of conduct as has been pointed out by Baade.[87] This implies that once a code has been adopted its content can be enacted as binding domestic law, *i.e.* 'OECD member countries are estopped from questioning the legality of legislation and regulatory acts by member states pursuing the same objective.'[88] Moreover, this legitimising effect also follows from the anti-consistency rule laid down in the *Nuclear Tests Cases* which states

> 'having committed themselves to the legal view that the substantive provisions of the instruments adopted are proper and even desirable objects of national policy, the declarant State can not in good faith subsequently adopt a legal position to the contrary.'[89]

Baade concludes that the adoption as well as the content of codes of conduct can encourage national legislation.[90] This legitimising effect of codes of conduct on national legislation is important in the light of this study. As will be discussed in chapter VII, national legislation is currently an important tool for holding corporations accountable for human rights violations.[91] Brownlie draws a parallel with the UDHR 'which was (…) designedly non-binding [and] was in a rather patchy way picked up (…) in various domestic courts'.[92] So far, this process is, however, not taking place, regarding the

85 Baade, *supra* n. 82,, p. 15.
86 S.C. van Bijsterveld and W.J.M. van Genugten, 'Gedragscodes voor het internationale bedrijfsleven; nuttig instrument of schild tegen bindende verantwoordelijkheid' [Codes of conduct for international business: useful instrument or a shield against binding responsibility?'], in: *Grondrechten en Zelfregulering [Fundamental rights and Selfregulation]*, Tjeenk Willink, Deventer, 1997, p.118.
87 Baade, *supra* n. 82, pp. 24-28.
88 Baade, *supra* n. 82, 1980, p. 27.
89 Baade, *supra* n. 82, 1980, p. 27.
90 Baade, *supra* n. 82, 1980, p. 29.
91 See pp. 177-216.
92 I. Brownlie, 'Legal effects of Codes of Conduct for MNEs: Commentary', in: *Legal Problems of Codes of Conduct for Multinational Enterprises*, Norbert Horn [ed.], Vol. 1, Kluwer, Deventer, 1980, p. 42.

codes of conduct discussed in this section. Having said this, a development can be detected towards national courts taking up the issue of corporate accountability for human rights violations. However, so far the OECD Guidelines and the ILO Tripartite Declaration have not played a major part in such cases.[93]

To sum up, it may be concluded that the codes discussed here, that directly address corporations at the international level are of a limited value with regard to effectively regulating corporate conduct in the light of human rights violations. At best it can be said that the codes generate a limited degree of normative force and provide some guidance and may legitimise the national regulation of corporations.

7 The United Nations

In the previous sections the main international codes of conduct directly addressing corporations have been discussed. Within the UN the regulation of corporations has also received attention. The attempts to adopt a code of conduct in the 1970s and the 1980s failed, however. Nevertheless, I find it useful to briefly discuss the –never finalised– UN Code of Conduct on Transnational Corporations, as it was an attempt to draft the most comprehensive international code regulating corporate behaviour. Moreover, it is interesting to examine the difficulties encountered during the drafting process of the code, which, as will become clear, were partly due to the political context at that time. Some of the problems encountered are, however, also relevant with regard to the present attempts to regulate corporate conduct. Recently, the issue of corporations and their impact on the enjoyment of human rights is again being discussed in the context of the UN. This will be dealt with in section 7.2.

7.1 The Draft UN Code of Conduct on Transnational Corporations

As was described in section 3, various developments in the 1970s resulted in a greater awareness within the UN concerning the lack of control with regard to the activities of corporations. Several resolutions were adopted affirming permanent sovereignty over natural resources.[94] It was during this decade that the rise of the developing countries, grouped together as 'the Group of 77', led to the call for a New International Economic Order (NIEO) in a resolution adopted by the UN General Assembly in 1974.[95]

---

93 An exception is the *BATCO* case where reference was made to the OECD Guidelines. This case is further discussed on p. 136.

94 In 1952 the General Assembly adopted resolution 626 (VII) affirming the right of peoples freely to use and exploit their natural wealth and resources as inherent in their sovereignty. In 1962 resolution 1803 (XVII) was adopted stating the rights of peoples and nations to permanent sovereignty over their natural wealth and resources. This right was reaffirmed in resolutions 3201 (S-VI), 3202 (S-VI), 3362 (S-VII) and 3281 (XXIX). This last resolution, known as the Charter of Economic Rights and Duties of States, was, however, not supported by some of the major market economies.

95 UN Doc. A/Res/3201 (S-VI), 1 May 1974.

The NIEO proposal arose from a perception by many Third World countries that they had not played a significant role in the establishment of the existing system of international ownership, finance and trade and that the system was seriously biased against their interests.[96] The NIEO would include, *inter alia*, the legal recognition of the right of a State to control the activities of corporations operating within its borders.

Several events further propelled the decision to draft a code of conduct. The adoption of the International Code of Marketing of Breast-milk Substitutes (better known as the Infant Formula Code)[97] by the 34th World Health Assembly on 21 May 1981 was a direct source of inspiration. The aggressive marketing of infant formula in developing countries led to a decrease in breast-feeding. However, the water needed for the infant formula was often contaminated and caused an increase in infant mortality. Furthermore, the decline in breast-feeding resulted in malnutrition. Pressure groups organised boycotts against the leading corporation in this field, the *Nestlé* Corporation. After years of protest the company agreed to a code of conduct restricting infant formula marketing. The infant formula campaign inspired the effort to establish a United Nations Code of Conduct for Transnational Corporations.

Formally, the UN attention became focussed on the issue of corporate conduct and its negative effects as a result of the 1972 protest by the Chilean representative Mr Santa Cruz, against the interference of the American corporation ITT in Chile's internal political affairs. ITT played a part, together with the American government, in overthrowing the democratically-chosen Marxist Allende government.[98] This was a clear example of the abuse of power by a corporation and gave rise to concern about the impossibility of holding these companies accountable for their behaviour.

In response to the concerns with regard to the activities of corporations the UN Economic and Social Council adopted resolution 1721 which requested the Secretary-General to establish a group of twenty eminent persons to study the impact of corporations on development and international relations. Following a report from this group,[99] the UN Centre on Transnational Corporations[100] and the UN Commission on Transnational Corporations were established. The main task of the Commission was to formu-

96 Lee E. Preston, 'The Evolution of Multinational Public Policy Towards Business: Codes of Conduct', *Multinational Culture, Social Impacts of a Global Economy. Contributions in Economics & Economic History*, No. 122, Cheryl R. Lehman and Russell M. Moore [eds.] Greenwood Press, New York, 1992, p.16.

97 UN Doc. WHA/Res/34.22 and Annex, 21 May 1981.

98 The role played by ITT was disclosed during hearings before the Subcommittee on Foreign Affairs of the US House of Representatives, *United States and Chile During the Allende Years*, 1970-1973, Hearings before the Subcommittee on Foreign Affairs, House of Representatives, US Government Printing Office, Washington, 1975. See also, Van Eyk, *supra* n. 13, pp. 15-16.

99 UN Doc. E/5500/Rev.1/Add 1 (Part 1), 24 May 1974.

100 In 1992 the UN Centre on Transnational Corporations was reorganised and renamed as the Transnational Corporations Management Division, one of the eight divisions of the United Nations Department of Economic and Social Development.

late a comprehensive and global code of conduct for corporations. By 1981, the Commission had formulated most of the provisions of the Code.

7.1.1 Content

The draft code addresses corporations and governments and is the most comprehensive code of conduct that has been drafted. The provisions in the draft code share a common goal, namely to maximise the contributions of corporations to the social and economic well-being of the host countries in which they operate.[101] Therefore, corporations must abstain from involvement in, and subversion of, domestic politics in host nations and respect host government priorities on employment, the environment and socio-economic policy.[102] Furthermore, corporations must 'respect human rights and fundamental freedoms in the countries in which they operate'[103] and 'shall not discriminate on the basis of race, colour, sex, religion, language, social, national and ethnic origin or political or other opinion.'[104] Moreover, corporations had to cease collaboration with racist politicians in South Africa.[105]

During the drafting process major disagreements with regard to the nature and the contents of the code came to the fore. The developed countries together with the corporations took the view that prevailed in earlier decades, namely that the code would especially have to protect foreign direct investment. Corporations needed to be protected and, therefore, the international framework had to be of a liberalising nature and had to focus on the protection of international investment. They did support the drafting of international guidelines, as they would subject all corporations to the same rules, which was a good thing from a competitive point of view.[106] International regulation would also enhance a stable investment climate. An example of this position is the viewpoint taken by the *Unilever* corporation during the hearing before the group of eminent persons:

> '(...) Too little is heard about the power of Governments; the power to act fairly or unfairly; the power to enforce the sale of shares at inadequate prices; the power to block dividend remittances for years; the power to discriminate through discrimination against foreign investment; the power to nationalise or take over a company (...) with inadequate or no compensation.'[107]

101 Preamble UN Doc. E/1990/94, 12 June 1990 (This is the latest version of the code).
102 Artts. 7-11, 13, 16 UN Doc. E/1990/94, 12 June 1990.
103 Art. 13 UN Doc. E/1990/94, 12 June 1990.
104 Art. 14 UN Doc. E/1990/94, 12 June 1990.
105 Art. 15 UN Doc. E/1990/94, 12 June 1990.
106 Van Eyk, *supra* n. 13, p.33.
107 Summary of the written and oral statement by Ernest G. Woodroofe and Gerrit D.A. Klijnstra, Second session, Geneva 2, 3, 5-8 and 15 November 1973. Summary of the Hearings Before the Group of Emi-

It became clear that the code would never be adopted without provisions aimed at providing basic guarantees for the protection and the freedom of corporate operations.

The position, which was defended by the developing countries, was that the capacity and the impact of corporations and the inadequate control-possibilities called for international guidelines for corporate behaviour. The power of corporations could threaten the national sovereignty of the host State. According to the developing countries, the code should, therefore, only address the corporations. The developed countries and corporations succeeded in the inclusion of a part on the treatment of corporations.[108] These contradictory views made the negotiations very difficult, as the discussion became part of the wider North-South discussion.

The socialist countries took a rather distinct position during the negotiations. They claimed that their centrally-guided system made the effective control of corporations possible and therefore international guidelines could not be applicable to their territories. International monitoring would be considered as interference in their national sovereignty. The socialist countries used the deliberations to oppose the Western world by supporting the viewpoint of the developing countries. As a result, the negotiations on the code not only became part of the North-South discussion but also became entangled in the political fencing between East and West.[109]

A further point of disagreement was the issue of a reference to general international law. As was mentioned earlier, a major incentive for the proposal for a NIEO was the fact that many developing countries felt that they had had no part in the realisation of the existing trade system. The developing countries, therefore, harboured a general distrust of international law that was seen as a tool for oppression by the developed countries. The developed countries and the business community were in favour of including a reference to international law as this would provide minimum standards regarding the treatment of foreign direct investment.[110]

7.1.2 Supervision

Disagreement not only existed regarding the contents of the code but the discussion also centred on the nature, the legal form, of the code. During the negotiations two basic positions appeared: the so-called minimalist position, supported by the developed

nent Persons to Study the Impact of Multinational Corporations on Development and on International Relations, Department of Economic and Social Affairs, United Nations, New York, 1974, p. 450.

108 Resolution 1980/60 of 24 July 1980 by the Economic and Social Council. Art. 55 UN Doc. E/1990/ 1994, 12 June 1990 .

109 Antonie de Kemp, 'Gedragscodes voor Multinationale Ondernemingen' [Codes Of Conduct for Multinational Enterprises], in: *Internationale Spectator*, (1986), pp. 371-381, see: p.373.

110 See also: Patrick Robertson, The Question of a Reference to International Law in the UN Code of Conduct on Transnational Corporations (July 1986, UNCTC Current Studies, Series A, No.1, UN Doc. ST/CTC/SER.A/2).

countries and the business community and the maximalist position, defended by the developing countries and the trade unions.[111] The minimalists opposed the idea of a binding code, as they feared it would obstruct business. This position promoted the notion of voluntary rather than legally enforceable rules. Minimalists claimed that the lack of uniformity, with regard to, *inter alia*, ideology, the level of development and national objectives, among the international actors, necessitated flexible, non-binding rules. The maximalists, on the other hand, favoured legally binding, internationally enforceable rules of conduct for corporations, either by means of an international treaty or customary international law.[112]

The first draft was presented to the Commission at its eighth session in 1982.[113] However, this draft was still very incomplete. Especially the provisions with regard to the treatment of corporations were heavily disputed. It was decided that a special session would be held by the Commission on Transnational Corporations in order to complete the draft.[114] Many sessions and many revised drafts followed. In the different versions of the draft code a process can be detected towards a less regulatory system with a more favourable code for the developed countries. The latest version of the code is the text proposed on 31 May 1990. In 1990, Kaufmann and Schrijver were still optimistic:

> '(…), after a long stalemate, there now seems to be an increasing willingness to complete the negotiations and to overcome differences. No doubt this change has been induced by a decrease of actual foreign investment in developing countries (especially Africa), on the one hand, and the establishment of transnational corporations with parent companies in developing countries on the other hand.'[115]

Nevertheless, the negotiations ended in an effective deadlock. They were finally suspended in July 1992.[116] By March 1993, the Centre for Transnational Corporations had been converted into a smaller agency within the UN Conference on Trade and Development. According to some observers, the main reason why the UN Code has never been finalised lies in its intended comprehensiveness.[117] The discussions on the UN Code became entangled in political interests. The fact that the work was being

---

111 See: Cynthia Day Wallace, *Legal Control of the Multinational Enterprise*, Martinus Nijhoff, The Hague etc., 1983.

112 A compromise between the Minimalist and the Maximalist position is the so-called 'Zebra Code'. This refers to an instrument that will consist of both binding and non-binding rules.

113 UN Doc. E/C.10/1982/6 of 5 June 1982.

114 Resolution 1982/68 of 27 October 1982.

115 Kaufmann and Schrijver, *supra* n. 9, p. 27.

116 International Chamber of Commerce, *Annual Report 1992,*(1992) p.24.

117 W. Fikentscher, 'United Nations Code of Conduct: New Paths in International Law', *American Journal of Comparative Law*, Vol. 30, 1982, pp. 577-604.

done by an intergovernmental working group instead of an independent group of persons contributed to this. Political interest quite soon dominated the discussions.[118]

From the above analysis, it is clear that the attempts to adopt a comprehensive code of conduct within the UN failed largely due to the political context at the time of drafting. However, the main points of disagreement between the different parties also remain obstacles to this day, as will be discussed below.[119]

7.2 Current Activities within the United Nations with Regard to Corporations and Human Rights

The issue of corporations and the impact of their activities has recently received renewed attention within the framework of the UN. Two parallel developments can be detected: the work on a regulatory system within the Sub-Commission on the Promotion and Protection of Human Rights and the initiative of the UN Secretary-General, Kofi Annan: *The Global Compact.*

7.2.1 The UN Sub-Commission on the Promotion and Protection of Human Rights

At its 50th session on August 28th, 1998, the Sub-Commission on the Promotion and Protection of Human Rights[120] decided to establish, for a three-year period, a sessional working group of the Sub-Commission to examine the working methods and activities of transnational corporations.[121] The mandate of the working group consists of six items. The Working Group shall: identify and examine the effects of the working methods and activities of corporations; examine, receive and gather information on the effects of the working methods; analyse the compatibility of the various international human rights instruments with the various investment agreements; make recommendations and proposals relating to the methods of work and activities of corporations; prepare a list of countries and corporations indicating their gross national product and financial turnover; consider the scope of the obligation of the States to regulate the activities of corporations. It was stressed by the Working Group that the new code of conduct should eventually have a binding character.[122]

The first draft prepared by David Weissbrodt entitled 'Draft Human Rights Guidelines for Companies' was discussed at the meeting of the Sub-Commission in 2000.[123]

---

118 Baade, *supra* n. 63, p. 417.

119 See p. 127 f.

120 At that time the Sub-Commission was called the Sub-Commission on Prevention of Discrimination and Protection of Minorities.

121 UN Doc. E/CN.4/Sub.2/Res/ 1998/8, 20 August 1998.

122 UN Doc. E/CN.4/Sub.2/1999/9, 12 August 1999, para. 26.

123 UN Doc. E/CN.4/Sub.2/2000/WG.2/WP.1, 25 May 2000, and the two addenda containing background information and a list of existing sources drawn on in the preparation of the draft: UN Doc. E/CN.4/ Sub.2/2000/WG.2/WP.1/ Add. 1 and Add.2, 25 May 2000.

The comments made during this session, together with other comments and recommendations received throughout the year[124], resulted in a new document: the 'Draft Universal Human Rights Guidelines for Companies.[125] This draft was discussed at the 53rd session of the Sub-Commission in 2001. During this meeting the Sub-Commission decided to extend the mandate of the working group for three years.[126]

In the latest version of the code, entitled 'Human Rights Principles and Responsibilities for Transnational Corporations and Other Business Enterprises',[127] the following obligations for corporations are identified. In general, while governments have the primary responsibility to promote and protect human rights, corporations, as organs of society, are also responsible for promoting and securing human rights elaborated in the UDHR[128] and other human rights instruments.[129] More specifically, the following obligations are enumerated:

/ Transnational corporations and other business enterprises shall ensure equality of opportunity and treatment for the purpose of eliminating discrimination (…) (art. 2).
/ Transnational corporations and other business enterprises shall not engage in nor benefit from war crimes, crimes against humanity, genocide, torture, forced disappearance, forced or compulsory labour, hostage-taking, other violations of humanitarian law, and other international crimes against the human person as defined by international law (art. 3).
/ Security arrangements of transnational corporations and other business enterprises shall observe international human rights norms as well as the laws and professional standards of the country in which they operate (art. 4).
/ Transnational corporations and other business enterprises shall not use forced or compulsory labour as forbidden by the relevant international instruments and national legislation (art. 5).

124 See, *inter alia*, the report of an international seminar held in March 2001, UN Doc. E/CN.4/Sub.2/2001/WG.2/WP.1/Add.3, 31 May 2001.

125 UN Doc.E/CN.4/Sub.2/2001/WG.2/WP.1/Add.1, 21 May 2001. Besides these Guidelines, the Sub-Commission also discussed a working paper drafted by Mr. Guissé: UN Doc.E/CN.4/Sub.2/2001/WG.2/WP.3,and a working paper prepared by Mr. Eide: UN Doc. E/CN.4/Sub.2/2001/WG.2/WP.2. For a summary of these discussions see UN Doc.E/CN.4/Sub.2/2001/9, 14 August 2001.

126 E/CN.4/Sub.2/Res/2001/3, 15 August 2001.

127 UN Doc. E/CN.4/Sub.2/2002/XX, E/CN.4/Sub.2/2002/WG.2/WP.1, February 2002 for discussion in July/August 2002. The document is available at: http://www1.umn.edu/humanrts/principlesW-OutCommentary5final.html (accessed on 20 May 2002). This document replaces the earlier 'Draft Fundamental Human Rights Principles for Business Enterprises', UN. Doc E/CN.4/Sub.2/2002/X/Add.1, E/CN.4/Sub.2/2002/WG.2/WP.1/Add.1 (Draft for discussion November 2001).

128 Paragraph 3 Preamble and art. 1 of the Draft Human Rights Principles and Responsibilities for Transnational Corporations and Other Business Enterprises, February 2002.

129 See paragraph 4 Preamble of the Draft Human Rights Principles and Responsibilities for Transnational Corporations and Other Business Enterprises, February 2002.

- Transnational corporations and other business enterprises shall respect the rights of children to be protected from economic exploitation as forbidden by the relevant international instruments and national legislation (art. 6).
- Transnational corporations and other business enterprises shall provide a safe and healthy working environment as provided by the relevant international instruments and national legislation (art. 7).
- Transnational corporations and other business enterprises shall compensate workers with remuneration that ensures an adequate standard of living for them and their families. Such renumeration shall take due account of their needs for adequate living conditions with a view towards progressive improvement (art. 8).
- Transnational corporations and other business enterprises shall ensure the freedom of association and effective recognition of the right to collective bargaining by protecting the right to establish and, subject only to the rules of the organization concerned, to join organizations of their own choosing without distinction, previous authorization, or interference, for the protection of their employment interests and for other collective bargaining puposes as provided in the relevant ILO conventions. (art. 9).
- Transnational corporations and other business enterprises shall recognise and respect applicable norms of international law; national laws; regulations; administrative practices; the rule of law; development objectives; social, economic and cultural policies; and authority of the countries in which enterprises operate (art. 10).
- Transnational corporations and other business enterprises shall not offer, promise, give, accept, condone, knowingly benefit from, or demand a bribe or other improper advantage. Nor shall they be solicited or expected to give a bribe or other improper advantage to any government, public official, candidate for elective post, or any other individual or organization (art. 11).
- Transnational corporations and other business enterprises shall respect civil, cultural, economic, political, and social rights, and contribute to their realisation, in particular the rights to development; adequate food; adequate health; adequate housing; education; freedom of thought, conscience, and religion; and freedom of opinion and expression; and refrain from actions which obstruct the realization of those rights. (art. 12).
- Transnational corporations and other business enterprises shall act in accordance with fair business, marketing and advertising practices and shall take all necessary steps to ensure the safety and quality of the goods and services they provide. They shall not produce, distribute, market, or advertise potentially harmful or harmful products for use by consumers (art. 13).
- Transnational corporations and other business enterprises shall carry out their activities in accordance with national laws, regulations, administrative practices, and policies relating to the preservation of the environment of the countries in which

they operate as well as in accordance with relevant international agreements, principles, objectives, and standards with regard to the environment as well as human rights, public health, and safety; and shall generally conduct their activities in a manner contributing to the wider goal of sustainable development (art. 14).

Finally, the Principles contain several provisions on implementation:

- As an initial step towards compliance with the Principles, transnational corporations or other business enterprises shall adopt, disseminate and implement internal rules of operation consistent with these principles. Further, they shall take other measures fully to implement these Principles and to provide at least for the prompt implementation of the protections set forth in these Principles (art. 15).
- Transnational corporations and other business enterprises shall be subject to periodic monitoring by national, international, governmental, and/or nongovernmental mechanisms regarding their application of the Principles. This monitoring shall be transparent, independent, and take into account input from relevant stakeholders. Further, transnational corporations and other business enterprises shall conduct periodic evaluations concerning the impact of their own activities on human rights under these Principles (art. 16).
- Transnational corporations and other business enterprises shall provide prompt, effective, and adequate reparation to those persons, entities, and communities who have been adversely affected by failures to comply with these Principles through restoring, replacing, or otherwise compensating for any damage done or property taken (art. 17).
- Nothing in these Principles shall be construed as diminishing, restricting, or adversely affecting the human rights obligations of States under national and international aw. Nor shall they be construed as diminishing, or adversely affecting more protective human rights norms.

This version of the Principles has been drafted taking the comments received during the 53rd meeting of the Sub-commission in August 2001 into account. An important issue that was brought up during this meeting was the question concerning the scope of the guidelines. Should the guidelines only apply to multinational corporations or also to domestic corporations? As put forward by some participants in the discussion, it may prove difficult to define multinational corporations. Moreover, it was observed that both multinational and domestic corporations can affect the enjoyment of human rights. On the other side, several speakers favoured a focus on multinational corporations as these entities, given their size and power, can have a notably far-reaching effect on the enjoyment of human rights.[130] In the February 2002 draft the following definition is applied:

> 'The term "transnational corporation" refers to a cluster of economic entities operating in two or more countries —whatever their legal form, whether in their home country of activity, and whether taken individually or collectively.
>
> The phrase "other business enterprise" includes any business entity, regardless of the international or domestic nature of its activities, including a transnational corporation; the corporate, partnership, or other legal form used to establish the business entity; and the nature of the ownership of the entity, including any privately-owned or government-owned entity'.[131]

Another issue that was discussed during the 53rd meeting of the Sub-Commission was the question of whether or not the draft guidelines should be binding. Most participants agreed that the code would eventually have to have a mandatory character.[132] In the light of this it was suggested that its name should be changed. Instead of the term 'guidelines', which implies 'non-binding', the term 'principles' is now used. The intention of ending up with a legally binding code is also expressed in resolution 2001/3 in which the working group is requested to continue its work, 'so that a binding document can be drafted'.[133]

The working group has been requested to present the principles at the 54th meeting of the Sub-Commission in August 2002. If, eventually, the 'Human Rights Principles and Responsibilities for Transnational Corporations and Other Business Enterprises' are adopted, this will, from a human rights perspective, be the most comprehensive code of conduct for corporations. It must, however, be borne in mind that the task of the Sub-Commission is merely to undertake studies and to make recommendations to the Commission on Human Rights. The adoption of the Principles by the Sub-Commission would therefore only be a first step in a long process towards a document with a legally binding character. The likelihood of the discussion becoming tangled up in political issues at the level of the Commission is indeed real as this organ consists of State representatives.

7.2.2 The Global Compact

Simultaneous to the activities of the Sub-Commission a certain development is taking place within the UN that focuses on the voluntary co-operation of corporations with

130 See for the summary of the discussion: E/CN.4/Sub.2/2001/9, 14 August 2001.

131 Art. 19 of the Draft Human Rights Principles and Responsibilities for Transnational corporations and Other Business Enterprises, February 2002.

132 See for the summary of the discussion: E/CN.4/Sub.2/2001/9, 14 August 2001.

133 UN Doc. E/CN.4/Sub.2/Res/2001/3, 15 August 2001, para.2.

the UN to further, *inter alia*, human rights. In an address to the World Economic Forum on 31 January 1999, UN Secretary-General Kofi Annan first called for a so-called Global Compact, a co-operation between the UN and major corporations, to promote nine key principles drawn from the UDHR, the ILO's Fundamental Principles on Rights at Work and the Rio Principles on Environment and Development. The Global Compact was officially launched on 26 July 2000 by the UN Secretary-General together with senior executives from some 50 major corporations and representatives of labour, human rights, environmental and development organizations. The Global Compact 'challenges [corporations] to embrace and enact within their sphere of influence in the areas of human rights, labour standards and the environment' the following principles: corporations should support and respect the protection of internationally proclaimed human rights; business should ensure that they are not complicit in human rights violations; business should uphold the freedom of association and the effective recognition of the right to collective bargaining; the elimination of all forms of forced and compulsory labour; the effective abolition of child labour; the elimination of discrimination in respect of employment and occupation; support for a precautionary approach to environmental challenges; corporations should undertake initiatives to promote greater environmental responsibility; and encourage the development and diffusion of environmentally friendly technologies.[134]

The Global Compact is of a voluntary nature. To participate, corporations are encouraged to publicly advocate the principles and the Global Compact. Moreover, corporations are asked once a year to provide the UN with a concrete example of progress made or a lesson learned in implementing the principles. The examples will be posted on the UN website. Finally, if a corporation wishes to, it is encouraged to join in with the UN in partnership projects.

The Global Compact has encountered a great deal of criticism from various NGOs.[135] The NGOs fear that collaboration with the UN will 'legitimise' corporations with a poor human rights or environmental record. According to these NGOs, several of the companies taking part in the Compact have been involved in human right violations.[136] Besides this possible misuse of the Global Compact, the criticism by

134 The nine principles of The Global Compact can be found on the website of the UN at: http://www.unglobalcompact.org (accessed on 19 December 2001).

135 See, for some critical notes regarding The Global Compact, *inter alia,* the website of the NGO Corpwatch: http://www.corpwatch.org. See also the report *Tangled Up In Blue Corporate Partnerships at the United Nations*, Kenny Bruno and Joshua Karliner, 2000, http://www.igc.org/trac/un/reports/tangled.html (accessed on 24 November 2001). And the article: 'The UN Courts Big Business In Whose Interest?', by Miloon Kothari and Peter Prove in *Human Rights Tribune*, September 1999, Vol. 6, No.3, pp.16-18. Some NGOs, however, support the initiative. Among these are: Human Rights Watch, Amnesty International and Lawyers Committee for Human Rights.

136 TRAC has posted a series of articles on its website that deal with corporate Global Compact participants that have allegedly violated the 9 principles of the Compact: see: http://www.corpwatch.org/un/updates/2001/gcseries.html (accessed on 24 November 2001).

NGOs focuses on the wholly voluntary nature of the initiative. The Global Compact does not provide for an enforcement mechanism or a monitoring system.

Basically, the Global Compact calls on corporations to conduct a form of self-regulation. The issue of self-regulation will be dealt with in section 9.

7.3 Concluding Remarks on the United Nations

Since the failure to adopt a comprehensive UN code of conduct, the issue of regulating corporate conduct has re-emerged on the UN agenda. Compared to the attempts in the 1970s and 1980s, the focus is now clearly on the protection and promotion of human rights, and corporations are considered to be partners in achieving this aim. The question whether corporations should be subjected to mandatory regulation or whether self-regulation is the best route to follow, remains a thorny issue in the debate within the UN.

8 Developments at the European Level

Within the European Union several developments are taking place with regard to the regulation of corporate conduct. Based on the standards of the UN, the ILO and the OECD, a code of conduct is being developed for European corporations. In 1999 the European Parliament adopted a 'Resolution on EU Standards for European Enterprises Operating in Developing Countries: Towards a European Code of Conduct', which, *inter alia*, recommends that a model code of conduct for European businesses should be adopted, which guarantees minimum internationally recognized standards on the environment, health and safety conditions in the workplace, and respect for basic human rights. As set forth in the resolution, there

> 'is a powerful case to answer that the European Union should take a more active role in standard-setting for the conduct of its enterprises in developing countries. Forty-two of the top 100 [multinational corporations] are based in Europe, only 35 in North America.'[137]

In the resolution the European Parliament requests the European Commission to establish a European Monitoring Platform which is to be an independent body of experts to monitor and verify the implementation of the code of conduct, identify best practices, and receive complaints about corporate conduct from interested parties.[138] The European Monitoring Platform should consist of representatives from the European business community and human rights and environmental organisations. The resolution further recommends that the European Monitoring Platform should be open

137 Explanatory statement to the European Parliament resolution A4-0508/98.

138 European Parliament resolution A4-0508/98 on EU Standards for European Enterprises operating in developing countries towards a European Code of Conduct, O.J. (1999) C104/180.

to receive complaints from people in the host country where the European corporation operates. Moreover, the resolution recommends that public hearings be organised regularly in the European Parliament in order to discuss specific cases, of both good and bad conduct, and that all persons concerned (including enterprises) be invited to attend them.[139] The first European Parliamentary hearings were held in November 2000. These hearings addressed the issues of infant nutrition and sportswear. The corporations that were invited to participate in these hearings decided not to co-operate.[140]

Furthermore, in July 2001 the European Commission presented a so-called 'Green Paper' entitled 'Promoting a European Framework for Corporate Social Responsibility'.[141] With this Green Paper, the Commission 'aims to launch a wide debate on how the European Commission could promote corporate social responsibility'.[142] This is clearly only a first step in a process towards, as the Commission hopes, 'a new framework for the promotion of corporate responsibility'.[143] In the Green Paper, the European Commission distinguishes two dimensions of corporate responsibility. Firstly, the internal dimension, which concerns mainly responsible management of natural and human resources.[144] Secondly, corporate social responsibility has an external dimension meaning that the responsibility of corporations extends beyond the doors of the corporation and beyond the borders of Europe.[145] The external dimension includes a responsibility for human rights. According to the European Commission,

> '[c]odes of conduct, however are not an alternative to national, European Union and international laws and binding rules: binding rules ensure minimum standards applicable to all, while codes of conduct and other voluntary initiatives can only complement these and promote higher standards for those who subscribe to them.'[146]

The initiatives undertaken within the context of the European Union would seem to be heading in the direction of the creation of a binding framework for regulating corporate responsibility. At the time of writing the initiatives are still at an embryonic stage, however.

139 Paragraph 17 of the European Parliament resolution A4-0508/98.
140 See for a brief report by the special Rapporteur Richard Howitt: http://www.cleanclothes.org/legal/01-04-10.htm (accessed on 28 November 2001).
141 European Commission, Directorate-General for Employment and Social Affairs, Unit EMPL/D.1, July 2001, http://www.europa.eu.int/comm/employment_social/soc-dial/csr/greenpaper.htm (accessed on 27 November 2001).
142 Executive summary para.7.
143 Introduction, para. 19.
144 See section 2.1.
145 See section 2.2.
146 See section 2.2.3, para. 54.

9 Self-Regulation

During the last two decades a fundamental shift in corporate attitude can be witnessed. Due to, *inter alia*, public pressure, corporations have started to rethink their role and responsibilities in society. This has resulted in a mushrooming of voluntary corporate codes of conduct in which corporations define the manner in which they conduct their business in line with their responsibilities. During the 1980s, the discussion on corporate codes of conduct took place mostly within the United States and was confined to business ethics. During the 1990s corporations elsewhere also started to draw up voluntary codes of conduct.[147]

An immense variety of corporate codes of conduct can be discerned. There are the codes drawn up by groups of corporations[148] or by individual companies.[149] Furthermore, codes exist that are drawn up by NGOs[150] and/or governments[151] usually in the form of guidelines aiming to help corporations in drawing up a code of conduct. Some codes deal with human rights obligations for corporations in general, others are aimed at a specific branch or product. This section deals with the internal codes drawn up by an individual corporation or a group of corporations.

Given the vast number of codes it is not feasible to discuss the various codes in any depth. The rapid proliferation of these codes, however, does warrant a brief discussion in this section. The major question relates to the significance of corporate codes of

147 According to a survey by VNO-NCW, a Dutch employers' organisation, 38 out of the 100 largest Dutch enterprises have an internal code of conduct and several others are in the process of drafting one. See also: Ans Kolk, Rob van Tulder and Carlijn Welters, 'International codes of conduct and corporate social responsibility: can transnational corporations regulate themselves?', in: *Transnational Corporations,* Vol. 8, No.1, April 1999, pp. 143-181 at p. 145.

148 To name but a few: in 1994, business leaders from the US, Japan and Europe adopted 'the Caux Round Table Principles for Business, http://www.cauxroundtable.org (accessed on 24 August 2000); in 1997, 14 Canadian companies announced an 'International Code of Ethics for Canadian Business', http://www.uottawa.ca/hrrec/busethics/codeint.html (accessed on 24 August 2000); in April 1998, the Confederation of Danish Industries published a guide to help associated corporations to develop their own code of conduct, *Industry and Human Rights* by Jens Schierbeck.

149 Individual corporate codes can be found on the websites of corporations. A few examples of business principles: http://www.shell.com, http://www.bpamoco.com, http://www.nestle.com (all accessed on 24 August 2000).

150 A few examples of Guidelines drawn up by NGOs dealing with human rights in general: The report by the Dutch sections of Amnesty International and Pax Christi International, *Multinational Enterprises and Human Rights*, Utrecht, November 1998; Amnesty International UK Business Group, *Human Rights Guidelines for Companies*, September 1998. A selection of codes drawn up by NGOs dealing with a specific branch or product: The Clean Clothes Campaign which calls on major retailers to adopt a code of practice and effective monitoring procedures: http://www.cleanclothes.org/codes.htm (accessed on 25 August 2000).

151 A selection of the codes drawn up together with or by governments: *The Ethical Trading Initiative*, http://www.ethicaltrade.org (accessed on 17 December 2001), *The Apparel Industry Partnership*, this agreement can be found on the website of the Fair Labor Association, an organisation that grew out of the Apparel Industry Partnership, http://www.fairlabor.org/ (accessed on 17 December 2001.

conduct in the light of the accountability of corporations for human rights violations. The findings in this section are based mainly on inventories and surveys of corporate codes of conduct as these have been conducted by the OECD[152] and the ILO[153] as well as studies carried out by various NGOs[154] and researchers.[155] It must be emphasised that the emergence of corporate codes of conduct is an extremely important development in the light of protecting and promoting human rights. It points towards an increasing recognition and support within the business community for corporate responsibility for human rights. Notwithstanding this positive development, several factors can limit the significance of corporate codes of conduct as a regulatory tool.

The first important factor that may limit the significance of corporate codes of conduct from the perspective of regulation is the fact that public pressure is frequently the main incentive for drawing up a corporate code of conduct.[156] This casts some doubts on the effectiveness of this form of self-regulation as not all industries are equally susceptible to public pressure. Research shows that codes of conduct are notably adopted by manufacturers of consumer goods, *i.e.* corporations sensitive to public opinion.[157] Corporations that are less 'visible' to the consumer might be less inclined to adopt a self-regulatory code.

The second factor is the considerable diversity and selectivity that can be discerned in the corporate codes of conduct. A study of 215 corporate codes of conduct conducted by the ILO in 1998 shows the diversity between the codes.[158] Corporations are

---

152 A working party of the Trade Committee of the OECD has produced an extensive inventory of codes of corporate conduct entitled *Codes of corporate conduct: an inventory* (TD/TC/WP(98)74/FINAL). The paper presents an overview of codes of corporate conduct based on information submitted by OECD member governments and non-governmental sources. This inventory comprises 233 codes, the majority of which were issued by individual companies. The survey can be found on the website of the OECD: www.oecd.org. (Accessed on: 25 August 2000).

153 International Labour Office, Governing Body, Working Party on the Social Dimensions of the Liberalization of International Trade, GB.273/WP/SDL/1, 273rd Session, Geneva, November 1998. *Overview of Global Developments and Office Activities concerning Codes of Conduct, Social Labelling and other Private Sector Initiatives addressing Labour Issues*. The ILO has only reviewed Codes that address labour practices.

154 For example, the study entitled *Commerce with Conscience* by Craig Forcese for the Canadian lawyers Association for International Human Rights (CLAIHR) in collaboration with the International Centre for Human Rights and Democratic Development, 1997.

155 The study by Kolk, Tulder and Welters, *supra* n. 147, Christopher L. Avery, *Business and Human Rights in a Time of Change*, February 2000. This report has been published by the Amnesty International UK Business Group, Mark B. Baker, 'Private Codes of Corporate Conduct; Should the Fox Guard the Henhouse?', in: *University of Miami Inter-American Law Review*, Vol. 24, No. 2, (1992-1993), pp. 399-433.

156 Kolk, Tulder and Welters, *supra* n. 147, pp. 151-152 and Avery, *supra* n. 155, p. 45.

157 'Most codes with a human rights component are found at apparel companies and oil companies. It is very disappointing that companies in other industries are usually silent on the subject.' Avery, *supra* n. 155, p. 48.

158 ILO report GB.273/WP/SDL/1, *Overview of Global Developments,* 1998.

very selective regarding which human rights issues are addressed. The ILO report states:

> '(...) the selective approach by which most codes address labour problems appears to promote uneven implementation of fundamental labour rights, both within a single enterprise and across the world's labour force.'[159]

Moreover, the ILO survey showed that corporations tend to use their own definitions of (specific) human rights. Corporate codes rarely refer to human rights as have been laid down in the international law of human rights.[160]

Finally, the manner in which corporate codes of conduct are frequently implemented in practice reduces their significance. For a code to be more than mere 'window-dressing' it is imperative that the code is implemented. In practice effective implementation is often lacking. An illustration of this can be found in a study on the effectiveness of the codes of several US corporations. This study revealed that workers are frequently not even aware of the existence of the corporate code of conduct.[161] Moreover, the existing codes mostly lack an independent system of monitoring. The survey by the ILO demonstrates that in general compliance with codes of conduct is poor and that codes rarely provide for independent, external monitoring. This makes it virtually impossible to verify the credibility of the claims made. In some cases the monitoring is performed by the auditing firms that also produce the financial reports. These firms are frequently ill-equipped to deal with human rights issues.

Given these considerations, should it be concluded that corporate codes of conduct are in practice of limited significance with regard to regulating corporate behaviour in the light of human rights? The fact that these codes are voluntary does not necessarily make them devoid of any meaning. In the first place, the voluntary codes can have normative force. Moreover, the corporate codes of conduct can also be legally binding if looked upon as 'contracts'. Corporate codes of conduct can be interpreted as self-imposed obligations that may be used against corporations. As Van Genugten points out:

---

159 ILO report GB.273/WP/SDL/1, *Overview of Global Developments,* 1998, para. 49.

160 ILO report GB.273/WP/SDL/1, *Overview of Global Developments,* 1998, paras. 50-52. Amnesty International has emphasised the importance of a reference to universal international standards in a corporate code of conduct. See: Amnesty International UK Business Group, *Human Rights Principles for Companies*, (AI Index ACT 70/01/98, January 1998). See also the report of Amnesty International and Pax Christi, *supra* n. 150, 1998, p. 57. The necessity for less diversity in corporate codes of conduct has been acknowledged in the Howitt Resolution (see p. 130) which calls for the standardisation of voluntary codes of conduct.

161 Forcese, *supra* n. 154, pp. 25-26. Forcese refers to the 1996 study by the US Department of Labour of 42 major US textile firms: *The Apparel Industry and Codes of Conduct: A Solution to the International Child Labour Problem?*

'if (...) the code states that the company will pay specific (levels) of wages for specific types of work, or if it explicitly says that the company will not make use of child labour, thereby specifying what it considers to be child labour, this creates controllable obligations, which can even be used within legal procedures. (...) A provision like the one related to child labour, for instance, creates expectations which are legally speaking relevant, and which come close to real contractual obligations.'[162]

For a code of conduct to come close to a contractual obligation that can be used as an argument in legal proceedings it is imperative that the wording of the corporate code of conduct is specific.[163]

An (so far unsuccessful) attempt to use corporate statements against a corporation in such a manner was the lawsuit filed against the corporation *Nike Inc.* in California, USA in 1998. The plaintiff in this civil lawsuit alleged that the corporation had engaged in false advertising by claiming that it does not use unfair labour practices in its factories in South-East Asia.[164] It was argued that workers who made *Nike* products in Asia were subjected to mistreatment.[165] This was a 'private attorney general action' for unlawful and unfair business practices' that violate California's Business and Professions Code. Such cases can be brought in the California State courts more easily than elsewhere because under California's broad consumer protection laws the plaintiff does not have to be a victim. It is sufficient to show that there was a likelihood of deception. According to the plaintiff the complaint venue was proper in the Californian court because the products at issue were advertised, promoted, sold and used in California and *Nike* received substantial compensation from the sale of the products at issue by doing business there and making numerous misrepresentations which had an effect in this state. Specific reference was made to the code of conduct and memorandum of understanding drawn up by *Nike* in 1992. According to the plaintiff the code of conduct was 'intended, among other things, to entice consumers who do not want to purchase products made in sweatshops and unsafe and/or inhumane conditions.'[166] *Nike* responded that the claims it made were of a non-commercial nature and protected by the freedom of speech in the First Amendment. The court in February 1999 held in

162 Willem J.M. van Genugten, 'The Status of Transnational Corporations in International Public Law. With Special reference to the Case of Shell', in: *Human Rights and the Oil Industry*, Asbjørn Eide, Helge Ole Bergesen and Pia Rudolfson Goyer [eds.], Intersentia, 2000, p. 72.

163 Van Genugten, *supra* n. 162, 2000, p.72.

164 Case of *Marc Kasky* v. *NIKE, INC* and DOES 1 through 200 inclusive, Demand for Trial, 20 April 1998, available at: http://www.corpwatch.org/trac/nike/lawsuit.html (accessed on 28 December 2000).

165 The allegations were *inter alia* that *NIKE* made misrepresentations by stating that: workers who made *NIKE* products are protected from and not subjected to punishment and/or sexual abuse; *NIKE* products are made in accordance with applicable governmental laws and regulations governing wages and hours, health and safety conditions; average line-workers who produce *NIKE* products are paid double the minimum wage in South-East Asia; workers receive free meals and health care; *NIKE* guarantees a 'living wage', *Kasky* v. *NIKE, INC,* Demand for Trial, 20 April 1998.

166 *Kasky* v. *NIKE, INC* Demand for Trial, 20 April 1998, paras. 23-24.

favour of *Nike* and dismissed the case. The plaintiffs appealed the decision claiming that the statements made by *Nike* were of a commercial nature and that the First Amendment does not protect commercial speech that is false, deceptive or misleading.[167] The Court of Appeal, however, upheld the judgment claiming that the corporation's defence of its Asian wages and benefits was speech on a public policy issue and was protected by the First Amendment. The case is currently being considered by the California Supreme Court.

A successful example where a self-imposed obligation was used against a corporation in a national court is the, somewhat dated, but well-known case against *Batco Tobacco* factory in the Netherlands.[168] In this case it did not concern an official corporate code of conduct but an annual report. In the annual report of 1978, *Batco* included a reference to the OECD Guidelines, stating that its policies would be in conformity with the OECD Guidelines. *Batco* was planning to partly move its factories without notifying to the trade unions. In the court case brought against *Batco* the reference to the OECD Guidelines in its annual report was cited. The court deemed the reference 'not without significance.'[169]

In sum, corporate codes of conduct can, given certain circumstances, constitute legally relevant and even binding instruments. The enforcement of the provisions in the corporate codes of conduct will be left to the national level. In chapter VII the developments at the national level concerning the regulation of corporations from a human rights perspective will be dealt with.

167 *Marc Kasky* v. *NIKE, INC.*, et al., No. A086142, In the Court of Appeal of the State of California, (First Appellate District), Filed 20 March 2000.

168 *The Batco Tobacco factory* was part of the *British American Tobacco Company*.

169 Court of Appeal of Amsterdam, 21 June 1979, *NJ* 1980, 71, *Batco*, para.6, and Van Genugten, *supra* n. 162, p.72.

CHAPTER VI
STATE RESPONSIBILITY

1 INTRODUCTION

According to the classical doctrine States are responsible for upholding human rights on the international level. Under most international treaties only States can be held responsible. Even though an increased awareness of the role that non-State entities play concerning human rights can be detected, the prime responsible entities regarding the protection and promotion of human rights remain States. This was once again confirmed in the *Vienna Declaration and Program of Action*.[1] It has also been reaffirmed in the case-law of international human rights bodies. For instance, according to the Inter-American Commission:

> 'the entire system for protecting human rights is designed on the basis of the State's acknowledgement of itself as a party to a fundamental legal contract on the matter of human rights and it is against the State that complaints alleging a violation of the rights upheld in the Convention are brought.'[2]

This primary responsibility of States for international law calls for an examination of the responsibility of the State for human rights violations by corporations.

This chapter will first examine the existing rules of general international law regarding State responsibility. The work of the International Law Commission (hereinafter ILC) on the law of State responsibility will be discussed in section 3.[3] Section 4 addresses the issue of State responsibility under international human rights law. In

1 'Human rights and fundamental freedoms are the birthright of all human beings; their protection and promotion is the *first responsibility* of Governments' (emphasis added), Part I, art. 1 *Vienna Declaration and Program of Action,* A/Conf.157/23, 12 July 1993. This prime responsibility of States was also stressed in the preamble of *The Declaration on the Right and Responsibility of Individuals, Groups and Organs of Society to Promote and Protect Universally Recognized Human Rights and Fundamental Freedoms*, General Assembly resolution 53/144, adopted on 8 March 1999: 'Stressing that the prime responsibility and duty to promote and protect human rights and fundamental freedoms lie with the State'. Amnesty International also stresses this in its work on corporations and human rights: 'We will continue to hold governments responsible -to insist that primary responsibility for human rights protection lies with the state. But the power and ensuing responsibilities of companies must be recognized and acted upon', *Summary Study on Company Approaches*, AI Index: ACT 70/03/98.

2 Inter American Yearbook on Human Rights, 1990, 358.

3 A comprehensive set of materials relating to the work of the ILC on the topic of State Responsibility can be found on the website of the Lauterpacht Research Centre for International Law: http://www.law.cam.ac.uk/rcil/ILCSR/Statresp.htm (accessed on 13 August 2001).

section 5 of this chapter, State responsibility for private acts under international human rights law will be addressed by examining the case-law of the supervisory organs to the international human rights treaties and the case-law of the International Labour Organisation (ILO). The final section will discuss the issue of home State responsibility, *i.e.* the responsibility of the State where a corporation is incorporated.

2 The State Responsibility Doctrine: the Classical View

Traditionally, the law of international responsibility of States has dealt primarily with the protection of aliens in respect of both their person and their property.[4] States are under an obligation to exercise due diligence in the protection of aliens. This implies that the State has to take reasonable measures to prevent or remedy a wrongdoing to an alien. As will be discussed below, the due diligence standard that was developed with regard to the protection of aliens is now applied to States as regards responsibility for human rights violations.[5]

At first sight the issue of State responsibility does not seem to be complicated: if a State violates an international obligation, it bears international responsibility for that violation. However, the doctrine of State responsibility has proven to be a very complex matter. It has taken the ILC some fifty years to draft a set of articles on State responsibility. In view of the complexities surrounding State responsibility, I find it useful to briefly discuss the concept in general before examining the problems particularly relating to State responsibility for private acts.

The doctrine of State responsibility gives rise to many questions. For instance: *what* can lead to State responsibility? In the *Corfu Channel* case it was established that acts contrary to international law that give rise to international responsibility can involve either a breach or non-performance of an international obligation.[6] Furthermore, what kind of responsibility is meant? Is State responsibility absolute, so-called objective responsibility, or must there be fault? In other words, is liability strict or must there be a degree of blameworthiness that can be attributed to the State? Arbitral and judicial decisions can be found supporting both points of view. With the proliferation of State organs, strict liability is increasingly being applied as fault liability has become too complicated to apply.[7]

---

4 Brownlie, *System of the Law of Nations. State responsibility*, Clarendon Press, Oxford, 1983, p. 9.

5 See p. 145.

6 The International Court of Justice found Albania liable for a failure to act because it knew or should have known of the illegal conduct involved, *Corfu Channel (U.K.* v. *Albania)*, judgement of April 9, 1949, I.C.J. Rep. (1949) p.4, 23.

7 See, *e.g.* the *Caire* Case *(France* v. *Mexico)* (1929) 5 UNRIAA 516, where it was decided that Mexico was liable for the acts of its soldiers, whether or not those soldiers had acted beyond their competence or contrary to the orders of their superiors.

Within the framework of the present study the question regarding attribution is particularly relevant; for whose acts can a State be held responsible? Can a State be held responsible for violations of human rights by corporations? And, if this question can be answered in the affirmative, does this responsibility also arise when the corporate activities take place outside the territorial boundaries of the State concerned? The latter question will be addressed in section 6. I will now first discuss the work of the ILC on State responsibility, especially with regard to the issue of attribution. The Draft Articles on the Responsibility of States for Internationally Wrongful Acts, drawn up by the ILC, are not a source of law in the formal sense, but they are widely invoked and considered to be authoritative and, therefore, merit examination.

3 The Work of the International Law Commission on State Responsibility

The ILC has been working on the topic of State responsibility since 1949. In 1996 the ILC completed its first reading of an entire sct of Draft Articles on International State Responsibility.[8] After this first reading the Draft Articles consisted of two parts. The first part dealt with those general conditions and circumstances that give rise to international responsibility. The second part dealt with the consequences once a case of international responsibility had arisen. Between 1998-2000 the drafting committee's second reading of the Draft Articles took place. During the second reading the previously adopted provisions were reviewed. At its 53rd session in August 2001, the ILC adopted the complete second reading of the Draft Articles together with the accompanying commentaries.[9] The Draft Articles now consist of four parts: the internationally wrongful act of a State; content of the international responsibility of a State; the implementation of the international responsibility of a State; and, the last part entitled general provisions. The Draft Articles have now been referred to the UN General Assembly with the recommendation that the General Assembly take note of the Articles in a resolution with a view to adopting a convention on the topic of State responsibility.

8 UN Doc. A/51/10, 6 May-26 July 1996.

9 UN Doc. A/CN.4/L.602/REV.1, 26 July 2001 and UN Doc. A/51/10, 23 April-1 June and 2 July-10 August 2001, pp. 29-365. See for an account of the main issues addressed during the second reading process: James Crawford, Jacqueline Peel and Simon Olleson, 'The ILC's Articles on Responsibility of States for Internationally Wrongful Acts: Completion of the Second Reading', in: *European Journal of International Law*, http://www.ejil.org/journal/new/new0109.html#fn4 (accessed on 14 September 2001).

3.1 Attribution of Conduct to the State

The provisions that deal with the question of what can be considered to be an act of State for which international responsibility can arise, were completed by the ILC in 1998, earlier on in the second reading. The special rapporteur, Professor James Crawford, dealt with the issue of attribution in his first report, which was discussed at the 50th session of the ILC in 1998.[10] This report reviewed chapters I (General Principles) and II (The "Act of the State" under International Law) of Part One of the Draft Articles.

State responsibility most clearly arises where organs of the State act in a way that violates international law.[11] According to the Draft Articles, for an entity to be considered an organ of the State, it is irrelevant what position that organ holds within the organisation of the State.[12] It is clear that the military forces of a State are State organs and their conduct may lead to the responsibility of the State.[13] The basis for attributing acts of State organs and agents to the State is wide. The State is responsible for this conduct even when the persons employed by the State act beyond their powers.[14]

The relevant question within the framework of the present study is under which circumstances acts by non-State entities may be attributed to the State and consequently give rise to State responsibility. According to the rules on attribution, provided for in chapter II of the Draft Articles, the conduct of non-State entities can be considered to be an act of State in the following circumstances.

In the first place, where individuals or groups empowered by the law of the State exercise elements of governmental authority this may be considered to be an act of State. These entities are not part of the formal State machinery but due to 'the special nature' of their activities their conduct is attributed to the State and the State is internationally responsible for such conduct.[15] The activities of corporations can, in some circumstances, fall within this category. The ILC mentions the case of a bank of issue and a transport company entitled to exercise police powers as examples.[16]

---

10 UN Doc. A/CN.4/490/Add.5, 22 July 1998.

11 Article 4 *Draft Articles on the Responsibility of States for Internationally Wrongful Acts,* UN Doc. A/CN.4/L.602/REV.1, 26 July 2001. See, for more information on the issue of State responsibility for State organs: Brownlie, *supra* n. 4, pp. 446-455.

12 Article 4, para. 1, *Draft Articles on the Responsibility of States for Internationally Wrongful Acts,* UN Doc. A/CN.4/L.602/REV.1, 26 July 2001.

13 See the *Thomas H. Youmans (USA)* v. *United Mexican States* (1926) 4 UNRIAA 110 (*Youmans Case*), *estate of Jean-Baptiste Caire (France)* v. *United Mexican States* (1929) 5 UNRIAA 516, *(Caire Case)* and Brownlie, *supra* n. 4, pp. 139-141.

14 Article 7, *Draft Articles on the Responsibility of States for Internationally Wrongful Acts*, UN Doc.A/CN.4/L.602/REV.1, 26 July 2001.

15 Article 5, *Draft Articles on the Responsibility of States for Internationally Wrongful Acts.* A/CN.4/ L.602/REV.1, 26 July 2001.

16 Commentary to Article 7, YBILC, Vol. II (part 1), 1974, p. 277, para.2 and p.282, para.18.

In the second place, State responsibility can arise for the conduct of organs placed at the disposal of a State by another State.[17] Such a situation might occur where a State 'lends' its armed forces to another State. The conduct of these armed forces can give rise to the international responsibility of the receiving State.

In the third place, State responsibility can arise in the case where private conduct is in fact directed or controlled by the State. In certain cases States may supplement their own action by authorising operations by private persons. These persons are not State organs but act on behalf of the State conferring authority. The conduct does not have to involve 'governmental authority'. This situation is reflected in Draft Article 8.[18] According to the ILC:

> 'Where the government is known to encourage and even promote the organisation of private groups, to provide them with financial assistance, training and weapons, and to co-ordinate their activities with those of its own forces for the purpose of possible operations, the groups in question cease to be individuals from the standpoint of international law. They become formations in concert with, and at the instigation of, the State, and perform missions authorised by or even entrusted to them by that State. They then fall into the category of persons or groups which are linked, in fact if not formally, with the State machinery and are frequently called 'de facto organs.'[19]

Security arrangements of oil companies illustrate this category of acts that can be attributed to the State. Oil companies frequently employ security forces to protect their installations against sabotage, hostage-taking and intimidation. The close collaboration between the host States and the oil companies as well as the secrecy surrounding the issue of security, however, can make it difficult to establish whether these security forces are of a private or public nature. An example of this situation is the security arrangement made by oil companies in Nigeria. All the oil companies in Nigeria hire special security forces, so-called supernumerary police, to protect their installations.[20]

17 Article 6 reads: 'The conduct of an organ placed at the disposal of a State by another State shall be considered an act of the former State under international law if the organ is acting in the exercise of elements of the governmental authority of the State at whose disposal it is placed'. *Draft Articles on the Responsibility of States for Internationally Wrongful Acts.* UN Doc.A/CN.4/L.602/REV.1, 26 July 2001.

18 Article 8 states: 'The conduct of a person or group of persons shall also be considered as an act of a State under international law if the person or group of persons was in fact acting on the instructions of, or under the direct control of, that State in carrying out the conduct'. *Draft Articles on the Responsibility of States for Internationally Wrongful Acts.* UN Doc.A/CN.4/L.602/REV.1, 26 July 2001.

19 'Commentary to article 11, Draft Articles on State responsibility after the first reading', *YBILC*, Vol. II, 1975, para. 32.

20 The Nigerian government has formed several special task forces such as the notorious Rivers State Internal Security Task Force, Operation Flush, the Mobile Police -called 'Kill-and-Go' by the Niger Delta population, Operation Storm, Operation Salvage etc. Human Rights Watch, *The Price of Oil. Corporate Responsibility and Human Rights Violations in Nigeria's Oil Producing Communities*, New

The special task forces are known for being notoriously abusive and responsible for many human rights violations.[21] These forces are equipped and paid by the oil companies. However, these forces are recruited and trained by the Nigerian police and remain accountable to Nigerian police command structures. The violations committed by these security units are to be considered acts of State for which State responsibility at the international level may arise. Article 8 of the Draft Articles, according to which acts of private entities are considered acts of State due to the fact that they are in fact directed or controlled by the State, refers primarily to acts of a military nature. It is conceivable, however, that corporate acts fall into this category. For example, the question can be asked whether acts of public enterprises, corporations owned or controlled by the State, fall within this category. As pointed out by Special Rapporteur Crawford, the acts of public enterprises are only attributable to the State when they exercise aspects of governmental authority or where the State is specifically using its ownership interest in or control over a corporation in order to achieve a particular result.[22] In practice it may prove difficult to determine whether the acts of such an enterprise can indeed be considered acts of State. For example, the case-law of the (former) European Commission on Human rights was still rather casuistic on this point.[23]

In the fourth place, according to Draft Article 9, private conduct can be attributable to the State if, in the absence or fault of official authorities, circumstances call for the private entity to exercise governmental authority.[24] One might think of a situation of war or after a natural disaster where private entities take over the functions of the State. This situation might also occur in so-called failed States. In such States there is a complete non-regulation of corporate activity. When a State has contributed to its ineffectiveness, the obligations of the State remain valid and State responsibility can occur for a breach of these obligations.

York, 1999, pp. 115-122. Available at: http://www.hrw.org/hrw/reports/1999/nigeria/index.htm (accessed on 17 January 2002).

21 A very serious case involving security forces was the incident at Umeuchem in 1990, where *Shell* asked for the assistance of MOPOL leading to the killing of eighty unarmed civilians and the destruction of hundreds of homes, Human Rights Watch, *supra* n. 20, p. 178.

22 UN Doc. A/CN.4/490/Add.5, 22 July 1998, paras. 213 and 214.

23 P. van Dijk and G.J.H. van Hoof, *Theory and Practice of the European Convention on Human Rights*, 3rd ed., Kluwer Law International, The Hague, 1998, p.122.

24 Article 9 reads: 'The conduct of a person or group of persons shall be considered an act of a State under international law if the person or group of persons is in fact exercising elements of the governmental authority in the absence or default of the official authorities and in circumstances such as to call for the exercise of those elements of authority.' *Draft Articles on the Responsibility of States for Internationally Wrongful Acts*. UN Doc.A/CN.4/L.602/REV.1, 26 July 2001.

In the fifth place, the conduct of an insurrectional movement is considered an act of State for which international responsibility can arise, provided that the movement becomes the new government or establishes a new State.[25]

Finally, the express approval by the State of the acts of individuals is a source for State responsibility. In the *Iranian Hostage case* the International Court of Justice held Iran responsible for the acts of the militants who seized the US embassy. Although the acts were not directly imputable to the Iranian State, the approval of the militants' actions by the Iranian government made them so.[26] This is reflected in Draft Article 11 which reads:

> 'Conduct which is not attributable to a State under the preceding articles shall nevertheless be considered an act of that State under international law if and to the extent that the State acknowledges and adopts the conduct in question as its own.'[27]

3.2 State Responsibility for Private Acts

The question arises whether private conduct in circumstances other than the ones enumerated above, can give rise to State responsibility. After the first reading by the Commission in 1996 the ILC Draft Articles contained a provision – article 11 – that explicitly dealt with this question. Article 11 read:

> *Conduct of persons not acting on behalf of the State*
>
> 1. The conduct of a person or a group of persons not acting on behalf of the State shall not be considered as an act of the State under international law.
>
> 2. Paragraph 1 is without prejudice to the attribution to the State of any other conduct which is related to that of the persons or groups of persons referred to in that paragraph and which is to be considered as an act of the State by virtue of articles 5 to 10.

Paragraph 2 referred to the circumstances described above where private conduct can be attributed to the State. Paragraph 1 is clear: In all other circumstances acts of private persons are not considered acts of State and cannot as such involve the responsibility of the State.

---

25 Article 10, *Draft Articles on the Responsibility of States for Internationally Wrongful Acts*. UN Doc. A/CN.4/L.602/REV.1, 26 July 2001. For a thorough study of State responsibility for the acts of insurrectional movements see, Liesbeth Zegveld, *Armed Opposition Groups in International Law: The Quest for Accountability*, Cambridge University Press, *forthcoming*, dissertation-copy, 2000, pp. 47-96.

26 *United Nations Diplomatic and Consular Staff in Teheran (U.S.* v. *Iran)*, Judgement of 24 May, 1980. I.C.J. Rep. (1980) 3.

27 *Draft Articles on the Responsibility of States for Internationally Wrongful Acts.* UN Doc. A/CN.4/L.602/REV.1, 26 July 2001.

During the 50th session of the Drafting Committee in 1998 it was decided to delete article 11. It was deemed unnecessary and even misleading to retain 'negative attribution' articles, *i.e.* stating the circumstances in which conduct is *not* attributable. Article 11, as it was formulated, said nothing more than that private conduct is not attributable to the State unless the conduct is attributable under other provisions. The content of article 11 is now included in the other articles or the commentaries as appropriate.[28]

Consequently, the latest version of the Draft Articles does not contain a provision explicitly stating that private acts cannot involve State responsibility. For an insight into the position taken by the ILC on the issue of State responsibility for private acts, the commentary of – the now deleted – article 11 is illuminating.

In the commentary the ILC distinguishes three schools of thought among writers on the subject of attribution of private acts to the State.[29] According to the first school of thought acts by individuals are attributable to the State regardless of the attitude of State organs. In the commentary the ILC points out that this idea – that the State should assume responsibility for all private acts – has not received wide support.[30] The second school of thought, to which many 19th century scholars belonged, proclaims the so-called 'theory of complicity'. According to the advocates of this school of thought an act committed by a private person is attributable to the State as a source of international responsibility on condition that other factors were involved in its commission, particularly a failure to prevent the act or to react *a posteriori*, and provided that such omissions were omissions of the State directly, *i.e.* of its organs. The common feature of the writers supporting this theory is that they 'place less emphasis on, or indeed abolish the distinction between acts of private persons and acts of State organs for the purpose of establishing individual conduct as an act of State'.[31] This distinguishes them from the adherents to the third school of thought. This school of thought, which was reflected in – the now deleted – article 11 of the Draft Articles, maintains that acts and omissions by private persons are not attributable to the State. They do not become acts of State. The acts of private persons, such as private companies, which result in damage to foreign States, their representatives and/or their subjects often amount to an internationally wrongful act by the State, but this wrongful act results from the conduct of State organs. The State is responsible for having breached, not the international obligation with which the individual's act might be in conflict, but the general or

28 See: *The Second Reading of the Draft Articles on State Responsibility: A Progress Report*, by James Crawford and Pierre Bodeau. This document can be found at www.law.cam.ac.uk/rcil/ILCSR/Forum2.doc (accessed on 4 January 2001).

29 UN Doc. A/CN.4/Ser.A/1975, Add. 1, 'Commentary to article 11, Draft Articles on State responsibility after the first reading', *YBILC,* Vol. II, 1975, pp. 70-83, at p. 80-82.

30 UN Doc. A/CN.4/Ser.A/1975, Add. 1, 'Commentary to article 11, Draft Articles on State responsibility after the first reading', *YBILC,* Vol. II, 1975, p. 80.

31 UN Doc. A/CN.4/Ser.A/1975, Add. 1, 'Commentary to article 11, Draft Articles on State responsibility after the first reading', *YBILC,* Vol. II, 1975, p. 81.

special obligation which imposes on its organs a duty to provide protection. The conduct of a private person *as such* cannot be the source of State responsibility. The wrongful conduct must be accompanied by wrongful conduct on the part of the State. The State is not responsible for the acts of the private entity but for the failure to prevent the act. The acts of private persons then constitute an external event, which serves as a catalyst for the wrongfulness of the State's conduct. This also becomes clear from the deliberations of the ILC on the issue of reparation. For the purposes of determining the damages that should be paid, it is the violation by the State that should be taken into account not the violation by the individual.[32] As was emphasised in the *Janes Claim*: the two delinquencies are different 'in their origin, character and effect'.[33]

Summarising, private acts constituting a violation of international law can involve State responsibility in two ways. Firstly, the conduct of non-State entities can be attributed to the State under certain circumstances: where non-State entities are empowered by law to exercise governmental authority; where a State has organs of another State placed at its disposal; where private conduct is directed or controlled by the State; where private conduct is correctly exercised in the absence of official authority; where an insurrectional movement becomes the new government; and where a State endorses private acts as its own. In these cases the private act is considered an act of State for which State responsibility may arise. The examples, mentioned above, demonstrate that under these rules of attribution, corporate activities can, on occasion, involve State responsibility.

Secondly, State responsibility arises where a State itself fails in its general obligation to protect from or respond to private acts that violate international law. In this case, the – what can be called – primary rule of attribution[34] comes into play: this failure is an act of the State for which responsibility will arise.

The ILC Draft Articles demonstrate that under general international law private acts may involve State responsibility through a variety of possibilities.

4 State Responsibility Under International Human Rights Law

In this section I will examine the practice of the human rights supervisory bodies with a view to analysing how they have dealt with the issue of State responsibility for human rights violations by private entities. But first an answer has to be provided to the question whether the rules that have been developed by the ILC equally apply to international human rights law. According to article 55, the Draft Articles do not apply where special rules of international law are applicable. Should international human

32 UN Doc. A/CN.4/Ser.A/1975, Add. 1, 'Commentary to article 11, Draft Articles onState responsibility after the first reading', *YBILC*, Vol. II, 1975, p. 81 see also: *Spain* v.*the United Kingdom (British Property in Spanish Marocco* case) 1925, 2, UNRIAA, p. 636.

33 *US* v. *Mexico*, 4 UNRIAA 82 (1926).

34 UN Doc. A/CN.4/490/Add.4, 22 July 1998, para.160.

rights law be considered *lex specialis,* allowing for a departure from the general principles? Clapham has argued that the international law on State responsibility is not appropriate in the context of human rights law. Referring to the ECHR he observes:

> 'The public international law framework, on its own, is considered insufficient for the following reasons: the Convention does not primarily operate as an inter-State treaty as it grants remedies to individuals; *effective* protection demands that the Convention controls private actors; the Convention takes effect in the national order of the Contracting Parties and constitutes a kind of European *ordre public*; a public/private dichotomy is arbitrary, unreasonably discriminatory and perpetrates the exclusion of certain kinds of violations of rights which are then "forgotten" (domestic violence, child abuse, discrimination against women in employment).'[35]

Notwithstanding these arguments, practice has shown that the international human rights bodies do in fact apply the general principles of State responsibility.[36] Furthermore, several authors have expressed the view that the general rules on State responsibility are equally applicable within the framework of human rights.[37]

It has been demonstrated that, according to the law of State responsibility, a general obligation exists for States to protect and to respond to private acts that violate international law. This general obligation can also be found in international human rights law and it has appeared in the case-law of international human rights bodies. The term used is, rather confusingly, 'due diligence.' As mentioned above,[38] the standard of due diligence was originally developed with regard to the protection of aliens, but now it is also applied to State responsibility arising from private acts in the context of human rights.

---

35 Andrew Clapham, 'The "Drittwirkung" of the Convention', in: *The European System for the Protection of Human Rights*, Ronald St. J. Macdonald *et al.* [eds.], Nijhoff, Dordrecht etc., 1993, pp. 163-206, at p. 170, footnote 32 and Andrew Clapham, *Human Rights in the Private Sphere*, Clarendon, Oxford, 1993, p.188, footnote 29.

36 See for a survey of the case-law of the ECHR: Rick Lawson, 'Out of Control. State Responsibility and Human Rights: Will the ILC's Definition of the "Act of State" Meet the Challenges of the 21st Century?', in: *The Role of the Nation-State in the 21st Century: human rights, international organisations and foreign policy: essays in honour of Peter Baehr*, Monique Castermans, Fried van Hoof and Jacqueline Smith [eds.], Kluwer Law International, The Hague, 1998, pp. 91-116. He concludes: 'the European Court of Human Rights has consistently applied the principles articulated in the ILC Draft Articles on State Responsibility, without, however, referring expressly to the Draft Articles', p. 115.

37 See Lawson, *supra* n. 36, p. 100, citing C. Warbrick, 'The European Convention on Human Rights and the Prevention on terrorism', *International and Comparative Law Quarterly*, Vol. 32, 1983, p. 4. Likewise, authors have come to the conclusion that the general rules of State Responsibility are applicable to individual complaints procedures under human rights treaties. See, *inter alia*, Preadviezen van Dr. M.T. Kamminga, Mr. L.A.D. Keus, *Staatsaansprakelijkheid jegens individuen: beginselen en procedures (State responsibility towards individuals: principles and procedures)* Nederlandse Vereniging voor Internationaal Recht (Netherlands International Law Association), 1997.

38 See p. 138.

The due diligence test in terms of the international law of human rights was first formulated within the framework of the American Convention of Human Rights (ACHR), *i.e.* in the *Velásquez Rodríguez* and *Godinez* cases. The *Velásquez Rodríguez* case concerned an individual who disappeared in 1981 and who was probably killed by the Honduran army or unknown attackers. The Inter-American Court decided that the State was responsible, even if the alleged human rights violations had not been carried out by agents acting under the cover of public authority. This was because the State apparatus failed to act to prevent these violations or to punish those responsible.[39] The Inter-American Court distinguished three kinds of obligations for State Parties to the ACHR. In the first place, States have the obligation to abstain from violating guaranteed human rights. In the second place, there exists the obligation to prevent violations by State and non-State actors. According to the Court:

> 'a State violates human rights when the State allows private persons or groups to act freely and with impunity to the detriment of the rights recognised by the Convention.'[40]

> 'An illegal act which violates human rights and which is initially not directly imputable to a State (for example, because it is an act of a private person or because the person responsible has not been identified) can lead to international responsibility of the State, not because of the act itself, but because of the lack of due diligence to prevent the violation or to respond to it as required by the Convention.'[41]

> 'The State has a legal duty to take reasonable steps to prevent human rights violations and to use the means at its disposal to carry out a serious investigation of violations committed within its jurisdiction, to identify those responsible, to impose the appropriate punishment and to ensure the victim adequate compensation. This obligation implies the duty of State Parties to organise the governmental apparatus and, in general, all the structures through which public power is exercised so that they are capable of juridically ensuring the free and full enjoyment of human rights.'[42]

The Court based its reasoning on Article 1 of the ACHR which reads: 'The State Parties to this Convention undertake to respect the rights and freedoms recognised herein and to ensure to all persons subject to their jurisdiction the free and full exercise

39 *Velásquez Rodríguez* case, Annual Report of the Inter-American Court of Human Rights, OAS/Ser.L/V/III.19, doc 13 (1988); *Godinez Cruz*, Inter-American Court of Human Rights, Decisions and Judgments (ser. C) No.5 (1989) These cases from 1988-1989 concerned petitions filed by the families of persons who had disappeared against the government of Honduras. In total, three cases were filed. In the third case *(Fairen Garbi and Solis Corrales* case) the Court held that there was insufficient evidence to establish Honduras' responsibility for the disappearances.

40 *Velásquez Rodríguez* case, OAS/Ser.L/V/III.19, doc. 13 (1988), para. 166.

41 *Velásquez Rodríguez* case, OAS/Ser.L/V/III.19, doc. 13 (1988), para. 172.

42 *Velásquez Rodríguez* case, OAS/Ser.L/V/III.19, doc. 13 (1988), paras. 174 and 175.

of those rights and freedoms'.[43] This applies to 'everyone within their jurisdiction', not only to foreigners. There is no clear definition of this obligation to exercise due diligence. The implications of the standard of due diligence depend on the circumstances of the case: 'appropriate measures are those measures which the State can reasonably be required to take in view of its own capabilities and the situation'.[44]

The third obligation for State Parties, according to the inter-American Court, is to investigate and punish both State and private human rights infringements. In the words of the Court: 'Where acts of private parties that violate the Convention are not seriously investigated, those parties are aided in a sense by the government, thereby making the State responsible on the international plane'.[45]

This decision of the Inter-American Court is of general importance for the protection of human rights. Many human rights instruments contain provisions similar to Article 1 of the ACHR for example: Article 2 [1] of the ICCPR,[46] Article 2 [1] of the ICESCR,[47] Article 2 (d) of the CERD,[48] Article 2 [1] of the CAT,[49] and Article 1 of the ECHR.[50]

Since the decision of the Inter-American Court in the *Velásquez Rodríguez* case, the due diligence test has been referred to in other human rights standards and by monitoring bodies. Especially in the field of women's rights there is increasing attention to the obligation of the State to protect women against domestic violence. According to article 4 (c) of the UN Declaration on the Elimination of Violence against Women (CEDAW) States 'must exercise due diligence to prevent, investigate and, in

43 American Convention on Human Rights, November 22, 1969.

44 *Velásquez Rodríguez* case, OAS/Ser.L/V/III.19, doc. 13 (1988), paras. 174-175.

45 *Velásquez Rodríguez* case, OAS/Ser.L/V/III.19, doc. 13 (1988), para. 177

46 Article 2 [1] ICCPR states: 'Each State Party to the present Covenant undertakes to respect and to ensure to all individuals within its territory and subject to its jurisdiction the rights recognised in the present Covenant (...)'. Specifically the Covenant requires each State Party to take the necessary steps to adopt such legislative or other measures required to give effect to the rights recognised in the Covenant, to ensure an effective remedy to any person whose rights or freedoms are violated, whether or not by persons acting in an official capacity, and to ensure that the competent authorities enforce the remedies granted. See M. Nowak, *U.N. Covenant on Civil and Political Rights: CCPR Commentary*, Engel, Kehl am Rhein, 1993, pp. 36-38.

47 Article 2 [1] ICESCR states: 'Each State Party to the present Covenant undertakes to take steps (...) with a view to achieving progressively the full realisation of the rights recognised in the present Covenant (...)'.

48 Article 2 (d) ICERD States: 'Each State Party shall prohibit and bring to an end, by all appropriate means, including legislation as required by circumstances, racial discrimination by any persons, group or organisation'. Article 6 states: 'The States Parties shall assure to everyone within their jurisdiction effective protection and remedies (...) as well as the right to seek (...) just and adequate reparation or satisfaction for any damage suffered as a result of such discrimination'.

49 Article 2 [1] CAT states: 'Each State Party shall take effective legislative, administrative, judicial or other measures to prevent acts of torture in any territory under its jurisdiction'. See also Article 16.

50 Article 1 ECHR states: 'The High Contracting Parties shall ensure to everyone within their jurisdiction the rights and freedoms defined in Section I of this Convention'.

accordance with national legislation, punish acts of violence against women, *whether those acts are perpetrated by the State or by private persons*' [emphasis added].[51] The due diligence obligation has also been acknowledged by the monitoring body of CEDAW, the UN Committee on the Elimination of Discrimination against Women, in its General Recommendation 19:

> 'Under general international law and specific human rights covenants, States may also be responsible for private acts if they fail to act with due diligence to prevent violations of rights or to investigate and punish acts of violence, and for providing compensation.'[52]

The obligation to exercise due diligence to prevent human rights violations comes under the category of the obligation to protect that has been identified in the tripartite typology, discussed earlier.[53] In the tripartite typology of obligations, States are under an obligation to respect human rights, *e.g.* not to violate human rights. Moreover, States must fulfil human rights which means that the State should take positive measures to ensure the enjoyment of human rights. Finally, States have the obligation to protect human rights which implies a duty to regulate the activities of private entities so as to avoid violations of human rights. As set forth in paragraph 18 of the *Maastricht Guidelines on Violations of Economic, Social and Cultural Rights*:

> 'The obligation to protect includes the State's responsibility to ensure that private entities or individuals, including transnational corporations over which they exercise jurisdiction, do not deprive individuals of their economic, social and cultural rights. States are responsible for violations of economic, social and cultural rights that result from their failure to exercise due diligence in controlling the behaviour of such non-state actors.'[54]

The discussion of the (indirect) horizontal effect of human rights in chapter II demonstrates that under international human rights law the distinction between public and private actors is being eroded. Obviously, a State cannot be held responsible for every private act that constitutes a violation of human rights, but States can and are being held responsible for not regulating private conduct.

---

51 Declaration on the Elimination of Violence against Women UN Doc.G.A. res. 48/104, 48 U.N. GAOR Supp. (No. 49) at 217, U.N. Doc. A/48/49, 1993. This has been reaffirmed in the Beijing Declaration & Platform for Action, see paras. 113 and 124 (b).

52 UN Doc. A/47/38, 30 January 1992, para.9.

53 See p. 82.

54 *Maastricht Guidelines on Violations of Economic, Social and Cultural Rights*, Maastricht, 22-26 January 1997, para.18.

5 Case-law of the Supervisory Bodies

After having demonstrated that (indirect) State responsibility may arise from private human rights violations, I will now turn to the issue of corporate human rights violations. In this section the case-law of various human rights bodies that has specifically dealt with corporate activity will be discussed. The aim is to determine how these organs have addressed the issue of State responsibility in cases where corporate activities amount to a human rights violation. As the following sections will show, in most cases State responsibility for corporate activities has arisen when there has been a failure to exercise due diligence in the State's obligation to prevent and repress human rights violations perpetrated by corporations. The case-law of the regional human rights bodies, the European Court of Human Rights, the Inter-American Commission and Court of Human Rights and the African Commission will be examined. Moreover, the case-law of the treaty bodies, the Human Rights Committee and the Committee on Economic, Social and Cultural Rights, will also be discussed.[55] Finally, attention will be paid to the case-law of the ILO. This case-law merits consideration given the vital role of the ILO in regulating the activities of corporations.

5.1 European Court of Human Rights

Under the ECHR States,[56] individuals, non-governmental organisations and groups[57] can bring a complaint concerning an alleged breach of the rights in the Convention before the Court.

The Court's case-law is in conformity with the relevant principles of international law governing State responsibility.[58] State responsibility may arise for the acts of the State's organs[59] as well as for those of private entities acting on behalf of the State (if exercising elements of governmental authority).[60] As is the case with the ACHR, the

55 See for a detailed survey of the case-law: Craig Scott, 'Multinational Enterprises and Emergent Jurisprudence on Violations of Economic, Social and Cultural Rights', in: *Economic, Social and Cultural Rights*, 2nd ed., Asbjørn Eide, Catarina Krause and Allan Rosas [eds.], Martinus Nijhoff, Dordrecht etc., 2001, pp. 563-595.

56 Art. 33 ECHR.

57 Art. 34 ECHR.

58 For example, in the *Loizidou* case the Court held that the responsibility of the State can arise when as a consequence of military action -whether lawful or unlawful- it exercises effective control over an area outside its national territory. Judgment of 23 March 1995, A.310, p. 24. See also, Appl. 852/60, *X* v. *Federal Republic of Germany*, Yearbook IV (1961), p. 346 (350-352). For more information on the issue of State responsibility under the ECHR see: Lawson, *supra* n. 36 , p. 115 and Van Dijk and Van Hoof, *supra* n. 23, pp. 120-122.

59 See, *inter alia*, *Ireland* v. *UK*, EcomHR, 25 January 1976, Appl. No. 5310/71, B.23-I. As referred to by Lawson, *supra* n. 36, p. 102

60 See, *inter alia*, *Van der Mussele* v. *Belgium*, 23 November 1983, A.70. As referred to by Lawson, *supra* n. 36, p. 103.

ECHR requires the State to 'secure' or 'to ensure' the rights recognised in the treaties. Acts by private entities may give rise to State responsibility if the State fails to 'secure' the rights in the Convention in its domestic legislation or if it fails to take 'reasonable' and 'appropriate' measures of protection.[61]

In the case of *Young, James and Webster* v. *The UK*,[62] three employees of British Rail were dismissed after they refused to join a trade union. As a result of a closed-shop agreement between British Rail and several trade unions all British Rail employees were required to join one of the unions. The Court decided that the responsibility of the UK had been brought about by the non-observance of article 1 ECHR according to which each contracting State shall secure within its jurisdiction the rights and freedoms defined in the Convention.

Another well-known case is *X and Y* v. *The Netherlands.* At issue in this case was the sexual abuse of a 16-year-old mentally handicapped girl in a private nursing home. Due to a shortcoming in the Dutch legal system it was not possible to prosecute the suspect. The Court held that the Netherlands had violated the right to privacy due to its failure to legislate.[63]

In three cases the Court has explicitly dealt with State responsibility that can arise in connection with the activities of corporations. All these cases concerned a violation of Article 8 ECHR, which protects privacy and family life.

In the case of *López Ostra* v. *Spain*[64] the European Court held that Spain was responsible for allowing a corporation to engage in acts contrary to human rights. The case concerned the contaminating activities of a company's plant for the treatment of liquid and solid waste. The plant had been built with a State subsidy. The Court held as follows:

> 'The Spanish authorities (...) were theoretically not directly responsible for the emissions in question. However (...) the town allowed the plant to be built on its land and the State subsidised the plant's construction.'[65]

According to the Court it was irrelevant whether the municipality in question was in fact fulfilling its legal duties under domestic law. The Court only needed to 'establish whether the national authorities took the measures necessary for protecting the appli-

---

61 For an analysis of the relevant case-law, see: Lawson, *supra* n. 36, pp. 91-116. See also: Clapham, *supra* n. 35. In his book Clapham analyses the European Convention on an article by article basis and concludes that the Convention covers not only violations by States but also the actions of private bodies and individuals. He argues that States are obliged to take preventive and punitive measures to protect people against any private abuse of their rights guaranteed under the Convention.

62 13 August 1981, *Young, James and Webster* v. *The UK,* A.44.

63 26 March 1985, *X and Y* v. *The Netherlands*, A. 91, para. 23. This line of reasoning has been confirmed by the Court on several other occasions, see, *inter alia Costello-Roberts* v. *The UK*, A.247-C.

64 9 December 1994, *López Ostra* v. *Spain*, A.303-C.

65 9 December 1994, *López Ostra* v. *Spain*, A.303-C, para. 52.

cant's right to respect for her home and for her private and family life under Article 8'.[66] It was concluded that the State failed in 'striking a fair balance between the interests of the town's well-being (...) and the applicant's effective enjoyment of her right to respect for her home and her private and family life.'[67]

In this case the Court did not specify whether the State was responsible because the conduct was considered to be a direct interference by a public organ or whether the conduct amounted to a failure to protect individuals against the harmful practices of third parties.

Later, in *Guerra* v. *Italy*,[68] which was a similar case, the Court explicitly based its decision on the failure of the State to fulfil its duty to protect the rights of private and family life. This case concerned a fertiliser plant that during the course of production released large quantities of inflammable gas and other toxic substances, a process which could lead to explosive chemical reactions. In fact, an accident had already occurred resulting in over 150 people having to be admitted to hospital with acute arsenic poisoning. Workers at the plant and families living in its vicinity were exposed to the pollution which had been caused by it. The government had taken some steps but overall the government's response had been such that the plant continued to operate for a considerable period of time before being shut down. The Court considered that:

> '(...) Italy cannot be said to have "interfered" with the applicants' private or family life; they complained not of an act by the State but of its failure to act. However, although the object of Article 8 is essentially that of protecting the individual against arbitrary interference by the public authorities, it does not merely compel the State to abstain from such interference: in addition to this primarily negative undertaking, there may be positive obligations inherent in effective respect for private or family life.'[69]

Referring to the case of *López Ostra* the Court continued:

> 'In the present case it need only be ascertained whether the national authorities took the necessary steps to ensure *effective* protection of the applicants' right to respect for their private and family life as guaranteed by Article 8. (...)The Court reiterates that severe environmental pollution may affect individuals' well-being and prevent them from enjoying their homes in such a way as to affect their private and family life adversely (...). In the instant case the applicants waited, right up until the production of fertilisers ceased in 1994, for essential information that would have enabled them to assess the

66 9 December 1994, *López Ostra* v. *Spain*, A.303-C, para. 54.

67 9 December 1994, *López Ostra* v. *Spain*, A.303-C, para. 58.

68 19 February 1998, *Guerra and Others* v. *Italy*, European Court of Human Rights, Reports of Judgments and Decisions 1998-I, No. 64.

69 19 February 1998, *Guerra and Others* v. *Italy*, European Court of Human Rights, Reports of Judgments and Decisions 1998-I, No. 64, para. 58.

> risks they and their families might run if they continued to live at Manfredonia, a town particularly exposed to danger in the event of an accident at the factory.'[70] [Emphasis added]

The Court reinforced the language used in *López Ostra* by adding the word 'effective'. A State should ensure 'effective protection' against the harmful activities of third parties.

In assessing whether a State has violated the right to privacy and family life the European Court must take into account the fair balance that the State must strike between the competing interests of the individual and the community as a whole.[71] In striking this balance States are accorded a margin of appreciation. In its judgment in the case of *López Ostra*, the Court ruled that Spain had failed in striking a fair balance. In the case of *Hatton and others* v. *The United Kingdom*[72] the Court addressed the issue of striking a fair balance in more detail. In this case the applicants complained of a violation of article 8 ECHR by virtue of an increase in the level of noise in their homes by aircrafts using Heathrow Airport at night. The Court, referring to *López Ostra,* held that in striking a balance 'in the particularly sensitive field of environmental protection, mere reference to the economic well-being of the country is not sufficient to outweigh the rights of others'.[73] This position taken by the Court is important for the content of the State's duty to protect individuals against harmful corporate activities. The activities of corporations are frequently detrimental to the environment. States are required to protect individuals against environmental pollution that is considered to be a violation of privacy and family life. The mere argument of economic interest will, according to the Court, not be sufficient to justify an interference with this right. The Court stated that

> 'States are required to minimise, as far as possible, the interference with these rights, by trying to find solutions and by generally seeking to achieve their aims in the least onerous way as regards human rights. In order to do that, a proper and complete investi-

70 19 February 1998, *Guerra and Others* v. *Italy*, European Court of Human Rights, Reports of Judgments and Decisions 1998-I, No. 64, paras. 58 and 60.

71 Article 8 [2] ECHR.

72 2 October 2001, *Hatton and others* v. *The United Kingdom*, European Court of Human Rights, Application no. 36022/97, not yet published, available at: www.coe.fr , (accessed on 5 October 2001). For earlier cases concerning complaints about noise at Heathrow Airport, see, *Arondelle* v. *the United Kingdom*, application no. 7889/77, DR 19 (1980), decision of 13 May 1982, DR 26 (1982); *Rayner* v. *the United Kingdom*, application no. 9310/81, decision of 17 July 1986, DR 47, p. 5. The case of *Hatton* differs from the previous cases as the applicant complained of noise at night.

73 2 October 2001, *Hatton and others* v. *The United Kingdom*, European Court of Human Rights, Application no. 36022/97, not yet published, available at: www.coe.fr , (accessed on 5 October 2001), para. 97.

gation and study with the aim of finding the best possible solution which will, in reality, strike the right balance should precede the relevant project.'[74]

With the case of *Hatton* the Court has solidified the obligation of States to protect individuals against harmful activities that infringe upon their right to privacy and family life. Moreover, in this case the Court has gone into considerable detail regarding the manner in which a State should fulfil this obligation.[75]

In sum, the European Court has firmly established that State responsibility can arise for a failure to protect individuals against harmful corporate activities. So far the cases have concerned article 8 ECHR, the right to privacy and family life. It should be noted that the extensive interpretation of article 8 ECHR to include environmental rights has encountered some criticism. In a dissenting opinion in the case of *Hatton*, Judge Greve opines that the environmental problems are of a different nature than the core right protected under article 8 ECHR. According to Judge Greve, the essence of article 8 ECHR is to 'secure the inviolability of one's home' and 'environmental rights are of a different character from the core right not to have one's home raided without a warrant'. In his opinion State responsibility for environmental problems may arise at most 'as a consequence of the impact of planning decisions, and potentially also when a State refrains from adequately addressing serious environmental problems'.[76]

At first sight it might indeed seem rather artificial to stretch article 8 ECHR to the extent to which the Court has done in these cases. On the other hand one has to take the evolving content of the concept of privacy into account. Given the origin of the Council of Europe as an organisation primarily designed to protect democracy and the rule of law in the context of the Cold War, the emphasis on protection against unwarranted interference by authorities, is understandable. However, the ECHR is a 'living instrument which (…) must be interpreted in the light of present day conditions'.[77] In the present circumstances the concept of privacy has changed. Nowadays environmental problems are also perceived as an intrusion of privacy. Besides privacy and family life, other rights might also be affected by the harmful activities of corporations. For instance, it is conceivable that severe environmental pollution might involve article 2 ECHR, which protects the right to life. It may be concluded that under the ECHR

---

74 2 October 2001, *Hatton and others* v. *The United Kingdom*, European Court of Human Rights, Application no. 36022/97, para. 97, not yet published, available at: www.coe.fr, (accessed on 5 October 2001).

75 In his dissenting opinion, Judge Kerr has criticised this rule. According to Kerr, the test formulated in *Hatton* 'denies to States any discretion as to how they wish to address socio-economic issues and instead requires that all policy decisions be dictated by a strict "minimum interference with fundamental rights" rule'.

76 *Partly dissenting opinion of Judge Greve*, 2 October 2001, *Hatton and others* v. *The United Kingdom*, European Court of Human Rights, Application no. 36022/97, not yet published, available at: www.coe.fr (accessed on 5 October 2001).

77 *Tyrer* v. *the United Kingdom*, Judgement of 25 April 1978, Series A, Vol. 26, p. 15.

States are, in principle, under an obligation to protect individuals against the harmful activities of corporations.

5.2 Inter-American Commission and Court

As pointed out above,[78] the State's obligation to protect individuals against human rights violations by third parties, the due diligence rule, was first explicitly formulated by the Inter-American Court in the *Velásquez* case. This case did not involve any corporate activities. Under the Inter-American system several cases have been heard that have dealt with the State's failure to regulate corporate conduct.

As far back as 1981 the Inter-American Commission had declared that Guatemala was responsible for human rights violations that involved a corporation. The communication to the Commission concerned the *Coca-Cola* bottling plant. In the communication it was alleged that the plant had a history of anti-union violence and that union leaders were murdered. It was alleged that the violence was a co-ordinated effort by the plant management and its US owner to destroy the union organisation. As the Guatemalan government did not reply to the Commission's requests for information, the Commission presumed the facts to be true[79] and declared that the State had violated the right to life, human treatment, personal liberty, fair trial, assembly and judicial protection.[80]

Most of the cases that have involved corporate activity have been brought before the Inter-American Commission and Court by, or on behalf of, indigenous peoples. The discovery of gold and oil has attracted corporations and led to corporate activities on indigenous lands. In the cases brought before the Inter-American Commission and Court it is claimed that the corporate activities pose a threat to the traditional way of life of many of the indigenous peoples.

In 1985 in the case of *Yanomami* v. *Brazil*,[81] the Inter-American Commission first formulated the basic obligation of States to protect individuals from harm caused by economic activity on the part of non-State entities in general. At issue in this case was the resource development in the Yanomami Indian territories in Brazil. The invasion by private oil workers and colonists of indigenous lands caused Indian inhabitants to leave their villages and resulted in a considerable number of deaths caused by epidemics and violence. The Commission held that the Brazilian government was responsible

---

78 See p. 147.

79 Article 39 IACHR.

80 Res. 38/81, Case 4425, 25 June 1981, para.1 IACH, *Annual Report 1980-1981*. Cited by Clapham, *supra* n. 35, p. 119-120. On 20 July 2001, the *Coca Cola Company* was sued in the US District Court for the Southern District of California, for working with death squads as part of a programme to intimidate trade union leaders. For more on the issue of enforcement at the national level, see chapter VII.

81 *Yanomami* v. *Brazil*, Case 7615, 5 March 1985, Res. No. 12/85, IACH, *Annual report*, 1985.

for having failed to take timely and effective measures to protect the human rights of the Yanomamis.[82]

In 1994 a petition was filed with the Inter-American Commission concerning the activities of multinational oil corporations in the Ecuadorian Amazon (the Oriente). In the process of extracting oil from this region toxic wastes and oil were directly released into the environment causing widespread damage to the environment and the health of the communities living there.[83] Indigenous groups claimed that the Ecuadorian government had failed in its obligation to protect the indigenous peoples. Instead of reaching a quasi-judicial decision, the Inter-American Commission decided to conduct an on-site visit in order to produce a country report.[84] As pointed out by one author, this allowed the Inter-American Commission to produce a very detailed analysis of the legal problems surrounding Ecuador's regulation of the oil companies. This might not have been possible if the Commission had continued to deal with the issue as a petition.[85]

Finally, in the *Awas Tingni Mayagna (Sumo) Indigenous Community* v. *The Republic of Nicaragua* case,[86] the Awas Tingni community in Nicaragua asserted that the government of Nicaragua had breached its obligation to guarantee the community's use and enjoyment of its ancestral lands by awarding a thirty-year concession for road construction and timber exploitation on those lands to a Korean corporation, *Sol del Caribe, S.A. (SOLCARSA).* The Awas Tingni community presented a petition to the Inter-American Commission in October 1995. The petition was declared admissible and, in 1997, the Inter-American Commission called for the suspension of the *SOLCARSA* concession to avoid irreparable harm to the lands. Subsequently, the case was presented to the Inter-American Court, which, in 2001, ruled that the State of Nicaragua had violated the rights of the Awas Tingni community to

> 'to the use and enjoyment of their property, and that it has granted concessions to third parties to utilize the property and resources located in an area which could correspond, fully or in part, to the lands which must be delimited, demarcated, and titled'.[87]

---

82 *Yanomami* v. *Brazil*, Case 7615, 5 March 1985, Res. No. 12/85, IACH, *Annual report*, 1985, paras. 10 and 11.

83 For a detailed report see, *Rights Violations in the Ecuadorian Amazon. The Human Consequences of Oil Development,* The Center For Economic and Social Rights, March 1994. http:www/cescr.org (accessed on 16 August 2001).

84 Inter-American Commission on Human Rights, *Report of the Situation of Human Rights in Equador*, OAS Doc. OEA/Ser.L/V/II.96 (1997).

85 Scott, *supra* n. 55, p. 578. Regarding the situation in The Oriente in Ecuador, several lawsuits have also been filled in the US. For a discussion of these cases see chapter VII, pp. 184-185.

86 Case No. 11.555. See also: Patrick Macklem and Ed Morgan, 'Indigenous Rights in the Inter-American System: the Amicus Brief of the Assembly of First Nations in Awas Tingni v. Republic of Nicaragua', in: *Human Rights Quarterly*, Vol. 22, 2000, pp. 569-602. pp. 569-602.

87 Inter-American Court on Human Rights, *The Mayagna (Sumo) Indigenous Community of Awas Tingni* v. *the Republic of Nicaragua*, decision of 31 August 2001, para. 153.

The Court continued,

> '(...) Together with the above, we must recall what has already been established by this court, based on article 1(1) of the American Convention, regarding the obligation of the State to respect the rights and freedoms recognized by the Convention and to organize public power so as to ensure the full enjoyment of human rights by the persons under its jurisdiction. According to the rules of law pertaining to the international responsibility of the State and applicable under International Human Rights Law, actions or omissions by any public authority, whatever its hierarchic position, are chargeable to the State which is responsible under the terms set forth in the American Convention.'[88]

The Court ordered Nicaragua to delimit, demark, and title the indigenous lands. Until this is done, Nicaragua must cease acts that could cause agents of the State, or third parties acting with its acquiescence or tolerance, to affect the existence, value, use or enjoyment of the indigenous property.

5.3 The African Commission

The African Commission, established under the African Charter on Human and People's Rights (ACHPR), has not yet produced a significant body of case-law. However, the issue of State responsibility has been addressed in a petition that has been filed with the African Commission by two NGOs, the Centre for Economic and Social Rights in the US together with the Social and Economic Rights Action Centre (SERAC). At issue is the responsibility of the Nigerian government for the adverse effects of oil exploitation on human rights in the Ogoni delta region. It is alleged that the activities of *Shell* and the *Nigerian National Petroleum Corporation* have had an adverse effect on, *inter alia*, the right to health and the right to food. According to the petitioners, the fact that a State corporation is involved implies that the State is directly responsible for the alleged violations. At the time of writing the petition was still under consideration.

5.4 The Human Rights Committee

In several General Comments the HRC has confirmed the obligations of the State to control private entities.[89] The issue has, however, only sporadically been addressed in the case-law of the HRC. As is the case under the Inter-American system, the issue of State obligations to protect individuals against harmful corporate activities has arisen

88 Inter-American Court on Human Rights, *The Mayagna (Sumo) Indigenous Community of Awas Tingni v. the Republic of Nicaragua*, decision of 31 August 2001, para. 153.
89 For a discussion of these General Comments, see chapter II.

mainly in the context of economic activity which poses a threat to indigenous populations. The *Länsman* cases concerned alleged violations by the Finnish government of article 27 ICCPR, the right of minorities to, *inter alia*, enjoy their own culture.[90] The *Länsman* cases were brought by reindeer breeders of Sami ethnic origin. They challenged the decision of the Central Forestry Board to award a four-year contract to a private company, *Arktinen Kivi Oy (Artic Stone Company),* which would allow the quarrying and transportation of stone. According to the authors of the claims these activities would disturb their reindeer herding, which, traditionally, is seen as an essential part of Sami culture.[91] Furthermore, the site of the quarry is a sacred place of the old Sami religion. In its views on this case, the HRC referred to General Comment No. 23 according to which article 27 ICCPR can require positive measures 'not only against the acts of the State Party itself (...) but also against the acts of other persons within the State party'.[92] Nevertheless, the HRC decided that Finland had not violated article 27 ICCPR noting that the amount of quarrying that had already taken place had not caused significant harm. Moreover, the HRC noted that the authors had been consulted during the proceedings leading to the issuing of a quarrying permit.[93]

Craig Scott has analysed the *Länsman* cases from the perspective of State obligations to protect human rights from corporate activity.[94] Scott observes that the HRC has approached the matter rather cautiously. Firstly, the *Länsman* cases show that the HRC 'requires a threshold of seriousness of harm before a state's duties to seek to prevent the harm are triggered'.[95] Secondly, in its finding that no violation had occurred, the HRC emphasised the importance of consultation. According to the HRC, if the effective participation of the affected groups is assured, the State meets its obligation. In the *Länsman* cases the HRC has clearly applied a due diligence approach to the issue of State responsibility for corporate activities. The State meets its obligation to protect against harmful corporate activity, where, in the context of the particular case, it exercises reasonable care. In his analysis Scott appears to find the reasoning of the HRC rather disappointing. He points out:

> 'the Committee has not yet interpreted the protection of human rights from corporate activity (at least where cultural rights are the issue) to create what would be called "obligations of result". That is to say, the State is not responsible for human rights

---

90 See Communication No. 511/1992 *I. Länsman et al.* v. *Finland* and Communication No. 671/1995, *J. Länsman et al.* v. *Finland.*

91 In an earlier decision the HRC had decided that certain kinds of economic activity, especially activity aimed at earning one's livelihood, is protected by article 27 ICCPR where that economic practice is sufficiently connected to cultural maintenance. Reindeer herding was considered a culturaly-valuable and thus protected practice. See *Ivan Kitok* v. *Sweden* (No. 197/1985).

92 A/49/40, Vol. I (1994), Annex V (p. 107-110); CCPR/C/21/Rev.1/Add.5, 6 April 1994, paras. 6.1.

93 511/1992, para. 9.6.

94 Scott, *supra* n. 55, 581-583.

95 Scott, *supra* n. 55, p. 582.

> violations simply because serious harm to human rights occur. Were a result-based responsibility to be found, this would amount to the vicarious liability of the state for the conduct of non-state actors, or in other words, the equivalent of a form of direct responsibility. The Committee does not appear willing at this time to treat states as guarantors of human rights in the private sphere in this strong sense.'[96]

Nevertheless, Scott acknowledges that the HRC has 'clearly laid the ground for a relevant body of jurisprudence if the right cases continue to come this way in the future'.[97]

In 1997 the HRC, for the first time, decided on a case concerning the obligations of the State for corporate activities outside the context of cultural rights. In the case of *Hopu and Bessert* v. *France*[98] two inhabitants of Tahiti, both ethnic Polynesians, brought claims against France for, *inter alia*, unlawful interference with family life.[99] At issue was the construction of a luxury hotel complex by the corporation *Société Hotelière RIVNAC* on land that the ethnic Polynesians considered an important place in their history, their culture and their life. The private company *RIVNAC* sub-leased the contested land from a corporation of which the government was the sole shareholder. The authors contended that embarking upon the construction work would destroy their traditional burial ground and ruinously affect their fishing activities. Together with their forceful removal from the site this allegedly constituted an unlawful interference with their private and family lives.[100] The HRC agreed with the authors, stating that the interference by the State party was not shown to be reasonable nor had the State party duly taken 'into account the importance of the burial grounds for the authors when it decided to lease the site for the building of the hotel complex'.[101] In its views on this case the HRC did not discuss the status of the corporation. As pointed out by Scott, the HRC's decision can therefore be interpreted in two ways.[102] On the one hand, the HRC's decision can be based on the fact that the State failed in its duty to protect the Polynesians against the harmful activities of the corporation. In other words, in that case, the State failed in its general obligation to exercise due diligence with respect to the corporate activity. On the other hand, the reasoning of the HRC could also have been based on the consideration that the private company was in fact acting as a government agent due to the leasing arrangement. This would involve the direct responsibility of the State.

---

96 Scott, *supra* n. 55, p. 582.
97 Scott, *supra* n. 55, pp. 582-583.
98 UN doc. CCPR/C/60/D/549/1993, 29 July 1997.
99 Article 17 ICCPR. Article 27 ICCPR could not be applied in this case due to a French reservation to this article. However, the HRC argued that article 17 could protect similar issues.
100 UN Doc. CCPR/C/60/D/549/1993, paras. 2.5 and 3.2.
101 UN doc. CCPR/C/60/D/549/1993, para. 10.3.
102 Scott, *supra* n. 55, pp. 585.

The difference between State responsibility for private acts arising from a failure to exercise due diligence, indirect State responsibility, and the direct State responsibility that arises for the acts of government agents, remains important. As pointed out by Scott:

> 'Were RIVNAC to be deemed a government actor (either because, hypothetically, it is 100 per cent government owned or because a lease is sufficient to give it that character) then each and every act that infringes on human interests by RIVNAC would constitute a violation by the government. In contrast, where RIVNAC remains purely private in status, the state's duty is generally considered to be more attenuated: the duty to take reasonable care in circumstances to prevent harm caused by RIVNAC. The simple fact of harm by a corporation, where a government does not have adequate prior or concurrent knowledge of that harm, will not necessarily be sufficient to trigger state responsibility.'[103]

In sum, the case-law, described above, shows that the HRC has, albeit cautiously, found that State responsibility may arise when there is a failure to control corporations.

5.5 The Committee on Economic, Social and Cultural Rights

Unlike the supervisory mechanisms discussed in the previous sections, the ICESCR does not provide for an individual complaint procedure. The implementation of the Covenant is monitored by means of a reporting procedure. State Parties are required to submit reports to the UN Secretary-General, who will transmit them to the Economic and Social Council (ECOSOC) for consideration. ECOSOC has delegated this task to the Committee on Economic, Social and Cultural Rights. In the reports States point out the measures adopted and the progress made in achieving the observance of the rights recognised in the ICESCR.[104] After the consideration of the reports the Committee draws up Concluding Observations, which include the positive aspects in a State, the difficulties in impeding the Covenant and the principal aspects of concern.

Under a reporting mechanism, the specific discussion of harmful corporate activities is less likely to occur than is the case under an individual complaint procedure. A few examples exist where the Committee has addressed the role played by corporations in human rights violations. For example, in 1998 the activities of *Shell* in Nigeria were brought to the attention of the Committee during the consideration of the Nigerian report. In its Concluding Observations, the Committee noted with alarm,

---

103 Scott, *supra* n. 55, p. 586.
104 Article 16 ICESCR.

> 'the extent of devastation that oil exploration has done to the environment and quality of life in the areas such as Ogoniland where oil has been discovered and extracted without due regard to the health and well-being of the people and their environment.'[105]

The Committee does not mention specific corporations and neither does it specify the manner in which State responsibility is involved. The role of the Committee could be enhanced if State Parties to the ICESCR were required to specifically report on the measures taken to control corporations and prevent harmful corporate activities.

5.6 The International Labour Organisation

As is the case with the human rights bodies discussed above, the ILO monitoring system deals solely with the obligations of States. Nevertheless, it follows from the fact that the ILO Conventions cover labour rights that the cases brought before the monitoring bodies of the ILO will mostly deal with the responsibility of the State that may arise in connection with corporate activities.

The monitoring system of the ILO is made up of an 'ordinary' system of supervision and three special mechanisms.[106] The ordinary system obliges a State to embark upon regular, periodic reporting on measures which have been taken to give effect to a ratified Convention.[107] The special systems of supervision, provided for in article 24 and article 26 of the ILO Constitution, involve cases of specific allegations against a member State. Moreover, the ILO has a special supervisory mechanism concerning freedom of association.[108]

Under the complaint procedure provided for in article 26 of the ILO Constitution, claims can be submitted by Member States against another Member State for a violation of ILO provisions. Claims may also be submitted by an ILO Conference delegate or by the Governing Body. The Governing Body decides whether to appoint a Commission of Inquiry. This Commission reports its findings, giving recommendations and

---

105 UN doc. E/C.12/1/Add.23, 13 May 1998, para. 29. Example mentioned by Sarah Joseph, 'An Overview of the Human Rights Accountability of Multinational Enterprises', in: *The Liability of Multinational Corporations Under International Law*, Menno T. Kamminga and Saman Zia-Zarifi [eds.], Kluwer Law International, The Hague etc. 2000, p. 78, nt. 7.

106 See, Lammy Betten, 'The International Implementation of Economic, Social and Cultural Rights by the ILO', in: *Netherlands Quarterly of Human Rights*, Vol. 6, No. 2, 1988, pp. 29-42 and W.J.M. van Genugten, *WTO, ILO en EG: handelen in vrijheid [WTO, ILO and EC: Trading in Freedom]*, W.E.J. Tjeenk Willink, Deventer, 1997, pp. 17-24.

107 Article 22 ILO Constitution. The reports are studied by the 'Committee of Experts on the Application of Conventions and Recommendations'. The Committee may issue a 'direct request' to the government for additional information. If violations are found the Committee may publish 'observations'. Moreover, the Committee may establish 'direct contact' with the government concerned by sending officials. Grave violations are discussed in the annual labour Conference and published in the annual report.

108 This procedure is based on an agreement between the UN Economic and Social Council and the ILO in 1950, ECOSOC Resolution 277 (x), 17 February 1950.

a time frame for their implementation. The report is sent to the government concerned, published, and transmitted to the Governing Body to take note. The Committee of Experts on the Application of Conventions and Recommendations follows up on the implementation of the recommendations. The government(s) concerned may refer the complaint to the International Court of Justice for a final decision.

In total, 26 cases have been submitted under this procedure.[109] It is interesting to note that of these cases, six have been initiated by governments.[110] These cases concern allegations of non-compliance with ILO Conventions concerning forced labour, protection of wages, discrimination and equality of treatment.[111] In 1961, Ghana filed a complaint against Portugal.[112] The case concerned Portugal's compliance with the ILO Convention on the Abolition of Forced Labour in its African territories of Mozambique, Angola and Guinea (at the time). A case filed in 1962, concerned Portugal's allegations of forced labour against Liberia.[113] Finally, in 1986, a case was filed by Tunisia against the Libyan Arab Jamahiriya concerning the alleged non-observance of three ILO Conventions regarding the protection of wages, discrimination and equality of treatment.[114]

Article 26 of the ILO Constitution provides that, in addition to States, complaints can be filed by the Governing body of the ILO and by a delegate to the Conference. This occurs more frequently than the Inter-State complaints, but still relatively rarely. Recently, such a case has reached an unprecedented phase in the procedure. In 1996 workers' representatives filed a complaint against Myanmar (formerly known as

109 See the website of the ILO: http://www.ilo.org/public/english/standards/norm/enforced/complnt/index.htm (accessed on 27 September 2001).

110 The cases before the human rights bodies, discussed in the previous sections, all emanated from the individual complaint procedures provided for in the IACHR, ECHR, and the ICCPR. Besides these individual complaint procedures these treaties provide the possibility for a State to lodge a complaint against another State. Practice shows, however, that States are extremely reluctant to use the inter-State complaint mechanisms. To date, 21 inter-State claims have been lodged under the ECHR (in 13 cases relating to no more than 7 situations), but none under the ICCPR and the IACHR. The inter-State claims filed under the European system have predominantly concerned cases of emergency rule and armed tension. No inter-State cases have been brought regarding the failure to exercise due diligence towards corporate activities. The inter-State complaints brought before the ILO are therefore more relevant for this study. For an overview of the inter-State claims procedures see: Scott Leckie, 'The Inter-State Complaint Procedure in International Human Rights Law: Hopeful Prospects or Wishful Thinking', in: *Human Rights Quarterly*, Vol. 10, 1988, pp. 249-303.

111 For a description of these cases see: Leckie, *supra* n. 110, pp. 278-289.

112 Complaint filed by Ghana concerning the observance by Portugal of the Abolition of Forced Labour Convention, 1957 (No. 105) (O.B., Vol. XLV, 1962, No. 2, Suppl.II).

113 Complaint filed by Portugal concerning the observance by Liberia of the Forced Labour Convention, 1930 (No. 29) (O.B., Vol. XLVI, 1963, No. 2, Suppl. II).

114 Complaint by the Government of Tunisia concerning the observance by the Libyan Arab Jamahiriya of the Protection of Wages Convention, 1949 (No. 95), the Discrimination (Employment and Occupation) Convention, 1958 (No. 111) and the Equality of Treatment (Social Security) Convention, 1962 (No. 118) (GB.232117/32,GB.238122/31, GB.240114/20, GB.240/14/26).

Burma) alleging a violation of the Forced Labour Convention (No. 29).[115] In November 2000, after various attempts to persuade the government of Myanmar to change its policies, the Governing Body of the ILO, for the first time in its history, recommended sanctions against a member. In this case, Myanmar is being held responsible for making use of forced labour. As will be discussed in chapter VII, several multinational corporations have been accused of being involved in these practices.[116] It can be said that by condemning Myanmar, the ILO is also scrutinising the activities of these corporations.

Besides the complaint procedure under article 26, article 24 of the ILO Constitution provides that employers' or workers' organisations can make a so-called 'representation' claiming that a given member State has failed to apply an ILO Convention which it has ratified. The matter is brought before the Governing Body, which determines whether the complaint is admissible. If the representation is admissible, it sets up an Ad Hoc committee of three members to examine the matter. The Governing Body considers the report of the Ad Hoc Committee and may decide to publish the representation. It may also decide to initiate a complaint under article 26 of the Constitution.

Finally, the ILO has established – in addition to the ordinary system of supervision – special machinery for the enforcement of Conventions 87 and 98 on the freedom of association. This procedure is particularly relevant in the light of corporate human rights violations, as the ILO Committee on Freedom of Association has explicitly named business enterprises implicated in certain State's failure to comply with ILO Conventions 87 and 98. The Committee on Freedom of Association and the Fact-Finding and Conciliation Commission on Freedom of Association examine complaints from governments, as well as workers' and employers' organisations that allege that Member States of the ILO are not respecting basic principles of freedom of association. Especially interesting in this procedure is that complaints may be examined whether or not the country concerned has ratified the ILO's Conventions on the subject. Mere membership of the organisation obliges States to observe the principle of freedom of association. This procedure has generated extensive case-law.[117]

The supervisory mechanisms of the ILO focus on the State and – except for the procedure on the freedom of association – the use made of the contentious procedures is relatively low. Nevertheless, in the light of the nature of the provisions of the ILO Conventions, it may be concluded that the ILO procedures offer potentially effective avenues for the indirect scrutiny of corporate activities. This especially applies to the procedure on the freedom of association where corporations have been explicitly

115 Complaint concerning the non-observance by Myanmar of the Forced Labour Convention, 1930 (No. 29), made by delegates to the 83rd (1996) Session of the Conference under article 26 of the Constitution of the ILO (GB.267/16/2, GB.268/14/8, GB.268/15/1).

116 See chapter VII, pp. 187-190.

117 At the time of writing over 2,000 cases have been examined. See, the website of the ILO: www.ilo.org (accessed on 1 October 2001).

named. In general, the ILO procedures supervising the behaviour of States are considered to be highly effective which can, *inter alia*, be attributed to the tripartite character of the ILO.[118] The fact that the ILO is made up of representatives of States, workers' organisations and employers' organisations contributes to well-balanced supervision. It should be noted, that, in the light of indirectly scrutinising corporate behaviour, the tripartite character at times might hamper the effectiveness as employers' organisations are in a position to block the indirect supervision of corporations.

5.7 Concluding Remarks on the Case-law

From the preceding survey of cases that have addressed State responsibility arising in connection with harmful corporate activities, it becomes apparent that the mechanisms under the international treaties offer a largely unexploited potential for the indirect scrutiny of corporate activities. The supervisory bodies, notably the European Court of Human Rights, have confirmed that States can be held responsible for corporate activities that violate human rights law by failing to exercise due diligence. Especially the individual complaint procedures prove to offer an effective mechanism to scrutinise corporate activity through the responsibility of the State. At the same time, the number of such cases brought before the international quasi-judicial bodies is relatively small.

The content of the due diligence obligation to regulate corporate activities depends on the circumstances of each case. At present, given the relatively small number of cases, the content is not fully elaborated yet. In the cases described above State responsibility has arisen for 'failure to strike a fair balance between the interests concerned',[119] 'failure to conduct a proper and complete investigation',[120] 'failure to take timely and effective measures',[121] 'failure to provide for essential information',[122] and 'failure to take due account of the importance of (in this case) burial grounds to the authors'.[123] In the *Ländsman* cases the HRC decided that, as the State provided for the effective participation of the interested groups, there was no human rights violation resulting in the responsibility of the State. In the discussed cases before the HRC, the contents of the due diligence obligation would appear first and foremost to consist of an obligation to provide information on corporate activities to the affected parties and to secure the latter's involvement in decision-making processes. The case-law of the ECHR, which

118 Van Genugten, *supra* n. 106, pp. 20-24.

119 *López Ostra* v. *Spain*, Judgment of 9 December 1994, Series A Vol. 303-C.para. 58.

120 *Hatton and others* v. *the United Kingdom*, para. 97. Judgement of 2 October 2001, Application No. 36022/97.

121 *Yanomamis* v. *Brasil*, Case No. 7615 (Brazil), 5 March 1985, O.A.S. Doc. OEA/Ser.L/V/II.66. doc.10, rev.1, 1985, paras. 10 and 11.

122 *Guerra* v. *Italy*, Judgment of 19 February 1998, Reports of Judgments and Decisions 1998-I, No. 64., para. 58 and 60.

123 *Hopu and Bessert* v. *France*, communication no. 549/1993, UN Doc. CCPR/C/60/D/549/1993, 29 July 1997, para. 10.3.

is the most developed, requires States to conduct a prior specific and complete study with the aim of finding the least onerous solution as regards human rights.

So far, this – embryonic – case-law has not yet explicitly stated that States should adopt legislation to prevent or repress corporate acts that constitute a human rights violation. However, the due diligence obligation is often perceived as an obligation to protect against human rights violations by means of legislation. The obligation to legislate is set forth in human rights treaties[124] and has been confirmed in several General Comments.[125]

6 Responsibility of the Host and the Home State

As was pointed out above, State responsibility may arise for a failure to exercise due diligence in controlling corporate activities. To avoid such responsibility States should take (legislative) measures to prevent and repress corporate activities that violate human rights.

The question can be posed whether State responsibility only arises following a failure to prevent corporate violations within the territory of the State or also when the violations occur outside of its territory. In other words, should a State adopt legislation that regulates corporate activity abroad? This question is closely related to the issue of *which* State can be held responsible for failing to regulate corporations. Can only the host State, on whose territory the corporation operates, be held responsible or can the home State, where the corporation is incorporated,[126] also be held responsible for failing to adopt legislation that regulates corporate activity?

This question is an important one. Holding home States responsible for failing to control their corporate citizens abroad could prove to be an effective way of controlling the activities of corporations with regard to human rights. Host States might be less inclined to act against corporations that violate human rights within their territory given the often very powerful positions which the corporations have within the host State.[127]

124 Article 2, para. 2 ICCPR, Art. 2, para. 1 ECHR, art. 4, para. 1 American Convention. In the *Velásquez Rodríguez* case, the Inter-American Court affirmed that the existence of a legal system is one of the means for a State to comply with its obligation to ensure [in that case] the right to life, para. 167.

125 See, *inter alia*, A/47/40 (1992), Annex VI (pp. 193-195), General Comment 20/44, 3 April 1992, which deals with article 7 ICCPR. In paragraph 2 the HRC stated that the State is obliged to protect persons from torture or cruel, inhuman and degrading treatment or punishment, also when committed by persons acting in a private capacity. According to the HRC it is the State's duty in this regard to take the necessary legislative measures.

126 *Case Concerning the Barcelona Traction Light and Power Co Ltd. (Belgium* v. *Spain)* I.C.J. Rep. (1970) p. 3, para. 70.

127 Most corporations' activities occur within the developed world. However, between one-third and two-fifths of all foreign direct investment occurs in the less-industrialised world, see European Parliament Resolution on 'EU Standards for European Enterprises: Towards a European Code of Conduct', 14 January 1999, Explanatory Memorandum on 'Globalisation, Foreign Investment and Development'.

Most corporations have revenues many times larger than the GNP of the States where they operate.[128] Moreover, in the event that the government of the host country colludes with a corporation in violating human rights, it will be doubtful, to say the least, that the host country will bring charges against the corporation, thereby allowing the corporation to act with impunity. Developed States, home to most multinational corporations, are more likely to have effective means and technical expertise to regulate and monitor corporate activities than is the case with developing host States. Moreover, the true centre of decision and control might be located in the home State. In some cases, corporate human rights violations in host countries may be the result of decisions taken by the parent-corporation in the home State.

In the light of these arguments it is important to examine whether home State responsibility can arise for failing to regulate extra-territorial corporate activities. In order to answer this question I will examine the general rules on the geographical scope of international State responsibility also on the basis of the case-law of the human rights bodies.

6.1 Principles of Territoriality and Actual/Effective Control

Traditionally, there is a connection between responsibility and territorial control. As was stated by Judge Huber in the case of *British Property in Spanish Morocco*, a State can, in principle, only be responsible for events occurring within its territory.[129] The territorial approach has been embraced by the ILC in its work on State responsibility. In principle State responsibility can only arise when the State where the harmful corporate activities take place, the host State, does not exercise due diligence in controlling these activities. Does this imply that a *home* State can never be held responsible for harm caused by the activities of its 'corporate nationals' outside that State's territorial boundaries? In other words, if the home State fails to exercise due diligence in preventing a violation of international law in another country, committed by a corporation, can this give rise to responsibility of the Home State?

In general a State is not under an obligation to control the activities of private individuals (being its nationals) beyond the bounds of State territory.[130] However, the territoriality principle, which was formulated in the particular context of the protection of foreign nationals, has been modified. While territoriality remains the predominant principle underlying a State's jurisdiction, under certain circumstances the principle should be moderated. As Brownlie points out:

128 An example is the position that the *Texaco* corporation has in Ecuador. For many years *Texaco* has operated in Ecuador as practically a State unto itself with annual global earnings four times the size of Ecuador's GNP and with the active support of the US government. See: Center for Economic and Social Rights, *supra* n. 83.

129 *Spain* v. *The United Kingdom*, 1925, 2, UNRIAA, 636.

130 Brownlie, *supra* n. 4, p. 165.

> 'This principle (...) is open to serious question and can operate, if at all, only as a weak presumption. In the first place circumstances, such as those in the *Trail Smelter Arbitration* dictate obvious and substantial qualifications to the principle.'[131]

In the *Trail Smelter* case the Arbitral Tribunal held that '[n]o State has the right to use or permit the use of its territory in such a manner as to cause injury by fumes in or to the territory of another or the properties therein'.[132] The ICJ followed the same line of reasoning in the *Corfu Channel* Case: '[It is] every State's obligation not to allow knowingly its territory to be used for acts contrary to the rights of other States'.[133] Brownlie adds:

> 'In general terms the test is that of physical control and not sovereignty. (...) The State is under the duty to control the activities of private persons within its State territory and the duty is no less applicable where the harm is caused to persons or other legal interests within the territory of another State.'[134]

It follows that a State has the obligation to prevent harm caused by its corporate citizens within the territory of another State. The State is under the obligation to control corporations operating within its jurisdiction, and where these operations cause harm in another State this may give rise to State responsibility. The crucial question is whether the State can in fact control the activities. A situation of control can be taken to exist when the State has either the possible victim or the possible perpetrator within its jurisdiction.

Under the ECHR it has been acknowledged that a party to the Convention may be responsible for acts of torture that occur outside its jurisdiction. In the *Soering* case,[135] the Court decided that a German national detained in the UK could not be extradited to Virginia in the United States in order to stand trial for murder and possibly be sentenced to death. The Court held that the conditions of the so-called death row phenomenon amounted to a violation of Article 3 ECHR (freedom from torture and other inhuman treatment). If the UK would extradite the applicant exposing him to this treatment, it would be responsible under the ECHR. The State was in a position of control, due to the fact that the potential victim of the human rights violation was within its jurisdiction. For the present study the more relevant issue concerns State responsibility where the perpetrator is under the control of the State.

131 Brownlie, *supra* n. 4, p. 165.
132 *Trail Smelter* case, 1941, 2, UNRIAA, para. 1165.
133 *Corfu Channel* case (*United Kingdom* v. *Albania*), I.C.J. Rep., 9 April 1949, p. 4 para. 22.
134 Brownlie, *supra* n. 4, p. 165.
135 Judgement of 7 July 1989, Series A, Vol. 161.

6.2 Extra Territorial Activities of State Organs

In the previous section it has been argued that the State's due diligence obligation is conditional upon its actual control over either the victim or the perpetrator. It follows that State responsibility can arise for acts committed on the territory of a State, assuming that the State has actual control over its territory. International practice shows that the State is presumed to have actual control over its State organs and that, consequently, State responsibility may arise for the acts of State organs even though they are committed outside the territory of the State concerned. This has been confirmed by the ILC in its work on State responsibility. The ILC has taken the position that the attribution to the State of the acts of its organs is not subject to any territorial limitation.[136] In the case of *Cyprus* v. *Turkey*[137] the European Commission dealt with the question of whether a State may be held responsible for acts by State organs outside its territorial boundaries. The Commission opined:

> 'It is clear (...) that the High Contracting Parties are bound to secure the said rights and freedoms to all persons under their actual authority and responsibility, whether that authority is exercised within their own territory or abroad.'[138]

The Commission equates the concept of jurisdiction with 'actual authority and responsibility'. The same line of reasoning is followed in the 1971 *Advisory Opinion on the Legal Consequences for States of the Continued Presence of South Africa in Namibia (South West Africa).* Here it was argued that:

> 'The fact that South Africa no longer has any title to administer the Territory does not release it from its obligations and responsibilities under international law towards other States in respect of the exercise of its powers in relation to this Territory. *Physical control* of a territory, and not sovereignty or legitimacy of title, is the basis of State liability for acts affecting other States.'[139] [Emphasis added]

Similarly, in early case-law concerning the activities of Uruguayan agents, the HRC noted that the geographical scope of application of the ICCPR is not limited to the territory of a Contracting Party. In the case of *Lopez Burgos* v. *Uruguay* the victim

---

136 UN Doc. A/CN.4/Ser.A/1975, *YBIL*, Vol. II, 1975, p. 83, para. 1.

137 Appls 6780/74 and 6950/75, *Cyprus* v. *Turkey*, Y.B. Eur. Conv.H.R. XVIII, 1975, p.82 The complaint which was filed by the government of Cyprus following Turkey's invasion of Cyprus, charged Turkey with violations of the Convention in that part of the island which had been invaded by Turkish troops.

138 *Cyprus* v. *Turkey*, p. 83. Some other cases before the European Commission and Court concerning the responsibility of Contracting States for acts of their organs that have been committed outside their territory are: Appl. 1611/62, *X* v. *Federal Republic of Germany*, Yearbook VIII (1965), p. 158 (163), *Loizidou* Case, Judgment of 23 March 1995, A. 310, p.24, Appl. 7289/75 and 7349/76, *X and Y* v. *Switzerland,* D&R 9 (1978), p. 57 (73). See Van Dijk and Van Hoof, *supra* n. 23, pp. 9-10.

139 I.C.J. Rep. 21 June 1971, p. 16, para. 118.

lived as a political refugee in Argentina where he was abducted and brought to Uruguay by Uruguayan agents. The HRC observed that,

> 'although the arrest and initial detention and mistreatment of Lopez Burgos allegedly took place on foreign territory, the Committee is not barred (...) by virtue of article 2 (1) of the Covenant ("...individuals within its territory and subject to its jurisdiction ...") from considering these allegations, together with the claim of subsequent abduction into Uruguayan territory, inasmuch as these acts were perpetrated by Uruguayan agents acting on foreign soil. Article 2 (1) of the Covenant places an obligation upon a State party to respect and to ensure rights "to all individuals within its territory and subject to its jurisdiction", but it does not imply that the State party concerned cannot be held accountable for violations of rights under the Covenant which its agents commit upon the territory of another State, whether with the acquiescence of the Government of that State or in opposition to it. In line with this, it would be unconscionable to so interpret the responsibility under article 2 of the Covenant as to permit a State party to perpetrate violations of the Covenant on the territory of another State, which violations it could not perpetrate on its own territory.'[140]

In sum, State responsibility may arise for a failure to control that State's organs irrespective of where the violation of international law takes place.

6.3 Extra Territorial Activities of Non-State Entities

State responsibility for the extra territorial acts of non-State entities is less evident. As was discussed in section 3.1, private acts can involve State responsibility in two ways. Either the private acts are considered as acts of State for which international responsibility may arise, or the State is held responsible for failing in its obligation to exercise due diligence in protecting against private harmful activities. The attribution of extra territorial private acts to the State was at stake in the *Case concerning Military and Paramilitary Activities in and against Nicaragua.*[141] The ICJ accepted that a State can in principle be liable for humanitarian violations committed by non-State actors outside its territory. The court held that the activities of the Nicaraguan *contras* were attributable to the US because of the planning, direction and support by US agents.[142] Never-

140 052/1979, *Delia Saldias de Lopez (alleged victim's wife) on behalf of Sergio Ruben Lopez Burgos* v. *Uruguay*, 29 July 1981, paras. 12.1 and 12.30. See, also 56/1979, *Francesco Cavallaro (alleged victim's legal representative) on behalf of Lilian Celiberti de Casariego* v. *Uruguay*, 29 July 1981, para. 10.3.

141 In this case Nicaragua sought to attribute responsibility to the US for the activities of the *contra* rebel military force, including the killing, wounding and kidnapping of Nicaraguan citizens. *Military and Paramilitary Activities* (*Nicaragua* v. *U.S.*), judgment of 27 June 1986, (Merits) I.C.J. Rep.,14.

142 *Military and Paramilitary Activities in and against Nicaragua* (*Nicaragua* v. *U.S.*) (Merits). I.C.J. Rep., 14, 1986, p.51.

theless, not all activities of the contras were attributable to the US. According to the Court:

> '(...) United States participation, even if preponderant or decisive, in the financing, organizing, training, supplying and equipping of the *contras*, the selection of its military or paramilitary targets, and the planning of the whole operation, is still insufficient in itself, on the basis of the evidence in the possession of the Court, for the purpose of attributing to the United States the acts committed by the *contras* in the course of their military or paramilitary operations in Nicaragua. All the forms of United States participation mentioned above, and even the general control by the respondent over a force with a high degree of dependency on it, would not in itself mean, without further evidence, that the United States directed or enforced the perpetration of the acts contrary to human rights and humanitarian law alleged by the applicant State. Such acts could well be committed by members of the *contras* without the control of the United States. For this conduct to give rise to legal responsibility of the United States, it would have to be proved that the State had effective control of the military or paramilitary operations in the course of which the alleged violations were committed.'[143]

The ICJ formulated a strict test for determining whether a State is responsible for the acts of private entities by requiring that the particular State had *effective* control over the private acts. As has been pointed out by several scholars, this test is stricter than the due diligence test.[144] For extra territorial private acts to be attributed to the State, the State should not only have neglected its obligation to prevent the violation or to respond to it, it is also required that the State had effective control over the private acts which violated human rights. To some authors this line of reasoning is considered a rather restrictive view on State responsibility and is therefore disappointing.[145] However, the limitation that State responsibility can only arise for private acts over which the State has effective control is realistic. It cannot be expected that a State can guarantee that private actors, over whom it has no effective control, will not commit human rights violations abroad.

At issue in the *Nicaragua* case was whether the *contras* had acted as *de facto* US agents for whose acts the responsibility of the US could arise. Despite the fact that the US financed, trained, equipped and advised the *contra* rebels, their acts were not considered as acts of State. Nevertheless, it is conceivable that in a military situation

143 Military and Paramilitary Activities in and against Nicaragua (*Nicaragua* v. *U.S.)* (Merits*)*. I.C.J. Rep., 14, 1986, p.51, para.115.

144 Rosalyn Higgins, *Problems and Process. International Law and How We Use It*, Clarendon Press, New York, 1994, p. 155, Dinah Shelton, 'State Responsibility for Covert and Indirect Forms of Violence', in: *Human Rights in the Twenty-First Century: a global challenge,* Kathleen E. Mahoney and Paul Mahoney [eds.],Martinus Nijhoff, Dordrecht etc., 1993. pp. 265-276, at p. 270.

145 Shelton, *supra* n. 144, p. 270. She argues that the Court's opinion is disappointing as it 'appears to retreat from the imposition of liability for complicity in internationally wrongful acts, imposed at Nuremberg'.

such a degree of control exists that it involves State responsibility. It is difficult to imagine a situation where a State exercises such a degree of control over corporate activities abroad that the corporate activities can be considered as acts of State.

Should it be concluded on the basis of the foregoing that home State responsibility can never arise for corporate extraterritorial activity? At most it can be argued that the home State may be held responsible for explicitly supporting harmful corporate activities abroad. In the *Nicaragua* case the Court held that the US could not be held responsible for the acts of the *contras*, but State responsibility did arise for its own support for the *contras*. In the light of the fact that home States may have effective means to regulate the parent companies, it can be argued that home States have a degree of control over extraterritorial corporate activities. Home States should exercise due diligence in controlling the parent company. As observed by Scott:

> '(…) if a state can violate the [ICCPR] by failing to exercise sufficient diligence with respect to corporate activity on its own territory, and it has sufficient knowledge to be able to do at least something to prevent harm on the territory of another state by a corporation that is *in some respects subject to its regulatory powers*, then it would seem that there is, at least *prima facie*, a duty on that state to do what it can to prevent such a violation.'[146] [Emphasis added]

It can be assumed that public enterprises, corporations owned by the State, are subject to the regulatory powers of the State. Regarding public enterprises the home State can have sufficient knowledge of harm caused on the territory of another State. In such a case the home State is under an obligation to take measures to prevent such a violation.

In the case of private corporations an argument can be made that effective control can flow from the economic, legal and political connection between the corporation and the home State. In particular the larger multinational corporations are conspicuous private actors for the purpose of implementing rules of due diligence. These corporations are more visible than small companies and are normally subjected to more extensive control by the authorities of the home State. The corporate conduct occurring in other States might be *de facto* within the reach of the headquarters of the corporation and therefore also within the home State's control. It may not always be easy for a home State to regulate the conduct of the parent company. One way in which the State can exercise control is by means of the issuing of permits and licences. For example, human rights may be violated by the export of hazardous industrial and technological activities.[147] This may result in a violation of the right to health. It can be argued that where the home State has sufficient knowledge of the potential damage, it is under an obligation to prevent and mitigate the risk by adopting legislation to this end. A failure

146 Scott, *supra* n. 55, p. 587.

147 Francesco Francioni and Tullio Scovazzi, *International Responsibility for Environmental Harm* Graham & Trotman/Martinus Nijhoff, London etc., 1991, p. 296.

to do so would amount to a breach of the international obligation to exercise due diligence, for which international responsibility arises. It is submitted that allowing harm to occur by not exercising due diligence in controlling the head office (where this can be effectively controlled by the home State) may amount to an internationally wrongful act for which State responsibility may arise.

In sum, the due diligence obligation to regulate the activities of corporations is conditioned by the degree of control over these activities and therefore rests first and foremost with the host State. For State responsibility to arise for private acts that occur outside the territory of the State a stricter test applies. However, it follows from the general principle formulated in the *Corfu Channel* case – that a State has the obligation not knowingly to allow its territory to be used for acts contrary to the rights of other States – that home State responsibility can arise where the home State has not exercised due diligence in controlling parent companies that are effectively under its control. Home States should take appropriate measures to prevent and repress the injurious acts of corporations abroad. As discussed above,[148] under international human rights law this obligation is, in the first place, perceived as an obligation to adopt legislation.

In the light of the foregoing it would seem useful to discuss several treaties that contain substantive obligations for States to regulate the extra territorial activities of corporations that are incorporated in these States.

6.4 Treaties Regulating Extra Territorial Activities of Corporations

The emergence of obligations susceptible of entailing State responsibility in relation to the behaviour of (legal) persons outside the territorial jurisdiction of that State is beginning to be realised in conventional law.

It is interesting to look at developments in the field of environmental protection. Several conventions and declarations dealing with responsibility for environmental harm point towards the existence of a duty of care on the part of States to prevent injury.[149] In certain conventions the duty of care is one of strict liability. This is the case in the 1967 Treaty on Principles Governing the Activities of States in the Exploration and Use of Outer Space, including the Moon and Other Celestial Bodies,[150] in the 1972 Convention on International Liability for Damage Caused by Space Objects[151] and in the 1982 Montego Bay Convention on the Law of the Sea.[152] In most cases, however, the standard of care is one of due diligence instead of strict liability. Article 21 of the

148 See p. 165.
149 Higgins, *supra* n. 144, p. 157.
150 UNTS, X, 205.
151 ILM (1971), 965.
152 See for example article 194 which states: ' States shall take (...) all measures... that are necessary to prevent, reduce and control pollution of the marine environment *from any source* (...)'. Emphasis added.

Stockholm Declaration on the Human Environment provides that the responsibility incumbent on States is 'to ensure that activities within their jurisdiction *or control* do not cause damage to the environment of other States or of areas beyond their jurisdiction' [emphasis added].[153] The content of this obligation is not limited to activities within a State's territory or jurisdiction but extends to activities under the *control* of the State. This language is also used in other declarations regarding the environment.[154] Article 30 of the Charter of Economic Rights and Duties of States provides:

> 'All States have the responsibility to ensure that activities within their jurisdiction *or control* do not cause damage to the environment of other States or of areas beyond the limits of national jurisdiction'.[155]

In sum, several international instruments dealing with the protection of the environment explicitly require States to adopt legislation with extra territorial reach. If a State does not adopt such legislation international responsibility arises.

The codification of the extra territorial obligations of home States is not confined to the protection of the environment. In the field of corruption several treaties exist that require States to criminalize corruption by both individuals and legal persons. A fairly recent example is the 1997 OECD Bribery Convention.[156] According to this Convention:

> '[e]ach Party shall take such measures as may be necessary in accordance with its legal principles, to establish the liability of legal persons for the bribery of a foreign public official.'[157]
>
> '[e]ach Party shall take such measures as may be necessary to establish its jurisdiction over the bribery of a foreign public official when the offence is committed in whole or in part in its territory.'[158]
> (…)
> 'Each Party shall review whether its current basis for jurisdiction is effective in the fight against bribery of foreign public officials and, if it is not, shall take remedial steps.'[159]

153 30 ILM 190 (1991).

154 See, for example, articles 139, 216(1) and 217(1) (b) of the Convention on the Law of the Sea according to which States must control pollution not only when it originates in the territory or in the areas of maritime jurisdiction of the transgressor State, but also when the pollution is caused by private activities under its control.

155 UN Doc. A/Res/3281 (XXIX), 12 December 1974.

156 OECD Convention on Combating Bribery of Foreign Public Officials in International Business (OECD Bribery Convention), adopted on 21 November 1997, entered into force on 15 February 1999. Text available at http://www. oecd.org (accessed on 18 September 2001).

157 Article 2 OECD Bribery Convention.

158 Article 4, para. 1 OECD Bribery Convention.

159 Article 4, para. 4 OECD Bribery Convention.

If a home State fails to adopt such legislation to regulate extra territorial activities, international responsibility arises.

Another example in the field of criminal law treaties that call on States to criminalize certain conduct, even if it occurs in other countries, is the Optional Protocol to the Convention on the Rights of the Child on the sale of children, child prostitution and child pornography.[160] Article 3, paragraph 4 reads:

> 'Subject to the provisions of its national law, each State Party shall take measures, where appropriate, to establish the liability of legal persons for [the prohibition of the sale of children, child prostitution and child pornography]. Subject to the legal principles of the State Party, such liability of legal persons may be criminal, civil or administrative.'

These steps to regulate the extraterritorial activities of corporations in the field of corruption, the environment and the exploitation of children, demonstrate that in various areas international law is moving towards obligating home States to adopt legislation that regulates activities of corporations abroad.
It may be argued that international human rights law imposes a similar obligation on home States to regulate extra territorial corporate activities that are effectively under their control.

7 Concluding Remarks

States are under the obligation to protect individuals against corporate activities that violate human rights. To avoid being held responsible for violating this obligation, the State should exercise due diligence in taking legislative and other measures. State responsibility may arise for corporate activities on a State's territory and, as has been demonstrated above, in certain circumstances, it is feasible that an obligation exists for a home State to adopt legislation controlling harmful corporate activities abroad. It has been demonstrated that in various areas, international law is moving towards an obligation on the part of the home State to control, by means of legislation and otherwise, the activities of corporations abroad. Holding the home State responsible for not using all possible measures to prevent human rights violations by their corporate citizens abroad offers interesting opportunities. However, this approach also raises many complex issues of a practical and political nature. The political obstacles to home State

160 Adopted and opened for signature, ratification and accession by General Assembly resolution A/RES/54/263 of25 May 2000, entered into force on 18 January 2002. Moreover, several States have assumed the responsibility of preventing that their nationals exploit child prostitutes abroad not only by providing legal remedies after the fact but also by attempting to prevent that such sex tours take place for example, by means of denying passports. Example used by M. Sornarajah, 'State Responsibility for Harms by Corporate Nationals Abroad', chapter 18 in: *Torture as Tort. Comparative Perspectives on the Development of Transnational Human Rigths Litigation,*, Graig Scott [ed.], Hart Publishing, Oxford etc. 2001, pp. 491-512, at p. 503.

responsibility must be taken into account. Host States might strongly resist regulation by the home State on their territory. Their reluctance may stem from the perceived interference that home States might have with Host State's choices and development programmes, which are seen as functions of the host States' domestic jurisdiction. Furthermore, in practice it will not be easy to establish in which State the true control lies due to the often extremely complicated corporate structures of corporations. Moreover, home States might be reluctant to regulate or hold corporations accountable, fearing that interference with the free market economy might lead to a competitive disadvantage.

The law of State responsibility offers an interesting, yet under-utilised tool for addressing human rights violations resulting from corporate activities. Several obstacles remain, however. This necessitates alternative approaches to the issue. It is interesting to examine the private law solutions that are emerging in various States. In this litigation the direct responsibility of corporations for human rights violations is addressed. This will be examined in the next chapter.

Chapter VII
Accountability at the National Level

1 Introduction

In the previous chapter it was demonstrated that the obligation to protect human rights requires that States regulate activities of corporations under their own jurisdiction. Moreover, it was pointed out that in various areas international law is moving towards an obligation on the part of the home State to control corporate activities abroad. It was submitted that such an obligation is also applicable in the field of human rights. It may be argued that the duty to protect not only requires that home States try to prevent corporate human rights violations abroad, but also provide a remedy if such a violation does occur. In the light of this it is interesting to discuss the developments in several national jurisdictions, notably in the field of civil litigation.

This chapter will first address the emergent civil case-law in the United States concerning corporations and human rights violations. Under the Alien Tort Claims Act, a civil law statute, actions have been initiated against private entities, including corporations, claiming violations of international human rights standards. Such violations may give rise to tortious liability.[1]

Secondly, this chapter will address developments in civil litigation against a corporation in its home State, *viz.* the State where the parent company is registered. In several States, civil actions have been brought against corporations for human rights violations committed by their subsidiaries abroad. The emphasis will be on civil actions in the British courts, where it has been decided that a parent company may owe a legal duty of care towards those who are affected by the overseas operations of their subsidiaries. A violation of this duty may constitute a (national) tort. As opposed to the litigation in the United States, these cases do not explicitly refer to international human rights law as the source of the tort. Nevertheless, these cases are relevant for our purpose for two reasons. Firstly, if national courts apply national law that incorporates

---

1 Tort is a national law construction. However, under the Alien Tort Claims Act, the norm that is violated is an international norm and, therefore, such a violation constitutes a distinct category: the international tort. See: Ian Seiderman, *Hierarchy in International Law. The Human Rights Dimension*, Intersentia, Antwerp etc., 2001, pp. 245-247. For a discussion of the specific category of international human rights torts, see: Michael Swan, 'International Human Rights Tort Claims and the Experience of United States Courts: An Introduction to the US Case-law, Key Statutes and Doctrines', in: *Torture as Tort. Comparative Perspectives on the Development of Transnational Human Rights Litigation*, Craig Scott [ed.], Hart Publishing, Oxford, 2001, pp. 65-107.

international law they indirectly give effect to international law. And, secondly, the British litigation is, as will be discussed below, particularly relevant in the light of 'piercing the corporate veil'.

Besides the cases in the United States and the United Kingdom, other national legal systems also offer opportunities in the field of civil law for claims against corporate perpetrators of human rights violations. Several cases in different countries will be discussed.

It is not intended – nor is it possible[2] – to present an exhaustive overview of national mechanisms for the liability of corporations. The purpose of this section is to highlight, by an examination of selected case-law, the possibilities and problems of holding corporations accountable in domestic courts. Moreover, the civil cases are interesting as they test the doctrinal and conceptual obstacles to litigating human rights claims against corporations and articulate the norms to which corporations can be held accountable.

2 Invoking International Law in Domestic Courts

In view of the fact that at present corporations cannot be held directly accountable before a tribunal or court at the international level,[3] national courts are the prime forums for holding these entities accountable for violations of international law. Before discussing the various cases a few preliminary remarks should be made with regard to the relationship between international law and the national legal systems in general. More specifically, the answer to the question whether international human rights obligations for corporations can be enforced in the national realm depends on the status of international law in the domestic legal system.

Two theories with regard to the relationship between international and national law can be discerned: the theories of monism and dualism. According to the doctrine of monism international law and national law exist alongside each other in one single system of law. In the dualist view, however, international law and national law are two distinct legal systems and there is no automatic interrelationship between the two.[4] It would seem that the implementation of international law is better guaranteed in a monistic system. However, this is certainly not always true. A restrictive interpretation by the judiciary may frustrate the application of international law in monistic systems.

2 The last two decades have witnessed a proliferation, notably in the United States, of the number of civil lawsuits that have been filed against corporations claiming corporate involvement in human rights violations. In most of these cases a final decision has not yet been delivered. The cases that will be discussed in this chapter are dealt with because they have advanced beyond the initial stages in the legal proceedings.

3 See chapter VIII.

4 Ian Brownlie, *Principles of Public International Law*, 5th ed., Clarendon Press, Oxford, 1998, pp. 31-34.

Several authors stress the important part which the national judiciary plays in the effective implementation of international law.[5] The important role played by the judiciary regarding the effective implementation of international law on the domestic level clearly comes to the fore in the case-law that will be discussed below.

3 Civil Litigation in the United States: the International Tort

In United States federal courts a potentially far-reaching development is taking place with regard to corporate liability for human rights violations on the basis of the application of the Alien Tort Claims Act (ATCA).[6] This Act enables aliens to seek civil remedies in American courts for violations of the law of nations. The ATCA was originally enacted as section 9 of the Judiciary Act of 1789.[7] One of the original purposes of the ATCA was to provide a remedy in the American courts for aliens who were mistreated on American soil.[8] In its current form the ATCA provides that district courts in the United States shall have jurisdiction over 'any civil action by an alien[9] for a tort only, committed in violation of the law of nations or a treaty of the United States'.[10]

The alien does not have to be physically present in the United States nor does the tort to have occurred there. Moreover, the defendant does not have to be American or to live in the United States. However, the defendant has to be properly served in order for personal jurisdiction to arise. Hence, an individual visiting the United States can be served and thereby become subject to the jurisdiction of United States courts. Where

5 Pieter van Dijk, 'Domestic Status of Human-Rights Treaties and the Attitude of the Judiciary: The Dutch case', in: *Fortschritt im Bewusstsein der Grund- und Menschenrechte*, Manfred Nowak, Dorothea Steurer, Hannes Tretter [eds], N.P. Engel Verlag Kehl, Strasbourg etc.,1988, pp. 631-650, see pp. 631-632; Fried van Hoof, 'International Human Rights Obligations for Companies and Domestic Courts: An Unlikely Combination?', in: *The Role of the Nation-State in the 21st Century: human rights, international organisations and foreign policy: essays in honour of Peter Baehr,* Monique Castermans-Holleman, Fried van Hoof and Jacqueline Smith [eds.], Kluwer, The Hague, 1998, pp. 47-59, at p.57-58; and Rosalyn Higgins, *Problems and Process. International Law and How We Use It,* Clarendon Press, New York, 1994, at p. 208.

6 28 U.S.C. para. 1350 (1994). The Alien Tort Claims Act is also referred to as the Alien Tort Act and the Alien Tort Statute. For the sake of consistency I will refer to its current formal title: Alien Tort Claims Act (ATCA). For a sound analysis of the ATCA, see: Beth Stephens and Michael Ratner, *International Human Rights Litigation in U.S. Courts*, Transnational Publishers, New York, 1996.

7 Judiciary Act of 1789, Ch. 20, para. 9 1 Stat. 73.

8 Adriane K. Sacharoff, 'Multinationals in Host Countries: Can They Be Held Liable Under the Alien Tort Claims Act for Human Rights Violations', in: *Brooklyn Journal of International Law*, Vol. XXIII, No.3, 1998, pp. 927-964, at p. 938. This view of the original purpose of the ATCA is held by the majority of scholars. However, the original intent of the ATCA is rather obscure and different views exist. For an overview, see: Seiderman, *supra* n. 1, p. 246, note 6 and the sources cited there.

9 An individual, his/her legal representative or a person who may be a claimant in an action for wrongful death. See: Stephens and Ratner, *supra* n. 6, pp. 42-47.

10 28 U.S.C. Sec. 1350 (1994).

the defendant is a corporation, the court will assume that it is physically present when that corporation 'conducts business' in the State where the complaint is filed.

Prior to 1980 the ATCA was a rather obscure statute for most of its 200-year existence, having only been successfully invoked twice.[11] Recently, the ATCA has been used by aliens seeking redress in United States courts for human rights violations abroad.

3.1 Evolution of the Alien Tort Claims Act

The interpretation of the ATCA by the American judiciary underscores the importance of the attitude of the judiciary regarding the effective implementation of international law. Several court decisions have considerably widened the scope of the ATCA, allowing aliens to seek civil redress for human rights violations committed outside the territory of the United States. In this section the evolution of the ATCA will be discussed, based on these court decisions, in order to establish the present scope of the ATCA.[12] In the next section, a number of recent cases in which the ATCA has been invoked against corporations will be analysed.

The first landmark case, filed in 1980, invoking the ATCA dealt with the question of what constitutes the law of nations. This was the *Filartiga v. Pena-Irala* case.[13] In this case two citizens of Paraguay, Mr and Mrs Filartiga, brought suit against another Paraguayan citizen, Mr Pena-Irala. The Filartigas alleged that in 1976 Pena, then Inspector General of Police in Asuncion, Paraguay, tortured and killed their son because of his father's political beliefs. While Pena was in the United States, he was served with a summons and a civil complaint. The district court dismissed the claim for lack of subject-matter jurisdiction.[14] The Second Circuit Court, however, reversed this decision and used the ATCA for the first time as a means for alien plaintiffs to assert jurisdiction in United States courts for human rights violations abroad. In this case there was clearly a tort and the claim was brought by an alien. Therefore, the question in this case was whether the alleged acts had violated the law of nations. In the *Filartiga* case, the court held that international law was derived from a plethora of

---

11 *Bolchos* v. *Darrell*, 3 F. Cas. 810 (D.S.C. 1795) involving cargo (slaves) seized as a prize of war and *Adra* v. *Clift* 195 F. Supp. 857 (D. Md. 1961) which was an international custody dispute.

12 Hoping to clarify the scope of the ATCA the Torture Victim Protection Act (TVPA) (Pub. L. No.1 102-256, 106 Stat. 73 (1992); 28 U.S.C. 1350) was enacted in 1992, which enables United States citizens and aliens to sue in the case of torture and extra-judicial killing. This Act, however, specifically excludes claims brought against purely private groups by stating that liability only arises when an *individual* is acting under '*actual or apparent authority, or color of law of any foreign nation*' [emphasis added]. Furthermore, in the case *Tom Beanal* v. *Freeport-McMoran* 969 F. Supp. 362 (E.D. La. 1997) at 381-382 (see p. 185) the court explicitly stated that the TVPA does not apply to corporations. Therefore the TVPA will not be considered any further in this study.

13 630 F. 2d 876 (2d Cir. 1980).

14 No. 79 C 917 (E.D.N.Y, May 15, 1979).

sources: '[T]he works of jurists, writing professedly on public law; or by the general usage and practice of nations; or by judicial decisions recognizing and enforcing that law'.[15] Furthermore, the court opined that international law is an evolving concept by observing that: 'courts must interpret international law not as it was in 1789 but as it has evolved and exists among the nations of the world today'.[16] This widened the range of norms of international law whose violations might give rise to international tortious liability under the ATCA.

The court decided that torture perpetrated under the colour of law, by a State against its own nationals, was nowadays to be considered a violation of the law of nations.[17] In this decision the Court extended the international law principle of universal jurisdiction to civil litigation in the United States. As the Court concluded in *Filartiga*: '[F]or purposes of civil liability the torturer has become – like the pirate and the slave trader before him – *hostis humani generis*, an enemy of all mankind.'[18]

A further important development concerned the applicability of the ATCA to other than State-actors. In the earliest ATCA cases the courts found that private actors could be liable under the ATCA.[19] Although the court in the *Filartiga* case did not explicitly determine that the ATCA does not extend to private action,[20] this decision did introduce the requirement that the defendant should be a State, by holding that torture *perpetrated under the colour of law* was a violation of the law of nations. The question whether the ATCA also covers private acts was not addressed until *Tel-Oren* v. *Libyan Arab Republic*.[21] In this case it was decided that international law was based on States and in 1984 had not been extended to hold non-state actors liable. The court, therefore, decided that it did not have jurisdiction over the plaintiffs' causes of action, which were of a non-State origin. Judge Edwards wrote a noteworthy dissenting opinion in this case. He commented that private individuals were considered to be bound by international law prior to the 19th century. However, at the time of this case, individual responsibility under international law remained available, in the face of the 19th century trend towards statism, for a handful of private acts only, including piracy and

15 *Filartiga* 630 F. 2d at 880.
16 *Filartiga* 630 F. 2d at 880-881.
17 *Filartiga* 630 F. 2d at 878.
18 *Filartiga* 630 F. 2d at 890.
19 See the cases *Bolchos* v. *Darrel* 3 F. Cas. 810 (D.S.C. 1795) and *Adra* v. *Clift* 195, F. Supp. 857 862-865 (D. Md. 1961).
20 *Filartiga* 630 F. 2d at 880.
21 726 F. 2d 774 (DC Cir 1984), see at 792-95. In this case the representatives of persons killed on a civilian bus in Israel, along with the injured survivors of the attack, sued the Libyan Arab Republic, the Palestine Liberation Organisation, the Palestine Information Office, the National Association of Arab Americans and the Palestine Congress of North America. The plaintiffs charged the defendants with multiple tortuous acts in violation of international law.

slave trading.[22] Edwards acknowledged that the recognition of a larger measure of individual responsibility under international law might be gaining strength. Nevertheless, he concluded that at that time the idea 'was not so widely accepted doctrinally or practically to represent the consensus among nations'.[23]

In a third significant case invoking the ATCA, *In Re Estate of Ferdinand E. Marcos Human Rights Litigation/Trajano* v. *Marcos*,[24] the court repeated that liability under the ATCA can only be triggered by State action. In this case, a citizen of Hawaii brought suit against the former president of the Philippines, Ferdinand E. Marcos, and his daughter, Imee Marcos-Manotoc, for the torture and wrongful death of her son. The court rejected the liability of purely private individuals and groups under the law of nations holding that a violation of international law can only be properly pleaded where the defendants have allegedly acted under the colour of official authority.[25]

The most expansive reading of the ATCA to include private actors as defendants is the 1995 United States Second Circuit Court decision in the case *Kadic* v. *Karadzic/ Doe* v. *Karadzic* (hereinafter *Kadic* case).[26] In this case, Croat and Muslim citizens of the internationally recognised nation of Bosnia-Herzegovina alleged that they had been victims of various atrocities, including rape, forced prostitution and impregnation, torture and other cruel, inhuman and degrading treatment, assault and battery, gender and ethnic inequality, summary execution and wrongful death. These atrocities formed part of a genocidal campaign conducted by military forces under the command of the Bosnian Serb leader Radovan Karadzic.[27] In early 1993 Karadzic was personally served with the summons and complaint in each action while he was physically present in Manhattan as an invitee of the United Nations. The judge decided that on the basis of case precedent, legislative history and scholarly work non-state activity was not covered by the law of nations. The ATCA did not therefore confer subject-matter jurisdiction.[28] In the decision of the Second Circuit reversing this lower court decision, the scope of the ATCA was widened to include the liability of private actors for certain human rights violations. The court disagreed with the proposition

22 *Tel-Oren*, 726 F .2d 774 (DC Cir 1984) at 794.

23 *Tel-Oren*, 726 F. 2d 774 (DC Cir 1984) at 793.

24 25 978 F. 2d 493 (9th Cir, 1992) This case was one of several cases brought against the estate of Ferdinand Marcos in District Courts in Hawaii and California by thousands of victims of human rights abuses during the Marcos regime in the Philippines.

25 In *re Estate of Ferdinand E. Marcos Human Rights Litigation,* 978 F. 2d 493 (9th Cir, 1992) at 501-502.

26 *Kadic* v. *Karadzic*, 70 F. 3d 232 (2nd Cir. 1995).

27 *Kadic*, 70 F. 3d at 237. Simultaneously another lawsuit was filed against Karadzic by two individuals representing a class suing for genocide, war crimes, crimes against humanity, rape and other torture, summary execution and other abuses. The two cases were consolidated for decision in the district court and Second Circuit.

28 866 F. Supp. 734 (S.D.N.Y. 1994). See at 739-741.

> 'that the law of nations, as understood, in the modern era, confines its reach to state action. Instead [the Court held] that certain forms of conduct violate the law of nations whether undertaken by those acting under the auspices of a state or only as private individuals.'[29]

The Court held that:

> 'participation in the slave trade violates the law of nations whether undertaken by those acting under the auspices of a state or only as private individuals.'[30]

In contrast, the court held that rape, torture and summary execution, when not perpetrated in the course of genocide or war crimes, are proscribed by international law only when the perpetrators are acting in an official capacity.[31]

The decision in this case has given rise to a great deal of discussion regarding the limits of the ATCA. Some authors argue that the second circuit court, in holding that the ATCA can be used to cover non-State conduct, overstepped the proper boundaries of the ATCA. For example, Lu argues that given the weight of American case precedent, legislative intent and concerns about United States courts meddling in foreign affairs by acting as an international watchdog, the second circuit court should have affirmed the district court's holding that the ATCA cannot be used to cover non-State activity.[32] However, as has been stressed by the courts in the above-mentioned cases, the ATCA must be interpreted in the light of present-day circumstances. The determination that the ATCA in some cases covers private action is in line with this rationale.

In sum, it may be concluded that over the past twenty years, decisions of the United States courts have expanded the reach of the ATCA, both with regard to subject-matter jurisdiction and personal jurisdiction.

3.2 The Alien Tort Claims Act and Corporations

Since the first landmark case under the ATCA, *Filartiga*, the range of defendants has widened to include private individuals. Recent decisions have included corporate

---

29 *Kadic* 70 F. 3d at 239.

30 *Kadic* 70 F. 3d at 239.

31 Outside the context of genocide or war crimes, rape, torture and summary execution are only considered a violation of international law when committed by state officials or under colour of law, *Kadic* 70 F. 3d at 243.

32 Justin Lu, 'Jurisdiction over Non-State Activity under the Alien Tort Claims Act', in: *Colombia Journal of Transnational Law*, Vol. 35, 1997, pp. 531-549, at pp. 549. See also: Lyal S. Sunga, *Individual Responsibility in International Law for Serious Human Rights Violations*, Martinus Nijhoff, Dordrecht, 1992.

entities within the range of defendants under the ATCA.[33] So far, in none of these cases has a decision been reached on the merits. Nevertheless, from the cases discussed in the previous section three principles emerge that make the ATCA potentially very important in the light of corporate liability for human rights violations.

Firstly, the court in the *Karadic* case decided that certain offences committed by private defendants also fall within the ATCA jurisdictional net. Secondly, in the *Filartiga* case the court held that international law is evolving and should be interpreted in its present-day context. This opens the possibility of expanding possible international tortious liability. Thirdly, in the *Filartiga* case the court affirmed that, despite the fact that the offence had occurred outside the United States, the United States federal court had jurisdiction as the tort follows the offender.[34] This implies that, in theory, a claim regarding a human rights violation, irrespective of where it occurs, can be brought before a United States court. The ATCA merely requires that the alleged offender is physically present in the United States. In the case of a corporation it must have contacts with the United States, such as an office or an official representative or it must be conducting business in this country.

To provide a better understanding of the ATCA and its implications for holding corporations accountable for human rights violations, the factual and procedural backgrounds to a selection of cases will be dealt with in the following sections.[35]

The Texaco cases

The first major case against a corporation that relied on the ATCA was the litigation addressing *Texaco's* oil-producing activities in Ecuador. The plaintiffs, rain-forest Indians from Ecuador and Peru, alleged that *Texaco*, in a joint venture with the national

---

33 So far, most of the cases invoking the ATCA have concerned corporations that deal with resource extraction. This is to be expected. These corporations tend to be among the largest companies in the world. The nature of their activities and the location of the resources tend to bring these corporations into situations where human rights are frequently abused. See: *Human Rights and the Oil Industry*, Asbjørn Eide, Helge Ole Bergesen and Pia Rudolfson Goyer [eds.], Intersentia, Antwerp etc., 2000.

34 *Filartiga*, 630 F. 2d at 885.

35 As already mentioned in note 2, I will, in the light of the overwhelming number of cases filed under the ATCA, only discuss the major cases, notably the ones that have advanced the furthest in the legal procedure. At the time of writing, complaints have also been filed against, *inter alia*, *Talisman* regarding its activities in Sudan, *DynCorp* regarding the company's conduct in Ecuador and Colombia, *The Coca Cola Company* for alleged complicity in human rights violations in Colombia, *ExxonMobil* for alleged harmful conduct in Aceh, Indonesia and *DelMonte* regarding activities in Colombia. For a detailed description and thorough analysis of the ATCA cases against corporations up until 1999, see Saman Zia-Zarifi, 'Suing multinational corporations in the U.S. for violating international law', in *UCLA Journal of International Law & Foreign Affairs*, Vol. 81, 1999, pp. 81-147. See also: Beth Stephens, 'Corporate Accountability: International Human Rights Litigation Against Corporations in US Courts' and Jennifer Green and Paul Hoffman, 'US Litigation Update', both in: *Liability of Multinational Corporations Under International Law*, Menno T. Kamminga and Saman Zia-Zarifi [eds.], Kluwer Law International, The Hague etc., 2000, pp. 209- 240.

Ecuadorian oil company, had damaged the natural environment and the way of life of the plaintiffs during their oil-extraction activities between 1972-1992. According to the plaintiffs, *Texaco* handled wastes improperly, several oil spills occurred and pipelines did burst, all of which resulted in extensive environmental damage. The first complaint in this case was dismissed by the federal court in 1994.[36] A different set of plaintiffs, with claims arising out of the same operations in Ecuador, sued *Texaco* in New York where the corporation is based.[37] The Second Circuit court held that the claim could be heard in New York and sent it back to the District Court for a review of jurisdictional and legal requirements.[38]

The environmental claims in these cases may constitute a violation of customary international law.[39] This would provide a valid cause of action under the ATCA. As the claims against *Texaco* relied solely on violations of international environmental law and did not cite international human rights law the *Texaco* cases will not be dealt with at any length here.[40] Nevertheless, the cases against *Texaco* make it clear that environmental destruction may trigger jurisdiction under the ATCA.

Beanal v. Freeport McMoRan

Several cases, invoking the ATCA, have been brought against the United States mining companies *Freeport-McMoran Inc.* and *Freeport-McMoran Copper & Gold* (hereinafter: *Freeport*). These companies have their headquarters in Louisiana, United States. *Freeport* operates the 'Grasberg Mine', an open-pit copper, gold and silver mine

---

36 The case was first filed in a State court against *Texaco* along with Ecuador's State-owned oil company, *Petroecuador*. Within five months it was removed to a federal court that dismissed it on grounds of *forum non conveniens* and international comity. This case had not yet invoked the ATCA. *Sequiha* v. *Texaco Inc.*, 847 F. Supp. 61 (S.D. Tex. 1994).

37 Two separate actions were filed in this suit. The first, *Aguinda* v. *Texaco*, S.D.N.Y. Dkt. No. 93 Civ. 7527, with plaintiffs from the Oriente region of Ecuador and the second, *Jota* v. *Texaco*, 157 F. 3d 153 (2nd Cir. 1998) filed by Peruvian farmers living downstream from Texaco's operations.

38 *Jota* v. *Texaco Inc*, 157 F. 3d 153 (2d Cir. 1998). The case was remanded and oral arguments were heard in February 1999. In January 2000, the Court ordered an additional briefing on whether the case could be heard in Ecuador in the light of the military coup that had occurred there on 21 January 2000. At the time of writing this case is still pending.

39 In the case of *Aguinda* v. *Texaco* and in the case of *Beanal* v. *Freeport* McMoran, discussed in the following section, the court held that environmental claims might be admissible under the ATCA as far as they refer to the principle of 'good neighborliness' and Principle 2 of the Rio Declaration (regarding the responsibility of the State not to harm their neighbours' environment). According to the Court these two principles could be considered to have reached the level of universality and specificity necessary to support ATCA-jurisdiction. See, Zia-Zarifi, *supra* n. 35, pp. 114-120.

40 This study concentrates on violations of human rights. Environmental deprivation will only be discussed when formulated as human rights violations. For more on the applicability of the ATCA in the context of international environmental law, see: Zia-Zarifi, *supra* n. 35, For a detailed analysis of the *Texaco* litigation, see: Zennith K. Rankins, 'U.S. Laws in the Rainforest: Can a U.S. Court Find Liability for Extraterritorial Pollution Caused by a U.S. Corporation?: An Analysis of *Aguinda* v.*Texaco*, in: *Boston College International and Comparative Law Review*, Vol. 18, 1995, pp. 221-263.

covering approximately 26,400 square kilometres in Irian Jaya, Indonesia. In 1997, Beanal, the leader of the Amungme tribe of Indonesia, filed a complaint in the United States federal district court.[41] In his first, amended, complaint Beanal alleged that the corporation had committed environmental torts, human rights violations by acting in conjunction with the Indonesian army (e.g. arbitrary arrest and detention, torture, and destruction of property) and cultural genocide[42] in the course of the extraction of gold and copper.

As has been discussed above,[43] for jurisdiction to arise under the ATCA over entities other than a State for violations of international law they must occur 'under the colour of law', except for slavery and some violations committed in the course of genocide and war crimes. The cases against *Freeport* combined claims that are actionable absent of State action, such as genocide, with claims that are only actionable if the alleged violations took place under the colour of State authority, such as torture. For the last-mentioned claim, the court had to examine whether the defendant *Freeport* had engaged in State action.

In *Beanal* the court listed the four tests formulated by the Supreme Court, which determine whether a private actor can be held to have acted under the colour of law.[44] Firstly, the *nexus test*, according to which a plaintiff must demonstrate that there is a sufficiently close nexus between the government and the challenged conduct such that the conduct may fairly be treated as that of the State itself. Secondly, under the *symbiotic relationship test*, State action is established if a State has brought itself into such a position of interdependence with a private party that it must be recognized as a joint participant in the challenged activity. The State and the private entity need to be physically and financially integral. Thirdly, according to the *joint action test*, State action is present where a private party is a wilful participant in joint action with the State or its agents. And, finally, the *public function test*, where State action is taken to exist when private entities perform a function that is traditionally the exclusive prerogative of the State.

41 *Beanal* v. *Freeport-McMoran Inc.*, 969 F. Supp. 362 (E.D. La. 1997). A case concerning the same matter was filed in a State court: *Yosofa Alomang* v. *Freeport-McMoran*, 97-1349 (La. App. 4th Cir., 03/04/98);718 So. 2d 971; 1998 La. App. LEXIS 335. In March 2000, the case was dismissed. The court stated that the plaintiffs failed to establish that the Indonesian subsidiary was the legal alterego of *Freeport-McMoran*.

42 Beanal claimed that the activities of *Freeport* resulted in the displacement, relocation and purposeful, deliberate, contrived and planned demise of a culture of indigenous people. The court found that the claim for genocide was not sufficiently clear. To prove genocide it has to be demonstrated that certain acts are committed with the intent to destroy a target group, in whole or in part. Beanal was given the opportunity to make a more definitive statement.

43 See p. 181.

44 *Beanal* v. *Freeport-McMoran Inc.*, 969 F. Supp. 362 (E.D. La. 1997) at 367, citing *Gallagher* v. *Neil Young Freedom Concert*, 49 F. 3d 1442, 1446 (10th Cir. 1995).

The complaint in this case was insufficient under all these tests to determine whether there was State action. The complaint failed to state the role that the Indonesian army had played in the challenged conduct. The plaintiff was required under the joint action test to allege that the Indonesian military 'jointly co-operated in the conduct, jointly participated in the conduct, influenced the conduct or played an integral part in the deprivation of human rights'.[45] Because Beanal failed, after several attempts, to do so, the court dismissed his claim of human rights violations under the ATCA.[46]

Doe v. Unocal

To date, the most advanced cases in which the ATCA has been held applicable to companies for human rights violations are the cases brought against the American corporation *Unocal.* In 1994 *Unocal* and *Total S.A.*, a French corporation, entered into a production-sharing contract with the *Myanmar Oil and Gas Enterprise (MOGE)* to develop and commercialise the Yadana oil field off the coast of Burma (Myanmar) by establishing platforms there and constructing a pipeline to transport gas from the field to the Thai border. *MOGE* is a company wholly owned by the *State Law and Order Restoration Council (SLORC). SLORC* is the current government of Burma and has been heavily criticised by the international community for human rights violations.[47] The joint venture hired *SLORC* to clear and level the ground and to provide for labour materials and security for the project.

A group of farmers from the Tenasserim region in Burma filed a complaint under the ATCA in the United States federal court of California against *Unocal Corp.*[48] *Total,*[49] *MOGE, SLORC*[50] and the president and chief executive officer of *Unocal*

45 *Beanal* v. *Freeport-McMoran Inc.*, 969 F. Supp. 362 (E.D. La. 1997), p. 18.

46 The court did grant the plaintiff the opportunity to amend his complaint in order to specifically underpin his claims for genocide and human rights violations. See: *Beanal* v. *Freeport-McMoran Inc.*, 969 F. Supp. 362 (E.D. La. 1997), p. 24. In the second amended complaint, Beanal added many new allegations without clarifying the statements on issues of genocide and State action. Therefore, the court dismissed this complaint in August 1997 and further granted leave to Beanal to amend his complaint, *Beanal* v. *Freeport-McMoran Inc.*, 1997, U.S.Dist. LEXIS 12001 (E.D. La. Aug. 8, 1997). On appeal, the fifth circuit upheld the District court's decision to dismiss the case, *Beanal* v. *Freeport-McMoran Inc.*, 197 F. 3d 161 (5th Cir. 1999). A *certiorari* petition was rejected by the United States Supreme Court as untimely on 6 March 2000.

47 See, *inter alia*, *Forced labour in Myanmar (Burma)*, Report of the Commission of Inquiry Appointed Under Article 26 of the Constitution of the International Labour Organisation to Examine the Observance by Myanmar of the Forced Labour Convention, 1930 (No. 29), ILO, Part IV, Geneva, 2 July 1998.

48 Based in California but with an additional headquarters in Kuala Lumpur.

49 The court decided that it lacked personal jurisdiction over the French corporation *Total.*

50 The court dismissed the claims against *SLORC* and *MOGE* on the grounds of sovereign immunity. For more on the doctrine of State immunity in the case of commercial activities, see: Robert Wai, 'The Commercial Activity Exception to Sovereign Immunity and the Boundaries of Contemporary International Legalism', in: *Torture as Tort. Comparative Perspectives on the Development of Transnational Human Rights Litigation*, Graig Scott [ed.], Hart Publishing, Oxford etc., 2001, pp. 213-247.

Corp. (hereinafter *Unocal I*).[51] A related action was brought against the same defendants by the Burmese government in exile (*the National Coalition Government of the Union of Burma (NCGUB)*), the federation of Trade Unions of Burma and four refugees from the Tenasserim region of Burma (hereinafter *Unocal II*).[52] According to the plaintiffs, *SLORC,* in providing for services, had committed numerous human rights violations; forced labour (enslaving farmers living in the area of the proposed pipeline); violence; intimidation; relocation of entire villages; stealing farmers' property; illegal detentions; murder; assault; rape; and other forms of torture.[53] The plaintiffs claimed that *Unocal* was put on notice that *SLORC* would use forced labour and commit other serious human rights abuses, but that the corporation dismissed those warnings.

The court decided that the ATCA was applicable in the case against *Unocal.* First, the court dealt with the claim of torture that requires State action. The court considered whether in this case private action could be deemed to be that of the State, based on the test of joint action.[54] In *Unocal I* the court held that 'where there is a "substantial degree of co-operative action" between the State and private actors in effecting the deprivation of rights, State action is present'.[55] According to the court in *Unocal II,*

> 'Joint action exists, not only where a conspiracy is alleged, but also where a private party is "a wilful participant in joint action with the State or its agents". (…) Nonetheless, a private person is only liable under a joint action theory if the particular actions challenged are inextricably intertwined with those of the government.'[56]

In the case of *Unocal II* the court decided that:

> 'the individual plaintiffs' allegations are sufficient to support subject-matter jurisdiction under the ATCA because, when construed in the light most favourable to plaintiffs, they suggest that Unocal may have been a wilful participant in joint action with the State or its agents.'[57]

This opinion of the court is significant in the light of the fact that corporations frequently enter into joint ventures with foreign governments and, as is shown in this

---

51 *John Doe I* v. *Unocal Corp.*, 963 F. Supp. 880 (C.D. Cal. 1997).

52 *National Coalition Government of the Union of Burma* v. *Unocal, Inc.*, 1997 U.S. Dist. Lexis 2097. The same judge, Judge Paez, dealt with both cases. In *Unocal II* Paez clarified his earlier decision in *Unocal I.*

53 *Unocal II*, 1997 U.S. Dist. Lexis 2097 p. 4.

54 See p. 186.

55 *Unocal I*, 963 F.Supp. 880 at 891.

56 *Unocal II*, 1997 U.S. Dist. Lexis 2097 at 349.

57 *Unocal II*, 1997 U.S. Dist. Lexis 2097 p. 20.

judgment, that such collaboration may result in labelling the corporate activities as State activities.[58]

More importantly, however, the Court also examined whether in the absence of State action *Unocal* could conceivably be liable for certain violations of international law. The court referred to the dissenting opinion of Judge Edwards in the *Tel-Oren* case[59] and the decision in the *Kadic* case,[60] where it was held that participation in slave trading is included in the handful of private acts to which the law of nations attributes individual responsibility even in the absence of State action. In *Unocal II* the Court ruled that forced labour may, under certain circumstances, amount to participation in slave trade. In the words of the court:

> 'The allegations of forced labour in this case may be sufficient to state a claim for participation in slave trading. Although plaintiffs do not allege that SLORC is physically selling Burmese citizens to the private defendants, plaintiffs allege that Unocal has knowingly accepted the benefit of and approved the use of forced labor in connection with the Project.'[61]

The court very easily equated forced labour with slave trading. After doing so the court had to ascertain whether the international norm against slavery could be applied against a corporate defendant. There were no allegations that the corporation had directly participated in the selling of Burmese citizens. The court held that it was sufficient that:

> 'the private defendants have paid and continue to pay SLORC to provide labor and security for the pipeline, essentially treating SLORC as an overseer, accepting the benefit of and approving the use of forced labor. These allegations are sufficient to establish subject-matter jurisdiction under the ATCA'.[62]

Zia-Zarifi points out that in this decision the court for the first time applied the principle of 'command responsibility' to corporate defenders.[63] This principle was first developed at the Nuremberg trials and imposes liability on persons in a command structure for allowing abuses that they knew or should have known were taking place. This principle offers an interesting solution to the problems that the often very complicated corporate structures pose.

---

58 Nevertheless, the factual requirements to satisfy the State action test are very high as came to the fore in the *Beanal* cases.

59 See p. 181.

60 See p. 182.

61 *Unocal II*, 1997 U.S. Dist. Lexis 2097, p. 21.

62 *Unocal I*, 963 F. Supp at 892.

63 Zia-Zarifi, *supra* n. 35, p. 106, note 101.

Finally, in September 2000, a federal district court dismissed the cases against *Unocal*. Judge Lew held that the fact that *Unocal* and *SLORC* 'shared the goal of a profitable project' was not enough to constitute joint action and *Unocal* could, therefore, not be held liable as a *de facto* State. According to the court, there was 'no evidence that Unocal "participated in or influenced" the military's unlawful conduct' nor that 'Unocal "conspired" with the military to commit the challenged conduct'.[64] Moreover, the court concluded that there was no evidence that *Unocal* controlled the decision of the Burmese military to commit the alleged tortious acts.[65] The court went on to conclude that *Unocal* could also not be held individually liable. According to the court, for individual liability to arise, participation or cooperation is required. Mere knowledge of someone else's abuses is not sufficient for liability to arise. According to Judge Lew

> '[t]he evidence does suggest that Unocal knew that forced labor was being utilized and that the Joint Venturers benefited from the practice. However, because such a showing is insufficient to establish liability under international law, Plaintiffs' claim against Unocal for forced labor under the Alien Tort Claims Act fails as a matter of law.'[66]

With this decision the district court has significantly narrowed the scope of the ATCA. For jurisdiction to arise, the corporation does not only have to be a 'wilful participant' in the alleged act, but it will have to be proven that the corporation in fact *controlled* the activities of the State. In this line of reasoning, instead of participation, control over the alleged violations has to be proven for ATCA jurisdiction to arise. Moreover, the decision of the district court dismissed the previous ruling that benefiting from a practice is sufficient to trigger jurisdiction under the ATCA. According to the judgment, it would have to be demonstrated that the corporation actually sought to, *in casu*, employ forced labour. The district court reached this conclusion after reviewing cases against corporations brought before the World War II Military Tribunal. This explains the more restrictive approach of the district court. As will be discussed in the following chapter, the legacy of the Nuremberg trials has resulted in a rather cautious approach to the concept of collective accountability.[67]

64 *John Doe I* v. *Unocal Corp./John Roe III* v. *Unocal Corp.*, Case Nos. CV 96-6959, CV 96-6112 (C.D. CA 2000) under section 3. At the time of writing, the claims are on appeal to the United States Ninth Circuit Court of Appeals. Moreover, the case will also be heard in a California State court. On 30 August 2001, California Superior Court Judge Victoria Chaney dismissed *Unocal's* motion to dismiss the State law claims.

65 *John Doe I* v. *Unocal Corp./John Roe III* v. *Unocal Corp.*, under section 4.

66 *John Doe I* v. *Unocal Corp./John Roe III* v. *Unocal Corp.*, under section 6.

67 Chapter VIII, pp. 222-225.

Owens Wiwa, Ken Wiwa and Blessing Kpuinen v. Royal Dutch/Shell
Another advanced case against a company based on the ATCA is the case of *Owens Wiwa, Ken Wiwa and Blessing Kpuinen* v. *Royal Dutch Petroleum Company and Shell Transport and Trading Company P.L.C.* (hereinafter: *Royal Dutch/Shell*).[68] These three Nigerians filed a lawsuit against the Dutch/Anglo corporation in the United States federal court of the Southern District of New York in November 1996. The plaintiffs claimed that the company was complicit in the hanging of Ken Saro-Wiwa and John Kpuinen, two leaders of MOSOP (Movement for the Survival of the Ogoni People),[69] the torture and detention of Owens Wiwa, and the shooting of a protestor by police officers, called in by *Shell Nigeria*.[70] While the human rights violations were perpetrated by the Nigerian military, they were allegedly instigated, orchestrated, planned and facilitated by *Shell Nigeria* under the direction of the defendants in this case. The background to the case was the resistance of the Ogoni people against the damaging activities of oil companies in Nigeria, of which *Royal Dutch/Shell* is the largest.

Soon after the filing of the lawsuit *Royal Dutch/Shell* served a multifaceted motion to dismiss.[71] On 25 September 1998, Judge Kimba Wood concluded that personal jurisdiction was appropriate in New York, but also ruled that the United Kingdom was a more convenient forum, and, therefore, that the defendants' motion to dismiss should be granted on the ground of *forum non conveniens*.[72] On 14 September 2000, the United States Court of Appeals of the 2nd Circuit, reversed the judgment of the district court, allowing the case to proceed in the United States courts.[73] The Court of Appeals argued that the continuous presence of an investor relations office representing *Royal Dutch/Shell* in New York was sufficient to fulfil the requirement of 'doing business'

68 *Ken Wiwa* v. *Royal Dutch Petroleum Co.* No. 96 Civ. 8386 (S.D.N.Y 1998).

69 Owens Wiwa and Ken Wiwa are the sons of Ken Saro-Wiwa and Blessing Kpuinen is the wife of John Kpuinen. These two Ogoni leaders were among the nine environmentalists that were condemned to death by a military tribunal and hanged on 10 November 1995. They were outspoken critics of the activities of *Shell* in the Ogoni regions of Nigeria. For more information on the Ogoni conflict, and the various actors involved see, Sigrun I. Skogly, 'Complexities in Human Rights Protection: Actors and Rights involved in the Ogoni Conflict in Nigeria', *Netherlands Quarterly of Human Rights,* Vol. 15, No. 1, 1997, pp. 47-60.

70 *Shell Nigeria (Shell Petroleum Development Company of Nigeria, Ltd.)* is a wholly-owned affiliated company of the *Royal Dutch/Shell Group.* The defendants in this case, *Royal Dutch Petroleum Company* and *Shell Transport and Trading Company Plc.*, jointly control and operate the *Royal Dutch Shell Group.*

71 The defendants' Motion to Dismiss the Complaint and their Memorandum of Law in Support of their Motion to Dismiss the Complaint were filed on 27 March 1997. On 9 April 1997, magistrate Judge Henry Pitman issued an order, permitting discovery on the issues of fact. On 16 May 1997, the defendants filed a motion to dismiss the amended complaint.

72 See p. 196.

73 *Ken Wiwa, Owens Wiwa* and *Blessing Kpuinen* v. *Royal Dutch Petroleum Company* and *Shell Transport and Trading Company. P.L.C.*, 226 F. 3d 88 (2nd Cir. 2000). This case only concerned the question of personal jurisdiction. The Court of Appeals did not therefore discuss the question of subject-matter jurisdiction. A judgment on this issue was rendered on 22 February 2002, see: p. 193.

and that consequently personal jurisdiction under the ATCA had arisen. Moreover, the court held that it was not 'unreasonable' for the case to proceed before a court in New York. In the words of the court:

> 'While it is true that certain factors normally used to assess the reasonableness of subjection to jurisdiction do favor the defendants (they are foreign corporations that face something of a burden if they litigate here, and the events in question did not occur in New York), litigation in New York would not represent any great inconvenience to the defendants. The defendants control a vast, wealthy, and far-flung business empire which operates in most parts of the globe. They have a physical presence in the forum state, have access to enormous resources, face little or no language barrier, have litigated in this country on previous occasions, have a four-decade long relationship with one of the nation's leading law firms, and are the parent companies of one of America's largest corporations, which has a very significant presence in New York. New York City, furthermore, where the trial would be held, is a major world capital which offers central location, easy access, and extensive facilities of all kinds.'[74]

Two of the plaintiffs in this case, Ken Wiwa and Owen Wiwa, were resident in the United States. This, according to the court, must also be taken into account, when reaching a decision on the appropriate forum as deference for the choice of forum should increase where it concerns United States residents.[75] Finally, the court opined that the case should proceed, as it is the policy of the United States to provide a forum for litigation with regard to violations of international human rights law. The court held that,

> '[i]f in cases of torture in violation of international law our courts exercise their jurisdiction conferred by [the ATCA] only for as long as it takes to dismiss the case for *forum non conveniens*, we will have done little to enforce the standards of the law of nations.'[76]

Royal Dutch/Shell responded to the decision of the Court of Appeals by petitioning the Supreme Court. In its petition the corporation requested the Supreme Court to review the Court of Appeals decision. Moreover, the petition included an argument seeking to overturn the *Filartiga* decision. The corporation asserted that with the *Filartiga* decision the United States federal courts had been transposed into

---

74 *Ken Wiwa, Owens Wiwa* and *Blessing Kpuinen* v. *Royal Dutch Petroleum Company* and *Shell Transport and Trading Company. Plc.*, 226 F. 3d 88 (2nd Cir. 2000).

75 *Wiwa* v. *Royal Dutch/ Shell*, 226 F. 3d 88 (2nd Cir. 2000).

76 *Wiwa* v. *Royal Dutch/ Shell*, 226 F. 3d 88 (2nd Cir. 2000).

> 'de facto international Courts of Justice with universal jurisdiction to apply international law to disputes arising out of alleged human rights abuses committed abroad against foreign nationals by their governments.'[77]

On 26 March 2001 the Supreme Court, without comment or dissent, denied *Royal Dutch/Shell*'s petition.

The question whether subject-matter jurisdiction could be established in the case of *Wiwa* versus *Royal Dutch/Shell* was decided upon on 22 February 2002.[78] The court decided that the plaintiffs adequately stated a claim with respect to alleged participation of *Royal Dutch/Shell* in: crimes against humanity; a violation of the rights to life, liberty and security of person;[79] peaceful assembly and association; torture and; cruel, inhuman or degrading treatment.[80] With regard to the latter, the court pointed out that judgments so far had been inconclusive whether 'cruel, inhuman or degrading treatment' is actionable under the ATCA. In this case the court held that, *inter alia*, the fact that Owens Wiwa was allegedly forced into exile under credible fear of arbitrary arrest, torture and death at the hands of the Nigerian military, constituted cruel, inhuman or degrading treatment.

The claims that according to the court were sufficiently grounded all require that the plaintiffs demonstrate that the corporate defendant acted under 'the colour of law'. According to the plaintiffs *Royal Dutch/Shell*, *inter alia*, met with Nigerian officials to formulate an anti-MOSOP campaign, made payments to the Nigerian military and police, provided the Nigerian military with boats and helicopters to facilitate attacks on Ogoni villages and bribed witnesses to give false testimony against Saro-Wiwa.[81]

---

77 Quotation from the *Royal Dutch Shell* petition to the Supreme Court on the website of World Monitors, Business and Human Rights Consulting (archive), www.worldmonitors.com (accessed on 1 January 2002). On file with the author.

78 *Wiwa et al.* v. *Royal Dutch Petroleum Company* and *Shell Transport and Trading Company* and *Wiwa et al.* v. *Brian Anderson*, 96 Civ. 8386 (KMW), United States District Court for the Southern District of New York, 2002, U.S. Dist. LEXIS 3293. Available at: http://www.earthrights.org/shell/mtd.02.html (accessed on 11 March 2002).

79 The court found this allegation was only sufficiently grounded with regard to the allegations made by *Doe,* an additional plaintiff, who remained anonymous for her safety. The court held that *Owens Wiwa* failed to plead facts that adequately supported his contention that *Royal Dutch/Shell* violated his right to life, liberty and personal security.

80 The court further held that plaintiff's allegations of arbitrary arrest and detention did not adequately demonstrate violations of international law and were therefore not actionable under the ATCA. *Wiwa et al.* v. *Royal Dutch Petroleum Company* and *Shell Transport and Trading Company* and *Wiwa et al.* v. *Brian Anderson*, 96 Civ. 8386 (KMW), United States District Court for the Southern District of New York, 2002, U.S. Dist. LEXIS 3293. Available at: http://www.earthrights.org/shell/mtd.02.html (accessed on 11 March 2002).

81 *Wiwa et al.* v. *Royal Dutch Petroleum Company* and *Shell Transport and Trading Company* and *Wiwa et al.* v. *Brian Anderson*, 96 Civ. 8386 (KMW), United States District Court for the Southern District of New York, 2002, U.S. Dist. LEXIS 3293, p. 21. Available at: http://www.earthrights.org/shell/mtd.02.html (accessed on 11 March 2002).

The court decided that the facts put forward by the plaintiffs would, if proven, be sufficient to demonstrate that a substantial degree of cooperative action between the corporate defendant and the Nigerian government existed and therefore would satisfy the joint action test.

With regard to the complex business structure of *Royal Dutch/Shell*, the court found that the plaintiffs adequately pled that the activities of *Shell Nigeria* could be imputed to the parent company. Plaintiffs alleged meetings between *Royal Dutch/Shell* and *Shell Nigeria* in London and the Netherlands concerning anti-MOSOP activities. The court held that

> '[s]uch factual allegation (...) are sufficient to give rise to an inference that the defendants did more that merely "hold stock" in Shell Nigeria. By involving themselves directly in Shell Nigeria's anti-MOSOP activities, and by directing these activities, defendants made Shell Nigeria their agent with respect to the torts alleged in the complaint.'[82]

Besides upholding the claims against *Royal Dutch/Shell,* the court also found that the former head of *Shell's* Nigerian subsidiary, Brian Anderson, could be sued under the Torture Victim Protection Act.[83]

Chevron

A class action complaint under the ATCA was filed in the District Court for the Northern District of California against the United States oil company *Chevron*.[84] The plaintiffs, a group of individuals from the Ilaji and Ijaw communities in Nigeria, alleged that the defendant *Chevron*, in conjunction with Nigeria's military and police force, wilfully, maliciously and systematically violated the plaintiffs' human rights, conducting, *inter alia*, summary execution, torture and unlawful arrest and detention. These violations were allegedly inflicted by the Nigerian military and police officers acting with the (financial) support and in co-operation with *Chevron* in May 1998, when they attacked the plaintiffs who were demonstrating on the company's oil-platform. The police were transported to the platform in *Chevron* helicopters. Later, in 1999, more Nigerian security troops, again travelling in *Chevron*-owned vehicles, looted several villages where protests against the oil company had taken place.

---

82 *Wiwa et al.* v. *Royal Dutch Petroleum Company* and *Shell Transport and Trading Company* and *Wiwa et al.* v. *Brian Anderson*, 96 Civ. 8386 (KMW), United States District Court for the Southern District of New York, 2002, U.S. Dist. LEXIS 3293. Available at: http://www.earthrights.org/shell/mtd.02.html (accessed on 11 March 2002).

83 *Wiwa et al.* v. *Royal Dutch Petroleum Company* and *Shell Transport and Trading Company* and *Wiwa et al.* v. *Brian Anderson*, 96 Civ. 8386 (KMW), United States District Court for the Southern District of New York, 2002, U.S. Dist. LEXIS 3293. Available at: http://www.earthrights.org/shell/mtd.02.html (accessed on 11 March 2002).

84 *Larry Bowoto et al.* v. *Chevron Corporation*, Case No. C99-2506 CAL (N.D. Cal 1999).

On 7 April 2000, the Court rejected *Chevron's* motion for dismissal based on the doctrine of *forum non conveniens*. *Chevron* argued that a court in Nigeria would be the proper venue for this suit, not the court in California. The Court rejected this argument, because *Chevron* did not consent to subject itself to jurisdiction in Nigeria. The Court also took public interest factors into account by noting that a court in California has a compelling interest in hearing cases involving allegations of international human rights violations against a California corporation.[85] Subsequently, *Chevron* filed several motions to dismiss the case. The corporation argued that the claims did not concern violations of international law and that litigation would interfere with United States foreign policy *vis-à-vis* Nigeria. The Court, however, concluded that the plaintiffs had adequately alleged violations of the prohibition of summary execution, torture and prolonged arbitrary detention which, according to the judge 'unquestionably constitute a violation of (…) norms of international law' covered by the ATCA.[86] Moreover, the Court rejected *Chevron*'s argument that the claims would interfere with United States foreign policy, concluding that it could not reach that conclusion at this stage of the litigation. Finally, *Chevron* claimed that the case should be dismissed on the grounds that the alleged acts, if true, were committed by the Nigerian subsidiary and not by *Chevron* itself. On 12 May 2001, the Court concluded that none of these assertions warranted dismissal of the case at this early stage of the proceedings. The motion by *Chevron* to dismiss was denied and the case was declared admissible.[87]

Holocaust cases
The ATCA is now also being used as a basis for claims with regard to corporate abuse of power during the Second World War. The first case as filed in March 1998[88] by the Belgian citizen Elsa Iwanowa, on behalf of herself and thousands of persons who were

---

85 *Larry Bowoto et al.* v. *Chevron Corporation*, Case No. C 99-2506, United States district court, Northern district of California, 7 April 2000. The transcript of the oral argument on Chevron's motion for dismissal based on *forum non conveniens* is available at: http://www.earthrights.org/chevron/0407transcript.rtf (accessed on 4 January 2002).

86 *Larry Bowoto et al.* v. *Chevron Corporation*, Case No. C 99-2506, United States district court, Northern district of California, 12 May 2000, p. 9 of the transcript of the oral argument on *Chevron*'s motion to dismiss and the plaintiff's motion for leave to amend the complaint. This document is available at: http://www.earthrights.org/chevron/0512transcript.rtf (accessed on 4 January 2002). For jurisdiction under the ATCA to arise based on these claims it is necessary that the defendants acted under the colour of official authority. As the alleged harms in this case occurred at the hands of the Nigerian military and the defendant allegedly took part in them, the court considered it clear that the alleged action took place under the colour of authority. The court therefore only needed to address the question whether the causes of action were properly pled as a violation of the law of nations.

87 At the time writing this case is in the discovery phase.

88 Prior to 5 November 1997 it was not possible for the plaintiff to seek compensation for forced labour during the Second World War from private corporations due to German Law. As a result of a ruling by the *Landgericht Bonn* forced labourers can now for the first time file individual claims for compensation against private corporations.

compelled to perform forced labour under inhuman conditions for *Ford Werke AG,* the German subsidiary of the defendant *Ford Motor Company*, between 1941 and 1945. *Ford* was never confiscated by the Nazi regime while the use of forced labour had been immensely profitable for the *Ford Motor Company*.[89] The plaintiff stated that *Ford Motor Company* and *Ford Werke AG* had violated the law of nations and were therefore liable for compensatory and punitive damages.[90] The district court denied *Ford's* motion to dismiss for lack of jurisdiction, finding that there was jurisdiction for the plaintiff's claims of slave labour under the ATCA. The court held that *Ford Werke's* 'use of unpaid, forced labor during World War II violated clearly established norms of customary international law'.[91]

Besides the case of *Iwanowa* v. *Ford*, more than 30 Holocaust survivors have filed complaints under the ATCA against German corporations, such as *Volkswagen* and *Siemens*. A smaller number of plaintiffs have also filed complaints against corporations that allegedly used forced labour in Japan during World War II. Moreover, a number of German, Swiss and Austrian banks which allegedly had illegally retained property belonging to Jews during the Holocaust have been sued.[92] Many of these cases have been settled out of court. For example, in July 2000, after extensive negotiations with the government of the United States, Germany and German industries agreed to establish a $5.1 billion fund, dedicated, in part, to compensating slave labour victims. In return for their contribution to the fund, the German government and industry were essentially given immunity from future lawsuits.

3.3 Legal Doctrines Limiting the Applicability of the Alien Tort Claims Act

The ATCA provides for the exercise of jurisdiction over alleged American *or* international violators in respect of acts that occur abroad. This, to say the least, 'stretches' the principles of jurisdiction and may affront the State of nationality of the corporation or the State where the activities took place. Partly in view of this, the American courts tend to take several legal doctrines that limit the reach of the ATCA into consideration.

Firstly, in an attempt to have the case dismissed, the defendants in ATCA actions frequently attempt to invoke the common law doctrine of *forum non conveniens.* Most federal States have adopted this common law doctrine.[93] According to this doctrine, a case can be dismissed, even when jurisdiction has been established, if the defendant

89 *Iwanowa* v. *Ford*, 98 Civ. 959 (D.N.J. filed 4 March, 1998).

90 See para. 40 of the Class Action Complaint and Jury Demand.

91 *Iwanowa* v. *Ford Motor Co.*, 67 F. Supp. 2d 424 (D.N.J. 1999) at 440.

92 See, *inter alia*: *Wasman* v. *Deutschbank,* No. 98 Civ 3938 (S.D.N.Y., June 1998); *Duveen* v. *Deutsch Bank*, No.98 Civ.06620 (E.D.N.Y. Oct.28, 1998).

93 For an overview of which States have adopted this doctrine see: Kathryeen Lee Boyd, 'The Inconvenience of Victims: Abolishing Forum Non Conveniens in US Human Rights Litigation', in: *Virginia Journal of International Law,* Vol. 39, 1998, pp. 41-87, note 15, p. 44.

can demonstrate that an alternative forum exists to provide some remedy to the plaintiffs and that certain discretionary public and private convenience factors, such as the location of evidence, shift the balance in the defendant's favour.[94] The defendants in ATCA actions frequently argue that, on the grounds of convenience, a case should be heard in the country where the alleged injury was inflicted. A well-known case against a US-based corporation where the *forum non conveniens* doctrine was successfully invoked is the case against *Union Carbide*.[95] With regard to corporate defendants, the *forum non conveniens* doctrine is likely to be successfully invoked as corporations, with offices in many different countries, have the option of proposing several alternative forums in addition to the country were the abuse occurred. The initial ruling in the case against *Royal Dutch/Shell* provides an example of this. This case was initially dismissed on the ground of *forum non conveniens*. The court held that the United Kingdom, being one of *Shell's* corporate headquarters, provided an alternative forum.[96]

An interesting thesis with regard to the *forum non conveniens* doctrine has been put forward by Kathryn Boyd. According to Boyd, the likelihood that the doctrine will be successfully invoked by corporate defendants in ATCA cases is greater than in other cases. Firstly, because corporate entities are not protected by governmental immunities, they tend to rely heavily on the doctrine. Besides, United States courts are historically reluctant to deal with politically-charged international issues. Moreover, the doctrine of *forum non conveniens* has a high success rate in ATCA cases, as the *inconveniens*

94 Other factors are e.g.: the costs of producing evidence at trial and translating documents and testimony, the relative effect of travel on the parties and the possibility that the Court will need to view or have access to the site of the cause of action, court congestion and familiarity with the law which will govern the action. Boyd, *supra* n. 93, pp. 67-68.

95 *Re Union Carbide Corp. Gas plant Disaster at Bhopal, India in December 1984,* 809 F. 2d 195 (2d Cir.1987), cert, denied, 484 US 871 (1987) The case was referred to the Indian courts. Dissatisfied with the settlement reached in the Indian courts in 1989, a new complaint was filed in 1999 against *Union Carbide*, as well as its former Chief Executive Officer, Warren Anderson, in the southern district court of New York, *Bano, et al.* v. *Union Carbide Corporation and Warren Anderson*, 99 Civ. 11329 (JFK) (S.D.N.Y. 1999). On 28 August 2000, Judge Keenan dismissed the case on the grounds that Indian legislation gave the government of India the sole and exclusive right to represent the interested Bhopal victims and that the Indian government had reached a binding settlement with *Union Carbide* resolving all civil claims arising out of the Bhopal disaster. There are numerous other cases in which the plaintiffs have been denied the opportunity to use United States courts to hold United States corporations liable for their conduct abroad resulting from the doctrine of *forum non conveniens*. See, *inter alia*, *Stewart* v. *Dow Chem Co.*, 865 F. 2d 103, 104 (6th Circuit 1989), *Sibaja* v. *Dow Chem. Co,* 757 F. 2d 1215, 1219 (11th Cir. 1985), cert. Denied, 474 US 948 (1985). These cases mostly concern environmental issues.

96 The judge took this decision even though the likelihood of success in the British courts is very low. The reasons for dismissal were: the presence of witnesses and evidence in Great Britain and the fact that 'none of the parties to this action is a citizen of the United States, there is no allegation that defendants' actions had an effect on the United States, and the conduct at issue was engaged in by an English corporation, in a nation formerly part of the Commonwealth of Nations, under a liability standard determined by English law'. *Wiwa*, 96 Civ. 8386 at 13-15. The Court of Appeals of the second circuit court, ruled that the American court was the appropriate forum, however.

per definition is present as the plaintiff must be an alien and the subject of litigation are abuses that have occurred on foreign soil. Obtaining witnesses and evidence may, therefore, be costly and the courts may be required to interpret the law of a foreign State.[97] According to Boyd, the doctrine therefore seems to contain a particularly high threshold for plaintiffs under the ATCA in cases against corporate defendants. Instead of promoting fairness and convenience, the doctrine, if successfully invoked, immunises corporations from liability. Boyd, therefore, suggests that the doctrine of *forum non conveniens* should be abolished in human rights cases.[98]

However, despite the doctrine, the dismissal of human rights cases in the United States has been prevented for the reason that the political and judicial systems in the countries where the alleged violations had taken place were considered dysfunctional. For example, in the *Unocal* case the lack of an alternative forum in Burma was manifestly clear to the court.[99]

The *forum non conveniens* doctrine reduces the possibility of holding corporations that are not based in the United States accountable under the ATCA. Most of the cases against corporations that have been declared admissible concern United States corporations. However, in several recent ATCA cases against non-US corporations, the courts have emphasised that a case should not be too readily dismissed on the grounds of *forum non conveniens.* In the case against *Chevron*, United States District judge Charles Legge ruled that defence motions based on the doctrine of *forum non conveniens* should be viewed sceptically and 'weighed in favor of the plaintiffs'.[100] And, as discussed above, on appeal in the *Wiwa* v. *Royal Dutch/Shell* case, the court decided that the case was admissible despite the doctrine of *forum non conveniens.* The court emphasised that it is the policy of the United States to offer a forum to victims of human rights violations.[101]

Other legal hurdles that have to be overcome by the plaintiffs under the ATCA are doctrines that take into account political considerations of a constitutional or international nature. In general, it can be said that these doctrines impede invoking the ATCA if this interferes with United States foreign policy or with domestic separation of powers. An example is the doctrine of the 'act of State'. The doctrine of the act of State precludes a United States court from considering a plaintiff's claim if this would require the court to determine that official acts committed by a foreign sovereign, recognised by the United States and performed in its own territory, were invalid. This

97 Boyd, *supra* n. 93, p. 61.
98 Boyd, *supra* n. 93, p. 86.
99 *Unocal I*, 963 F. Supp. At 886.
100 *Larry Bowoto et al.* v. *Chevron Corporation*, Case No. C 99-2506, United States district court, Northern district of California, 7 April 2000, p. 11 of the transcript of the oral argument on Chevron's motion for dismissal based on forum non conveniens. This document is available at: http://www.earthrights.org/chevron/0407transcript.rtf (accessed on 4 January 2002).
101 See p. 191.

could give rise to constitutional difficulties (the executive and legislative branches of the US government might have a different policy) and international problems (interference in a sovereign State).[102] The act of State doctrine requires that the court considers, *inter alia*, whether the case might 'touch (...) sharply on national nerves'.[103] In theory, the act of State doctrine may bar an ATCA suit where a court is dealing with a corporation that operates in the context of a joint venture with a government that is involved in gross human rights violations. However, in general this doctrine is not likely to be successfully invoked in the case of human rights violations as such violations will seldom be official acts of State. The act of State doctrine might apply when the contested act is taken in pursuit of public interest. However, it is hard to envision that a United States court will consider such reasoning in the case of a violation of a *jus cogens* norm. In the words of the court in the *Unocal* case:

> 'In the context of *jus cogens* violations of international law, which are, by definition, internationally denounced, the high degree of international consensus severely undermines defendants' argument that SLORC and MOGE's alleged activities should be treated as acts of State [...] Because nations do not, and cannot under international law, claim a right to torture or enslave their own citizens, a finding that a nation has committed such acts, particularly where, as here, that finding comports with the prior conclusions of the coordinate branches of government, would not have the detrimental effect on the policies underlying the act of state doctrine.'[104]

The court clearly considered that the act of State doctrine did not pose an obstacle in the *Unocal* case, not only due to the *jus cogens* character of the applicable norms, but also because the United States' government had already spoken out against Burma.

Another potentially limiting doctrine is the doctrine of political question. The doctrine is concerned with constitutional aspects. The doctrine comes into play when there exists: '[1] a textually demonstrable constitutional commitment of the issue to a coordinate political department; or [2] a lack of judicially discoverable and manageable standards for resolving it; or [3] the impossibility of deciding without an initial policy determination of a kind clearly for non-judicial discretion; or [4] the impossibility of a court's undertaking independent resolution without expressing lack of the respect due to the coordinate branches of government; or [5] an unusual need for unquestioning adherence to a political decision already made; or [6] the potentiality of embarrassment from multifarious pronouncements by various departments on one question'.[105] ATCA-

102 The doctrine of the Act of State is similar to the doctrine of international comity which states that United States courts 'ordinarily refuse to review acts of foreign governments and defer to proceedings taking place in foreign countries, allowing those acts and proceedings to have extraterritorial effect in the United States', *Hilton* v. *Guyot*, 159 US 113, 164 (1895).

103 *Banco Naccional de Cuba* v. *Sabbatino*, 376 U.S. 398, 428 (1964).

104 *Unocal I*, 963 F. Supp. at 894.

105 *Baker* v. *Carr*, 369 U.S. 186, 216 (1962).

cases involving human rights will frequently deal with politically charged situation. Nevertheless, in general, the political question doctrine has not been accepted as a ground for dismissal in such cases.[106] The doctrine has not been explicitly addressed in the described case-law against corporations.

3.4 Concluding Remarks on the Alien Tort Claims Act

A development can be discerned towards widening the reach of the ATCA, both regarding the circle of defendants and the applicable human rights norms. The ATCA litigation is unique in that the subject matter of the lawsuits derives directly from international law. With regard to individuals, the courts have accepted that under the ATCA, international tortious liability may arise for genocide, war crimes and crimes against humanity. Currently, with regard to corporations, the United States courts have held that absent of State action, slave trade (forced labour) can trigger jurisdiction under the ATCA. Moreover, jurisdiction over corporations may also arise where a corporation is complicit in State acts of; summary execution; crimes against humanity; cruel, inhuman or degrading treatment; torture; violation of the right to life, liberty and security of person; prolonged arbitrary detention and; peaceful assembly.

In view of the described cases and the doctrines that potentially limit the reach of the ATCA, what are the implications of the ATCA as a tool for holding corporations accountable for human rights violations? The rulings in the cases against *Unocal, Royal Dutch/Shell* and *Chevron*, seem promising for victims of corporate human rights violations. In the *Chevron* and *Royal Dutch/Shell* cases the doctrine of *forum non conveniens* did not prove to be an obstacle. Moreover, in both the *Chevron* case and the *Royal Dutch/Shell* case the court 'pierced the corporate veil' by dismissing the argument that the actions of the Nigerian subsidiaries cannot be viewed as actions of the parent corporations. In the cases against *Unocal* and *Royal Dutch/Shell* jurisdiction over corporations was relatively easily established for acts committed 'under the colour of official authority'. Furthermore, in the *Unocal* case forced labour was equated with slavery (slave trade), giving rise to jurisdiction even without State action. Finally, in the *Unocal* case, the principle of command responsibility was applied to corporations, providing a useful tool to pierce the frequently very complicated corporate structures. On the other hand, the latest ruling in this case has restricted the scope of the ATCA in the field of corporate liability for human rights violations.

Overall, it is clear that the potential of the ATCA as a remedy for victims of corporate human rights violations should not be overestimated. Besides the potentially

106 A notable exception is the decision in the *Tel Oren* case. In this case the court held that human rights cases should be left to the competence of the political branches of government'. *Tel Oren*, 726 F 2d. at 823-27.This decision has, however, not been followed.

limiting legal doctrines referred to above, several other considerations may considerably reduce the likelihood that the ATCA will offer a substantial remedy.

In the first place, the threshold for a case to be declared admissible under the ATCA is still high. The plaintiffs must identify an enforceable and universal international norm and properly allege its violation by the corporation concerned. This requires a very specific account of the facts, which are often difficult to establish for the plaintiffs. The case of *Beanal* v. *Freeport McMoran* provides an example. Contrary to judge Paez in the *Unocal* case, who relatively readily accepted the claim that torture was committed 'under colour of official authority', the plaintiffs in the *Beanal* case proved unable – despite the fact that they were given several opportunities to improve the complaint – to satisfy the very specific details demanded by judge Duval to underpin the claims that required State action.[107] The differences between these two decisions reflect the lack of uniformity that may occur in this kind of litigation.

In the second place, to date, in the cases against corporations for activities absent State action, the courts have only excepted the exercise of subject-matter jurisdiction in case of a violation of a human right with a *jus cogens* character, *viz*. the slave trade.[108] But, it is feasible that the range of actionable norms will broaden. In the *Unocal* case the court did not appear to have much difficulty in accepting that forced labour is to be equated with participation in slave trade and, consequently, constitutes a violation of a *jus cogens* norm. Moreover, as pointed out by Seiderman the understanding that the scope of the ATCA is limited to violations of *jus cogens* norms is 'at best dubious'.[109] The statutory language of the ATCA and previous case-law does not suggest that actionable claims under the ATCA should refer to a violation of a *jus cogens* norm.[110] For determining the norms for whose violation subject-matter jurisdiction under the ATCA might arise, the test is whether these norms are 'definable, obligatory, and universally condemned.[111] It is important to note here that the court in

107 In the *Unocal* case Judge Paez decided that it was enough that the allegations suggested that the corporation might have been a wilful participant in the joint action with the State. *Unocal II,* p.20. In the *Beanal*-case in which the plaintiffs presented similar allegations, judge Duval was much more stringent. For example, he held that the fact that the Indonesian government was a major shareholder in the corporation and a principle source of income was not enough to determine State action. *Beanal*, 1998, U.S. Dist LEXIS 2522. pp.17-18. As Zia-Zarifi states: 'it is difficult to imagine what other evidence could have been presented at the pleading [in the Beanal case] to satisfy the court', Zia-Zarifi, *supra* n. 35, p.113.

108 The idea that, in the case of a private defendant, only violations of a *jus cogens* norm is actionable, comes to the fore in the decision of the court in *Unocal II*. Here the court opined that 'a foreign sovereign's expropriation of its national's property does not constitute a *jus cogens* violation of the law of nations and, therefore is not cognizable under (ATCA)'. *Unocal II*, 963 F. Supp. 880 (C.D. Cal. 1997).

109 Seiderman, *supra* n. 1, p. 256.

110 Seiderman, *supra* n. 1, p. 255.

111 *Forti* v. *Suarez-Mason*, 672 F. Supp.1531, 1539-40 (N.D. Cal. 1987), amended in part, 694 F. Supp. 7-7 (N.D. Cal. 1989).

the *Filartiga* case stressed the evolving character of international law. As new norms emerge and ripen, the courts possibly will consider more norms 'definable, obligatory, and universally condemned', turning these norms into a basis for civil lawsuits against corporations under the ATCA.[112]

A third potential limitation inherent in the ATCA as a remedy for corporate human rights violations is the prerequisite that the defendant must have certain minimum contacts with the jurisdiction of the United States. This can pose a problem for plaintiffs suing corporations that are not based in the United States. In the ATCA cases, the courts are clearly struggling with the question of what kind of tie the defendant corporation should have in order for jurisdiction to arise. In the *Unocal* case, the court ruled against jurisdiction with regard to the claims against *Total,* despite the nationwide contacts of the corporation and its direct contact with *Unocal*.[113] In the case against *Royal Dutch Petroleum/Shell*, it was upheld, in the first instance, that the activities of various subsidiaries to the parent companies, the actions of the defendant's agent in New York and the nationwide contacts, were not enough to trigger jurisdiction.[114] However, on appeal the court argued that the presence of the agent in New York was sufficient for jurisdiction to arise.[115]

The possibilities for victims of any nationality to bring suit in American courts under the ATCA for violations committed anywhere in the world, has given rise to some concern that this will lead to a considerable increase in suits, especially considering the fact that the compensation that can be awarded is often significantly higher in United States courts than elsewhere.[116] However, notwithstanding the potential opportunities which the ATCA offers plaintiffs attempting to hold corporations directly accountable for human rights violations, it is clear that the potential of the ATCA as a substantial redress for victims of corporate human rights violations must not be overestimated. It must be reiterated that none of the cases against corporations have yet been determined on the merits or heard before the Supreme Court.[117] Therefore, it

112 In their book published in 1996, Stephens and Ratner have listed a number of violations that in the future might be found to trigger ATCA jurisdiction. These include: slavery and the slave trade; piracy; violations of safe conduct and the rights of ambassadors; racial discrimination; systematic violations of human rights; gender violence and gender discrimination; environmental harm; and terrorism, hijacking and hostage-taking, Stephens and Ratner, *supra* n. 6, pp.79-94. At the time of writing the slave trade and possibly environmental harm have already been recognised by United States courts as falling under the ATCA.

113 *Doe I* v. *Unocal Corp.*, 27 F.Supp.2d 1174 (C.D. Cal. 1998) (Order granting *Total's* Motion to Dismiss).

114 *Shell*, 96 Civ. 8386, at 7-10.

115 *Ken Wiwa, Owens Wiwa* and *Blessing Kpuinen* v. *Royal Dutch Petroleum Company* and *Shell Transport and Trading Company. Plc.*, 226 F. 3d 88 (2nd Cir. 2000).

116 This especially comes to the fore in the legislative history of the Torture Victim Protection Act. Boyd, *supra* n. 93, pp. 44-47.

117 Except for the petition filed by *Royal Dutch/Shell.* The Supreme Court denied this petition without comment or dissent, see pp. 193.

remains to be seen how far the American judiciary will go in stretching the (jurisdictional) limits of the ATCA.

In the light of the applicability of international human rights law to corporations the developments under the ATCA are very significant. Despite considerable legal hurdles, plaintiffs have succeeded in passing the admissibility stages in a couple of cases. The United States courts have recognised that corporations, acting alone or in concert with the State, may be liable for violations of certain provisions of *international* human rights law. It remains to be seen how the embryonic case-law will develop but there does not appear to be a reason why the number of corporate human rights violations that might be actionable under the ATCA should not broaden. The developments in the United States courts are in very early stages which gives rise to some legal uncertainty. The jurisdiction of United States courts under the ATCA is very broad, as hardly any ties between the alleged tort, the defendant, plaintiff and the United States are required for jurisdiction to be triggered. In the light of legal certainty, it might be argued that litigation against corporations can best take place either in the State where the tort occurs or in the State where the corporation has its headquarters.

In the following sections the developments with regard to litigation in the home State will be discussed. In several home States, civil litigation is emerging against corporations for human right violations abroad.

4 Civil Litigation in the Home State

The most noteworthy cases with regard to civil litigation brought against a corporation in its home State, are the cases that have been brought before the British courts against British mining corporations for violations of human rights in Africa. Before addressing these cases, a few preliminary remarks will be made with regard to the accountability of corporations for human rights violations in European States in general.

In chapter V, it was pointed out that within the European Union a development may be discerned towards binding regulation for corporations with regard to international human rights.[118] Nevertheless, at present, there is no binding legislation for corporations on the level of the European Union. Unlike the American federal situation,[119] each country in the European Union has its own codified and case-law bases for the exercise of jurisdiction. In addition, each Member State has acceded to multilateral and/or bilateral conventions which govern jurisdiction between Member State courts. Nevertheless, the 1968 Convention on Jurisdiction and the Enforcement of Judgments

118 See pp. 130-131.

119 In the United States, federal courts exercise jurisdiction to the extent authorised by Congress and allowable by the Constitution.

in Civil and Commercial Matters (hereinafter: Brussels Convention)[120] provides for the possibility of dismissing national law for the purposes of jurisdiction. According to the Brussels Convention, domestic courts in European States can be the forum to deal with corporate violations of internationally agreed standards. As a general rule, Article 2 of the Brussels Convention provides that

> 'Subject to the provisions of this Convention, persons domiciled in a Contracting State shall, whatever their nationality, be sued in the courts of that State. Persons who are not nationals of the State in which they are domiciled shall be governed by the rules of jurisdiction applicable to nationals of that State'.

What is to be considered the domicile of the defendant is left to the rules of private international law that are administered by the court.[121] Most Member States currently interpret article 2 of the Brussels Convention as implying that cases can be brought from any country throughout the world.[122] Under the Brussels Convention, a judge essentially has no discretion either to accept or reject jurisdiction on a *forum non conveniens* basis, as is the case in the United States. However, as will be discussed in the following sections, not all European Union Member States interpret this Convention in the same way.

4.1 Civil Litigation in the United Kingdom

Several interesting civil actions have recently been instigated in the British courts against British corporations for violations of human rights abroad.[123] The United Kingdom is a party to the Brussels Convention. However, whereas most European Union Member States interpret this Convention as being applicable to plaintiffs from

---

120 1968 Brussels Convention on Jurisdiction and the Enforcement of Judgments in Civil and Commercial Matters, O.J. (1998) C27/1. In March 2002 the Brussels Convention will become an European Union (EU) regulation as the EU will take over competence as regards civil justice under the Amsterdam Treaty.

121 Gerrit Betlem, 'Transnational Litigation Against Multinational Corporations Before Dutch Civil Courts', in: *Liability of Multinational Corporations Under International Law*, Menno T. Kamminga and Saman Zia-Zarifi [eds.], Kluwer Law International, The Hague etc., 2000, pp. 283-305, at p. 285. Betlem points out that in the case of a civil suit before a Dutch court, the doctrine of incorporation will apply. This means that a corporation that is incorporated under Dutch law can be sued in a Dutch court.

122 Report on EU standards for European enterprises operating in developing countries: towards a European Code of Conduct, Committee on Development and Cooperation, 17 December 1998, p. 16

123 See, for a detailed account: Richard Meeran, 'The Unveiling of Transnational Corporations', in: *Human Rights Standards and the Responsibility of Transnational Corporations*, Michael K. Addo [ed.], Kluwer Law International, The Hague, 1999, pp. 161-169 and Richard Meeran, 'Liability of Multinational Corporations: A Critical Stage in the UK, *Liability of Multinational Corporations Under International Law*, Menno T. Kamminga and Saman Zia-Zarifi [eds.], Kluwer Law International, The Hague etc., 2000, pp. 251-264. The barrister Richard Meeran has represented all the plaintiffs in the cases discussed here.

countries outside the European Union, the United Kingdom judiciary does not. Furthermore, just as in the US courts, cases in British courts are subject to the doctrine of *forum non conveniens*.[124] Nevertheless, an interesting trend can be discerned in British civil litigation towards a less stringent application of this concept. Employees from third countries have been successful in having their cases against British parent companies heard in British courts. Moreover, these civil cases are noteworthy in relation to the frequently extremely complex structures of corporations, which may present an obstacle in the quest for accountability. Multinational corporations operate in many countries and their legal identity is often separated between different limited companies. This may be used to shield the parent company from legal accountability for violations committed by its subsidiaries. As will be discussed below, in several civil cases the courts in the United Kingdom have pierced this corporate veil.

Connelly v. R.T.Z. Corporation plc

In this landmark judgment it was decided that the victim of throat cancer, which had developed after working in an uranium mine in Namibia, could bring his claim for damages in the United Kingdom against *R.T.Z.*, the British parent company. The plaintiff argued that the British courts were the appropriate forum given the fact that the parent company devised and implemented the subsidiary's policy on health, safety and the environment. Initially, in 1995, the court rejected this line of reasoning and argued that Namibia was the most appropriate forum in this case, despite the fact that it was highly unlikely that a case would be heard before a Namibian court, as no legal aid was available to the plaintiffs there.[125] The case was appealed twice. In the first appeal, the Court held that the availability of legal aid could not be taken into account in determining whether the courts in the United Kingdom were the appropriate forum.[126] However, on appeal in 1996, it was decided, with specific reference to article 6 ECHR and article 14 ICCPR, that the case would be allowed to proceed.[127] The decisive consideration was that financial assistance for legal representation was available in the United Kingdom and not in Namibia. Lord Thomas Bingham M.R. considered the following:

124 In *Harrods (Buenos Aires) Ltd.*, (1991) 4 All ER 334, CA, the Court of Appeal held that, despite the mandatory language of Article 2 of the Brussels Convention, the British court had jurisdiction to order a stay if an alternative forum was available in a non-contracting State. The principles applicable to the identification of the appropriate forum have been formulated in *Spiliada Maritime Corporation* v. *Consulex Ltd.* (1987) A.C. 460. Besides the United Kingdom, Ireland is the only EU State where the doctrine of forum non conveniens is applied.

125 Judgment of the High Court in London, 28 February 1995.

126 This decision was based on section 33 (1) (b) Legal Aid Act 1988 which provides that the receipt of legal aid shall not affect the principles upon which any judicial discretion is normally exercised. *Connelly* v. *RTZ Corporation Plc*, 1996, 2 W.L.R. p. 251.

127 *Connelly* v. *RTZ Corporation Plc*, 1997, 3 W.L.R. p. 373.

> '(...) faced with a stark choice between one jurisdiction, albeit not the most appropriate in which there could in fact be a trial, and another jurisdiction, the most appropriate in which there never could, in my judgment, the interests of justice would tend to weigh, and weigh strongly in favour of that forum in which the plaintiff could assert his rights.'[128]

The Law Lords held that the case could not be properly pursued in Namibia because the highly professional representation from legal and scientific experts was not available there. For the achievement of substantial justice it was reasonable that the case should be heard in the United Kingdom.

The circumstances which the court referred to, are not uncommon in cases of human rights violations resulting from corporate activities overseas. In such cases, the facts and underlying scientific evidence will frequently be technically complex while the plaintiffs tend to be impecunious. In a dissenting opinion, Lord Hoffmann pointed to the far-reaching consequences of the judgment. He argued that to allow the case to proceed on the basis that legal aid was not available in Namibia meant that an action,

> 'of a rich plaintiff will be stayed while the action of a poor plaintiff in respect of precisely the same transaction will not. It means that the more speculative and difficult the action, the more likely it is to be allowed to proceed in this country with the support of public funds. Such distinctions will do the law no credit.'[129]

Hoffmann continued:

> 'The defendant is a multinational company, present almost everywhere and certainly present and ready to be sued in Namibia. I would therefore regard the presence of the defendants in the jurisdiction as a neutral factor. If the presence of the defendants, as parent company and local subsidiary of a multinational, can enable them to be sued here, any multinational with its parent company in England will be liable to be sued here in respect of its activities anywhere in the world.'[130]

Finally, in December 1998, the case was dismissed on limitation grounds. However, another cancer victim who worked at the same mine, Peter Carlson, has also brought a claim against *R.T.Z.* The court decided not to dismiss this case, once again because of a lack of sufficient legal aid in Namibia.[131]

---

128 *Connelly* v. *RTZ Corporation Plc*, 1997, 3 W.L.R. p. 373.
129 *Connelly* v. *RTZ Corporation Plc,* 1997, 3 W.L.R. p. 387. Dissenting opinion of Lord Hoffmann.
130 *Connelly* v. *RTZ Corporation Plc.,* 1997, W.L.R. p. 388. Dissenting opinion of Lord Hoffmann.
131 *Carlson* v. *RTZ Corporation Plc.,* Decision of Wright J. [November 1998, unreported]. Meeran, *supra* n. 124, p. 258.

The Cape plc. case

This case was brought by asbestos victims who had previously been employed by the British corporation *Cape plc.* to work in a mine in South Africa. The asbestos dust levels at this South African mine were 12-35 times higher than the levels permitted in Great Britain. The operations at the mine were carried out by a subsidiary that was wholly owned by the British parent company *Cape plc*. Initially, in January 1998, the case was dismissed on the ground of *forum non conveniens*. However, on appeal, in July 1998, the Court of Appeal agreed with the plaintiff that, even if the operations were not unlawful under South African law, this does not mean that the corporate defendant was not negligent. The corporation ought reasonably to have taken into account the scientific knowledge that was available to it as it was situated in England.[132] Furthermore, even though the injuries occurred in South Africa and, therefore, strong and compelling reasons existed why the action should be heard in the local courts, the judge decided as follows:

> 'that [the] directors and senior personnel [of the defendant company] were responsible for the decisions which led to the business being carried on in the way that it was. (...) The alleged breaches of duty occurred essentially in England.'[133]

The Court therefore decided that the victims could bring their case against *Cape plc.* before the English High Court.

It is interesting that on appeal the plaintiffs submitted that the stay in the first instance was contrary to the Brussels Convention, referred to above,[134] and requested that the matter should be remitted to the European Court of Justice for a ruling as to whether the Brussels Convention applies. However, as the judge ruled in favour of the plaintiff, the need for a European Court ruling in this case did not arise. A civil action was also brought against *Cape plc.* by Italian plaintiffs for alleged harmful activities at a subsidiary of *Cape plc.* in Italy. In this case, the Brussels Convention did prevent the dismissal of the case on the ground of *forum non conveniens*. As *Cape plc.* is registered in the United Kingdom the British courts, under article 2 Brussels Convention, were the appropriate forum.

In January 1999, further civil actions were brought against *Cape plc.* relating to its operations in South Africa. These actions comprised over 2,000 claims against the corporation.[135] *Cape plc.* petitioned the English court to stay all the actions. At first instance, the judge granted this petition ordering a stay of all the cases. The judge ruled, based *inter alia* on public policy considerations, that South Africa was the most

---

132 *Rachel Lubbe* v. *Cape plc.*, 1998, C.L.C. 1559.

133 *Rachel Lubbe* v. *Cape plc.*, 1998, C.L.C. 1559.

134 See p. 204.

135 *Africa and 1539 others* v. *Cape plc.*, (1999) A No. 40 and *Mphahlele and 336 others* v. *Cape plc.* (1999) M No. 146.

appropriate forum.[136] Finally, in 2000, the highest court in the United Kingdom, the House of Lords, unanimously ruled that the mass tort action could proceed in the English courts.[137] In reaching this decision, the lack of funding and access to legal representation in South Africa were decisive. According to the court, under such circumstances a stay would constitute a denial of justice.[138] Lord Hope of Craighead added that public policy considerations should not play a role in reaching a decision concerning which court is the appropriate forum. He explicitly referred to the decision of the United States court to dismiss the claim against *Union Carbide* for the disaster at Bhopal.[139] He considered that:

> '[h]owever tempting it may be to give effect to concerns about the expense and inconvenience to the administration of justice in litigating actions (…), the argument must only be resolved upon an examination of their effect upon the interests of the parties who are before the court and securing the ends of justice in their case.'[140]

Furthermore, the argument was again advanced by the plaintiffs that a stay was precluded by article 2 of the Brussels Convention. As the court ruled in favour of the plaintiffs, it was not considered necessary to deal with the question whether applying the doctrine of *forum non conveniens* was in violation of article 2 of the Brussels Convention. The judge opined that '[h]ad it been necessary to resolve that question, I would have thought it necessary to seek a ruling on the applicability on Article 2 from the European Court of Justice, since I do not consider the answer to that question to be clear'.[141]

In December 2001, *Cape* eventually agreed out of court to a settlement with 7,500 South African victims.[142]

The Thor cases

South African workers claiming to have suffered potentially lethal mercury poisoning in a factory in South Africa brought suit against the United Kingdom parent company, *Thor Chemicals* and its Chairman. The mercury levels at the subsidiary of *Thor*

136 Judgment of 30 July 1999: 2000 1 Lloyd's Rep. 139 at 141. On appeal the cases were also dismissed on the ground of *forum non conveniens*: the second Court of Appeal. Judgment of 29 November 1999, 2000, 1 Lloyd's Rep. 139 at p. 160.

137 *Lubbe and 4 others* and *Cape Plc. and Afrika and others* v. *same*, 2000, Lloyds Rep. P. 383, H.L.. Lord Justice Wright set 9 April 2002 as the date for the case against *Cape Plc.*

138 *Lubbe and and Afrika and others* v. *same*, 2000, Lloyds Rep. P. 383, H.L, p. 393.

139 *Union Carbide Corporation Gas Plant Disaster at Bhopal*. 1986, 643 F. Supp. 842.

140 *Lubbe and Afrika and others* v. *same*, 2000, Lloyds Rep. P. 383, H.L., p. 398.

141 *Lubbe and Afrika and others* v. *same*, 2000, Lloyds Rep. P. 383, H.L. p. 394.

142 According to this settlement *Cape Plc.* will pay 21 million British pounds into a trust fund to be established in South Africa which will make payment to the victims. One condition was that the South African government confirmed that it will not fund future claims against *Cape*.

Chemicals in South Africa were consistently in excess of United Kingdom standards. The defendants applied for a stay on the ground that the convenient forum was South Africa. However, the plaintiffs contended that, although the damage had occurred in South Africa, the breach of the duty of care had occurred in the United Kingdom. The British courts ruled that even though the South African courts seemed the more appropriate forum for the suit, the parent company's negligence was firmly based in the United Kingdom, and, therefore, the victims had a right to claim compensation in the British courts.[143] After filing claims for damages in the High Court in London, *Thor Chemicals* agreed to a settlement of 1.3. million British pounds. Further claims have been filed. The request to stay these actions on the basis of *forum non conveniens* was dismissed and the court of appeal refused leave to appeal.[144]

4.2 Concluding Remarks on the Civil Litigation in the United Kingdom

The source of the tort in the cases before the English courts is municipal tort law. It might be argued that it is not appropriate to deal with violations of international law in the context of municipal tort law, as it might belittle the grave nature of the violations. Notwithstanding this argument, the importance of these decisions in the English courts for the liability of corporations for human rights violations is twofold.

Firstly, the implications of the judgments are important for British-based corporations operating in developing countries with low health and safety standards. It was decided that parent companies which are aware that the operations of foreign subsidiaries involve risks for their employees and others, owe a 'duty of care'. British-based corporations may be liable for injuries when their subsidiaries apply lower standards than those applicable in the United Kingdom. These cases tackle the 'double standards' which corporations can employ when operating overseas.

Secondly, the importance of these cases before the British courts lies in the fact that they successfully 'pierce the corporate veil'. Corporations regularly escape being held responsible for human rights violations due to their complex business structures, claiming that subsidiaries are separate legal entities that must be brought to trial in the countries in which they operate. However, in these countries the applicable standards might often be significantly lower than those which are applicable in the United Kingdom. These cases have successfully established that a breach of the duty of care had taken place in the United Kingdom.

In all the above-mentioned British cases the defending corporations relied on the doctrine of *forum non conveniens.* As has been demonstrated a trend can be detected in British litigation towards weighing the factors in the convenient forum test in favour of the plaintiffs.

143 *Ngcobo and others* v. *Thor Chemicals Holdings Ltd. and Another*, 1995, T.L.R. p. 579.
144 *Sithole and others* v. *Thor Chemicals Holdings Ltd. and Another*, 1999, T.L.R. p. 110.

4.3 Possibilities for Civil Litigation in the Netherlands

As was discussed in section 4, in theory, European States are required under the Brussels Convention to allow plaintiffs to sue corporations which are domiciled in these States for harmful acts committed abroad. At the same time, it was pointed out that the British courts do not pay much attention to article 2 of the Brussels Convention. The British courts maintain the doctrine of *forum non conveniens,* albeit a tendency can be discerned towards leniency when applying this doctrine. In European countries with a civil law tradition the *forum non conveniens* doctrine is not applied. Thus, it may be argued that the plaintiffs who bring suit before these domestic courts may stand a greater chance of success.

I will now briefly explore the possibilities in the Netherlands for bringing a civil lawsuit against a corporation for an alleged violation of international human rights law committed by a subsidiary abroad. At the time of writing, there has not yet been such a case brought under Dutch civil law. However, several authors have addressed the question whether in theory this possibility exists.[145]

For a corporation to be sued in a domestic court for a alleged violation of international human rights law, a couple of conditions need to be fulfilled. A first prerequisite, is that the national law recognises that a corporation is a legal person. In the Netherlands this is the case under article 2:3 of the Dutch Civil Code. The subsequent question is whether international human rights law can provide a direct basis for a civil action. Under Dutch law, international human rights norms can be the direct basis of a civil action provided that the norms have direct[146] ànd horizontal effect. As discussed by Nollkaemper, the Dutch courts have accepted that a small number of human rights can have direct and horizontal effect, in particular the right to privacy (art. 8 ECHR) and the prohibition of discrimination (art.26 ICCPR).[147] Nollkaemper reaches the following interesting conclusion,

> '[h]aving (...) accepted the fundamental principle that international human rights norms that can have direct effect also can have horizontal effect, there does not seem to be a principle reason why not other international human rights norms that are capable of having direct effect also are capable of having horizontal effect. Large parts of the norms contained in the ECHR and the ICCPR – that have been accepted as having direct effect

145 See, chapters 11 and 12 in: *Liability of Multinational Corporations Under International Law*, Menno T. Kamminga and Saman Zia-Zarifi [eds.], Kluwer Law International, The Hague etc., 2000: Andre Nollkaemper, 'Public International Law in Transnational Litigation Against Multinational Corporations: Prospects and Problems in the Courts of the Netherlands', pp. 265-283 and Gerrit Betlem, *supra* n. 121

146 This is required under article 93 of the Dutch Constitution.

147 Nollkeamper, *supra* n. 145, p. 272.

– then could pass the test. In addition to the rights to privacy and non-discrimination, this could apply to freedom of speech or freedom from torture.'[148]

Certain provisions in the European Social Charter and the ICESCR will, however, not stand the test as the Dutch courts have explicitly held that these provisions lack direct effect.[149] These social, economic and cultural provisions cannot, therefore, constitute the basis for a civil action against a corporation in the Netherlands.

Apart from the case of direct applicability of international law, a tort action could also be brought against a corporation for a violation of a duty of care under article 6:162 of the Dutch Civil Code. In such a case international law is applied indirectly. Parties to the case have the choice to invoke Dutch or foreign civil law. If they choose Dutch civil law, the connection between the main office of the defendant and the subsidiary will become very important for such a case to be declared admissible. In a civil suit, it would have to be demonstrated that the subsidiary and the head office in fact operate as one unit. It would have to be argued, as has been done in the cases before the British courts discussed earlier, that the harm resulted from an activity (or lack of activity) at the head office that is situated in the Netherlands.[150] It is pointed out by Betlem that it is currently unclear whether such a line of reasoning would be accepted by the Dutch courts.[151]

To sum up, in theory, possibilities exist for suing corporations that are incorporated in the Netherlands, either by directly invoking international law or under Dutch tort law. Whether such actions would in fact be successful remains to be seen.

4.4 Civil Litigation in Other Home States

In this section a few noteworthy civil suits that have been brought against corporations in other 'home' jurisdictions, will be briefly addressed. In Australia, a case has been filed against the mining company *Broken Hill Properties (BHP)* for allegedly destroying the livelihood of 25,000 people in Papua New Guinea. The *Ok Tedi Mining Ltd.*, a subsidiary owned by *BHP*, dumped several tonnes of toxic waste in the Fly river. After the Australian court had ruled that it had jurisdiction, the case was settled out of court on 12 June 1996 with an agreement according to which *BHP* agreed to clear up some of the environmental damage and to compensate some of the people involved.[152] The settlement contained a provision that any disputes arising during the course of its implementation would be heard by the courts in Melbourne, rather than in Papua New Guinea. In April 2000 a new case was filed against *BHP* for not adhering to the terms

148 Nollkaemper, *supra* n. 145, p. 272.
149 Nollkaemper, *supra* n. 145, p. 273.
150 Betlem, *supra* n. 121, pp. 290-292.
151 Betlem, *supra* n. 121, p. 291.
152 *Dagi* v. *Broken Hill Properties* (No. 2), 1997, 1 V.R. 428 (S.C. Vic.).

of the settlement. The harmful overseas activities of *BHP* and other Australian mining companies prompted the Australian Democrats in September 2000 to introduce to the Senate the 'Corporate Code of Conduct Bill 2000' which aimed to impose human rights and environmental standards on the conduct of Australian corporations which undertake business activities in other countries. The Parliamentary Joint Statutory Committee on Corporations and Securities compiled a report on the provisions of the bill and decided that, instead of a law, self-regulation would be preferable. In 2001, the Corporate Code of Conduct Bill 2000 was rejected.[153]

The developments in the field of civil litigation discussed in sections 3 and 4 concerned cases in the United States and the United Kingdom, which are both common law countries. However, as was pointed out in the previous section with regard to the Netherlands, there is no apparent reason why corporations could not be litigated against in civil law countries. An example is provided by the civil action that was (unsuccessfully) instigated in a court in Quebec, Canada. Quebec has a largely civil-law system, albeit with strong common law influences. In this case, some 23,000 Guyanese residents were mentioned as victims who had allegedly suffered damage in connection with a dam failure and resulting spillage at a gold mine, in Guyana, in August 1995. The Canadian-based company operating the gold mine had allegedly used methods that had been illegal in Canada for over 25 years. The Superior Court of Quebec held that, in theory, it could hear such a case but that in this case, however, the High Court in Guyana would be the better forum.[154]

Finally, it should be mentioned that at the time of writing, negotiations are taking place with regard to a global Convention on Jurisdiction and the Enforcement of Judgements at the Hague Conference on Private International Law. The aim of the draft is to enable civil judgements in one State to be enforced in other Member States. In June 2001, a draft Convention was formulated. The intention is to finalise it in May-June 2002. One of the stumbling blocks is whether the *forum non conveniens* doctrine should be included in the Convention. If this Convention is adopted it would potentially facilitate civil actions against corporations.

5 Civil Liability versus Criminal Responsibility

In this chapter, the focus has been on remedies offered to plaintiffs in the field of civil law. This emphasis on civil litigation is not meant to imply that criminal prosecution at the national level is not an important mechanism for holding corporations account-

153 For a detailed report on the 'Corporate Code of Conduct Bill 2000', see the submission to the Joint Parliamentary Committee on Securities and Corporations inquiry into the Corporate Code of Conduct Bill 2000 by Oxfam, Australia, available at: http://www.caa.org.au/campaigns/submissions/corporate (accessed on 28 December 2001).

154 *Recherches Internationales du Quebec* v. *Cambior Inc.*, 1998, Q.J. No. 2554 (Q.L.).

able for violations of international law. However, criminal prosecution has proved to be more problematic at the national level than civil litigation.

In the first place, there are differences as regards the issue of jurisdiction. Generally speaking, international law recognises five bases for jurisdiction in criminal cases. The primary basis is the territorial principle, which recognises the right of a State to prescribe and apply its law over acts committed within its territorial boundaries. The nationality principle applies where a State exercises jurisdiction over an offender who is one of its nationals, regardless of where the violation occurred. Under the protective principle, jurisdiction is granted to protect important interests of the State. The passive personality principle applies when the victim of the offence is a national of the State seeking to exercise jurisdiction. Finally, the principle of universality permits a State to exercise jurisdiction over perpetrators of certain offences considered to be particularly heinous or harmful to the interests of the international community.[155]

There is an essential difference between jurisdiction in criminal matters and jurisdiction in civil matters. As has been demonstrated by the case-law discussed above, jurisdiction in civil matters is frequently more readily assumed on the basis of the (temporary) presence of the defendant, the presence of assets (*forum patrimonii*) and/or nationality, domicile or the residence of the alleged offender.

The criminal prosecution of corporations at the national level may prove problematic as not every national system accepts the concept of criminal liability of legal persons. Moreover, some of the elements of criminal liability, such as the requisite intent, may be difficult to prove in the case of a corporate defendant. Finally, in general, the burden of proof is stricter in criminal cases than in civil cases. For these reasons, the criminal accountability of corporations before national courts might prove complex and difficult to achieve.

As has been described above, national civil law offers significant possibilities in the field of corporate liability for human rights violations. Some authors claim that the use of civil remedies belittles human rights violations, as torts are considered to be less grave than crimes.[156] Nevertheless, several arguments, mostly of a practical nature, speak in favour of applying civil law to address corporate human rights violations. In the first place, under civil law victims can instigate proceedings without having to await action on the part of public authorities. This is especially important in the light of corporate complicity in human rights violations that are committed by States.[157] States will frequently not be very inclined to investigate and prosecute their own

155 Brownlie, *supra* n. 4, pp. 303-310.

156 Lyal S. Sunga, *Individual Responsibilty in International Law for Serious Human Rights Violations*, Martinus Nijhoff Publishers, Dordrecht 1992, pp. 111-116.

157 See the conclusion of the special rapporteur to the Sub-commission of Human Rights: 'States that benefit from [the] activities [of corporations] pass legislation in their favour.[…] Moreover, certain transnational corporations encourage States to violate their people's rights'. UN Doc. E/CN.4/Sub2/1998/6, 10 June 1998, at 16.

agents' human rights violations. Furthermore, private civil lawsuits offer victims of human rights violations a possibility to receive compensation for their injuries. In practice, however, such compensation might prove difficult and arduous to collect.[158] Nevertheless, the symbolic value of being awarded compensation should not be underestimated. Moreover, the civil law cases described above focus attention on human rights violations, thus creating a public record of the events. This type of litigation contributes to identifying corporations as violators of human rights. Such cases may, therefore, also serve to deter future abuses. Particularly, in the case of litigation against corporations the negative publicity that these suits may generate constitutes an important factor in preventing corporate violations of human rights. Finally, these suits contribute to the development of certain concepts of international law. For example, the concept of corporations as violators of international human rights as such is not considered to be problematic anymore by American courts in the ATCA cases.

6 Extraterritorial Jurisdiction

The litigation in the domestic courts discussed above involves the controversial issue of extraterritorial jurisdiction. In the United States, the Supreme Court has laid down the general presumption that United States' laws do not apply extraterritorially.[159] However, in certain cases the United States' courts may exercise extraterritorial jurisdiction, so long as this is the intention of the Congress.[160] The exceptions to the territoriality principle have been applied where the harmful effects are felt in the United States, most notably in the field of economic regulation (especially in the field of anti-trust) and criminal law.[161] Gibney and Emerick point out that the :

> 'governing institutions in the United States have been very quick to apply U.S. law to phenomena in other countries that appear to have some negative "effect" on [the United States, however they] have been very slow to apply U.S. law (...) where entities of the United States help to bring about negative effects in other countries.'[162]

---

158 In most of the ATCA cases the damages awarded have never been collected, see: Stephans and Ratner, *supra* n. 6.

159 This was most explicitly expressed in *American Banana Co.* v. *United Fruit Co.*, 213 US 347 (1909).

160 Mark Gibney and R. David Emerick, 'The extraterritorial application of United States law and the protection of human rights: holding multinational corporations to domestic and international standards' in: *Temple International & Comparative Law Journal*, Vol. 10, 1996, pp. 123-145, at p.125.

161 This is known as the 'effects doctrine'. See: Brownlie, *supra* n. 4, p. 311.

162 Gibney and Emerick, *supra* n. 160, p. 132. See also: M. Sornarajah, 'State Responsibility for Harms by Corporate Nationals Abroad', in: Scott, *Torture as Tort. Comparative Perpectives on the Development of Transnational Human Rights Litigation*, Hart Publishing, Oxford, 2001, p. 506 who makes the same point stating that the United States has exercised its jurisdiction outside its territory when it has been advantageous to its interests but never on purely altruistic grounds.

Gibney and Emerick argue that the nationality of a corporation should be an important consideration for the United States' courts in 'determining the degree to which domestic laws and standards apply extraterritorially'.[163] There should not be a dichotomy between the standards which a corporation applies domestically and the standards applied in overseas operations. As discussed above, the British courts do take the nationality of the corporation into consideration. Moreover, they apply a broad interpretation of what constitutes conduct within a territory. The litigation in the United Kingdom can be seen as an extension of the territorial principle (some parts of the act can be said to have occurred on the State's territory) and the nationality principle.

Despite the unwillingness of some United States courts to extend the scope of domestic laws that protect human rights extra territorially, it has been demonstrated in the previous sections that other United States courts are willing to apply their tort laws beyond the United States' borders with regard to *international* human rights standards. In the *Filartiga* decision, the court affirmed that the fact that the subject offence occurred outside of the United States does not exclude the exercise of jurisdiction, since under the transitory tort doctrine, the tort follows the offender wherever he goes.[164] In the *Wiwa* case, the court held that a case against a non-American corporation should proceed, as it was the policy of the United States to provide a forum for litigation with regard to violations of international human rights law.[165]

7 Concluding Remarks

In the previous chapter it was concluded that States should have the obligation to protect human rights by regulating corporate activities abroad. Furthermore, if regulation fails, the duty to protect requires that the State offers a means of redress to the victims of the corporate human rights violations. Failure to do so gives rise to State responsibility. The civil remedies at the national level, discussed in this chapter, constitute a way in which States can fulfil their obligation to protect.

Two different types of corporate liability for human rights violations have been discussed: liability arising from an international tort and liability that may arise under the domestic law of the home State. For a claim concerning the first type of liability to be possible it is necessary that States adopt legislation that expands the jurisdiction of their domestic courts over corporate activities that violate *international* human rights law abroad, irrespective of the nationality of the corporation or *locus delicti*.

The second type of liability that was discussed was the liability that may arise in the home State, *i.e.* the State where the corporation has its headquarters. In practice, the host State, *i.e.* the State were the corporation operates, often is not in a position to

163 Gibney and Emerick, *supra* n. 160, pp. 142-143.

164 *Filartiga*, 630 F. 2d at 885.

165 See p. 192.

effectively control corporations operating in their jurisdiction. Corporations may be very powerful and mobile entities that can threaten to disinvest when a State decides to adopt regulations that are considered disadvantageous by the corporation. Moreover, violations of human rights by corporations frequently take place in developing countries that lack the legal machinery which is necessary to hold corporations accountable.[166] In the light of these arguments, a case can be made for making civil remedies available in home State jurisdictions. It is argued here that existing national civil law in national jurisdictions may be sufficient for holding corporations liable for human rights violations, without the need to resort to the next step and make international law the direct basis of action as is the case under the ATCA in the United States. On the basis of the territoriality principle or the nationality principle home States are required, as a result of the obligation to protect human rights, to enact legislation expanding the jurisdiction of their domestic courts to cover the harmful activities of their corporations abroad. If a home State fails to provide civil remedies for victims of corporate human rights violations abroad, this State should be held accountable under international law. As was pointed out in the previous chapter, the international responsibility of the home State for the activities of its corporations abroad is not unprecedented.[167]

Corporate accountability through domestic courts remains unpredictable and uncertain. To guarantee the uniform application of human rights, an international mechanism for accountability is preferable. This issue will be discussed in the following chapter.

---

166 See, for example, on the judiciary in Nigeria, a report by Human Rights Watch:' A major factor in the cycle of protest and repression in the oil areas is the lack of a properly functioning legal system which could promptly and fairly rule in cases of compensation and corruption.', Human Rights Watch, *The Price Of Oil: Corporate Responsibility and Human Rights Violations in Nigeria's Oil Producing Communities,* New York, 1999, This report is available at http://www.hrw.org/hrw/reports/1999/nigeria (accessed on 12 October 2001).

167 See chapter VI, pp. 172-174.

CHAPTER VIII
JUDICIAL ENFORCEMENT AT THE INTERNATIONAL LEVEL

1 INTRODUCTION

In the preceding chapters, the question has been addressed of whether human rights obligations for corporations can actually be enforced. In chapter V an analysis was made of the non-binding instruments that directly address corporations at the international level. It was concluded that these international instruments are of limited value with regard to effectively regulating corporate activities. In the previous chapter, it was demonstrated that a range of possibilities to deal with corporations exist at the national level. The concept of corporate liability arising from a human rights violation is increasingly being accepted in domestic courts. Nevertheless, the fact that large corporations operate at the international level requires an answer to the question whether there are judicial organs at the international and supra-national level that can directly enforce obligations on corporations. The question regarding corporate accountability at the international level is part of the broader theoretical query regarding the horizontal effect of human rights and the status of corporations under international law. This has been dealt with in part A of this study.[1] The purpose of this chapter is to assess the procedural possibilities for holding corporations directly accountable at the international level. This will be done by describing and analysing international procedures that either aim to hold violators of human rights accountable, or could possibly function as such. Several international and supranational human rights mechanisms will be examined. Firstly, the international human rights organs, both at the international and regional level, will be dealt with. Secondly, developments in international criminal law will be discussed. Finally, a brief excursion into the field of international trade agreements will be made in order to assess whether these agreements offer any possibilities for holding corporations directly accountable for human rights violations. In that respect the focus will be on the procedures created under the World Trade Organisation (WTO) and the North American Free Trade Association (NAFTA).

2 INTERNATIONAL HUMAN RIGHTS MECHANISMS

Since World War II, a range of mechanisms has been developed both at the international and the regional level which aim to ensure that human rights obligations are

1 See chapters II and III, pp. 19-74.

complied with. The treaties establishing these mechanisms have been drawn up and ratified by States and States are the entities that can be held directly accountable before these mechanisms.[2]

At the European level two instruments deal with human rights: the European Convention on Human Rights (ECHR) and the European Social Charter (ESC). Under the ECHR, States and individuals can submit a complaint. As was discussed in chapter III, it can be deduced from the case-law of the European Court that the European Convention covers the protection of human rights against actions by private bodies and not only against State actions.[3] Nevertheless, complaints regarding human rights violations can only be brought before the European Court when a State has not complied with its obligations arising from the European Convention.[4] Corporations cannot be accused of human rights violations before the Court.

The supervisory mechanism of the ESC consists of a reporting procedure.[5] The contracting States are required to submit, on a regular basis, reports on the implementation of the Charter. On 1 July 1998, an additional Protocol to the ESC entered into force. This Protocol provides for a collective complaints procedure. States, having accepted this procedure, allow the following organisations to file a complaint alleging a breach of the Charter:

> '(...) international organisations of employers and trade unions [and] other international non-governmental organisations which have consultative status with the Council of Europe and have been put on a list established for this purpose by the Governmental Committee (...).'[6]

Again, complaints can only be brought against a State party.[7]

---

2 See also chapter VI.

3 See pp. 48-72.

4 See art. 34 of Protocol No. 11 of the Convention For The Protection Of Human Rights And Fundamental Freedoms, Strasbourg, 11.V.1994: 'The Court may receive applications from any person, non-governmental organisation or group of individuals claiming to be the victim of a violation by one of the High Contracting Parties of the rights set forth in the Convention or the protocols thereto'.

5 Art. 21 of the European Social Charter, *European Treaty Series - No. 163*, 3.V.1996.

6 Art. 1 of the Additional Protocol to the European Social Charter Providing for a System of Collective Complaints, Strasbourg, 9.XI.1995.

7 Art. 4 of the Additional Protocol reads: 'The complaint shall be lodged in writing, relate to a provision of the Charter accepted by the Contracting Party concerned and indicate in what respect the latter has not ensured the satisfactory application of this provision'. The first collective complaint under this protocol has been lodged by the International Commission of Jurists (IComJ) against Portugal concerning child labour: complaint 1/1998, lodged on 12 October 1998. This complaint concerned children set to work in corporations in the north of Portugal. According to Article 7, para. 1 of the ESC, States are required not just to set the minimum age of admission to employment at 15 but also to take the necessary measures to ensure the satisfactory application of this rule. According to the IComJ, Portugal has violated this article. The European Committee of Social Rights found that Portugal was indeed responsible. See Chapter III, p. 66. (note 102).

Likewise, in the Inter-American system, it is not possible to lodge a complaint against a legal person. Article 44 of the American Convention on Human Rights (ACHR) reads: 'any person or group of persons, or any non-governmental entity legally recognised in one or more member States of the Organisation, may lodge petitions with the Commission containing denunciations or complaints of violation of this Convention by a State Party'.[8]

Finally, the regional human rights system of Africa does not provide for a mechanism where private entities can be held directly accountable for human rights violations either. In 1981, the Eighteenth Assembly of the Heads of State and Government of the Organisation of African Unity (OAU) adopted the African Charter on Human and Peoples' Rights. Strictly speaking, a judicial or quasi-judicial organ is still absent.[9] The relevant organ is the African Commission on Human and Peoples' Rights. This Commission has a very wide and general mandate, including interpretation of the Charter and investigation.[10] The Commission's mandate only extends to supervising the behaviour of State Parties.[11]

As is the case with the judicial supervisory organs, the mandate of the monitoring bodies of the United Nations human rights treaties are equally limited to assessing the behaviour of States. All the United Nations human rights treaties provide for a reporting system according to which States have the obligation to submit reports on the measures taken to implement the treaty.[12] Moreover, optional protocols have been added to some of the human rights treaties allowing individuals to submit complaints with regard to the alleged violations by the State. For example, according to article 1 of the Optional Protocol to the ICCPR, the Human Rights Committee (HRC) can 'receive and consider communications from individuals subject to its jurisdiction who

8 American Convention on Human Rights, O.A.S. Treaty Series No. 36, 1144 U.N.T.S. 123 which entered into force July 18, 1978, reprinted in Basic Documents Pertaining to Human Rights in the Inter-American System, OEA/Ser.L.V/II.82 doc.6 rev.1 at 25 (1992).

9 On 10 June 1998, at the 34th Ordinary Session of the OAU held in Ouagadougou, Burkina Faso, the Assembly of Heads of State and Government of the OAU adopted the Protocol to the African Charter on Human and Peoples' Rights on the Establishment of an African Court on Human and Peoples' Rights. This Protocol has not yet entered into force.

10 See arts. 45-59 of the African Charter on Human Rights and Peoples' Rights.

11 This can be deduced from art. 47 which states: 'If a State party to the present Charter has good reason to believe that another State Party (...) has violated the provisions of the Charter it may draw the attention of that State to the matter. The communication shall also be addressed to (...) the Chairman of the Committee'.

12 Art. 16, para. 1 ICESCR and art. 40 ICCPR. Other human rights treaties also provide for a reporting procedure: art. 9 ICERD, art. 18 CEDAW, art. 19 CAT, art. 44 CRC and art. 22 of the ILO Covenant.

claim to be victims of a violation [of their rights] by [a] State Party'.[13] Hence, a corporation cannot be a defendant before the HRC.

None of the above mentioned international bodies dealing with human rights have jurisdiction over legal persons directly. As has been discussed in the previous chapters, this does not mean that legal persons do not have obligations under international law. Nevertheless, enforcing these human rights obligations at the international level is currently only possible if the harmful corporate activities can be traced back to a breach of obligations by a State. In the mechanisms according to which States are required to submit reports, more attention should be paid to the measures taken by States to regulate the behaviour of corporations. As was discussed in chapter VI, States have a due diligence obligation, *viz.* they must ensure that human rights are protected in their jurisdiction. A breach of this obligation can give rise to State responsibility.[14] Moreover, the individual complaints procedures can be used to scrutinise the behaviour of corporations indirectly by bringing a claim against a State for violation of its due diligence obligation.

It is feasible that, with the increasing attention to the role which corporations sometimes play in human rights violations, States at some point in the future might decide to draw up an international treaty laying down the international human rights obligations of corporations coupled with a supervisory mechanism that will ensure that corporations fulfil their obligations. However, in the light of probable political obstacles this will unquestionably be tremendously difficult to achieve. Pending such an agreement, it is crucial that the existing mechanisms, described above, are used to scrutinise corporate behaviour.

3 International Criminal Tribunals and Corporate Criminal Responsibility

The concept of the direct accountability of entities other than States at the international level is more accepted in the area of international criminal law, where individuals can be held accountable before international criminal tribunals. The question whether, next to natural persons, legal entities might also be held criminally accountable at the international level has been discussed in the context of the International Criminal Court (ICC). Consequently, I consider it useful to elaborate on the issue of international criminal responsibility.

The creation of international criminal tribunals dealing with individuals that violate international law is a revolutionary development in a system originally aimed at

13 Optional Protocol to the International Covenant on Civil and Political Rights, G.A. Res. 2200A (XXI), 21 U.N. GAOR Supp. (No. 16) at 59, UN Doc.A/6316 (1966), 999 U.N.T.S. 302, which entered into force March 23, 1976. An individual complaint procedure also exists under ICERD (art. 14), Optional protocol CEDAW (not yet in force) (art.1) and CAT (art.22).

14 See chapter VI, pp. 145-149.

protecting the individual from the State. The 20th century witnessed the realisation of several international criminal tribunals.[15] Article 227 of the Treaty of Versailles, drawn up after World War I, provided for the establishment of a tribunal to try the former Kaiser Wilhelm II. After the Kaiser fled to the Netherlands, the idea of an international court was abandoned. During and after World War II the Allies declared that they were committed to bringing German and Japanese war criminals to justice, which resulted in the establishment of the *ad hoc* tribunals in Nuremberg and Tokyo. The wars in Rwanda and the former Yugoslavia also led to the creation of two *ad hoc* tribunals. Finally, with the adoption of the Rome Statute for an International Criminal Court in 1998, a permanent international criminal court will now be established.

The question is what role, if any, corporations play (or have played) before these criminal tribunals? Before assessing the different tribunals – from the oldest to the newest – some preliminary remarks will be made about corporate criminal responsibility in general.

In addition to the individual criminal responsibility of the senior personnel of a corporation, a corporation may itself be criminally responsible for the actions or omissions of agents acting on its behalf. This is the case in the national law of several States.[16] Some authors find the concept of corporate criminal responsibility on the national level somewhat troublesome. In their view, legal persons are not endowed with reason or conscience and are therefore unsusceptible to guilt and punishment and, consequently, they cannot play a part in criminal law.[17] However, when punishment is considered in a functional manner it is possible to punish a corporation. The penalty can consist of fines, expropriation or dissolution.[18] It is important to keep in mind that

15 However, international criminal tribunals are not a twentieth century phenomenon. The earliest precedent for an international criminal tribunal can be traced back to 1474 with the trial of the Burgundian Governor of Breisach, Peter von Hagenback. Despite this precedent it would be nearly 500 years before another criminal tribunal would be created.

16 In the common law systems the concept of corporate criminal responsibility is more widely accepted than it is in the continental systems. In the United States criminal responsibility on the part of legal persons has been accepted to a greater degree than in other countries. In the United Kingdom corporate responsibility for most acts, except the typically individual crimes (for example, rape or manslaughter), has been accepted. In the Netherlands, criminal responsibility on the part of legal persons was introduced into the Criminal Code in 1976, article 51, Criminal Code. See: J. Remmelink, *D. Hazewinkel-Suringa's Inleiding tot de Studie van het Nederlandse Strafrecht [Introduction to Dutch Criminal Law],* 15th ed., Gouda Quint, Deventer, 1996, pp. 137-160. In France, the concept of responsibility on the part of *personnes morales* (*i.e.* non-human entities) was introduced into the French Criminal Code in 1994. For more on corporate criminal responsibility in general, see: Celia Wells, *Corporations and Criminal Responsibility*, Clarendon Press, Oxford, 1994. For detailed information on corporate criminal responsibility in national legal systems, see: Hans de Doelder and Klaus Tiedemann, *La Criminalisation du Comportement Collectif, XIVe Congres International de Droit Compare,* Kluwer Law International, The Hague, 1996.

17 Remmelink, *supra* n. 16, pp. 159-160.

18 Remmelink does not object to this functional approach, 'when the purpose of the prosecution is to improve or abolish an undesirable economic, fiscal or social situation'; Remmelink, *supra* n. 16, p. 160.

criminal attribution in international criminal law differs from criminal attribution in national criminal law: While in the latter case normally a concrete criminal result caused by a person's individual act is punished, under international criminal law for responsibility to arise the acts should be committed in a collective context and systematic manner.[19] The attribution of criminal responsibility to corporate entities on the international level therefore poses additional difficulties, especially concerning the required evidence.

The advantages of the criminal prosecution of corporations may not be obvious. In fact, criminal prosecution usually requires a higher burden of proof and penalties are mostly designed around imprisonment. The criminal prosecution of legal persons does, however, have certain advantages. Criminal law can be viewed either from an instrumental perspective or a symbolic perspective.[20] From the instrumental point of view, it might prove advantageous, as regards the question of possible compensation and reparation for the victims, to hold a corporation criminally responsible as opposed to an individual. Individuals might not have the assets to pay the reparation ordered by the court. From a symbolic point of view, the labelling of certain violations of international law by legal persons as crimes, might be more appropriate than torts, given the grave character of these violations.

3.1 The International Military Tribunals in Nuremberg and Tokyo

In 1945, France, Great Britain, the Soviet Union and the United States decided to establish an *ad hoc* International Military Tribunal (IMT) in Nuremberg to bring the Nazi war criminals to trial.[21] In addition, the International Military Tribunal for the Far East (Tokyo 1948) was established by a special proclamation of General MacArthur as the Supreme Commander in the Far East for the Allied Powers.[22]

---

19 Kai Ambos, 'Individual criminal responsibility', in: Otto Triffterer, *Commentary on the Rome Statute of the international Criminal Court: Observer's Notes, Article by Article*, Nomos, Baden Baden, 1999, p. 95.

20 Wells, *supra* n. 16, p. 15.

21 Agreement for the Prosecution and Punishment of Major War Criminals of the European Axis (London Agreement), signed in London, August 1945, 82 U.N.T.S 280, 59, E.A.S. No. 472 (entered into force, 8 August 1945); Charter of the International Military Tribunal (annexed to the London Agreement). These documents and the case-law of the IMT can be accessed at the website of the *Avalon project* of the University of Yale: http://www.yale.edu/lawweb/avalon/imt/proc/v1menu.htm (accessed on 18 December 2001). For a detailed analysis of the case-law with regard to corporations, see: Andrew Clapham, 'The Question of Jurisdiction Under International Criminal Law Over Legal Persons: Lessons from the Rome Conference on an International Criminal Court', in: *Liability of Multinational Corporations Under International Law*, Menno T.Kamminga and Saman Zia-Zarifi (eds)., 2000, pp. 139-195.

22 Charter of the International Military Tribunal for the Far East, 19 January 1946, amended on 26 April 1946, 82 U.N.T.S. 284.

At the IMT in Nuremberg private entities, such as corporations, could not be brought to trial. The competence of the IMT was held to extend only to natural persons. In its judgment the IMT stated that,

> 'enough has been said to show that individuals can be punished for violations of International Law. Crimes against International Law are committed by men not by abstract entities, and only by punishing individuals who commit such crimes can the provisions of International Law be enforced.'[23]

Although legal persons could not be tried in Nuremberg, the IMT did deal with legal entities. The IMT was vested with discretion to declare that an organisation was deemed criminal.[24] Article 10 of the IMT Charter read:

> 'In cases where a group or organization is declared criminal by the Tribunal, the competent national authority of any Signatory shall have the right to bring individuals to trial for membership therein before national, military or occupation courts. In any such case the criminal nature of the group or organization is considered proved and shall not be questioned.'[25]

The declaration stating that an organisation was deemed criminal thus fixed the criminality of the members of that organisation. It was then possible to bring individuals to trial for membership of such a group or organisation. Hence, in the words of Clapham, 'the Prosecutors in Nuremberg in fact started with the investigation of the legal person and chose their human defendants in order to be able to ensure the representation and defence of the legal person'.[26] Membership of a criminal organisation was punishable by death, imprisonment or fines.[27] Linking the criminality of natural persons to their membership of a criminal organisation is a far-reaching concept. It can result in prosecutions of thousands of defendants who may not have had the sort of criminal intent which would justify such harsh measures as the death penalty. Aware of this problem, the IMT, in its judgement, limited the notion of collective criminal responsibility as follows:

> '[s]ince the declaration with respect to the organisations and groups will (...) fix the criminality of its members, that definition should exclude persons who had no knowledge of the criminal purposes or acts of the organization (...), unless they were personally implicated in the commission of acts declared criminal by Article 6 of the Charter

23 Nuremberg Judgment, Law Reports of Trials of War Criminals, Vol. XXII, p. 447.
24 Art. 9 IMT Charter 82 UNTS 280, signed 8 August 1945, London.
25 82 UNTS 280, signed 8 August 1945, London.
26 Clapham *supra* n. 21, p. 164.
27 Law Number 10 of the Control Council of Germany passed on 20 December 1945.

> as members of the organization. Membership alone is not enough to come within the scope of these declarations.'[28]

The IMT declared the leadership corps of the Nazi Party, the Gestapo and the *Sicherheitsdienst des Reichfuehrer SS* (SD) and the *Schutzstaffel* (SS) to be criminal organisations. The Tribunal did not convict any natural persons for membership of these criminal organisations, however. This did occur with regard to corporations that were declared to be criminal organisations by the IMT. In the case against *I.G. Farben* the United States Military Tribunal declared that the corporation was criminal as a result of its involvement in war crimes, such as, *inter alia*, deportation, slave labour, terrorisation, torture, killings, plunder and spoliation of invaded countries and the production and supply of drugs and poison gas for experimental and extermination purposes.[29] The Tribunal emphasised that the *Farben* corporation was not on trial and could not be subjected to criminal penalties in these proceedings. However, according to the prosecution the defendants individually and collectively used the *Farben* corporation as an instrument through which they committed the crimes charged.[30] The Tribunal found that,

> 'the result was the enrichment of Farben and the building of its greater chemical empire through the medium of occupancy at the expense of the former owners. Such action on the part of Farben constituted a violation of the Hague Regulations. It was in violation of the rights of private property, protected by the Laws and Customs of War (…). The form of the transactions were varied and intricate, and were reflected in corporate agreements to create the illusion of legality. But the objective of pillage, plunder and spoliation stands out, and there can be no uncertainty as to the actual result.'[31]

The Tribunal subsequently convicted all members of the governing body of *Farben.* Clapham comes to the conclusion that the '*Farben* judgment can be read as implying that the Farben company itself had committed the relevant war crime, even though the

---

28 International Military Tribunal (Nuremberg) Judgment and Sentence, 1 October 1946, 41 American Journal of International Law, January 1947, pp. 172-333 at p. 251.

29 Case No. 57, the *I.G. Farben Trial* (United States Military Tribunal, Nuremberg, 14 August 1947-29 July 1948), *Law Reports of Trials of War Criminals*, Vol. X, p. 1. Other trials involving businessmen for crimes committed as such, were: Case No. 48, *Trial of Friedrich Flick and Five others*, 20 April-22 December 1947, *Law Reports of the Trials of War Criminals*, Vol. IX, p. 1 and Case No. 58 *The Krupp Trial*, 17 November 1947-30 June 1948, *Law Reports of Trials of War Criminals*, Vol. X, p. 69. A well-known case before a British Military Court is the *Zyklon B* trial, in which the director of a company was convicted for having sold large amounts of poison gas to German concentration camps knowing that it would be used for mass extermination, Case No. 9, *The Zyklon B Case*, 1-8 March 1946, *Law Reports of the Trials of War Criminals*, Vol. I, p. 93.

30 Case No. 57, the *I.G. Farben Trial* (United States Military Tribunal, Nuremberg, 14 August 1947-29 July 1948), *Law Reports of Trials of War Criminals*, Vol. X, at p. 1153.

31 Case No. 57, the *I.G. Farben Trial* (United States Military Tribunal, Nuremberg, 14 August 1947-29 July 1948), *Law Reports of Trials of War Criminals*, Vol. X, at p.50.

Tribunal had no jurisdiction over Farben as such'.[32] The prime interest of the IMT in the prosecution of the corporation rather than the individual was very clear in the case against *Krupp von Bohlen und Halbach*, the owner of *Krupp* enterprises, which was the chief supplier of armaments and munitions to Hitler. Due to senile dementia *Gustav Krupp von Bohlen* was in fact not fit to stand trial. However, the prosecutor argued that it would be contrary to the public interest to dismiss *Krupp von Bohlen*, unless his place was substituted by his son.[33]

The Charter of the International Military Tribunal for the Far East (The Tokyo Tribunal) was modelled largely on the Nuremberg Charter. However, while at Nuremberg both individuals and organisations were brought to trial, the Tokyo Charter contained no provision regarding allegedly criminal organisations.[34]

3.2 International Convention on the Suppression and Punishment of the Crime of Apartheid

A convention worth mentioning in the context of bringing criminal activities of legal persons within the jurisdiction of an international criminal tribunal, is the International Convention on the Suppression and Punishment of the Crime of Apartheid. Under this Convention, it is possible for an International Criminal Tribunal to 'declare criminal those organisations, institutions and individuals committing the crime of apartheid'.[35]

In 1980, a Draft Statute for an international criminal tribunal to prosecute apartheid was elaborated, but the project has thus far not been acted upon. Even though the prohibitions in the Convention were not intended to apply exclusively to the specific case of South Africa, the future of the Convention, in the light of the end of apartheid in South Africa, is uncertain. The Convention is associated with the South African situation and States have not yet shown much inclination to apply the Apartheid Convention as a potential source of law.[36]

3.3 International Criminal Tribunal for the Former Yugoslavia

On 25 May 1993, the Security Council adopted Resolution 827, which created the International Criminal Tribunal for the Former Yugoslavia (ICTFY). Under the Statute

32 Clapham *supra* n. 21, pp. 170-171.

33 Answer of the United States Prosecutor to the Motion on Behalf of the defendant *Gustav Krupp von Bohlen*, Robert Jackson, 12 November 1945. Available at: www.yale.edu/lawweb/avalon/imt/proc/v11l.htm (accessed on 18 December 2001).

34 B.V.A. Röling and Antonio Cassese, *The Tokyo Trial and Beyond, Reflections of a Peacemonger*, Polity Press, Cambridge etc., 1994, p. 3.

35 Art. I, sub. 2 International Convention on the Suppression and Punishment of the Crime of Apartheid, adopted by the General Assembly on 30 November 1973.

36 Steven R. Ratner and Jason S. Abrams, *Accountability for Human Rights Atrocities in International Law. Beyond the Nuremberg Legacy*, Clarendon Press, Oxford, 1997, p.116.

of the ICTFY it is not possible to prosecute legal persons. According to article 6 of the Statute 'the International Tribunal shall have jurisdiction over natural persons (...)'.[37] In the report establishing the ICTY Statute, the Secretary-General did address the question how the term 'persons' should be interpreted. Clearly rejecting the 'Nuremberg construction' the Secretary-General stated that,

> '(...) the ordinary meaning of the term "persons responsible for serious violations of international humanitarian law" would be natural persons to the exclusion of juridical persons. The questions arises, however, whether a juridical person, such as an association or organisation, may be considered criminal as such and thus its members, for that reason alone, be made subject to the jurisdiction of the International Tribunal. The Secretary-General believes that this concept should not be retained in regard to the International Tribunal. The criminal acts set out in this statute are carried out by natural persons; such persons would be subject to the jurisdiction of the International Tribunal irrespective of membership in groups.'[38]

3.4 International Criminal Tribunal for Rwanda

On 8 November 1994, the Security Council adopted resolution 955 (1994) creating the International Criminal Tribunal for Rwanda (ICTR). The history of the ICTR mirrors that of the ICTFY in many respects. The Tribunal was established,

> 'for the sole purpose of prosecuting persons responsible for genocide and other serious violations of international humanitarian law committed in the territory of Rwanda and Rwandan citizens responsible for genocide and other such violations committed in the Territory of neighbouring states, between 1 January 1994 and 31 December 1994.'[39]

Corporations played an important role in the genocide that took place in Rwanda. For example, coffee companies in Rwanda assisted in the genocide by storing arms and equipment. Furthermore, construction companies and radio stations were also actively involved in the Rwanda genocide.[40] Despite the role which corporations apparently played in the genocide in Rwanda, these entities are not included within the jurisdiction of the ICTR. According to article 5 of the Statute only natural persons fall within the jurisdicion of the ICTR.

---

37 Art. 6 of the Statute of the International Tribunal for the Prosecution of Persons Responsible for Serious Violations of International Humanitarian Law Committed in the Territory of the Former Yugoslavia since 1991.

38 Report of the Secretary-General S/1993/25704 of 3 May 1993, pursuant to para. 2 of Security Council Resolution 808 (1993), UN doc. S/INF/49 (1994), p. 14.

39 UN Doc. S/RES/955 (1994), 8 November 1994, para. 1.

40 Clapham *supra* n. 21, p. 148. He refers to statements made by the Tanzanian representative at the negotiations on the ICC Statute. As will be discussed in the following section, the issue of international criminal responsibility for corporations arose during the negotiations on the Rome Statute.

3.5 The Permanent International Criminal Court

The criminal tribunals discussed above are all of an *ad hoc* nature. The idea to establish a permanent international court first emerged in 1948 when the General Assembly asked the ILC to study the desirability of a Criminal Chamber for the International Court of Justice (ICJ).[41] In the deliberations that followed, the question was also addressed whether the ICJ should be competent to judge corporations. It was argued that the criminal responsibility of corporations was not excluded either by doctrine or by case-law as criminal responsibility on the part of private corporations was not unknown in some criminal legal systems.[42] It was further argued that the mere fact that the responsibility of corporations under existing international law was not entirely clear should not mean that every possibility of conferring jurisdiction over them should be denied.[43] However, eventually it was concluded that it was undesirable to include so novel a principle as corporate criminal responsibility in the statute.[44] Under the present Statute corporations cannot be a party before the ICJ. The Statute is clear regarding jurisdiction; only States may be parties in cases before the ICJ.[45]

An international criminal court could have been established based on the 1948 Genocide Convention. This Convention recognised the jurisdiction of an international criminal tribunal, should one be established, but the Convention did not require that such a court must be established.[46]

The idea of a permanent international criminal court lay dormant, partly as a result of the Cold War, for over forty years. The idea was again taken up in 1989 by the General Assembly at the request of Trinidad and Tobago, a small nation which thought that a permanent international criminal court would assist it in combating drug trafficking and crimes that small nations simply could not deal with on their own.[47] In 1992,

41 UN Doc.A/Res/260 B (III), 9 December 1948.

42 Other national legal systems, however, did not recognize such a criminal responsibility on the part of legal entities and it was therefore felt by most members of the Committee that the introduction of such a responsibility in international law would be a matter of considerable controversy. A/2136 Report of the Committee on International Criminal Jurisdiction, 1-31 August 1951, General Assembly, Official records: seventh session, Supplement No. 11, para. 88.

43 A/2136 Report of the Committee on International Criminal Jurisdiction, 1-31 August 1951, General Assembly, Official records: seventh session, Supplement No. 11, para. 88.

44 By 11 votes to none, with three abstentions, the Committee therefore expressed itself in favour of the principle that the court should be competent to pass judgment on the criminal responsibility of individuals only. A/2136 Report of the Committee on International Criminal Jurisdiction, 1-31 August 1951, General Assembly, Official records: seventh session, Supplement No. 11, para. 88.

45 Art. 34, sub. 1 Statute of the International Court of Justice.

46 Art. IV, Convention on the Prevention and Punishment of the Crime of Genocide, 9 December 1948.

47 See Jelena Pejic's comments at an NGO Coalition for an International Criminal Court press briefing held in New York on 13 August 1996, http://www.lchr.org/lchr/icc/press2.htm (accessed on 17 December 2001).

the General Assembly directed the ILC to elaborate a draft statute for a permanent international criminal court.

In July 1998, the United Nations Diplomatic Conference of Plenipotentiaries on the Establishment of an International Criminal Court signed the Rome Statute of the ICC.[48] The Rome Statute is directed towards ending impunity for crimes against humanity, the crime of genocide and war crimes committed by governments and government officials.[49]

Under the Rome Statute only natural persons can be brought to trial before the ICC.[50] However, the issue whether the jurisdiction of the ICC should include corporations was discussed during the negotiations on the Rome Statute. The French delegation proposed the inclusion of legal persons within the jurisdiction of the ICC. The initial proposal was clearly modelled on the Nuremberg precedent as it stated that when a crime had been committed by a natural person on behalf or with the assent of a group, the ICC could declare the group to be a criminal organisation. Such a declaration would oblige State parties to take measures in response. The proposal was further discussed and elaborated upon, resulting in a final French proposal,[51] which was discussed at the Conference in Rome. If this text would have been adopted, the ICC would have had jurisdiction not only over natural persons but also over legal persons. In the final French proposal article 23, paragraphs 5 and 6 read as follows:

> '5. Without prejudice to any individual criminal responsibility of natural persons under this Statute, the Court may also have jurisdiction over a juridical person for a crime under this Statute. Charges may be filed by the Prosecutor against a juridical person, and the Court may render a judgement over a juridical person for the crime charged, if:
> (…)
> b) The natural person charged was in a position of control within the juridical person under the national law of the State where the juridical person was registered at the time the crime was committed; and
> c) The crime was committed by the natural person acting on behalf of and with the explicit consent of that juridical person and in the course of its activities; and
> d) The natural person has been convicted of the crime charged.
> For the purpose of this Statute, 'juridical' person means a corporation whose concrete, real or dominant objective is seeking private profit or benefit, and not a State or other public body in the exercise of State authority, a public international body or an organi-

48 166 States, 33 governmental organizations and 36 NGOs took part in the conference. The Statute was adopted by a vote of 120 in favour, 7 against with 21 abstentions. Those who stated on the record that they voted against the Statute are: the United States of America, Israel and China. It seems that the other negative votes were cast by Iraq, Qatar, Sri Lanka and Sudan. On 2 January 2002, the Rome Statute had 139 signatory States of which 48 States had ratified the Rome Statute. The ICC will be formally established after 60 States have ratified the Rome Statute.

49 Art. 5 of the ICC Statute.

50 Art. 25, sub. 1 of the ICC Statute.

51 UN Doc. A/Conf.183/C.1/WGGP/L.5/Rev.2, 3 July 1998.

sation registered, and acting under the national law of a State as a non-profit organisation.
6. (...) The Prosecutor may file charges against the natural and juridical persons jointly or separately. The natural and the juridical person may be jointly tried.
If convicted, the juridical person may incur the penalties referred to in article 76. (...).'[52]

The essential difference with the initial proposal, based on the Nuremberg precedent, was that, rather than implicating an individual by association with a legal person, the drafters of this proposal sought to implicate the legal person, once the natural person had been convicted of a crime. This is clearly the result of the negative experiences with the concept of collective corporate responsibility at the Nuremberg trials. The adverse effect of the responsibility of natural persons for grave crimes such as genocide, merely because of membership of such an organisation, is avoided in this construction. According to the proposal, if an individual has already been tried and found guilty and that individual was in a position of control in the corporation, then there may be grounds to hold the corporation responsible.

The proposal gave rise to controversy within the Preparatory Committee. There was a deep divergence of views as to the advisability of including the criminal responsibility of corporations within the jurisdiction of the ICC. Many delegations were strongly opposed, whereas some strongly favoured its inclusion. Some delegations held the view that only providing for the civil or administrative liability of legal persons could provide a middle ground.[53] After three weeks of negotiations and the circulation and discussion of a number of texts, the proposal was finally withdrawn by the French delegation. No agreement could be found to include jurisdiction over legal persons.

There were several stumbling blocks.[54] Firstly, the question arose who would represent the legal person before the ICC and how assets could be taken without affecting the rights of third persons. Secondly, it proved impossible to satisfy those who feared that this provision could be used against entities struggling for self-determination or against State entities. According to Clapham, the latter concern especially proved an obstacle as States feared possible prosecution and were wary of having to defend themselves or their corporations before the ICC.[55] This fear becomes apparent from the explicit exclusion of States from the definition in the final proposal. However, not only States were opposed to widening the ICC's jurisdiction. For example, Am-

52 UN Doc. A/Conf.183/C.1/WGGP/L.5/Rev.2, 3 July 1998 [footnotes omitted].
53 UN Doc. A/Conf.183/2/Add.1, 14 April 1998, Art. 23, para. 6 note 3. For a detailed discussion of the deliberations on this French proposal see: Clapham *supra* n. 21, pp. 139-195, especially pp. 150-158. Professor Clapham acted as a legal advisor to the Government of the Solomon Islands for the duration of the United Nations Diplomatic Conference of Plenipotentiaries on the Establishment of an International Criminal Court. The Solomon Islands delegation was approached by the French delegation and asked to assist France in organizing the consultations regarding the proposal relating to legal persons.
54 Kai Ambos, *supra* n. 19, p. 96 and Clapham *supra* n. 21, pp. 156-158.
55 Clapham *supra* n. 21, p. 156.

nesty International was also opposed to including legal persons within the jurisdiction of the court arguing that

> 'Article 23 (5) and (6), both of which provide for criminal responsibility of legal persons (such as corporations or political parties) are inconsistent with the prohibition of collective criminal responsibility and should be deleted. Of course, legal persons should be civilly responsible in certain cases for the acts of their personnel.'[56]

In the third place, the negotiators feared that the inclusion of collective responsibility would detract from the ICC's jurisdictional focus, which is on individuals. Moreover, on a practical level, many delegations felt that there was simply no time to elaborate acceptable solutions. Finally, the fact that the concept of corporate criminal responsibility has not been recognised in various national criminal law systems, presented a stumbling block. The absence of corporate criminal responsibility in many States would render the principle of complementarity[57] unworkable.

In the final version of the Statute no reference was made to legal persons in the article on the jurisdiction of the ICC. However, under the current ICC Statute the possibility does exist to convict *corporate officers* for their activities. Moreover, some provisions in the ICC Statute leave open the possibility that corporations will be included within the jurisdiction of the ICC in the future.

As correctly pointed out by Clapham, the concept of criminalizing individual participation in a crime committed by a collective entity is present and operative in the final Statute. In article 25, paragraph 3 (d) it is stated that individual criminal responsibility is incurred where the individual contributes to the commission of a crime within the jurisdiction of the court, committed by a group of persons acting with a common purpose. It is added that such contribution shall be intentional and shall either be made with the aim of furthering the criminal activity or criminal purpose of the group, where such activity or purpose involves the commission of a crime within the jurisdiction of the court, or be made in the knowledge of the intention of the group to commit the crime. Complicity includes 'providing the means for its commission or its attempted commission' or contributing 'in any other way to the commission or the attempted commission' of a covered crime.[58] The mental state requires 'knowledge of the intention of the group' that commits the offence. Knowledge is defined as 'awareness that a circumstance exists or a consequence will occur in the ordinary course of events'.[59] Regarding possible difficulties in finding the responsible person within a

56 Amnesty International - Report - IOR 40/10/98 May 1998 United Nations (UN), The International Criminal Court Making the Right Choices - Part V, Recommendations to the Diplomatic Conference.

57 The complementarity principle implies that the ICC can only act when it is manifest that a state Party is unwilling or unable genuinely to carry out the investigation or prosecution, Article 17 Statute ICC. The jurisdiction of the ICC is therefore tempered as it is subject to national jurisdictions.

58 Art. 25, para. 3 (c) and (d) of the ICC Statute.

59 Art. 30, para. 2, of the ICC Statute.

corporation, article 28 of the ICC Statute offers a solution. This article deals with the responsibility of commanders. The first paragraph deals with military commanders.[60] The second paragraph, however, deals with other superiors:

> '28 (2) With respect to superior and subordinate relationships not described in paragraph 1, a superior shall be criminally responsible for crimes within the jurisdiction of the Court committed by subordinates under his or her effective authority and control, as a result of his or her failure to exercise control properly over such subordinates, where:
> The superior either knew, or consciously disregarded information which clearly indicated, that the subordinates were committing or about to commit crimes;
> The crimes concerned activities that were within the effective responsibility and control of the superior; and
> The superior failed to take all necessary and reasonable measures within his or her power to prevent or repress their commission or to submit the matter to the competent authorities for investigation and prosecution.'[61]

In addition to locating the responsible officers, the concept of command responsibility offers interesting opportunities in pinpointing accountability on parent companies, as was discussed in chapter VII with regard to accountability at the national level.[62]

Moreover, the ICC Statute contains provisions that allow for the possible expansion of the jurisdiction of the ICC to include corporations in the future.[63] The 1994 draft Statute stated that imprisonment and fines would be the penalties applicable to persons convicted of a crime.[64] In the 1998 draft text, available at the start of the conference in Rome, the penalties applicable to the convicted (legal) person were broader: fines, dissolution, prohibition of activities, closure of the premises used in the commission of the crime, forfeiture of proceeds, property and assets obtained by criminal conduct and appropriate forms of reparation.[65] In the final text of the Statute the possibility of reparations, fines and forfeiture has been retained (for natural persons). It has been

---

60 Art. 28, para. 1 ICC Statute reads. 'A military commander or person effectively acting as a military commander shall be criminally responsible for crimes within the jurisdiction of the Court committed by forces under his or her effective command and control, or effective authority and control as the case may be, as a result of his or her failure to exercise control properly over such forces, where:
(a) That military commander or person either knew or, owing to circumstances at the time should have known that the forces were committing or about to commit such crimes; and
(b) That military commander or person failed to take all necessary and reasonable measures within his or her power to prevent or repress their commission or to submit the matter to the competent authorities for investigation and prosecution'.

61 Art. 28, of the ICC Statute.

62 See p. 189.

63 The ICC Statute can be amended. For the first seven years after the Statute enters into force there is no possibility of proposing non-institutional amendments. According to Article 123, seven years after the Statute enters into force, a Review Conference will be held to consider amendments to the Statute.

64 UN Doc. A/49/10, Art. 47.

65 UN Doc. A/Conf.183/2/Add.1, 14 April 1998, Artt. 79 and 99.

agreed that punishment can extend beyond imprisonment. This leaves room for including legal persons in the Statute at a later stage.

3.6 Concluding Remarks on International Criminal Law Mechanisms

The existing mechanisms created for prosecuting violators of international criminal law currently offer no possibilities for the prosecution of corporations. Nevertheless, the process towards the establishment of international criminal tribunals has been discussed at some length here, as it demonstrates that the concept of the international responsibility of legal entities for human rights violations *as such* is not alien to international criminal law. It can be argued that even though corporations such as *I.G. Farben, Flick* and *Krupp* were not parties to any treaty, the IMT recognised that these corporations had violated international law and went on to attach individual criminal responsibility. From the discussion above, it can be deduced that the main arguments against including legal persons within the jurisdiction of the ICC were not of a legal nature, but rather of a practical and political nature. As Clapham concludes: 'The question *whether* legal persons are bound by international law was never posed. (…) [T]he real preoccupation was with shielding the public sphere from the jurisdiction of this new Court.'[66]

At present, there are no international mechanisms where corporations can be held directly accountable for human rights violations. The developments in international criminal law demonstrate, however (as is the case with human rights obligations), that the fact that corporations cannot be brought to trial does not mean that they do not fall under international criminal law.

4 Enforcement of Human Rights through Trade Agreements

The international organisations that aim to facilitate trade and economic co-operation have created dispute settlement systems that are commonly considered highly effective.[67] This warrants a brief excursion into the field of international trade agreements. This section aims to describe how these mechanisms function and whether they can play a role as regards regulating corporate conduct in the light of human rights. It can be argued that enforcing the human rights obligations of corporations will be the most effective when these obligations are incorporated into a trade agreement. Firstly,

66 Clapham, *supra* n. 21, p. 191.

67 See, for example, with regard to the WTO the report of the International Council on Human Rights Policy, *Beyond Voluntarism. Human rights and the developing international legal obligations of companies* 2002, p. 112: 'The WTO has one of the most effective systems for peacefully resolving inter-state disputes. (…) The procedures are not dormant paper provisions; they are regularly and successfully invoked to enforce trade rules'.

the effective dispute settlement systems that exist under these agreements could be invoked to enforce corporate human rights obligations. Secondly, if human rights obligations are balanced with regulations aimed at facilitating and protecting corporate activities, this may prove to be an incentive for corporations to fulfil their obligations. In this section the World Trade Organisation (WTO)[68] and the North American Free Trade Agreement (NAFTA)[69] will be discussed.[70]

4.1 The World Trade Organisation

The World Trade Organisation[71] was established in 1995, succeeding the 1947 General Agreement on Tariffs and Trade (GATT).[72] The main objective of the WTO is to 'liberalize international trade and place it on a secure basis' which will 'thereby contribut[e] to the economic growth, development and welfare of the world's people'.[73] The WTO administers a series of international agreements which can be divided into three pillars: trade in goods, trade in services and intellectual property. Throughout these agreements, three core principles can be found. Firstly, thc 'most-favoured-nation treatment', which requires States to grant all their trading partners the same treatment. Secondly, the principle of 'national treatment' demands that a State will treat imported goods no less favourably than similar domestic goods. Finally, quantitative restrictions, such as quotas, import bans, and export bans are prohibited. The main aim of these principles is to secure the equality of competitive trading opportunities between States.

Under the WTO a highly effective trade dispute settlement system has been created. If a State feels that another State has violated the WTO rules, it can refer the trade dispute to the WTO Dispute Settlement Body.[74] If negotiations fail, a panel will make

68 See the WTO's website: http://www.wto.org (accessed on: 17 December 2001).

69 The full text of the NAFTA can be found at the following site: http://www-tech.mit.edp.u/Bulletins/nafta.html (accessed on 15 August 2000).

70 This section deals with the dispute settlement mechanisms that specifically deal with trade. The international financial institutions, the World Bank and the International Monetary Fund, are not dealt with in this study. See, for a detailed study: Sigrun I, Skogly, *The Human Rights Obligations of the World Bank & the International Monetary Fund*, London, Cavendish Publishing, 2001.

71 Agreement establishing the World Trade Organization, opened for signature on 5 April 1994, 33 I.L.M. 1144. The WTO was established during the Uruguay Round of trade negotiations on the 15 April 1994. On 1 January 1995 the Agreement entered into force.

72 General Agreement on Tariffs and Trade, 30 October 1947, 55 U.N.T.S. 188, 262.

73 Final Act Embodying the Results of the Uruguay Round of Multilateral Trade Negotiations, Agreement establishing the Multilateral Trade Organization.

74 Art. 3, Understanding on Rules and Procedures Governing the Settlement of Disputes, 15 April 1994, 33 I.L.M. 1226.

the first ruling.[75] A party can appeal the decision based on points of law.[76] All final rulings or decisions are adopted automatically, unless WTO members decide by consensus not to do so.[77] The effectiveness of this system follows from the fact that, if a State fails to change the practice or regulations that have been found to be in violation of WTO rules, the aggrieved State has the right to impose trade sanctions against this State.[78] The dispute settlement system is an inter-State system. It has become clear that States will bring trade disputes before the Dispute Settlement Body in order to protect the commercial interests of their corporations. A well-known example is the dispute between the United States and the European Union concerning European subsidies to Caribbean banana exporters. It has been suggested that the US corporations *Chiquita* and *Dole* were behind the complaint filed by the United States.

What role, if any, does this strong and effective mechanism play as regards enforcing human rights obligations? In reaching a decision the WTO Appellate Body is required to take all relevant rules of international law into account. However, human rights considerations have so far not played a role. In fact, the WTO and the dispute settlement system are frequently considered to be detrimental to the protection and promotion of human rights. The above mentioned core principles of the WTO – the 'most-favoured-nation treatment' and the principle of 'national treatment'– are potentially in conflict with human rights objectives. Under human rights treaties, States are required to take steps to implement the rights contained in the treaties. These steps may very well be contradictory to the WTO principle of national treatment, however. For example, the right to health requires that States ensure access to medicine. The intellectual property protection offered by the WTO Agreement on Trade-Related Intellectual Property rights (TRIPs Agreements) can have adverse consequences for the possibilities of States to realise the right to health. Subsequently, the WTO has encountered a great deal of criticism from the human rights community.[79] For example, in 2000 the UN Sub-Commission published a highly critical report.[80] According to this report, the WTO's.

75 Art. 8, Understanding on Rules and Procedures Governing the Settlement of Disputes, 15 April 1994, 33 I.L.M. 1226.

76 Art. 17, Understanding on Rules and Procedures Governing the Settlement of Disputes, 15 April 1994, 33 I.L.M. 1226.

77 Arts. 16.4, 17.14, Understanding on Rules and Procedures Governing the Settlement of Disputes, 15 April 1994, 33 I.L.M. 1226.

78 Art. 22, Understanding on Rules and Procedures Governing the Settlement of Disputes, 15 April 1994, 33 I.L.M. 1226.

79 Besides the fact that the principles of the WTO may undermine the objective of the human rights system, the WTO has been criticised for its lack of transparency and accountability. The criticism with regard to the WTO culminated in protests on the streets of Seattle in 1999 during the summit of the WTO.

80 UN Doc. E/CN.4/Sub.2/2000/13, 15 June 2000.

> '(...) trade and commerce activities have serious human rights implications. This is compounded by the fact that the founding instruments of WTO make scant (indeed only oblique) reference to the principles of human rights. The net result is that for certain sectors of humanity – particularly the developing countries in the South – the WTO is a veritable nightmare.'[81]

The Committee on Economic, Social and Cultural Rights has also paid attention to the impact of the policies of the WTO on human rights. In a statement to the WTO's Third Ministerial Conference, the Committee noted that human rights norms must shape the process of international economic policy formulation so that the benefits for human development of the evolving international trade regime will be shared equitably by all, in particular the most vulnerable sectors. The Committee stated its willingness to work together with the WTO in the realisation of economic, social and cultural rights.[82]

The need to take the social impact of trade into account in the context of the WTO has repeatedly been discussed. During the Uruguay round of the GATT negotiations, a proposal was put forward to include a – so-called – social clause in the WTO Agreement which would aim to prevent and redress violations of workers' rights. The question whether a social clause should be included in the WTO proved to be one of the thorniest problems at the WTO First Ministerial Conference in Singapore in 1996. Eventually the proposal was rejected due to fierce opposition from the business community and developing nations. The latter viewed a social clause as a disguised form of protectionism. It was decided that the ILO was the relevant institution to deal with such issues.[83] Consequently, the WTO deals exclusively with WTO rules on trade liberalisation.

In sum, the rules of the WTO are potentially in conflict with the objectives of the human rights regime. The strong dispute settlement mechanism can be detrimental to human rights. In theory it is possible that a State, in order to protect the commercial interests of a corporation, will file a complaint against another State in order to remove a measure that is perceived as a trade restriction but has been taken in the light of the State's human rights obligations.

---

81 UN Doc. E/CN.4/Sub.2/2000/13, 15 June 2000, para. 15.

82 UN Doc. E/C.12/1999/9, 26 November 1999, para. 8.

83 The ILO does not have an observer status in the WTO General Council, however. For a proposal as to how the ILO and the WTO could work together in enforcing labour standards, see: Erika de Wet, 'Labor Standards in the Globalized Economy: The Inclusion of a Social Clause in the General Agreement on Tariff and Trade/World Trade Organization, in: *Human Rights Quarterly*, Vol.17, 1995, pp. 443-462. See also: W.J.M. van Genugten, *WTO, ILO en EG: handelen in vrijheid [WTO, ILO and EC: Trading in Freedom*, W.E.J. Tjeenk Willink, Deventer, 1997. He points out that, notwithstanding procedurale problems in the relationship between the WTO and the ILO, the ILO is the appropriate organisation to watch over the social issues. Especially in the light of the effective supervisory procedures of the ILO.

As mentioned above, under the rules of the WTO, States are generally prohibited from creating rules that constitute trade limitations. However, several exceptions allow States to restrict trade when certain conditions are met. According to the general exception clause – article XX of the 1974 General Agreement on Tariffs and Trade – States, if *necessary*, may use trade-restrictive measures in order to, *inter alia*, protect public morals;[84] protect human, animal or plant life or health;[85] preserve exhaustible natural resources;[86] and they may also take measures relating to products of prison labour.[87] Nevertheless, to date, the practice of the panels show little or no willingness to invoke the general exceptions provided for under Article XX.[88] An exception is the 1998 *Import Prohibition of Certain Shrimp and Shrimp Products* case. In this case the WTO Appellate Body gave a more expansive reading of Article XX by suggesting that exceptions to the prohibition on trade restrictions might be considered necessary to enable a State to conform with its international obligations.

Another development that might offer a possibility to restrict trade in the light of concurring human rights obligation is if the WTO allows States to impose trade restrictions with regard to the *way* in which products are produced. Some commentators suggest that the WTO is moving closer towards allowing such restrictions.[89]

4.2 Concluding Remarks on the World Trade Organisation

The WTO dispute settlement system can be considered to be highly effective because of the possibility of applying trade sanctions if a decision is not followed. This effective system does not impose human rights obligations on corporations, however. Firstly, it is an inter-State system. But, more importantly, human rights so far have not been taken into consideration in the WTO dispute settlement system. In fact, the non-discriminatory principles of the WTO, which are enforced by the dispute settlement mechanism, can undermine the ability of states to fulfil their human rights obligations. Moreover, in accordance with article 23 of the WTO Dispute Settlement Understanding, if a dispute involves an allegation of a violation of WTO law, recourse to the WTO dispute settlement mechanism is compulsory and exclusive. This provision excludes recourse to any other jurisdiction if human rights are violated as a result of WTO rules.

84 Art. XX (a), GATT, 30 October 1947, 55 U.N.T.S. 188, 262.
85 Art. XX (b), GATT, 30 October 1947, 55 U.N.T.S. 188, 262.
86 Art. XX (g), GATT, 30 October 1947, 55 U.N.T.S. 188, 262.
87 Art. XX (e), GATT, 30 October 1947, 55 U.N.T.S. 188, 262.
88 Paul J.I.M. de Waart, Quality of Life at the Mercy of WTO Panels: GATT's Article XX an Empty Shell?', chapter 6 in: *International Economic Law with a Human Face*, Friedl Weiss, Erik Denters and Paul de Waart [eds.], Kluwer Law International, The Hague etc., 1998, pp.109-131. See also: Steve Charnovitz, 'The Moral Exception in Trade Policy', in: *Virginia Journal of International Law*, Vol. 38, 1998, pp. 689-744.
89 Report of the In-Depth Study Session on the WTO for Human Rights Professionals, Morges, Switzerland, 27-28 July 2001.

Some scholars argue that human rights law has primacy over WTO law, as the UDHR is generally considered to be customary international law, while some of the human rights norms are also *jus cogens* principles. Hence, the provisions of the WTO should be interpreted in a way which is consistent with the human rights norms in the UDHR.[90] Nevertheless, the present-day reality is that two international systems have developed in total isolation of each other and the strong enforcement system established by the WTO, rather than benefiting human rights, may in fact undermine them.

4.3 The North American Free Trade Agreement

The 1992 NAFTA aims to liberalise trade between Canada, the United States and Mexico. Contrary to the WTO, where regulations to protect human rights are largely perceived as camouflaged trade barriers, under the NAFTA trade restriction is permissible if the demonstrated purpose of the measure is to achieve a legitimate objective. Complying with an international standard is presumed to be such a legitimate objective. Moreover, States are allowed to establish higher standards than internationally required.[91] Notwithstanding this, the NAFTA resembles the WTO in many ways, especially with regard to the dispute settlement system. Under chapter 11 of the NAFTA, corporations have recourse to a binding dispute settlement system according to which they can bring a case against one of the participating States for a regulation or government decision which they feel violates the investor protection provisions under the NAFTA.[92] In several instances corporations have successfully sued States and received large sums of money as compensation for violations of the NAFTA. For example, in the case of *Ethyl Corporation* v. *Canada*, a United States' corporation sued Canada for implementing an environmental law which prohibited the import of a gasoline additive, MMT. Under the environmental law, the Canadian subsidiary of *Ethyl Corporation* would be prohibited from importing the additive. The arbitrators agreed with the corporation that this violated the investor protection provisions under NAFTA, and Canada decided to settle the dispute by paying $13 million and withdrew the legislation which *Ethyl* opposed.

In August 2001 the Trade Ministers of the NAFTA States modified the chapter 11 dispute regulation. They issued a binding interpretation that directs the chapter 11 arbitration panels to abide by the narrow standard of 'customary international law' in deciding whether companies have been denied 'fair and equitable treatment'.

It can be concluded that the NAFTA provides an effective dispute settlement mechanism. This system does not, however, offer any opportunities with regard to

90 Warren Allmand, *Trading in Human Rights: The need for human rights sensitivity at the World Trade Organization*, A brief to the Standing Committee on Foreign Affairs and International Trade, 24 March, 1999, International Centre for Human Rights and Democratic Development.

91 Art. 904(4)(a), 905(2) and 905(3) NAFTA.

92 Arts. 1115-1138 of the NAFTA.

enforcing obligations on corporations. Corporations can request a binding decision, but they cannot themselves be brought before an arbitration panel.

Two other complaint mechanisms that have been created under NAFTA warrant discussion. Partly as a result of pressure from the public,[93] two complaint mechanisms for individuals have been created that are interesting in the light of scrutinising, albeit indirectly, the behaviour of corporations. These so-called side agreements aim to protect labour rights and the environment.

4.3.1 The NAFTA Side Agreements

The two side agreements that have been added to the NAFTA are: the North American Agreement on Environmental Co-operation (the NAAEC) and the North American Agreement on Labor Co-operation (NAALC). In the light of the fact that the NAAEC deals exclusively with environmental regulations, the focus in this section will be on the NAALC which deals with labour rights.[94]

The NAALC can be considered as the first attempt to reconcile trade objectives and social values. Under the NAALC dispute settlement mechanism it is only possible to file a complaint against a State for not enforcing labour laws. It does not allow for a direct complaint against a corporation. The NAALC has, however, been called 'the most extensive, internationally enforceable mechanism' for the protection of workers' rights containing 'real sanctions for an entire range of violations, though not all'.[95] It therefore merits discussion.

The NAFTA and the two side agreements on labour and the environment entered into force on 1 January 1994. The fact that the supplements were a part of NAFTA and that the package needed to be adopted in its entirety, resulted in a weakened agreement.[96] The emphasis is on the enforcement of national standards; there is no reference to internationally recognised labour standards. There was strong opposition against including international labour standards in the agreement. The main reason given for this exclusion was that the majority of the ILO Conventions in which these labour standards are codified, were not yet ratified by the United States. Moreover, the

---

93 Jack I. Garvey, 'Trade Law and Quality of Life-Dispute Resolution under the NAFTA Side Accords on Labor and the Environment', in: *The American Journal of International Law,* Current Developments, Vol. 89, 1995, pp. 439-453, p. 440.

94 For more information on the NAALC, see: Laura Okin Pomeroy in 'Note: The Labor Side Agreement under the NAFTA: Analysis of its failure to include strong enforcement provisions and recommendations for future labor agreements negotiated with developing countries', in: *George Washington Journal of International Law and Economics*, Vol. 29, 1996, pp. 769-801, p. 772.

95 This was said by Lael Brainard during an interdisciplinary discussion held at Harvard Law School in December 1997 on the topic of Business and Human Rights. The transcript of this meeting can be found at www:law.harvard.edu/programs/HRP/Publications/bussession1.html (accessed on 11 August 2000).

96 Pomeroy, *supra* n. 94, p. 775.

Mexican government feared an infringement of its sovereignty.[97] As a result of this strong opposition the NAALC merely requires that each participating State shall enforce its own domestic labour standards. The NAALC states that,

> 'while recognizing the right of each Party to establish its own domestic labor standards (...) each Party shall ensure that its labor laws and regulations provide for high labor standards, consistent with high quality and productivity workplaces, and shall continue to strive to improve those standards in that light.'[98]

Despite the absence of a reference to international standards, the NAALC could potentially contribute significantly to the protection of workers, as the national labour laws of some of the participating States offer a high level of protection. For instance, on paper the domestic labour standards in Mexico offer a great deal of protection for workers.[99]

4.3.2 Follow-Up

As stated above, the NAALC contains no minimum labour standards, it merely requires States to enforce their own national labour standards.[100] The implementation mechanism of the NAALC is rather complicated.[101] A trilateral commission, the 'Commission for Labor Co-operation', has been set up. This Commission acts as a governing body in overseeing the implementation of the NAALC and addressing conflicts that arise.[102] A complaint must first be directed at the National Administrative Offices that, according to the NAALC, must be established at the federal level in each country. These offices review complaints regarding a country's failure to comply with its domestic labour laws and determine whether to accept the complaint for review.[103] Complaints that one of the other countries is failing to enforce its labour laws can be filed by

97 Pomeroy, *supra* n. 94, p. 776.
98 NAALC Part 2, article 2.
99 Pomeroy, *supra* n. 94, p. 798.
100 Under the NAFTA a State is required to enforce its labour laws as they relate directly to the following labour rights: the freedom of association and protection of the right to organise; the right to bargain collectively; the right to strike; the prohibition of forced labour; labour protection for children and young persons; minimum employment standards, such as minimum wages and overtime pay, covering wage earners, including those not covered by collective agreements; the elimination of employment discrimination on the basis of race, religion, age, sex, or other grounds as determined by each country's domestic laws; equal pay for men and women; the prevention of occupational injuries and illnesses; and the protection of migrant workers.
101 See for a detailed analysis: Pomeroy, *supra* n. 94 and Garvey, *supra* n. 93.
102 The Commission is also responsible for promoting cooperative activities between the three countries and for establishing the rules of procedure of -and electing members for- the Evaluation Committee of Experts, NAALC, Part III, Sections A, B.
103 NAALC, Part III, Section C.

governments of the signatory countries, individuals and non-governmental organisations. If the National Administrative Office finds a complaint to be admissible it will convene a public meeting to assess the credibility of the allegations. During these proceedings the claim is publicly identified and a public report is filed. Subsequently, the National Administrative Office can recommend consultation at the ministerial level. With regard to complaints concerning the freedom of association, the right to strike and the right to bargain collectively, no further steps are possible under the NAALC procedure. If, with regard to claims concerning other rights, the ministerial consultations do not lead to an adequate resolution a State party may request the establishment of an Evaluation Committee of Experts.[104] This group of independent experts will study the claim and make recommendations. If, again, the outcome does not lead to a solution additional consultations with other countries can be held. When these consultations fail a special session of the Council can be convened. Finally, if all this does not lead to a satisfactory result, two out of three labour ministers can decide to establish an Arbitration Panel. To date, such an Arbitration Panel has not been set up. The Panel can decide, when a country has *persistently* failed to effectively enforce its occupational safety and health, child-labour or minimum wage standards, to apply monetary or trade sanctions. If so, recommendations are made. Only if the recommendation is not followed within sixty days, the country may be subjected to a fine of no more than .007 per cent of the total trade in goods between the three countries. After a period of six months, additional trade sanctions are possible if the country continues to refuse to comply. However, such sanctions are only possible in relation to labour laws that are trade-related and common to the three NAFTA countries.[105]

In April 2001, a total of twenty-three cases had been handled under the NAALC. In none of these cases monetary or trade sanctions were applied.

The question arises whether this detailed follow-up mechanism can be considered to be effective?[106] At each stage of the implementation mechanism, the range of areas that are investigated becomes more limited. Only violations of occupational safety and health, child labour or minimum wage standards can be the subject of sanctions. Basic workers' rights, such as the right to organise, can never reach the sanctions stage. It can be concluded that, given the amount of time[107] and the number of steps required to reach the arbitration stage, it is very unlikely that a monetary penalty will ever be

104 NAALC, Part III, Section B, art. 29.

105 NAALC, Part III, Section B, art.29.

106 For a detailed study of the effectiveness of the NAALC from the perspective of human rights, see Human Rights Watch, *Trading Away Rights. The Unfulfilled Promise of NAFTA's Labor Side Agreement*, Vol. 13 No. 2 (B), April 2001, this document is available at: http://www.hrw.org/reports/2001/nafta/index.htm (accessed on 18 December 2001).

107 According to Garvey a minimum of about 1,225 days are required from the initiation of the complaint to the sanctions stage, Garvey, *supra* n. 93, p. 442.

imposed on a country failing to enforce its labour laws.[108] At each step of the procedure, the possibility exists for the accused government to enter into negotiations well before any sanction is possible. This is considered a major weakness of the system.[109] Enforcement is further weakened by the various exceptions and vague terms contained in the Side Agreement.[110] An important aspect regarding the protection of workers is the relative openness of the system under NAFTA. The Side Agreements welcome input from NGOs and experts.[111]

4.4 Concluding Remarks on the NAFTA

It can be concluded that, from the perspective of directly addressing corporate human rights violations, the NAFTA does not offer any possibilities. Nevertheless, the Side Agreements attached to the NAFTA are interesting as they provide for the possibility to file complaints regarding another (NAFTA) country's inadequate response to corporate practices that violate workers' rights. Despite the fact that the NAALC does not refer to international standards, the implementation mechanism of the NAALC can provide a means for the indirect scrutiny of corporate behaviour. The NAALC has been criticised for lacking strong enforcement provisions, however.[112] The only available remedy for workers is discussion between governments. Employers cannot be forced to re-employ discharged workers and the basic labour rights, such as the freedom of association, are not subject to monetary sanctions.[113] Moreover, the mechanism is extremely lengthy and complicated.

5 Concluding Remarks on International Judicial Mechanisms

The purpose of this chapter was to answer the question whether corporations can be held directly accountable for human rights violations at the international level. Currently, the answer to this question is in the negative. There are no international mechanisms where corporations can be directly addressed for such violations. The international human rights supervisory mechanisms have in common that they only allow for complaints concerning human rights violations against State parties. Hence, corporate human rights violations can, as was described in chapter VI, only be addressed indirectly. It is possible that in the future, States might decide to draw up a special Convention that binds corporations directly to human rights norms. As this is currently not the

108 Pomeroy, *supra* n. 94, p. 784.
109 Garvey, *supra* n. 93, p. 443
110 Garvey, *supra* n. 93, p. 442.
111 Garvey, *supra* n. 93, p. 449-450
112 Pomeroy, *supra* n. 94, p. 791-792
113 Only the use of child labour, violation of minimum wages and occupational and safety standards are open to these sanctions.

case, it has been necessary to broaden the scope of the analysis in this chapter to other areas where corporations can possibly be held accountable.

The excursion into the field of international criminal law shows that the concept of holding corporate entities accountable for human rights violations is neither impossible nor a novelty. From the analysis of the developments during the negotiations leading up to the establishment of the ICC, it can be concluded that the current obstacles as regards the inclusion of corporations within the jurisdiction of the ICC are not based on issues of doctrine but that they are largely of a political nature. It is therefore conceivable that in the not too distant future the possibility of holding corporations accountable before the ICC for war crimes, genocide and crimes against humanity may indeed be possible.

Finally, this chapter has assessed the major international trade agreements, the WTO and the NAFTA, in order to see what role human rights considerations play within these agreements. This question has been deemed to be particularly interesting in the light of the strong enforcement mechanisms that have been created under these trade agreements. However, the dispute settlement mechanisms are only open to States and only scrutinise the behaviour of States. Moreover, it has been concluded that the objectives of the WTO and the NAFTA are potentially in conflict with human rights objectives.

PART C

SUMMARY, CONCLUSIONS AND RECOMMENDATIONS

CHAPTER IX
SUMMARY, CONCLUSIONS AND RECOMMENDATIONS

1 INTRODUCTION

The present study deals with the question if and to what extent corporations have human rights obligations and, if such obligations can be discerned, how these can be enforced. It was taken as a point of departure that, in the light of the impact of corporations on human rights the present human rights system, according to which primarily States bear obligations, is deficient. The examples of corporate influence on human rights violations that have been discussed throughout this study show the need to bring the legal reality into line with the requirements of practice.

In this final chapter the content and the findings in the foregoing chapters will first be summarized. Subsequently, some concluding observations will be presented in sections 3 and 4.

2 SUMMARY

In Part A I dealt with the theoretical questions that arise with regard to the issue of human rights obligations for corporations. Before embarking upon the analysis of the main question of whether corporations have human rights obligations, some conceptual issues needed to be clarified that potentially might constitute obstacles with regard to corporate human rights obligations.

First it was necessary to revisit the doctrine of international legal personality as the rights and duties that corporations may have depend on their position under international law (chapter II). Whether an entity is considered to have legal personality mainly depends on the definition that is used and on which elements of the definition are considered decisive. In this study the approach used by Nørgaard was applied in an effort to establish the position of corporations under international law. Nørgaard distinguishes four constitutive elements of legal personality. For an entity to have international legal personality it must be the subject of rights, proceedings, duties and responsibility/examinations. As far as the position of corporations under international law is concerned all four constitutive elements were found to be present. On that basis it was concluded that corporations may be considered to have international legal personality.

The number of entities that can be considered legal persons under international law is growing and the traditional subject-object dichotomy is under increasing pressure.

Nevertheless, even if one insists on examining the status of corporations in the light of the traditional concept of legal personality, the conclusion that these entities are not subjects of international law is no longer valid. This conclusion is important as it implies that no inherent conceptual reason exists why corporations cannot be endowed with international human rights obligations.

Just as is the case with international organisations, the international legal personality of corporations differs from that of States. The resistance to the recognition of corporations as legal subjects – based primarily on the fear that corporations might be enabled to interfere in the affairs of States – is, therefore, unfounded. Recognising the legal personality of corporations does not pose a threat to the status of States as the prime bearers of rights and duties on the international plane.

The observation that corporations have rights and duties in the international realm does not help us to settle the question whether companies have obligations under international law in the field of human rights, let alone what these obligations might be. Consequently, in the second section of chapter II, attention was turned to international human rights law. In the aftermath of World War II human rights law was developed to protect human dignity from unwarranted interference by the State. The concept of corporate human rights obligations deviates from the traditional concept that human rights apply only in a vertical relationship, *i.e.* the individual has rights *vis-à-vis* the State. Consequently, any further discussion of corporate human rights obligations requires dealing with, the concept of the horizontal application of human rights, also known as *Drittwirkung*, first.

Most provisions in the UDHR, the ICESCR and the ICCPR, which together make up the International Bill of Rights, were developed with States in mind. Nevertheless, support for the concept that human rights provisions can also be applicable in horizontal relations can be inferred both from the nature of human rights and from several general provisions in the human rights treaties. The fundamental nature of human rights as protecting the dignity of the individual, requires that these rights are not protected merely *vis-à-vis* the State. Arguments in favour of *Drittwirkung* can also be derived from several of the general provisions in the International Bill of Rights. Illustrative is the clause in the preamble of the UDHR which provides that the rights in the Declaration apply to 'every individual and every organ of society'. This is a clear recognition of the fact that non-State entities were also considered to bear responsibility at the time the UDHR was drafted. It was similarly pointed out that the formulation of several other general provisions can also be taken to imply support for the existence of *Drittwirkung.* Nevertheless, the general provisions in the core human rights documents have been susceptible to different interpretations by scholars. Consequently, these provisions cannot be said to independently provide strong enough evidence for the conclusion that norms of international human rights law can be applied horizontally. All that can be said is that the general provisions do not 'stand in the way' of horizontal effect; they provide for the possibility of *Drittwirkung.* On the basis of this conclusion, I examined each provision in the International Bill of Rights separately in order to establish whether the provision in question, *prima facie*, is applicable to non-State actors (chapter III).

The object and purpose of the International Bill of Rights is to protect human dignity by promoting respect for human rights. In chapter III, I argued that if the interpretation of the provisions in the International Bill of Rights, in the light of the object and purpose of these core human rights documents, is geared to the changing circumstances, the horizontal effect of many of the provisions cannot be denied. In other words, if the interest that is to be protected is taken as the point of departure, it is clear that many provisions in the International Bill of Rights are applicable to corporations. It has been observed that the object and purpose of the provisions in the human rights documents increasingly require that the obligations apply to private entities. Besides references to the direct applicability of a provision to a non-State entity, the provisions are frequently interpreted as being applicable to a non-State entity *indirectly*, that is to say, the norm works horizontally, but the State is ultimately held responsible for a violation. Reference to the direct responsibilities of non-State entities is most explicit in the interpretative documents regarding social, economic and cultural rights.

In the practice of the human rights supervisory bodies a trend may be discerned towards increased acceptance of the horizontal application of several human rights provisions. On the basis of rules of interpretation set forth in articles 31-2 of the Vienna Convention on the Law of Treaties (1969), it was concluded that certain provisions in the International Bill of Rights are applicable to the legal relations of corporations (in some cases pre-eminently so) while others are clearly not. In my view the peremptory character of some of these norms offer an additional argument in support of their applicability to corporations.

Obligations flowing from the following rights were distinguished as applicable to non-State entities, notably to corporations: the right to life; equality and the prohibition of discrimination; the prohibition of slavery, slave trade and forced labour; and the prohibition of torture, cruel and degrading treatment; the right to freedom of thought, conscience and religion, the right to privacy; the right to freedom of movement; the right to family-life; the prohibition of the exploitation of children; the right to property; the right to freedom of opinion, expression and information; the right to participation in cultural life and the protection of minorities; the right to form a trade union; the right to freedom of assembly; the right to favourable conditions of work; the right to liberty and security of person; the right to an adequate standard of living; the right to free disposal of natural wealth and resources, the right to health; the right to education and; the prohibition of war propaganda.

After having established which human rights provisions are applicable to corporations in chapter III, the following chapter aimed to identify the ensuing obligations of companies. This was done by drawing a parallel with the typology of human rights obligations for States that has been developed in human rights scholarly writing. According to this typology, obligations 'to respect, protect and fulfil' may result from each separate human right. On the basis of this typology, it was demonstrated that human rights do not only give rise to the negative obligation for corporations to 'respect', but may also embrace the more positive obligations 'to protect' and 'to fulfil'. Examples of corporate activities were used to illustrate possible violations of the various obligations. The sole purpose of these examples was to illustrate the *kind* of corporate obligations that in a given circumstance may arise. It would be to conjecture too far to attempt to compile a comprehensive list of human rights obligations for corporations. This is not possible as the question which specific human rights obligation exists, depends, for a large part, upon an evaluation of each specific right in a specific setting.

The answer to the question of which kind of obligation may arise for a corporation depends on the 'proximity' of the corporation to the human rights violation. The duty to respect may arise with respect to a large group of people: the corporation's own employees, the people residing on the land where the corporation operates and the community in general.

A new layer was added to the typology of human rights obligations in this study by distinguishing the duty *not to co-operate*. This was done to accommodate for, the not uncommon, situation where corporations operate in States with an egregious human rights record. In such cases the duty not to co-operate may arise, when a corporation itself is not directly violating human rights but when its nexus to the violating State in fact amounts to participation in the violation. The duty not to co-operate requires from the corporation that operates in States where widespread and systematic human rights violations occur, to either abstain from operations or to take measures to ensure that its operations do not amount to complicity in these human rights violations.

The duty to protect is likely to arise with respect to a smaller group of individuals. That is to say, a corporation must regulate the activities of the individuals or groups within its sphere of influence to prevent the violation of human rights by others. For example, with regard to the prohibition of slavery and forced labour, the obligation to protect implies that a corporation takes measures to prevent third parties, such as subcontractors and other business partners, from violating the prohibition of slavery and forced labour.

The obligation to fulfil is of an even more restricted applicability. Only in exceptional cases does a corporation have the obligation to fulfil a right. This is most likely to arise in cases where a corporation operates in a remote area where the State is unable to fulfil certain human rights and/or where a corporation has taken on a duty that is usually considered to be a typical State duty, such as health care or the prison system.

Depending on the situation, different levels of obligations may arise. In some cases a corporation might have the duty to respect as well as the duty to protect. Moreover, it is feasible that a corporation has the duty to protect, while, if it becomes clear that notorious human rights violations occur the obligation not to co-operate may arise.

Identifying obligations is of limited usefulness if there are no possibilities of enforcement. Therefore, Part B sought to map out and analyse the possibilities of redressing violations of human rights obligations by corporations. In the chapters V to VIII the existing structures for enforcement and implementation of human rights obligations under international and national law were discussed.

The most noticeable activities at the international level aimed at regulating the policies of corporations in this field have taken place within three international organisations, *viz.* the Organisation for Economic Co-operation and Development (OECD); the International Labour Organisation (ILO) and; the United Nations (UN). The codes of conduct and the guidelines that have been drafted within the framework of these organisations are all of a voluntary nature. Their effectiveness was analysed in chapter V.

The main focus of the 'Guidelines for Multinational Enterprises' that were adopted by the OECD is to facilitate international trade. However, since the Guidelines have been reviewed in 2000, more attention is now being paid to the human rights obligations of corporations. Nevertheless, it cannot be denied that the supervision under the OECD Guidelines to date is not very effective, as a result of the confidentiality of the proceedings and the lack of sanctions. Moreover, the use made of the Guidelines has been limited. It remains to be seen whether the adjustments to the supervisory system carried out under the 2000 review will improve the effectiveness of the OECD Guidelines.

As is the case with the OECD Guidelines, the use made of the ILO 'Tripartite Declaration of Principles Concerning Multinational Enterprises and Social Policy' is limited in practice. The voluntary nature of the Tripartite Declaration implies that its effectiveness relies on the commitment of corporations to use the Declaration as a point of reference. However, in practice the ILO Declaration is seldom referred to. Moreover, from a legal point of view the supervisory mechanism is hampered by the tripartite structure of the ILO.

The efforts during the 1970s and 1980s to come to a comprehensive code of conduct within the United Nations failed largely as a result of the political context at the time of drafting. However, the issue of regulating corporate behaviour has re-emerged on the United Nations agenda. The focus is now more clearly on the protection and promotion of human rights. Two initiatives can be distinguished. On the one hand the voluntary approach where corporations are seen as partners in achieving a better protection and promotion of human rights, the Global Compact; and, on the other hand, the efforts towards a more binding form of regulation, undertaken within the Sub-Commission for the Protection an Promotion of Human Rights. NGOs have been increasingly critical of the non-obligatory character of the Global Compact initiative.

The code that is currently under discussion in the Sub-Commission, if eventually accepted, would possibly offer a more binding regulatory framework.

The initiatives undertaken within the context of the European Union were also briefly addressed in this study. A cautious movement towards the creation of a binding framework for regulating corporate responsibility has surfaced. These initiatives are at an embryonic stage, however, and no definite conclusions can be drawn yet.

The overall conclusion is that the existing non-binding codes of conduct at the international level are of limited value in view of regulating corporate behaviour. At best, it can be argued that they imply some normative force and may provide guidance and encourage the adoption of national legislation.

In chapter V, I addressed the legal relevance of voluntary corporate codes of conduct. This was deemed necessary in the light of the proliferation of these codes in the 1990s. Overall, the conclusion was drawn that the exclusive reliance on self-regulation in its present form has serious shortcomings, as a significant risk exists that the voluntary codes are mere or mainly window-dressing. A system of independent verification and monitoring is frequently nonexistent. Moreover, the codes are very diverse and seldom comprehensive.

While the main objective of the present study is to analyse the question whether corporations have obligations in the field of human rights, it is important not to lose sight of the fact that States remain the cornerstone of the human rights system. In the light of this, it was deemed imperative to discuss the responsibilities of the State for human rights violations committed by corporations. This issue was dealt with in chapter VI.

In its work on a code of State responsibility, the International Law Commission (ILC) has dealt with the question whether acts by non-State entities may be attributed to the State and as such give rise to State responsibility. According to the draft Articles on State responsibility that were finalised in 2001, private acts constituting a violation of international law may entail State responsibility in two ways. Firstly, the conduct of non-State entities may be attributed to the State under certain circumstances: where non-State entities are empowered by law to exercise governmental authority; where a State has organs of another State placed at its disposal; where private conduct is directed or controlled by the State; where private conduct is exercised in the absence of official authority; where an insurrectional movement becomes the new government; and where a State endorses private acts as its own. In these cases, the private act is considered an act of State for which State responsibility may arise. According to this rule of attribution, corporate activities may, on occasion, involve State responsibility. Secondly, State responsibility may arise where a State itself fails in its general obligation to protect or respond to private acts that violate international law. In this case, the primary rule of attribution comes into play: this failure is considered an act of the State for which responsibility arises.

The general obligation for States to protect and thereby to respond to private acts that violate international law can also be found in international human rights law. This has appeared in the case-law of international human rights bodies as the 'due diligence test'. This test was first formulated by the Inter-American Court on Human Rights (IACHR) in the *Velásquez Rodríguez* and *Gondinez* cases. Since these decisions, the due diligence test has been referred to in other human rights standards and by monitoring bodies.

In chapter VI, I examined the case-law of the supervisory bodies where the responsibility of the State in connection with harmful corporate activities was at stake. The supervisory bodies, notably the European Court of Human Rights (ECrtHR), have confirmed that States can be held responsible for corporate activities that violate human rights law by failing to exercise due diligence towards these corporations. Particularly, the individual complaint procedures offer effective mechanisms to scrutinise corporate activity through the responsibility of the State. Nevertheless, the number of such cases brought before the international judicial bodies is relatively small.

The contents of the due diligence obligation to regulate corporate activities depends on the circumstances of each case. At present, given the relatively small number of cases, the content is still rather undetermined. So far, the case-law has not yet explicitly concluded that States should adopt legislation to prevent or repress corporate acts that constitute a human rights violation. However, the due diligence obligation is frequently perceived as an obligation to protect against human rights violations by means of legislation.

In chapter VI, the question was addressed whether State responsibility may also arise when the corporate violations occur outside of the State's territory. This question was deemed particularly important in the light of the fact that developed States, home to most multinational corporations, are more likely to have effective means and technical expertise to regulate and monitor corporate activities than is the case with developing host States. With regard to a failure to control the State's organs, State responsibility can arise irrespective of where the violation of international law takes place. The due diligence obligation to regulate the activities of corporations is conditioned by the degree of control over these activities and therefore rests first and foremost with the host State. However, it follows from the general principle formulated in the *Corfu Channel* case – that a State has the obligation not knowingly to allow its territory to be used for acts contrary to the rights of other States – that home State responsibility may arise where the home State has not exercised due diligence in controlling parent companies that are effectively under its control. Consequently, the home States should undertake appropriate measures to prevent and repress injurious acts of corporations abroad. Under international human rights law this obligation is, in the first place, perceived as an obligation to adopt legislation. Obligations to regulate the extraterritorial activities of corporations are not unprecedented as can be deduced from the developments in the field of corruption, the environment and the exploitation of children. In various areas international law is moving towards obligating home States to adopt legislation that regulates the activities of corporations abroad. It may be argued that international human rights law imposes a similar obligation on home States to regulate extra-territorial corporate activities that are effectively under their control.

The law of State responsibility offers an interesting yet under-utilised tool for addressing human rights violations resulting from corporate activities. Several obstacles, notably of a political and economic nature, remain, however. This necessitated an examination of alternative approaches to the issue of enforcing human rights obligations on corporations

In chapter VII, I discussed the current developments at the national level in the field of judicial enforcement of human rights obligations on corporations. At the national level, alternative approaches are emerging, notably in the area of civil law. In this civil litigation the *direct* responsibility of corporations for human rights violations is becoming accepted. Two different types of corporate liability for human rights violations have been discussed: liability arising from a violation of international law – the international tort – and liability arising from a violation of the domestic law of the home State.

International tort cases have been brought before US courts under the Alien Tort Claims Act (ATCA). Under this 200-year-old statute non-US plaintiffs may bring suit for violations of international law irrespective of the nationality of the defendant or the place where the alleged violation has taken place. A development can be discerned towards widening the scope of the ATCA, both regarding the circle of defendants and the applicable human rights norms. Recently, cases against corporations for alleged violations of international law outside of the United States have been declared admissible. To date, US courts have held that absent of State action, slave trade (forced labour) and, possibly, certain environmental offences may trigger jurisdiction under the ATCA. Moreover, jurisdiction over corporations may also arise where a corporation is complicit in State acts involving: summary execution; crimes against humanity; cruel, inhuman or degrading treatment; torture; violation of the right to life, liberty and security of person; prolonged arbitrary detention; and peaceful assembly. All the ATCA-cases discussed in chapter VII were still ongoing at the time of writing. Any conclusion regarding the potential of the ATCA as a tool for holding corporations accountable for human rights violations is therefore a precarious undertaking. Nevertheless, the extensive interpretations in several rulings seem promising for victims of corporate human rights violations. A potentially major obstacle for plaintiffs is the doctrine of *forum non conveniens*, according to which plaintiffs can be required to bring their cases in other, more convenient courts. However, in recent rulings in the corporate ATCA cases, US courts expressed the view that the *forum non conveniens* doctrine should not stand in the way of the aspiration of the United States to provide a forum for victims of human rights violations around the world.

The ATCA cases are also relevant in the light of overcoming the obstacle posed by the often extremely complicated business structures. Corporations regularly escape being held responsible for human rights violations due to their complex business structures, claiming that subsidiaries are separate legal entities that must be brought to trial in the countries in which they operate. In cases under the ATCA, US courts have 'pierced the corporate veil'. However, it remains to be seen whether the ATCA will live up to the expectations that exist as to its potential as an effective remedy for victims of human rights violations. Several obstacles might prove to be too high thresholds. The plaintiffs must identify an enforceable and universal international norm and properly allege its violation by the corporation. This requires a very specific account of the facts, which are often difficult to obtain for the plaintiffs. Moreover, to date, the courts have only accepted the exercise of jurisdiction in the case of corporate defendants allegedly violating a human right with a *jus cogens* character, *viz.* the slave trade. However, there does not seem to be a reason why other human rights norms should not become the basis for civil lawsuits against corporations under the ATCA. The prerequisite that the defendant must have certain minimum contacts with the jurisdiction of the United States may also prove to constitute an insurmountable hurdle.

For the topic op the present study the developments under the ATCA are very important. Despite considerable legal hurdles, plaintiffs have succeeded in passing the admissibility stages in a couple of cases. The US courts have recognised that corporations, acting alone or in concert with the State, may be liable for violations of certain provisions of *international* human rights law. The developments in the US courts are in very early stages which gives rise to some legal uncertainty. The jurisdiction of US courts under the ATCA is very broad, as hardly any ties between the alleged tort, the defendant, plaintiff and the United States are required for jurisdiction to be triggered. In the light of legal certainty, it might be argued that litigation against corporations can best take place either in the State where the tort occurs or in the State where the corporation has its headquarters. In several States civil litigation is emerging against corporations for human rights violations abroad which constitute a domestic tort, as opposed to the ATCA litigation which deals with a violation of international law. A selection of cases, notably in the United Kingdom, was discussed in chapter VII.

Cases have been brought before the UK courts by plaintiffs that have suffered health problems related to their work for subsidiaries of British based corporations. These cases have also yet to be decided on their merits. Nevertheless, the decisions to allow several cases to proceed are important in the light of regulating overseas corporate behaviour. In these cases, it was decided that parent companies which were aware that the operations of foreign subsidiaries involved risks for their employees and others, owed a 'duty of care'. British-based corporations may be liable for injuries when their subsidiaries apply lower standards than those applicable in the United Kingdom. These cases tackle the double standards which corporations can employ when operating overseas. As is the case in the ATCA litigation, the cases before the British courts successfully 'pierce the corporate veil'. In these cases, it has been established that a breach of the duty of care had taken place in the United Kingdom. A trend may be discerned in British litigation towards weighing the factors in the convenient forum, a line of defence recurrently advanced by defendants, in favour of the plaintiffs.

It is concluded in this study that the existing possibilities offered under civil law in several national jurisdictions may be sufficient for holding corporations liable for human rights violations without the need to resort to the next step and make international law the direct cause of action as is the case under the ATCA in the United States. On the basis of the territoriality principle or the nationality principle, home States could be required, as a result of the obligation to protect human rights, to adopt legislation expanding the jurisdiction of their domestic courts to cover the harmful activities of their corporations abroad.

Finally, I examined the question whether human rights obligations for corporations can be directly enforced at the international level (chapter VIII). Currently, the answer to this question is in the negative. There are no international judicial mechanisms where corporations can be directly held accountable for such violations. The international human rights supervisory mechanisms have in common that they only allow for complaints concerning human rights violations against States. Hence, corporate human rights violations can, as was described in chapter VI, only be addressed indirectly. As there presently is no international human rights treaty that directly addresses corporations, it was necessary to broaden the scope of the analysis in chapter VIII to other areas where corporations can possibly be held accountable.

The excursion into the field of international criminal law showed that the concept of holding corporate entities responsible for human rights violations is neither impossible nor a novelty. After World War II – even though corporations were not parties to any treaty – the International Military Tribunal recognised that certain corporations had violated international law and went on to attach criminal responsibility to individuals. Moreover, from the analysis of the developments during the negotiations leading up to the establishment of the International Criminal Court (ICC), it can be concluded that the current obstacles as regards the inclusion of corporations within the jurisdiction of the ICC are not matters of principle but are largely of a political nature. It is, therefore, conceivable that in the not too distant future the possibility of holding corporations accountable before the ICC for war crimes, genocide and crimes against humanity may indeed be possible.

Finally, I examined the major international trade agreements, *i.e.* the treaty establishing the World Trade Organisation (WTO) and the North American Free Trade Agreement (NAFTA), in order to assess the role human rights considerations play within these agreements. This question was deemed to be particularly interesting in the light of the issue of enforcement. As opposed to the human rights instruments, the trade agreements have successfully established strong enforcement mechanisms. However, the WTO dispute settlement mechanism is only open to States. Corporations play a larger role in the NAFTA dispute settlement procedure as they are allowed to file a complaint against a State if they feel that State has violated the rules of the NAFTA. But, like the WTO, the NAFTA does not offer any possibilities for the scrutiny of corporate behaviour. Moreover, the objectives of the WTO and the NAFTA are potentially in conflict with human rights considerations. In the course of removing non-tariff barriers to trade, public interest constraints may be loosened. The Side Agreement on Labor Co-operation, attached to the NAFTA, was discussed at some length as it provides for the possibility to file complaints regarding another NAFTA country's inadequate response to corporate practices that violate workers' rights. The Side Agreement thus offers a mechanism to indirectly scrutinise corporate behaviour. In practice, the effectiveness of the side agreement has proven to be of limited value, however.

3 Conclusions

The main questions that I have set out to answer in this study can be divided into five sub-questions:

I. Can corporations have human rights obligations seen from a conceptual point of view?
II. Do corporations have human rights obligations?

And if so:

III. What kind of human rights obligations for corporations can be discerned?
IV. Can human rights obligations for corporations be enforced?
V. How can the supervision of corporate human rights obligations be improved?

3.1 Can Corporations have Human Rights Obligations seen from a Conceptual Point of View?

The analysis in this study shows that the question whether corporations *can* have human rights obligations should be answered in the affirmative. Traditional theoretical concepts such as the doctrine of legal personality and the private-public dichotomy impart no reasons that effectively stand in the way of human rights obligations for corporations. Corporations have international rights and duties while avenues of enforcing their rights exist, *i.e.* corporations have legal personality. Moreover, it is increasingly accepted that the protection offered by human rights norms extends beyond the vertical relationship to horizontal relationships.

3.2 Do Corporations have Human Rights Obligations?

Human rights aim to protect the dignity of each human being. In order to effectively satisfy this objective it is imperative that human right provisions are interpreted in conformity with the present-day circumstances. This implies that a human rights provision should be interpreted taking into account, besides the language and the context of a provision, its object and purpose. Applying such a teleological interpretation of human rights provisions leads to the conclusion that certain human rights are applicable to corporations and that, therefore, corporate human rights obligations may arise. Compelling arguments of effectiveness support this approach to human rights. It is necessary to apply a broad interpretation of human rights provisions encompassing private action, if human rights law is to be effective in the present-day circumstances where human rights protection is frequently dependant on private action. By analysing interpretative statements regarding human rights it has been concluded that a trend may be discerned towards increased recognition of the applicability of several human rights provisions to corporations.

3.3 What Kind of Corporate Human Rights Obligations can be discerned?

It has been demonstrated that of the different levels of obligations that can be derived from each human right, each and every one can be applicable to corporations. Depending on the circumstances, corporations may not only have the negative obligation to respect, but also the more positive obligations to protect and to fulfil. Moreover, in certain circumstances the obligation not to co-operate may arise. It is important to be somewhat cautious with regard to corporate responsibility for human rights. First and foremost, the duty to respect and to protect should be the focal point in view of the pressing urgency to combat the most flagrant violations of human rights by corporations.

3.4 Can Corporate Human Rights Obligations be enforced?

Part B of this study has made clear that the difficulties centre on the enforcement of corporate human rights obligations. It is important to bear in mind that the fact whether a victim of corporate human rights violations is able to bring legal action against a corporation should not be considered a test for the existence of human rights obligations for corporations. In Part A it has been demonstrated that there are no legal obstacles with regard to human rights obligations for corporations and that certain human rights can be applicable to the legal relations of corporations. The bottleneck is the enforcement of these obligations.

Apart from the existing – rather deficient – non-binding regulation of corporate activities, there are no direct enforcement possibilities at the international level. None of the international bodies dealing with human rights have jurisdiction over legal persons directly. Judicial enforcement of these human rights obligations at the international level is currently only possible if the harmful corporate activities can be traced back to a breach of obligations by a State. Thus, corporate human rights violations can only be addressed indirectly.

At the national level, some avenues do exist for holding corporations directly accountable for human rights violations. This is clear in the case where a violation occurs within the territory of the forum State. However, gradually States are also offering their courts as a forum in cases where the corporate human rights violations occur abroad. Enabling victims of corporate human rights violations to address the alleged corporate violator in the courts of the home State of that violator is an important asset to ensuring an effective system for the protection of human rights against corporate infringements.

3.5 How can the Supervision of Corporate Human Rights Obligations be improved?

From the analysis of the existing avenues of enforcement and implementation it becomes clear that no single mechanism provides an adequate answer to the problem of redressing corporate human rights violations. A comprehensive approach is needed to effectively redress these violations. It is necessary to integrate a systematic scrutiny of corporate activities into the human rights system.

At the international level, State responsibility offers an important avenue for indirectly addressing corporate human rights violations. States are under the obligation to protect human rights against corporate infringements. The supervisory mechanisms under the international treaties offer a largely unexploited potential for the indirect scrutiny of corporate activities by examining the obligation of States to protect. In the mechanisms under which States are required to submit reports, systematic reviews should take place with regard to the measures taken by States to regulate their corporate citizens. In order for the supervisory mechanisms to effectively assess whether a State is living up to its obligation to regulate corporations, the State should be required to provide information on the activities of corporations domiciled in these States. A State could acquire such information by obliging corporations to annually report on the human rights impact of their activities in the particular State *and* abroad.

Moreover, the complaint based mechanisms – both the procedures under which States can file a complaint and those were individuals have a right to complain – could be used more effectively to scrutinise the behaviour of corporations indirectly, by bringing a claim against a State for an alleged violation of its due diligence obligation. A more frequent utilisation of these avenues would increase the pressure upon States to effectively regulate the activities of corporations in the light of human rights.

The obligation to protect implies that, on the one hand, a positive duty can arise for States to regulate the activities of their corporations on their own territory but also abroad. On the other hand, if regulation fails, the duty to protect will require the home State to provide for redress for the victims. Enabling victims of corporate human rights violations to litigate at the national level constitutes a way in which States can fulfil their obligation to protect. The national courts are a largely untapped source for holding corporations accountable for human rights violations. As has been pointed out in this study, national law, *i.e.* criminal and notably civil law, offers opportunities to hold corporations accountable for human rights violations.

Furthermore, it is vital that the attention for human rights is made an integral part of the international mechanisms that aim to facilitate free trade. The systems that endeavour to protect and promote human rights and the systems aimed at facilitating free trade continue to develop in virtually complete isolation from each other. Contrary to the frequently deficient human rights enforcement mechanisms, the free trade agreements have set up comparatively effective enforcement machineries which should, given the customary law and often *jus cogens* character of human rights law, be used to benefit the protection and promotion of human rights. For that reason more attention should be paid to mainstreaming human rights into WTO law.

Ultimately, it can be considered desirable to draw up a multilateral treaty codifying the international human rights obligations of corporations combined with a supervisory mechanism that will directly ensure that corporations fulfil their obligations. An additional advantage of such an agreement would be the level playing field that would ensue. The reluctance corporations and governments currently show with regard to pursuing corporate social responsibility, is allegedly based on arguments of competition. An international agreement would remove such restraints, as all players would be subjected to the same rules. It is feasible that, with the increasing attention for the role that corporations have proven to play in human rights matters, States at some point might decide to draw up a multilateral agreement on corporate human rights responsibility and accountability. However, in the light of economic interests and the foreseeable political considerations this route might seem daunting and will unquestionably be a tremendously arduous undertaking. Pending such an agreement, it is crucial that the existing supervisory human rights mechanisms are used to their full potential by including a systematic scrutiny of corporate behaviour. It is submitted here that, notwithstanding the desirability of a directly binding instrument, such a document is not a necessity. The existing structures offer sufficient avenues for holding corporations accountable for human rights violations, albeit often in an indirect manner.

3.6 Final Observations

The accountability of corporations for human rights violations has received mounting attention during the last couple of years. Propelled by a number of highly publicized cases of corporate involvement in human rights violations in the 1990s, NGOs and consumers are increasingly demanding socially responsible behaviour from corporations. Even though a range of corporate activities indicates an acceptance by corporations to take on human rights responsibility, the focus is strongly placed on voluntarism and self-regulation. Corporate human rights obligations and legal accountability remain a somewhat contested area in international law.

In attempting to clarify the issue, this study has challenged several traditional ideas and dichotomies. In the first place, the traditional dichotomy between the horizontal application and the vertical application of international human rights law has been further questioned. The analysis of the (indirect) horizontal effect of human rights in chapter II demonstrates that under international human rights law the distinction between public and private actors is fading. Nevertheless, the State for the time being remains the primary duty-holder under international human right law. Against the background of the foregoing a number of observations are in place.

A first observation concerns the 'special character' of human rights. The fear may exist that bringing private acts under the human rights umbrella may constitute a devaluation of the special status attached to a human rights violation. As human rights are considered fundamental legal guarantees against the State, the extension of human rights to encompass private acts might be considered to entail the risk of undermining human rights altogether. However, recognising the horizontal effect of human rights does not lead to devaluation. On the contrary, the *denial* of the applicability of human rights in horizontal relations may eventually detract from the human rights system. Infringements of fundamental rights by private actors need to be brought within the ambit of the human rights system in order for the system to be significantly effective.

Throughout this study, I have reiterated that the identification of corporate human rights obligations does not in any way diminish any of the existing obligations incumbent on the traditional bearers of obligations: the States. The recognition of the horizontal effect of human rights does not imply that the State should divest itself of its responsibility to ensure human rights and freedoms. Corporate obligations exist in addition to the obligations of States. The central and superior position of the State in international law is essential as it secures stability and legal certainty. Therefore, corporate obligations are not, and should not, be the same as those of States. The human rights obligations for corporations are different and distinct in kind from those of the State.

Another issue that has addressed in this study, is that of international law versus domestic law. The present study has underlined the role of national law and national courts in the effective implementation of international law. Domestic courts play a crucial role in the field of corporate accountability, particularly given the fact that international remedies in this field are still lacking. The present study has advocated civil proceedings as an avenue for corporate accountability. It should be reiterated that civil proceedings are not a belittlement of the nature of human rights violations. On the contrary, civil law offers several significant advantages, not in the least the fact that compensation can be awarded to the victims of corporate human rights violations. In addition, in civil actions the initiative rests with the victim, making him or her independent from the decision of a State to initiate actions, as is the case under criminal law. Moreover, civil jurisdiction over corporate activities in practice may be more easily established than criminal jurisdiction.

Finally, some remarks should be made regarding the power to regulate versus the duty to regulate. In the light of the fundamental importance of human rights for the dignity of human beings, it is tempting to place a duty to regulate on those who have the power to regulate. This study has demonstrated that such claims in the field of corporate responsibility for human rights are more than mere aspirations. Corporate human rights obligations are not merely a question of self-imposed obligations emanating from ethical or policy considerations. Corporate obligations in the field of human rights derive from the trend towards a broad and dynamic interpretation of international human rights law. However, corporate responsibility has yet to be transformed into rules and procedures through which corporations can be held directly accountable under international law. This presents a major challenge for human rights proponents in the years to come.

Nederlandse Samenvatting

1 Inleiding (Hoofdstuk 1)

Sinds de aanvaarding van de Universele Verklaring voor de Rechten van de Mens (UVRM), meer dan 50 jaar geleden, hebben zich ingrijpende veranderingen in de internationale betrekkingen voorgedaan. Door processen van liberalisering, deregulering en privatisering zijn naast Staten andere actoren zoals bedrijven een belangrijke rol gaan spelen. Gesteld kan worden dat bedrijven soms een verdergaande invloed uitoefenen op het welzijn van veel burgers dan (sommige) Staten. Vanuit een traditioneel perspectief draagt echter uitsluitend de soevereine Staat verplichtingen met betrekking tot de rechten van de mens. De veranderde situatie vereist een heroverweging van het traditionele perspectief op de bescherming van de rechten van de mens. In dit onderzoek wordt de vraag gesteld of bedrijven verplichtingen hebben op het terrein van de mensenrechten. Deze vraag moet worden gezien tegen de achtergrond van globalisering. Deze vaak gebruikte term refereert aan de politieke, wetenschappelijke, culturele en met name economische ontwikkelingen die hebben plaatsgevonden sinds de Tweede Wereldoorlog. Deze processen hebben geleid tot de toegenomen invloed van bedrijven op het internationale vlak in het algemeen en op de rechten van de mens in het bijzonder. Het uitgangspunt van dit onderzoek is dat de traditionele benadering waarin Staten de exclusieve drager zijn van verplichtingen op het gebied van mensenrechten in de huidige context tekortschiet.

De centrale vraag van dit onderzoek is:

Kunnen er binnen het internationale recht verplichtingen voor bedrijven op het terrein van de rechten van de mens worden onderscheiden en, indien dit het geval is, hoe kunnen deze verplichtingen worden afgedwongen?

Deze centrale vraag kan worden onderverdeeld in een vijftal deelvragen die in dit onderzoek zijn behandeld.

1. Kunnen bedrijven, vanuit een conceptueel perspectief, verplichtingen hebben met betrekking tot mensenrechten? (Hoofdstuk II)

De vraag of bedrijven mensenrechtenverplichtingen *kunnen* dragen vereist een heroverweging van een aantal traditionele concepten. Traditioneel is de Staat immers de geadresseerde van mensenrechtenverdragen. Allereerst moet de vraag gesteld worden of de status van bedrijven in het internationale recht het dragen van plichten mogelijk maakt. Met andere woorden: kunnen bedrijven internationale rechtspersoonlijkheid bezitten? Uit de analyse in hoofdstuk II blijkt dat bedrijven reeds rechten en plichten op het internationale vlak bezitten. Bovendien bestaan er mogelijkheden voor bedrijven om deze rechten af te dwingen en kunnen bedrijven in (semi-juridische) procedures aan een onderzoek naar de nakoming van hun verplichtingen worden onderworpen. Er is derhalve geconcludeerd dat de doctrine van internationale rechtspersoonlijkheid geen conceptueel obstakel vormt in het licht van het identificeren van mensenrechtenverplichtingen voor bedrijven. Belangrijk is evenwel om op te merken dat de internationale rechtspersoonlijkheid van Staten verschilt van de status van bedrijven.

In hoofdstuk II wordt uitvoerig ingegaan op de traditionele publieke-private dichotomie. Traditioneel gezien werken mensenrechten alleen tussen de Staat en het individu, dat wil zeggen in een verticale verhouding. In toenemende mate wordt echter geaccepteerd dat mensenrechten ook werking kunnen hebben in een horizontale verhouding, bijvoorbeeld tussen bedrijven en individuen. De bepalingen in de belangrijkste mensenrechteninstrumenten, de UVRM, het Internationale Verdrag inzake Burgerrechten en Politieke Rechten (IVBPR) en het Internationale Verdrag inzake Economische, Sociale en Culturele Rechten (IVESCR), richten zich primair tot Staten. Echter, gesteld kan worden dat uit het karakter van mensenrechten voortvloeit dat deze bepalingen ook horizontale werking, ook wel aangeduid als *Drittwirkung*, toekomt. Mensenrechten beogen de waardigheid van het individu te beschermen. In het licht van dit fundamentele karakter is het noodzakelijk om de bescherming die deze rechten bieden niet te beperken tot de bescherming *vis-à-vis* de Staat maar ook tegen private inmenging. Argumenten ter ondersteuning van de stelling dat mensenrechten ook horizontale werking hebben kunnen verder worden afgeleid uit enkele algemene bepalingen in de internationale mensenrechtenverdragen en de UVRM. Illustratief is de bepaling in de preambule van de UVRM dat 'ieder individu en *elk orgaan* van de gemeenschap, (…) er naar zal streven (…) de eerbied voor deze rechten en vrijheden te bevorderen'. Op grond van, onder andere, deze algemene bepaling kan worden gesteld dat de bepalingen in de sfeer van de internationaal erkende mensenrechten naast Staten ook op andere entiteiten, zoals bedrijven, van toepassing kunnen zijn. Het voert echter te ver om te concluderen dat alle mensenrechtenbepalingen van toepassing kunnen zijn op bedrijven indien dit slechts gebaseerd wordt op de bovengenoemde argumenten. Hooguit kan worden betoogd dat het karakter van mensenrechten en de algemene bepalingen in de mensenrechteninstrumenten de mogelijkheid van horizontale werking open laten.

2. Hebben bedrijven verplichtingen op het terrein van de rechten van de mens?

Nadat is vastgesteld dat het karakter van mensenrechten en enkele algemene bepalingen in de mensenrechteninstrumenten de mogelijkheid van horizontale werking scheppen, is in hoofdstuk III een analyse gemaakt van elke afzonderlijke inhoudelijke bepaling in de UVRM, het IVBPR en het IVESCR. In deze analyse wordt een antwoord gezocht op de vraag welke specifieke bepalingen van toepassing kunnen zijn op bedrijven. Uitgangspunt bij de interpretatie van deze bepalingen is de constante dynamiek van het internationale recht en de evolutie van rechten. Om het doel van mensenrechten – het beschermen van de waardigheid van het individu – te bereiken is het noodzakelijk dat mensenrechtenbepalingen dynamisch worden geïnterpreteerd, dat wil zeggen in het licht van de hedendaagse omstandigheden. Een ruime interpretatie van mensenrechten die private handelingen omvat is essentieel in de huidige context waar de effectieve bescherming van mensenrechten dikwijls door private handelingen wordt gefrustreerd. In de analyse wordt, naast de strekking en het doel van de bepaling, ook de taal en de context in overweging genomen. Verder zijn interpretatieve teksten zoals, onder andere, de 'General Comments' (algemene commentaren) van de toezichthoudende organen betrokken bij de analyse. Dit is in overeenstemming met de regels van verdragsinterpretatie zoals die zijn neergelegd in de artikelen 30 en 31 van het Weens verdragenverdrag van 1969.

De analyse van de bepalingen van de UVRM, het IVBPR en het IVESCR leidt tot de conclusie dat sommige mensenrechtenbepalingen van toepassing zijn op bedrijven en dat daaruit derhalve verplichtingen voor bedrijven op het terrein van de rechten van de mens kunnen voortvloeien. Dit geldt voor de volgende bepalingen: het recht op leven; het recht op gelijke behandeling en het verbod van discriminatie; het verbod van slavernij, slavenhandel en dwangarbeid; het verbod van foltering en wrede, onmenselijke of vernederende behandeling; de vrijheid van gedachte, geweten en godsdienst; het recht op privacy; het recht zich vrijelijk te verplaatsen; het recht op familieleven; het verbod op uitbuiting van kinderen; het recht op eigendom; de vrijheid van meningsuiting; het recht om deel te nemen aan het culturele leven en de bescherming van minderheden; de vrijheid van (vak)vereniging; het recht op billijke en gunstige arbeidsvoorwaarden; het recht op vrijheid en veiligheid van persoon; het recht op een behoorlijke levensstandaard; het recht om vrijelijk te beschikken over natuurlijke rijkdommen en hulpbronnen; het recht op gezondheid; het recht op onderwijs en het verbod op oorlogspropaganda. Het feit dat sommige van deze bepalingen behoren tot de categorie van dwingend internationaal recht kan, naar mijn mening, een additioneel argument vormen ter ondersteuning van de stelling dat deze normen op bedrijven van toepassing kunnen zijn.

Kortom, in deze analyse is geconcludeerd dat een trend waarneembaar is naar een toenemende horizontalisering van de internationale mensenrechten hetgeen impliceert dat in toenemende mate mensenrechtennormen van toepassing worden geacht te zijn op niet-Statelijke entiteiten zoals bedrijven. Hierbij past evenwel de aantekening dat het vaak gaat om zogenaamde 'indirecte' horizontale werking. Dat wil zeggen dat uiteindelijk Staten rechtens worden aangesproken voor private schendingen van mensenrechten. Dit doet echter niet af aan de stelling dat de *norm* van toepassing is op bedrijven.

3. Wat voor soort mensenrechtenverplichtingen voor bedrijven kunnen worden onderscheiden? (Hoofdstuk IV)

Teneinde het soort mensenrechtenverplichtingen van bedrijven te verhelderen is gebruik gemaakt van de tripartiete typologie van verplichtingen zoals die in de mensenrechtendoctrine tot ontwikkeling is gekomen. Volgens deze typologie kunnen uit ieder mensenrecht verschillende soorten verplichtingen worden afgeleid: de verplichting tot 'respect', tot 'bescherming' en tot 'verwezenlijking. Om de verlichtingen voor bedrijven te verduidelijken is deze typologie in hoofdstuk IV toegepast op een viertal rechten, te weten: het recht op voedsel, het recht op gezondheid, het recht op leven en het verbod op slavernij.

Verplichtingen tot 'respect' zijn negatieve verplichtingen en vereisen onthouding van inbreuk op rechten door bedrijven. De verplichting tot 'respect' geldt niet alleen tegenover de werknemers en de mensen in de directe omgeving van een bedrijf maar ook tegenover de samenleving in het algemeen. Met betrekking tot het recht op voedsel kan hierbij gedacht worden aan de verplichting van bedrijven om zich te onthouden van milieuvervuilende activiteiten die burgers belemmeren in hun mogelijkheden om aan adequaat voedsel te komen. Verplichtingen tot 'bescherming' en 'verwezenlijking' zijn positief van karakter en vereisen een zekere mate van actief optreden door bedrijven. De toepasselijkheid van dit soort verplichtingen ligt minder voor de hand dan het geval is bij de verplichting tot 'respect'. De verplichting tot 'bescherming' betreft maatregelen die een bedrijf zal moeten nemen om burgers te beschermen tegen schendingen van mensenrechten door derden. Bedrijven zullen moeten optreden tegen diegenen die zich in hun invloedssfeer bevinden zoals zakenpartners, leveranciers en onderaannemers. Indien deze mensenrechten schenden zal het bedrijf maatregelen moeten treffen. De verplichting tot 'verwezenlijking' van een mensenrecht zal zich alleen voordoen indien een bedrijf een taak op zich neemt die als een 'typische' taak van de Staat kan worden betiteld, zoals de gezondheidszorg of het gevangeniswezen. Verder wordt betoogd dat de verplichting tot 'verwezenlijking' zich zou kunnen voordoen indien een bedrijf opereert in een land dat niet in staat is om aan deze verplichting te voldoen. Tenslotte wordt in dit hoofdstuk nog een verkennend onderzoek gedaan naar een mogelijk vierde soort verplichting: het verbod op 'samenwerking'. Deze additionele laag van verplichtingen is noodzakelijk omdat de tripartiete typologie geen antwoord biedt in alle situaties waarin bedrijven zich kunnen bevinden. Gedacht kan worden aan de situatie waarin een bedrijf in een Staat opereert dat zich schuldig maakt aan grove, systematische mensenrechtenschendingen. In dit soort situaties kan de verplichting om 'niet samen te werken' zich voordoen. De in hoofdstuk IV geïdentificeerde verplichtingen zijn geïllustreerd met een aantal voorbeelden van concrete schendingen.

4. Hoe kunnen mensenrechtenverplichtingen van bedrijven worden afgedwongen? (Hoofdstukken V-VIII)

Het identificeren van verplichtingen voor bedrijven op het terrein van de rechten van de mens heeft beperkte waarde als er geen mogelijkheden zijn om die verplichtingen af te dwingen. Deel B van dit boek, dat de hoofdstukken V-VIII beslaat, richt zich daarom op de mogelijkheden om de mensenrechtenverplichtingen voor bedrijven af te dwingen, waarbij zowel de zogenaamde *hard law* als de zogenaamde *soft law* instrumenten in de beschouwingen worden betrokken.

In hoofdstuk V staan een aantal juridisch niet-bindende internationale instrumenten centraal. Er bestaan diverse internationale codes die beogen het gedrag van bedrijven te reguleren met het oog op mogelijke negatieve sociale gevolgen van hun activiteiten. In dit hoofdstuk wordt de juridische betekenis van deze codes onderzocht en de vraag beantwoord wat de waarde is van deze instrumenten vanuit het perspectief van het reguleren van bedrijven in relatie tot mensenrechten. In deze analyse worden de (recentelijk herziene) Richtlijnen voor Multinationals van de Organisatie voor Economische Samenwerking en Ontwikkeling (OESO) uit 1976, en de Tripartiete Verklaring betreffende Multinationale Ondernemingen en Sociaal Beleid van de Internationale Arbeids Organisatie (IAO) uit 1977, besproken. Verder wordt in dit hoofdstuk aandacht besteed aan de ontwikkelingen binnen de Verenigde Naties (VN). Aan bod komen de ontwerpcode van de VN van 1978 en meer recente initiatieven zoals het 'Global Compact' en de ontwerpcode van de VN Subcommissie voor de Rechten van de Mens. Tenslotte wordt in dit hoofdstuk ingegaan op de ontwikkelingen binnen de Europese Unie (EU).

Aan de hand van een analyse van de inhoud en met name de implementatiemethodes wordt geconcludeerd dat de bestaande codes slechts beperkte waarde hebben als het gaat om het effectief reguleren van het gedrag van bedrijven met betrekking tot de rechten van de mens. In de praktijk wordt er weinig gebruik gemaakt van de codes en effectieve sanctiemechanismen ontbreken. Hoogstens kan worden gesteld dat de codes enige normatieve kracht bezitten.

In hoofdstuk V wordt ook ingegaan op het mechanisme van zelfregulering. De laatste jaren is er sprake van een ware proliferatie van vrijwillige interne gedragscodes.

Niettegenstaande het belang van deze ontwikkeling moet worden geconcludeerd dat een exclusief vertrouwen op het mechanisme van zelfregulering door middel van interne bedrijfscodes niet terecht is. Diverse argumenten worden aangevoerd om aan te tonen dat interne gedragscodes niet afdoende zijn om de rol van bedrijven in relatie tot mensenrechten te reguleren. De gedragscodes komen vaak tot stand als gevolg van zware druk van de publieke opinie. Bedrijven die minder gevoelig zijn voor de publieke opinie zullen wellicht minder geneigd zijn een gedragscode aan te nemen. Daar waar wel gedragscodes worden opgesteld wordt zelden verwezen naar de bestaande internationale mensenrechtenstandaarden en ontbreekt vaak een onafhankelijk toezicht die het gedrag van de bedrijven toetst aan de eigen gedragscode.

In hoofdstuk VI wordt ingegaan op de aansprakelijkheid van de Staat. Weliswaar staan in dit onderzoek de verplichtingen van bedrijven centraal maar er mag niet uit het oog worden verloren dat de Staat de hoeksteen is van het internationale recht. De Staat draagt de primaire verantwoordelijkheid voor de verwezenlijking van de rechten van de mens. In het licht hiervan wordt in hoofdstuk VI de vraag gesteld in hoeverre de Staat aansprakelijk is voor mensenrechtenschendingen die door bedrijven worden begaan.

Uit de regels omtrent staatsaansprakelijkheid opgesteld door de *International Law Commission* (ILC) in 2001 blijkt dat de Staat op twee manieren aansprakelijk kan zijn voor schendingen van mensenrechten door private entiteiten. Ten eerste kunnen, onder zekere voorwaarden, de handelingen van private entiteiten worden toegeschreven aan de Staat. Ten tweede heeft de Staat een zorgplicht *(due diligence)* om burgers te beschermen tegen mensenrechtenschendingen door private entiteiten. Deze zorgplicht is erkend door de toezichthoudende organen van de mensenrechtenverdragen. Hoofdstuk VI bevat een analyse van de (quasi)rechtspraak van deze organen waaruit naar voren komt dat Staten aansprakelijk kunnen zijn voor het schenden van de zorgplicht wanneer burgers het slachtoffer worden van mensenrechtenschendingen door bedrijven. Geconcludeerd wordt dat het individuele klachtrecht een, tot op heden onderbenut, instrument biedt om mensenrechtenschendingen door bedrijven, zij het indirect, aan de kaak te stellen.

In hoofdstuk VI wordt voorts de vraag gesteld of staatsaansprakelijkheid ook kan ontstaan indien een bedrijf zich buiten de landsgrenzen schuldig maakt aan mensenrechtenschendingen. Deze vraag is relevant met het oog op het feit dat ontwikkelde landen – vaak de thuisstaat van multinationale ondernemingen – in het algemeen over effectievere middelen zullen beschikken om bedrijven te reguleren dan het geval is bij zich nog ontwikkelende Staten. De vraag naar de reikwijdte van de plicht van de Staat om bedrijven te reguleren is afhankelijk van de mate van controle die de Staat heeft over de bedrijfsactiviteiten. Betoogd wordt dat – in navolging van ontwikkelingen op het terrein van milieu en corruptie – thuisstaten verplicht zouden kunnen worden om de extraterritoriale activiteiten van bedrijven die zich effectief onder hun controle bevinden, te reguleren met betrekking tot de rechten van de mens.

Hoofdstuk VII onderzoekt de mogelijkheden om bedrijven op nationaal niveau direct aansprakelijk te houden voor mensenrechtenschendingen. Met name de ontwikkelingen in de Verenigde Staten en Groot-Brittannië betreffende civiele aansprakelijkheid van bedrijven staan in dit hoofdstuk centraal. In de Verenigde Staten zijn verschillende civiele procedures aanhangig gemaakt wegens een zogenaamde internationale onrechtmatige daad op grond van de *Alien Tort Claims Act* (ATCA). Op basis van deze 200 jaar oude wet zijn civiele procedures aangespannen tegen bedrijven (ongeacht hun nationaliteit) voor schendingen in andere landen van bepalingen uit internationale mensenrechtenstandaarden. Rechters in verschillende federale jurisdicties hebben zaken ontvankelijk verklaard waarin bedrijven aansprakelijk worden gesteld voor het schenden van het verbod op slavernij (dwangarbeid). Bovendien zijn zaken ontvankelijk verklaard waarin bedrijven worden beschuldigd van medeplichtigheid aan schendingen door Staten begaan zoals, onder andere, een schending van het verbod op foltering en onmenselijke behandeling en het recht op leven. In hoofdstuk VII worden deze zaken geanalyseerd. Het is te vroeg om uitspraken te doen over de afloop van deze zaken. Voor slachtoffers van mensenrechtenschendingen door bedrijven is het evenwel hoopgevend dat de klagers in deze zaken er in zijn geslaagd, in weerwil van aanzienlijke juridische obstakels, aan de ontvankelijkheidscriteria te voldoen. Vanuit een juridisch perspectief zijn de ATCA-zaken met name interessant omdat erkend wordt dat bedrijven aansprakelijk kunnen zijn voor schendingen van het *internationale* recht.

Het feit dat bedrijven in de Verenigde Staten kunnen worden aangeklaagd ongeacht hun nationaliteit en ogeacht waar de schending zich heeft afgespeeld, kan rechtsonzekerheid met zich mee brengen. Dat gevaar is minder groot bij de ontwikkelingen in de Britse civiele rechtspraak. In Groot-Brittannië zijn rechtszaken tegen Britse moederbedrijven voor mensenrechtenschendingen in het buitenland aangespannen. De Britse rechters hebben deze zaken ontvankelijk verklaard stellend dat wanneer een dochteronderneming mensenrechten in het buitenland schendt dit een onrechtmatige daad onder *nationaal* recht in de thuisstaat kan opleveren. Volgens de Britse rechters hebben bedrijven een zorgplicht die ook geldt voor de activiteiten van dochterondernemingen. Deze rechtspraak is met name interessant in het licht van de complexe bedrijfsstructuren die de vraag naar aansprakelijkheid van bedrijven voor mensenrechtenschendingen kunnen bemoeilijken.

In hoofdstuk VIII is aandacht besteed aan de mogelijkheden om bedrijven op internationaal niveau direct aansprakelijk te stellen voor het schenden van mensenrechten. Op basis van de internationale mensenrechtenverdragen is het niet mogelijk om bedrijven rechtstreeks aan te spreken.

Omdat het direct aansprakelijk stellen van bedrijven onder deze verdragen niet mogelijk is, wordt in hoofdstuk VIII gekeken naar de mogelijkheden die het internationale strafrecht biedt. Uit de verkenning van het internationale strafrecht blijkt dat het idee dat bedrijven zich schuldig kunnen maken aan schendingen van internationaal recht niet nieuw is. Tijdens de processen voor het internationale militaire tribunaal in Neurenberg na de Tweede Wereldoorlog werd erkend dat bedrijven zich schuldig hadden gemaakt aan schendingen van het internationale recht. De strafrechtelijke aansprakelijkheid werd echter gekoppeld aan individuen en niet aan de rechtspersonen. In de onderhandelingen in de aanloop naar de oprichting van het permanente internationale strafhof is het voorstel gedaan om bedrijven binnen de rechtsmacht van het strafhof te laten vallen. Uit de analyse van de besprekingen over dit voorstel kan worden geconcludeerd dat de uiteindelijke beslissing, om de rechtsmacht van het strafhof te beperken tot natuurlijke personen, niet zozeer op juridische gronden als wel op grond van politieke overwegingen is genomen. Betoogd wordt dat het niet ondenkbaar is dat bedrijven in de toekomst wel binnen de rechtsmacht van het strafhof zullen komen te vallen. Desalniettemin biedt het internationale strafrecht op dit moment nog geen mogelijkheden om bedrijven direct aansprakelijk te stellen voor mensenrechtenschendingen.

Tenslotte wordt in hoofdstuk VII ingegaan op de vraag of mensenrechtennormen kunnen worden afgedwongen door middel van de internationale handelsverdragen. Centraal staan het verdrag van de Wereldhandelsorganisatie (WTO) en het Vrijhandelsverdrag tussen de Verenigde Staten, Canada en Mexico (NAFTA). Deze vraag is met name interessant met het oog op de effectieve stelsels voor geschillenbeslechting die in de WTO en de NAFTA tot stand zijn gebracht. Geconcludeerd moet echter worden dat in deze procedures weinig aandacht is voor de invloed van bedrijven op mensenrechten.

Concluderend kan worden gesteld dat momenteel de effectieve afdwinging van mensenrechtenverplichtingen voor bedrijven slechts op nationaal niveau mogelijk is. Op het internationale niveau bestaan, behalve de tekortschietende regulering vanuit de OESO en de ILO, geen mogelijkheden om bedrijven rechtstreeks aan te spreken op hun mensenrechtenverplichtingen.

5. *Hoe kan het toezicht op de naleving van mensenrechtenverplichtingen van bedrijven worden verbeterd? (Hoofdstuk IX)*

In hoofdstuk IX worden de bevindingen van de voorafgaande hoofdstukken kort samengevat en de belangrijkste conclusies gepresenteerd. Bovendien worden er enkele aanbevelingen gedaan ter verbetering van de regulering van bedrijven in relatie tot de rechten van de mens. Op basis van de voorafgaande analyse kan worden geconcludeerd dat geen van de bestaande instrumenten op zichzelf voldoende is om mensenrechtenverplichtingen voor bedrijven af te dwingen. In dit hoofdstuk wordt gepleit voor een geïntegreerde aanpak. Aandacht voor de invloed van bedrijven op mensenrechten moet systematisch onderdeel worden gemaakt van de bestaande implementatiestructuren op het terrein van de rechten van de mens.

Tenslotte worden enkele opmerkingen gemaakt over de wenselijkheid van een meer actieve rol van het bedrijfsleven bij mensenrechten. De vraag rijst of het identificeren van verplichtingen van bedrijven op dit terrein geen afbreuk doet aan het 'speciale karakter' van mensenrechten zijnde fundamentele waarborgen tegen de Staat. Bovendien kan de vraag gesteld worden of mensenrechtenverplichtingen voor andere entiteiten dan de Staat het systeem van bescherming van de rechten van de mens niet ondermijnt. Benadrukt dient te worden dat dit onderzoek op generlei wijze afbreuk wil doen aan de primaire verantwoordelijkheid van de Staat op het terrein van de rechten van de mens. De conclusie van dit onderzoek dat bedrijven zijn gebonden aan de rechten van de mens laat onverlet dat de Staat primair gehouden is deze rechten te verwezenlijken. Echter het ontkennen van de verplichtingen van bedrijven op dit terrein vormt, in het licht van de hedendaagse uitdagingen, een ware bedreiging voor de adequate bescherming van de rechten van de mens.

Terugkerend op de centrale vraagstelling van deze studie, kan worden geconcludeerd dat mensenrechtenverplichtingen voor bedrijven uit de bestaande mensenrechtencatalogus kunnen worden afgeleid. De afdwinging van deze verplichtingen is echter problematisch. De bestaande implementatiemechanismen dienen beter te worden benut om de invloed van bedrijven op de bescherming van mensenrechten kritisch tegen het licht te houden.

SELECTED BIBLIOGRAPHY

Addo, Michael K., 'The Corporation as a Victim of Human Rights Violations', in: *Human Rights Standards and the Responsibility of Transnational Corporations,* Michael K. Addo (ed.), Kluwer law International, The Hague etc., 1999, pp. 187-196.

Addo, Michael K., *Human Rights Standards and the Responsibility of Transnational Corporations,* Kluwer law International, The Hague etc., 1999.

Alkema, Evert Albert, 'The Third-party Applicability or "Drittwirkung" of the European Convention on Human Rights', in: *Protecting Human Rights: The European Dimension. Studies in Honour of Gerard J. Wiarda*, Franz Matscher and Herbert Petzold (eds.), Carl Heymanns Verlag, Cologne etc, 1988, pp. 33-45.

Allmand, Warren, *Trading in Human Rights: The need for human rights sensitivity at the World Trade Organization*, A brief to the Standing Committee in Foreign Affairs and International Trade, 24 March 1999, International Centre for Human Rights and Democratic Development, Montreal, Canada.

Alston, Philip (ed.), *The EU and Human Rights*, Oxford University Press, Oxford, 1999.

Alston, Philip, *Leading by Example: A Human Rights Agenda for the European Union for the Year 2000. Agenda of the* Comite des Sages *and Final Project Report*, European University Institute, Florence, 1998.

Alston, Philip, 'The Myopia of the Handmaidens: International Lawyers and Globalization', in: *European Journal of International Law*, Vol. 8, No.3, 1997, pp. 435-448.

Alston, Philip, 'Labor Rights Provisions in U.S. Trade Law "Aggressive Unilateralism"?', in: *Human Rights, Labor Rights, and International Trade*, Lance A. Compa and Stephen F. Diamond (eds.), University of Pennsylvania Press, Philadelphia, 1996, pp. 71-95.

Alston, Philip and Gerard Quinn, 'The Nature and Scope of State Parties' Obligations under the International Covenant on Economic, Social and Cultural Rights', in: *Human Rights Quarterly*, Vol. 9, 1987, pp. 156-229.

Alston, P. and K. Tomaševski (eds.), *The Right to Food*, International Studies in Human Rights, Netherlands Institute of Human Rights, Martinus Nijhoff Publishers, Utrecht, 1984.

Ambos, Kai, 'Article 25: Individual Criminal Responsibility' in: *Commentary on the Rome Statute of the International Criminal Court-Observers' Notes, Article by Article*, Otto Triffterer (ed.), 1999, Nomos, Baden-Baden, pp. 93-110.

Amerasinghe, C.F., *State Responsibility for Injuries to Aliens*, Clarendon Press, Oxford, 1967.

Amnesty International, *Sudan. Sudan - The Human Price of Oil*, 3 May 2000, AI Index: AFR 54/01/00, 2000.

Amnesty International UK Business Group, *Human Rights Guidelines for Companies*, Amnesty International, London, 1998.

Amnesty International/Pax Christi (Dutch sections), *Multinational Enterprises and Human Rights*, Utrecht, November 1998.

Amnesty International, *Human Rights are Everybody's Business*, AI Index, ASA 17/18/96, 1996.

Amnesty International, *Nigeria. Time to end contempt for human rights*, 6 November 1996, AI Index: AFR 44/14/96, 1996.
Asante, S.K.B., 'The Concept of the Good Corporate Citizen in International Business', in: *ICSID Review-Foreign Investment Law Journal*, Vol. 4, 1989, pp. 1-38
Avery, Christopher L., *Business and Human Rights in a Time of Change*, Amnesty International UK Section, February 2000.
Baade, Hans W., 'The Legal Effects of Codes of Conduct for Multinational Enterprises', in: *Legal Problems of Codes of Conduct for Multinational Enterprises*, Norbert Horn (ed.), Studies in Transnational Economic Law, Kluwer, The Hague etc., Vol.1, 1980, pp. 3-39.
Baade, Hans W., 'Codes of Conduct for Multinational Enterprises: An Introductory Survey', in: *Legal Problems of Codes of Conduct for Multinational Enterprises*, Norbert Horn (ed.), Studies in Transnational Economic Law, Kluwer, The Hague etc., Vol.1, 1980, pp. 407-441.
Baker, Mark B., 'Private Codes of Corporate Conduct: Should the Fox Guard the Henhouse?', in: *University of Miami Inter-American Law Review*, Vol. 24, No.3, 1992-1993, pp. 399-433.
Banning, Th. R.G. van, *The Human Right to Property*, Intersentia, Antwerp, 2002 *(forthcoming)*.
Betlem, Gerrit, 'Transnational Litigation Against Multinational Corporations Before Dutch Civil Courts', in: *Liability of Multinational Corporations Under International Law*, Menno T. Kamminga and Saman Zia-Zarifi (eds.), Kluwer Law International, The Hague, 2000, pp. 283-305.
Betten, Lammy, 'The International Implementation of Economic, Social and Cultural Rights by the ILO', in: *Netherlands Quarterly of Human* Rights, Vol. 6. No. 2, 1998, pp. 29-42.
BIAC, 'Contribution on the employment and industrial relations chapter of the OECD Guidelines for Multinational Enterprises', in: 'Multinational Enterprises and the Social Challenges of the XXIst Century. The ILO Declaration on Fundamental Principles at Work. Public and Private Codes of Conduct', Roger Blanpain (ed.), *Bulletin of Comparative Labour Relations* Vol. 37, 2000, pp. 99-106.
Biesheuvel, M.B.W., 'Horizontale werking van grondrechten (II)' [third-party applicability of fundamental rights (II)], in: *NJCM-Bulletin* 6-4, 1981, pp. 205-225.
Biesheuvel, M.B.W., 'Horizontale werking van grondrechten (I)' [third-party applicability of fundamental rights (I)], in: *NJCM-Bulletin* 6-3, 1981, pp. 147-169.
Blanpain, Roger, 'Review of the OECD Guidelines for Multinational Enterprises: Possible revisions to the chapter on employment and industrial relations', in: 'Multinational Enterprises and the Social Challenges of the XXIst Century. The ILO Declaration on Fundamental Principles at Work. Public and Private Codes of Conduct', Roger Blanpain (ed.), *Bulletin of Comparative Labour Relations*, Vol. 37, 2000, pp. 29-67.
Blanpain, Roger (ed.), 'Multinational Enterprises and the Social Challenges of the XXIst Century, in: 'The ILO Declaration on Fundamental Principles at Work. Public and Private Codes of Conduct', *Bulletin of Comparative Labour Relations*, Vol. 37, 2000.
Blanpain, Roger, 'The OECD Guidelines and Labour Relations: Badger and Beyond', in: *Legal Problems of Codes of Conduct for Multinational Enterprises*, Norbert Horn (ed.), Studies in Transnational Economic Law, Kluwer, The Hague, Vol. 1, 1980, pp. 145-155.
Boerefijn, Ineke, *The Reporting Procedure under the Covenant on Civil and Political Rights. Practice and Procedures of the Human Rights Committee*, Intersentia, Antwerp etc., 1999.

Boesjes, J., 'De horizontale werking van grondrechten', [The third-party applicability of fundamental rights], in: *Nederlands Juristen Blad*, 8 September, 1973, Vol. 29, pp. 905-916.
Bossuyt, Marc J., *Guide to the 'Travaux Préparatoires' of the ICCPR*, Martinus Nijhoff, Dordrecht, 1987, p. 120.
Boven, Theo C. van, Cees Flinterman, Fred Grünfeld, Rita Hur (eds.), *The Legitimacy of the United Nations: Towards an Enhanced Legal Status of Non-State Actors*, SIM Special No. 19, Utrecht, 1997.
Boyd, Kathryn Lee, 'The Inconvenience of Victims: Abolishing Forum Non Conveniens in US Human Rights Litigation', in: *Virginia Journal of International Law*, Vol. 39, No.1, 1998, pp. 41-87.
Brownlie, Ian, *Principles of Public International Law*, 5th edition, Clarendon Press, Oxford, 1998.
Brownlie, Ian, *System of the Law of Nations. State Responsibility. Part I*, Clarendon Press, Oxford, 1983.
Brownlie, Ian, 'Legal Effects of Codes of Conduct for Multinational Enterprises: Commentary', in: *Legal Problems of Codes of Conduct for Multinational Enterprises*, Vol. 1, Norbert Horn (ed.), 1980, pp. 39-45.
Buergenthal, Thomas, 'To Respect and to Ensure: State Obligations and Permissible Derogations', in: *The International Bill of Rights: The Covenant on Civil and Political Rights*, Louis Henkin (ed.), Columbia University Press, New York, 1981, pp. 72-91.
Buikema, R.H., *De Multinational Onderneming in Juridisch Perspectief: Enkele Rechtsvragen naar Aanleiding van de Discussie over Multinationale Ondernemingen [The Multinational Corporation in Perspective: Some Legal Questions Resulting from the Discussion on Multinational Corporations]*, T.C.Asser Instituut, The Hague, 1992.
Bijsterveld, S.C. van en W.J.M. van Genugten, 'Gedragscodes voor het internationale bedrijfsleven: nuttig instrument of schild tegen bindende verantwoordelijkheid ?' [Codes of Conduct for Multinational Enterprises: Useful Instrument or a Shield against Binding Responsibility], in: *Grondrechten en zelfregulering*, H.R.B.M. Kummeling and S.C. Bijsterveld (eds.), Tjeenk Willink, Deventer, 1997, pp. 105-125.
Byers, Michael, 'English Courts and Serious Human Rights Violations Abroad: A Preliminary Assessment', in: *Liability of Multinational Corporations Under International Law*, Menno T. Kamminga and Saman Zia-Zarifi (eds.), Kluwer Law International, The Hague etc., 2000, pp. 241-251.
Cassese, Antonio, *International Law in a Divided World*, Oxford University Press, Oxford, 1986, pp. 74-104
Castermans-Holleman, Monique, Fried van Hoof and Jacqueline Smith (eds.), *The Role of the Nation-State in the 21st Century, human rights, international organisations and foreign policy: essays in honour of Peter Baehr*, Kluwer Law International, The Hague, 1998.
Center For Economic and Social Rights, *Rights Violations in the Ecuadorian Amazon. The Human Consequences of Oil Development,* March 1994. Available at: http://www.cescr.org (accessed on 16 August 2001).
Charnovitz, Steve, 'The Moral Exception in Trade Policy', in: *Virginia Journal of International Law*, Vol. 38, 1998, pp. 689-744.
Cheng, Bin, 'Introduction to Subjects of International Law', in: *International Law: Achievements and Prospects*, M. Bedjaoui (ed.), UNESCO, 1991, pp. 23-40.

Clapham, Andrew and Scott Jerbi, *Towards a Common Understanding of Business Complicity in Human Rights Abuses*, Background paper for the Global Compact dialogue on the role of the private sector in zones of conflict, New York, 21-22 March 2001, Available at: http://www.globaldimensions.net/articles/cr/complicity.html (accessed on 26 July 2001).

Clapham, Andrew, 'The Question of Jurisdiction under International Criminal Law over Legal Persons: Lessons from the Rome Conference on an International Criminal Court', in: *Liability of Multinational Corporations Under International law*, Menno T. Kamminga and Saman Zia-Zarifi (eds.), Kluwer Law International, The Hague etc., 2000, pp. 139-195.

Clapham, Andrew, 'The "Drittwirkung" of the Convention', in: *The European System for the Protection of Human Rights*, R. St. J. Macdonald *et al.*, (eds.), Martinus Nijhoff Publishers, Dordrecht etc., 1993.

Clapham, Andrew, *Human Rights in the Private Sphere*, Clarendon Press, Oxford, 1993.

Colucci, Michele, 'Implementation and monitoring of codes of conduct. How to make codes effective?', in: 'Multinational Enterprises and the Social Challenges of the XXIst Century. The ILO Declaration on Fundamental Principles at Work. Public and Private Codes of Conduct', Roger Blanpain (ed.), *Bulletin of Comparative Labour Relations,* Vol. 37, 2000, pp. 277-289.

Colvin, Eric, 'Corporate Personality and Criminal Liability', in: *Criminal Law Forum,* Vol. 6 No. 1, 1995, pp. 1-44.

Compa, Lance A. and Tashia Hinchliffe Darrcarrere, 'Private Labor Rights Enforcement Through Corporate Codes of Conduct', in: *Human Rights, Labor Rights and International Trade*, Lance A Compa and Stephen Diamond (eds.), Pennsylvania Press, Philadelphia, 1996, pp. 181-198.

Compa, Lance A. and Stephen Diamond (eds.), *Human Rights, Labor Rights and International Trade,* Pennsylvania Press, Philadelphia, 1996.

Confederation of Danish Industries, Danish Centre for Human Rights and the Danish Industrialization Fund, *Defining the Scope of Business Responsibility for Human Rights Abroad*, 2000. Available at: http://www.e-chef.dk/humanrightsbusiness/ (accessed on 10 march 2002).

Conforti Benedetto, and Francesco Francioni. 'Enforcing international human rights in domestic courts', *International studies in human rights* vol. 49, Nijhoff, The Hague etc., 1997.

Coomans, Fons and Fried van Hoof, *The Right to Complain About Economic, Social and Cultural Rights*, SIM Special No. 18, Utrecht, 1995.

Coomans, A.P.M., *De internationale bescherming van het recht op Onderwijs*, proefschrift, Stichting NJCM-Boekerij, Leiden, 1992.

Craven, Matthew, *The International Covenant on Economic, Social and Cultural Rights. A Perspective on its Development*, Clarendon Press, Oxford, 1995.

Crawford, James, Jacqueline Peel and Simon Olleson, 'The ILC's Articles on Responsibility of States for Internationally Wrongful Acts: Completion of the Second Reading', in: *European Journal of International Law.* Available at: http://www.ejil.org/journal/new/new0109.html#fn4 (accessed on 14 September 2001).

Crawford, James and Pierre Bodeau, *The Second Reading of the Draft Articles on State Responsibility: A Progress Report*, by James Crawford and Pierre Bodeau. Available at: www.law.cam.ac.uk/rcil/ILCSR/Forum2.doc (accessed on 4 January 2001).

Daes, Erica-Irene A., *Freedom of the Individual under Law. A Study on the Individual's Duties to the Community and the Limitations on Human Rights and Freedoms under Article 29 of the Universal Declaration of Human* Rights, United Nations, New York, 1990.

Daly, Kieran, *The Business Response to HIV/AIDS: Impact and lessons learned*, Joint United Nations Programme on HIV/AIDS, The Prince of Wales Business Leaders Forum and the Global Business Council on HIV and AIDS, 2000.

De George, Richard T., *Competing with integrity in international business*, Oxford University Press, Oxford, 1993.

Diamond, Stephen F., 'Labor Rights in the Global Economy: A Case Study of the North American Free Trade Agreement', in: *Human Rights, Labor Rights, and International Trade,* Lance A. Compa and Stephen F. Diamond (eds.), University of Pennsylvania Press, Philadelphia, 1996, pp. 199-227.

Dine, J. 'Human Rights and Company Law', in: *Human Rights Standards and the Responsibility of Transnational Corporations,* Michael K. Addo (ed.), Kluwer law International, The Hague etc., 1999, pp. 209-235.

Doelder, Hans de, and Klaus Tiedemann, *La criminalisation du comportement collectif, XIVe Congres International de Droit Compare,* Kluwer Law International, The Hague etc., 1996.

Donaldson, Thomas, 'Ethiek over dc grens: dilemma's rond internationaal ondernemen', [Ethics across borders: dilemma's surrounding international business] in: *Holland/Belgium Management Review*, No. 50, 1996, p. 39-47

Donnelly, Jack, 'Human Rights, Globalisation and the State', in: *The Role of the Nation-State in the 21st Century: human rights, international organisations and foreign policy: essays in honour of Peter Baehr*, Monique Castermans-Holleman, Fried van Hoof and Jacqueline Smith (eds.), Kluwer Law International, The Hague, 1998, pp. 401-410.

Donnelly, Jack and Rhoda E. Howard, Assessing National Human Rights Performance: A Theoretical Framework', in: *Human Rights Quarterly*, Vol. 10, 1998, pp. 214-248.

Donnelly, Jack, *Universal Human Rights in Theory and in Practice*, Cornell University Press, New York, 1989.

Drzemczewski, A., 'The European Human Rights Convention and Relations between Private Parties', Netherlands International Law Review, Vol. XXVI, 1979, pp. 163-181.

Dubin, Laurence, 'The Direct Application of Human Rights Standards to, and by, Transnational Corporations', in: *Globalisation, Human Rights and the Rule of Law, The Review.* International Commission of Jurists, Adama Dieng (ed.), 1999, No. 61, pp. 35-66.

Dunoff, Jeffrey L., 'Does Globalisation Advance Human Rights?' in: Symposium: The Universal Declaration of Human Rights at 50 and the challenges of global markets: The global market as friend or poe of human rights, in: *Brooklyn Journal of International Law*, Vol. XXV, 1999, No. 1, pp. 125-139.

Dijk, P. van and G.J.H. van Hoof, *Theory and Practice of the European Convention on Human Rights*, 3rd edition, Kluwer Law International, The Hague etc., 1998.

Dijk, Pieter van, 'Domestic Status of Human-Rights Treaties and the Attitude of the Judiciary: The Dutch case', in: *Fortschritt im Bewusstsein der grund- und Menschenrechte*, Manfred Nowak, Dorothea Steurer, Hannes Tretter (eds.), N.P. Engel Verlag Kehl, Strasbourg etc., 1988, pp. 631-650.

Ehrenberg, Daniel S., 'From Intention to Action: An ILO-GATT/WTO Enforcement Regime for International Labor Rights', in: *Human Rights, Labor Rights and International Trade,*

Lance A. Compa and Stephen F. Diamond, University of Pennsylvania Press, Philadelphia, 1996, pp. 163-181.
Eide, Asbjørn, 'Promoting economic, social and cultural rights: obligations of States and accountability of non-state actors', Available at: http://www.undp.org/hdro/Rioforum.html (accessed on 25 January 2001)
Eide, Asbjørn, Helge Ole Bergesen and Pia Rudolfson Goyer (eds.), *Human Rights and the Oil Industry*, Intersentia, Antwerpen, 2000.
Eide, Asbjørn, Catarina Krause and Allan Rosas (eds.), *Economic, Social and Cultural Rights*, Martinus Nijhoff Publishers, Dordrecht etc., 1995.
Eide, Asbjørn, 'Economic, Social and Cultural Rights as Human Rights', in: *Economic, Social and Cultural Rights*, Asbjørn Eide, Catarina Krause and Allan Rosas (eds.), Martinus Nijhoff Publishers, Dordrecht etc., 1995, pp. 21-40.
Eissen M.A., 'The European Convention on Human Rights and the Duties of the Individual', in: *Nordisk Tidsskrift for International Ret*, Vol. 32, 1962.
Elkind, Jerome B. and Antony Shaw, *A Standard for Justice. A Critical Commentary on the Proposed Bill of Rights for New Zealand.* Oxford University Press, Oxford etc., 1986.
Eyk, S.C. van, *The OECD Declaration and Decisions Concerning Multinational Enterprises. An Attempt to Tame the Shrew,* Ars Aequi, Nijmegen, 1995.
Fabig, Heike, 'The Body Shop and the Ogoni', in: *Human Rights Standards and the Responsibility of Transnational Corporations*, Michael Addo (ed.), Kluwer Law International, the Hague, 1999, pp. 309-321.
Fatouros, A.A., 'Introduction: Looking for an International Legal Framework for Transnational Corporations', in: *Transnational Corporations: The International Legal framework.* The United Nations Library on Transnational Corporations. Volume 20, A.A. Fatouros, (ed.), Routeledge, London, 1994, pp. 1-38.
Fatouros, A.A., 'On the Implementation of International Codes of Conduct: An Analysis of Future Experience', in: *American University Law Review*, Vol. 30, 1981, pp. 941-972.
Fatouros, A.A., 'The UN Code of Conduct on Transnational Corporations: A Critical Discussion of the First Drafting Phase', in: *Legal Problems of Codes of Conduct for Multinational Enterprises*, Norbert Horn (ed.), Studies in Transnational Economic Law,, Vol. 1, Kluwer, Deventer, 1980, pp. 103-127.
Feyter, Koen de, *World Trade Development Law. Sharing Responsibility for Development*, Intersentia, Antwerp etc., 2001.
Fikentscher, W., 'United Nations Codes of Conduct: New Paths in International Law', in: *American Journal of Comparative Law*, Vol. 30, 1982, pp. 577-604.
Fischer, Peter, and Heribert Fransz Kock, *Algemeines Volkerrecht*, 4th ed., Linde Verlag, Wien, 1994.
Fischer, Peter, 'Transnational Enterprises', in: *Encyclopaedia of Public International Law, Human Rights and the Individual in International Law. International Economic Relations*, published under the auspices of the Max Planck Institute for Comparative Public Law and International law under the direction of Rudolf Bernhardt, Vol.8, North Holland, Amsterdam etc., 1985, pp. 515-519.
Fisse, Brent and John Braithwaite, *Corporations, Crime and Accountability,* Series: Theories of Institutional Design, Cambridge University Press, New York etc., 1993.
Flinterman, C., B. Kwiatkowska and J.G. Lammers (eds.), *Transboundary Air Pollution,* Martinus Nijhoff Publishers, The Hague, 1986.

Forde, M., 'Non-governmental interference with human rights', in: *British Yearbook of International Law,* Vol. 56, 1985, pp. 253-280.

Forcese, Craig, *Putting Commerce into Conscience: Strategies for Making Human Rights Business as Usual*, Canadian Lawyers Association for International Human Rights in collaboration with the International Centre for Human Rights and Democratic Development, Vol. 2, 1997.

Forcese, Craig, *Commerce With Conscience ? Human Rights and Corporate Codes of Conduct*, Canadian Lawyers Association for International Human Rights in collaboration with the International Centre for Human Rights and Democratic Development, Vol. 1, 1997.

Forsythe, David P., 'Transnational corporations and human rights', in: *Human Rights in International Relations*, Cambridge, Cambridge University Press, 2000, pp. 191-213.

Francioni, Fancesco and Tullio Scovazzi (eds.), *International Responsibility for Environmental Harm*, International Environmental Law and Policy Series, Graham and Trotman, Martinus Nijhoff Publishers, London etc., 1993.

Friedman, M, 'The social responsibilities of business is to increase its profits', in: *Business ethics readings and cases in corporate morality*, Hoffman, W.M. and R.E. Frederick (eds.), 3rd edition, Mc Graw-Hill, New York, 1995, pp. 137-141.

Friedmann, Wolfgang, *The Changing Structure of International Law,* Steven and sons, London, 1964.

Gagnon, Georgette and John Ryle, *Report on an Investigation into Oil Development, Conflict and Displacement in Western Upper Nile Sudan*, October 2001. The report can be found at: http://www.worldvision.ca/ (accessed on 14 November 2001).

Garcia, Frank J., Mark A.A. Warner and Steve Charnovitz, Symposium: The Universal Declaration of Human Rights at 50 and the Challenges of Global Markets: The global market as friend or poe of human rights, in: *Brooklyn Journal of International Law,* Vol. XXV, No. 1, 1999, pp. 51-140.

Garvey, Jack L., 'Trade Law and Quality of Life -Dispute Resolution under the NAFTA Side Accords on Labor and the Environment', in: *The American Journal of International Law,* Current Developments, Vol. 89, 1995, pp. 439-453.

Geer, Martin A., 'Foreigners in Their Own Land: Cultural Land and Transnational Corporations – Emergent International Rights and Wrongs', in: *Virginia Journal of International Law*, Vol. 38, No. 3, 1998, pp. 331-399.

Genugten, W.J.M. van, 'Bescherming van de rechten van de mens: de taakverdeling tussen staten en ondernemingen [Protection of human rights: the division of tasks between States and corporations], in: *Civis Mundi. Tijdschrift voor politieke filosofie en cultuur. Internationale dimensies van maatschappelijk verantwoord ondernemen*, Vol. 41, No. 2, January 2002, pp. 5-10.

Genugten, W.J.M. van, 'Multinationale ondernemingen en de rechten van de mens: van voorzichtige toenadering tot paradigmawisseling, [Multinational corporations and human rights: from a careful rapprochement to a change of change of paradigm] in: *Nederlands Juristenblad*, Vol. 25, 23 June 2000, pp. 1231-1236.

Genugten, Willem J.M. van, The Status of Transnational Corporations in International Law. With Special Reference to the Case of Shell', in: *Human Rights and the Oil Industry*, Asbjørn Eide, Helge Ole Bergesen and Pia Rudolfson Goyer (eds.), Intersentia, 2000, pp. 71-89.

Genugten, W.J.M. van, *WTO, ILO en EG: handelen in vrijheid [WTO, ILO and EC: trading in freedom]*, W.E.J. Tjeenk Willink, Deventer, 1997.
Getz, Kathleen A., 'International Codes of Conduct: An Analysis of Ethical Reasoning', in: *Journal of Business Ethics*, Vol. 9, 1990, pp. 567-577.
Gibney, M. and R.D. Emerick, 'The Extraterritorial Application of United States Law and the Protection of Human Rights: Holding Multinational Corporations to Domestic and International Standards', in: *Temple International and Comparative Law Journal*, Vol. 10, No. 1, 1996, pp. 123-145.
Gordon, Kathryn and Maiko Miyake, 'Deciphering Codes of Corporate Conduct: A Review of their Contents', in: *Working Papers on International Investment*, OECD/OCDE, Number 99/2, December 1999.
Green, Jennifer and Paul Hoffman, 'US Litigation Update', in: *Liability of Multinational Corporations Under International Law*, Menno T. Kamminga and Saman Zia-Zarifi (eds.), Kluwer Law International, The Hague, 2000, pp. 231-241.
Grossfeld, Berhard, 'Legal Controls of Transnational Enterprises', in: *Legal Issues in International Trade*, Petar Sarcevíc and Hans van Houtte (eds.), Graham and Trotman/Martinus Nijhoff Publishers, Dordrecht, 1990, pp. 176-186.
Guertin, Don L., 'A Business View on the Implementation of Codes of Conduct', in: *Legal Problems of Codes of Conduct for Multinational Enterprises,* Norbert Horn (ed.), Studies in Transnational Economic Law, Vol. 1, Kluwer, Deventer, 1980, pp. 295-309.
Günter, Hans, 'The Tripartite Declaration of Principles (ILO): Standards and Follow-Up', in: *Legal Problems of Codes of Conduct for Multinational Enterprises*, Norbert Horn (ed.), Studies in Transnational Economic Law, Vol. 1, Kluwerd, Deventer, 1980, pp. 155-177.
Handl, G.F., W.M. Reisman, B. Simma, P.M. Dupuy and C.Chinkin, 'A Hard Look at Soft Law', in: *Transnational Corporations: The International Legal Framework. The United Nations Library on Transnational Corporations*, A.A. Fatouros, (ed.), Vol. 20, Routledge, London, 1994, pp. 333-361.
Handl, Gunther, 'State Liability for Accidental Transnational Environmental Damage by Private Actors', in: *American Journal of International Law*, Vol. 74, 1980, pp. 525-565.
Hansen, Peter, Victoria Aranda, 'An Emerging International Framework for Transnational Corporations', *Fordham International Law Journal*, 1990-1991, pp. 881-981.
Harris, D.J., M. O'Boyle, and C. Warbrick, *Law of the European Convention on Human Rights*, Butterworths, London, 1995.
Henkin, Louis, 'The Universal Declaration at 50 and the Challenge of Global Markets', in: *Brooklyn Journal of International Law*, Vol. XXV, No. 1, 1999, pp. 17-25.
Henkin, Louis, *International Law: Politics and Values*, Martinus Nijhoff Publishers, Dordrecht etc., 1995.
Hepple, Bob, 'The Importance of Law, Guidelines and Codes of Conduct in Monitoring Corporate Behaviour', in: 'Multinational Enterprises and the Social Challenges of the XXIst Century. The ILO Declaration on Fundamental Principles at Work. Public and Private Codes of Conduct', Roger Blanpain (ed.), *Bulletin of Comparative Labour Relations*, Vol. 37, 2000, pp. 3-9.
Herdegen, Matthias, *Internationales Wirtshaftsrecht*, 2nd edition, Beck, Muchen, 1993.
Hessel, Bart and Patrick de Graaf, *Over Recht en Bedrijfsethiek. Pleidooien voor Samenwerking [on Law and Business Ethics. Pleas for Cooperation]*, Ars Aequi Libri, 1998.

Higgins, Rosalyn, *Problems and Process. International Law and How We Use It*, Clarendon Press, New York, 1994.

Higgins, Rosalyn, 'A Multinational Corporation or an International Organisation', in: *New Diplomacy in the Post-Cold War World. Essays for Susan Strange*, Roger Morgan *et al.* (ed.), McMillan, Basingstoke etc., 1993, pp. 182-190.

Hochstedler, Ellen (ed.), *Corporations as Criminals*, perspectives in criminal justice 6, Sage Publications, Beverly Hills/London/New Dehli, 1984.

Hoof, Fried van, 'International Human Rights Obligations for Companies and Domestic Courts; An Unlikely Combination?', in: *The Role of the Nation-State in the 21st Century: human rights, international organisations and foreign policy: essays in honour of Peter Baehr,* Monique Castermans-Holleman, Fried van Hoof and Jacqueline Smith (eds.), Kluwer Law International, The Hague, 1998, pp. 47-59.

Hoof, G.J.H. van, 'The Legal Nature of Economic, Social and Cultural Rights: a Rebuttal of Some Traditional Views', in: *The Right to Food*, P. Alston, K. Tomaševski (eds.), Studie- en Informatie centrum Mensenrechten-SIM/Martinus Nijhoff Publishers, Utrecht/Dordrecht, 1984.

Hoof, G.J.H. van, *Rethinking the Fundamental Sources of International Law*, Deventer, Kluwer, 1983.

Hoof. G.J.H. van and Karel de Vey Mestdagh, *Mechanisms of International Supervision*, Europa Instituut, Universiteit Utrecht, 1979.

Horn, Norbert (ed.), *Legal Problems of Codes of Conduct for Multinational Enterprises*, Studies in Transnationial Economic Law, Vol. 1, Kluwer, Deventer, 1980.

Hossain, Kamal, 'Globalization and the promotion of human rights', in: *Reflections on International Law from the Low Countries. In honour of Paul de Waart.* Erik Denters and Nico Schrijver (eds.), Martinus Nijhoff Publishers, The Hague etc., 1998, pp. 101-115.

Howitt, Richard, *Report on EU Standards for European Enterprises Operating in Developing Countries: Towards a European Code of Conduct, Committee on Development and Cooperation,* 17 December 1998, A-4-0508/98, PE 228.198/fin.

Howse, Robert and Makau Mutua, *Protecting Human Rights in a Global Economy. Challenges for the World Trade Organisation*, International Centre for Human Rights and Democratic Development, available at: http://www.ichrdd.ca/111/english/contentsEnglish.html (accessed on 12 June 2001)

Human Rights Committee, International Law Association (British Branch), 'Report on Civil Actions in the English Courts for Serious Human Rights Violations Abroad', in: *European Human Rights Law Review*, Issue 2, 2001, pp. 129-166.

Human Rights Program Harvard Law School and the Lawyers' Committee for Human Rights, *Business and Human Rights. An Interdisciplinary Discussion Held at Harvard Law School in December 1997*, Publication of the Harvard Law School Human Rights Program, 1999, Available at: http://www.law.harvard.edu/programs/HRP/Publications/bussession1.html (accessed on 18-05-00).

Human Rights Watch, *Trading Away Rights. The Unfulfilled Promise of NAFTA's Labor Side Agreement*, Vol. 13 No. 2 (B), April 2001. Available at: http://www.hrw.org/reports/2001/nafta/index.htm (accessed on 18 December 2001).

Human Rights Watch, *The Price of Oil. Corporate Responsibility and Human Rights Violations in Nigeria's Oil Producing Communities*, New York, 1999. Available at: http://www.hrw.org/hrw/reports/1999/nigeria/index.htm (accessed on 17 January 2002).

Human Rights Watch, *World Report 1999*, New York, 1999.

Human Rights Watch, *The Enron Corporation: Corporate Complicity in Human Rights Violations,* New York, 1999. Available at: http.hrw.org/hrw/reports/1999/enron (accessed on 17 January 2002).

Human Rights Watch, *Colombia: Human Rights ConcernsRraised by the Security Arrangements of Transnational Oil Companies*, 1998. Available at: http://www.hrw.org/hrw/advocay/corporations/colombia/index.htm (accessed on 17 January 2002).

Human Rights Watch Africa, *Nigeria, Permanent Transition,* September 1996, Vol. 8, No. 3 (A)

Human Rights Watch, *Nigeria, the Ogoni crisis: a case study of military repression in South East Nigeria*, New York, 1995.

Huner, Jan, 'The Multilateral Agreement on Investment and the Review of the OECD Guidelines for Multinational Enterprises', in: *Liability of Multinational Corporations Under International Law,* Menno T. Kamminga and Saman Zia-Zarifi (eds.), Kluwer Law International, The Hague etc., 2000, pp. 197-207.

International Centre for Human Rights and Democratic Development, *Summary Report. Globalization, Trade and Human Rights: The Canadian Business Perspective*, Toronto, 22 February 1996.

International Council on Human Rights Policy, *Beyond Voluntarism. Human rights and the developing international legal obligations of companies*, February 2002.

International Labour Organisation, *Forced labour in Myanmar (Burma)*, Report of the Commission of Inquiry Appointed Under Article 26 of the Constitution of the International Labour Organisation to Examine the Observance by Myanmar of the Forced Labour Convention, 1930 (No. 29), ILO, Part IV, Geneva, 2 July 1998.

International Labour Organisation, *Overview of Global Development and Office Activities Concerning Codes of Conduct, Social Labelling and other Private Sector Initiatives Addressing Labour Issues*, Working Party on the Social Dimensions of the Liberalization of International Trade, International Labour Office, GB. 273/WP/SDL/1, 273rd session, Geneva, November 1998.

International NGO Committee on Human Rights in Trade and Investment, *Investment, Trade and Finance: The Human Rights Framework. Focussing on the Multilateral Agreement on Investment (MAI)*, Policy Statement, 1998.

IRENE (International Restructuring Education Network Europe), *Controlling Corporate Wrongs: The Liability of Multinational Corporations/ Legal Possibilities, Initiatives and Strategies for Civil Society. Report of the international IRENE seminar on corporate liability and workers' rights held at the University of Warwick, Coventry, United Kingdom*, 20 and 21 March 2000.

Jägers, Nicola, 'The entrepreneur and man; a reaction to Bram Rutgers van der Loeff's presentation, in: *Divisions of Roles in the International and Legal Order. Enterprises, Governments, Trade Unions, NGO's and Human Rights*, Willem van Genugten en Ruud Lubbers (eds.), Wolf Legal Publishers, Nijmegen, 2002, pp. 75-79.

Jägers, Nicola, 'The Legal Status of the multinational Corporation Under International Law', in: *Human Rights Standards and the Responsibility of Transnational Corporations,* Michael K. Addo (ed.), Kluwer Law International, The Hague, 1999, pp. 259-270.

Jägers, Nicola, 'Transnational Corporations and Human Rights', in: *To Baehr in Our Minds. Essays from the Heart of the Netherlands*, Mielle Bulterman, Aart Hendriks and Jacqueline

Smith (eds.), Studie- en Informatiecentrum Mensenrechten [Netherlands Institute of Human Rights], SIM Special No. 21, Utrecht, 1998.

Janis, M.W., 'Individuals as subjects of international law', in: *Cornell International Law Journal*, 1984, Vol. 17, No. 1, pp. 61-78.

Jennings, Robert and Arthur Watts, *Oppenheims International Law*, 9th edition, Volume I Peace, Longman, 1992.

Jochnick, Chris, 'Confronting the Impunity of Non-State Actors: New Fields for the Promotion of Human Rights', in: *Human Rights Quarterly,* Vol. 21No. 1, 1999, pp. 56-79.

Jones, Roy, 'The 1999 Review of OECD Guidelines for Multinational Enterprises', in: 'Multinational Enterprises and the Social Challenges of the XXIst Century. The ILO Declaration on Fundamental Principles at Work. Public and Private Codes of Conduct', Roger Blanpain (ed.), *Bulletin of Comparative Labour Relations* Vol. 37, 2000, pp. 141-149.

Joseph, Sarah, Jenny Schultz and Melissa Castan, *The International Covenant on Civil and Political Rights. Cases, Materials and Commentary*, Oxford University Press, Oxford, 2000.

Joseph, Sarah, 'An Overview of the Human Rights Accountability of Multinational Enterprises', in: *The Liability of Multinational Corporations Under International Law,* Menno T. Kamminga and Saman Zia-Zarifi (eds.), Kluwer Law International, The Hague etc., 2000, pp. 75-95.

Joseph, Sarah, 'Taming the Leviathans: Multinational Enterprises and Human Rights', in: *Netherlands International law Review*, Vol. XLVI, 1999, pp. 171-203.

Jungk, Margaret, *Deciding whether to do Business in States with Bad Governments*, The Confederation of Danish Industries, The Danish Centre for Human Rights, The Danish Industrialization Fund for Developing Countries, 2001.

Jungk, M., 'A Practical Guide to Addressing Human Rights Concerns for Companies Operating Abroad', in: *Human Rights Standards and the Responsibility of Transnational Corporations*, Michael K. Addo (ed.), Kluwer Law International, The Hague etc., 1999, pp. 171-186.

Kaptein, Muel, Huib Klamer and Bram Rutgers van der Loeff, *Business Ethics and Company Codes in the Netherlands: Translation, Summary and Update of a brochure of the 'Nederlands Christelijk Werkgeversverbond (NCW)'*, NCW, The Hague, 1992.

Kapur, R., 'From Human Tragedy to Human Rights: Multinational Corporate Accountability for Human Rights Violations': in: *Boston College of Third World Law Journal,* Vol. 10, No. 1, 1990, p. 15.

Kamminga, Menno T. and Saman Zia-Zarifi (eds.), *Liability of Multinational Corporations Under International Law,* Kluwer law International, The Hague etc., 2000.

Kamminga, Menno, 'Holding Multinational Corporations Accountable for Human Rights Abuses: A Challenge for the EC', in: *The EU and Human Rights*, Philip Alston (ed.), Oxford University Press, Oxford, 1999, pp. 553-569.

Kamminga, M.T. en L.A.D. Keus, 'Staatsaansprakelijkheid jegens individuen: beginselen en procedures', [State Responsibility towards individuals: principles and procedures] Preadviezen, *Mededelingen van de Nederlandse Vereniging voor Internationaal Recht 116*, inclusief: Verslag van de Algemene Ledenvergadering, 7 november 1997, Kluwer.

Kamminga, Menno, 'Aansprakelijkheid van multinationale ondernemingen voor schendingen van internationaal recht', [accountability of multinational corporations for violations of international law] *NJCM-Bulletin Bulletin. Nederlands Tijdschrift voor de Mensenrechten*, Vol. 6, September, 1997.

Kamminga, Menno T., *Inter-State Accountability for Violations of Human Rights*, University of Pennsylvania Press, Philadelphia, 1992.

Kaufmann, Johan and Nico Schrijver, *Changing Global Needs: Expanding Roles for the United Nations System*, the Academic Council on the United Nations System, Report and Papers 1990-5, Hannover, 1990.

Karl, J., 'The OECD Guidelines for Multinational Enterprises', in: *Human Rights Standards and the Responsibility of Transnational Corporations*, Michael K. Addo, Kluwer Law International, The Hague etc., 1999, pp. 89-106.

Kemp, Antonie de, 'Gedragscodes voor multinationale ondernemingen'[codes of conduct for multinational corporations] in: *Internationale Spectator,* 1986, pp. 371-381.

Kingsbury, Benedict, 'Claims by Non-State Groups in International Law', in: *Cornell International Law Journal,* Vol. 25, 1992, pp. 481-513.

Klip, André and Göran Sluiter (eds.), *Annotated Leading Cases of International Criminal Tribunals. The International Criminal Tribunal of Rwanda 1994-1999*, Intersentia, Antwerp etc., 2001.

Kline, John M., 'International regulation of transnational business: providing the missing leg of global investment standards', in: *Transnational Corporations*, Vol. 2, No. 1, February 1993, pp. 153-164.

Kochan, Donald J., 'Constitutional Structure as a Limitation on the Scope of "The Law of Nations" in the Alien Tort Claims Act', in: *Cornell International Law Journal*, Vol. 31, No. 1, 1998, pp. 153-191.

Kokkini-Iatridou, D. and P.J.I.M. de Waart, 'Foreign Investments in Developing Countries - Legal Personality of Multinationals in International Law', in: *Netherlands Yearbook of International law*, Vol. XIV 1983, Martinus Nijhoff Publishers, Dordrecht, 1983, pp. 87-131.

Kolk, Ans, Rob van Tulder and Carlijn Welters, 'International codes of conduct and corporate social responsibility: can transnational corporations regulate themselves ?', in: *Transnational Corporations*, Vol. 8, No. 1, April 1999, pp. 143-181.

Kothari, Miloon en Peter Prove, 'The UN Courts Big Business. In Whose Interest ?', in: *The Human Rights Tribune*, September 1999, Vol. 6, No. 3, pp. 16-18.

Kothari, Miloon en Peter Prove, 'Issues for debate. International Trade and Investment: A Human Rights Framework', in: *Lokayan Bulletin*, 14.6, 1998, pp. 37-43.

Krause, Catarina and Gudmundur Alfredsson, 'Article 17', in: *The Universal Declaration of Human Rights: a common standard of achievement*, Gudmundur Alfredsson and Asbjørn Eide (eds.), Martinus Nijhoff Publishers, The Hague, 1999.

Lauterpacht, H. *The International Protection of Human Rights*, *Recueil des Cours*, 1947.

Law Reports of Trials of War Criminals, Volume I, IX, X, Published for the United Nations War Crimes Commission by His Majesty's Stationery Office, London, 1949.

Lawson, Rick, 'Out of Control. State Responsibility and Human Rights: Will the ILC's Definition of the 'Act of State' Meet the Challenges of the 21st Century ?', in: *The Role of the Nation-State in the 21st Century: human rights, international organisations and foreign policy: essays in honour of Peter Baehr*, Monique Castermans-Holleman, Fried van Hoof and Jacqueline Smith (eds.), Kluwer, The Hague, 1998, pp. 91-116.

Leary, Virginia A., 'The Paradox of Workers' Rights as Human Rights', in: *Human Rights, Labor Rights, and International Trade*, Lance A. Compa and Stephen F. Diamond (eds.), University of Pennsylvania Press, Philadelphia, 1996, pp. 22-47.

Leckie, Scott, 'The Inter-State Complaint Procedure in International Human Rights Law: Hopeful Prospects or Wishful Thinking', in: *Human Rights Quarterly*, Vol. 10, 1988, pp. 249-303.

Lehman, Cheryl R. and Russell M. Moore, (eds.), *Multinational Culture. Social Impacts of a Global Economy*. Contributions in Economics and Economic History, No. 122, Greenwood Press, Westport etc., 1992.

Leeson, Helena, 'Human Rights, Corporate Wrongs', in: *The World Today*, August/September 1998, pp. 228-230.

Loomis, W., 'The Responsibility of Parent Corporations for the Human Rights Violations of Their Subsidiaries': in: *Human Rights Standards and the Responsibility of Transnational Corporations*, Michael K. Addo (ed.), Kluwer Law International, The Hague etc., 1999, pp. 145-159.

Lu, Justin, 'Jurisdiction over Non-State Activity Under the Alien Tort Claims Act', in: *Columbia Journal of Transnational Law*, Vol. 35, 1997, pp. 531-549.

Lyons, Beth S., 'Getting to Accountability: Business, Apartheid and Human Rights', in: *Netherlands Quarterly of Human Rights*, Kluwer Law International, Vol. 17, No. 2, June 1999, pp. 135-160.

Macklem, Patrick and Ed Morgan, 'Indigenous Rights in the Inter-American System: the Amicus Brief of the Assembly of First Nations in Awas Tingni v. Republic of Nicaragua', in: *Human Rights Quarterly*, Vol. 22, 2000, pp. 569-602.

MacShane, Denis, 'Human Rights and Labor Rights. A European Perspective', in: *Human Rights, Labor Rights, and International Trade*, Lance A. Compa and Stephen F. Diamond (eds.), University of Pennsylvania Press, Philadelphia, 1996, pp. 48-69.

Malanczuk, Peter, 'Multinational Enterprises and Treaty-Making – A Contribution to the Discussion on Non-State Actors and the "Subjects" of International law', in: *Multilateral Treaty-Making. The Current Status of Challenges to and Reforms Needed in the International Legislative Process*, Vera Gowlland-Debbas (ed.), Proceedings of the American Society of International Law/ Graduate Institute of International Studies, Forum Geneva, May 16 1998, Geneva, Switzerland, Martinus Nijhoff Publishers, 2000, pp. 35-62.

Malanczuk, Peter, 'Globalization and the future role of sovereign states', in: *International Economic Law with a Human Face*, Friedl Weiss, Erik Denters and Paul de Waart (eds.), Kluwer Law International, The Hague etc., 1998, pp. 45-64.

Malanczuk, Peter, *Akehurst's Modern Introduction to International Law -7th rev.*, Routledge, London, 1997.

McCorquodale, Robert and Richard Fairbrother, 'Globalization and Human Rights', in *Human Rights Quarterly*, Vol. 21, 1999, pp. 735-766.

McGoldrick, Dominic, *The Human Rights Committee. Its Role in the Development of the International Covenant on Civil and Political Rights*, Clarendon Press, Oxford, 1994.

Meeran, Richard, 'Liability of Multinational Corporations: A Critical Stage in the UK', in: *Liability of Multinational Corporations Under International Law*, Menno T. Kamminga and Saman Zia-Zarifi, Kluwer Law International, The Hague, 2000, pp. 251-264.

Meeran, Richard, 'The Unveiling of Transnational Corporations', in: *Human Rights Standards and the Responsibility of Transnational Corporations*, Michael K. Addo (ed.), Kluwer Law International, The Hague, 1999, pp. 161-169.

Meron, Theodor, 'Is International Law Moving Towards Criminalization?', in: *European Journal of International Law*, Vol. 9, 1998, pp. 18-31.

Meron, Theodor, *Human Rights and Humanitarian Norms as Customary Law*, Clarendon Press, Oxford, 1989.

Meuwissen, D.H.M., *De Europese Conventie en het Nederlandse Recht [The European Convention and Dutch Law]*, Sijthof, Leiden, 1968.

Meijknecht, Anne, *Towards International Personality: The Position of Minorities and Indigenous Peoples in International Law*, Intersentia, Antwerp etc., 2001.

Meyer, William H., 'Confirming, Infirming and "Falsifying" Theories of Human Rights: Reflections on Smith, Bolyard, and Ippolito Through the Lens of Lakatos', in: *Human Rights Quarterly*, Vol. 21, No. 1, 1999, pp. 220-228.

Meyer, William, *Human Rights and International Political Economy in Third World Nations: Multinational Corporations, Foreign Aid, and Repression*, Westport, Connecticut, 1998.

Meyer, William H., 'Human Rights and MNCs: Theory versus Quantitative Analysis', in: *Human Rights Quarterly*, Vol. 2, 1996, pp. 368-397.

Morehouse, Ward and M. Arun, 'The Bhopal Tragedy. What Really Happened and What it Means for American Workers and Communities at Risk', A Preliminary Report for the Citizens Commission on Bhopal, 1986, New York.

Morris, Virginia and Michael P. Scharf, *An Insiders Guide to the International Criminal Tribunal for the Former Yugoslavia*, Vol. I, Transnational Publishers, New York etc., 1995.

Morsink, Johannes, *The Universal Declaration on Human Rights: origins, drafting and intent*, PENN, Philadelphia, 1999.

Muchlinski, Peter T., 'Human Rights and Multinationals', in: *International Affairs*, Vol. 77, No.1, January 2001, The Royal Institute of International Affairs, pp. 31 - 47.

Muchlinski, Peter T., 'Attempts to Extend the Accountability of Transnational Corporations: The Role of UNCTAD, in: *Liability of Multinational Corporations Under International Law*, Menno T. Kamminga and Saman Zia-Zarifi (eds.), Kluwer Law International, The Hague etc., 2000, pp. 97-119.

Muchlinski, P.T., *Multinationals Enterprises and the Law*, Blackwell, Oxford, 1995.

Nieuwenhuys, Eva, 'Het Multilaterale Akkoord inzake Investeringen. Een stelsel voor een wereldomvattende economie of een stelsel van transatlantisch machtsoverwicht?' [The Multilateral Agreement of Investments. A system for a global economy or a system of transatlantic dominance] in: *Internationale Spectator*, October 1998, Vol. 10, pp. 509-515.

Nieuwenhuis, E.C.,'Transnationale Ondernemingen en Mensenrechten', [Transnational Corporations and Human Rights] in: *NJCM-Bulletin*, 22, Vol. 6, September 1997, pp. 696-702.

Niklasson, Sten, 'The OECD Guidelines for Multinational Enterprises and the UN Draft Code of Conduct: Some Political Considerations', in: *Legal Problems of Codes of Conduct for Multinational Enterprises*, Norbert Horn (ed.), Studies in Transnational Economic Law, Vol. 1, Kluwer, Deventer, 1980, pp. 141-145.

Nollkaemper, Andre, 'Public International Law in Transnational Litigation Against Multinational Corporations: Prospects and Problems in the Courts of the Netherlands', in: *Liability of Multinational Corporations Under International Law*, Menno T. Kamminga and Saman Zia-Zarifi (eds.), Kluwer Law International, The Hague, 2000, pp. 265-283.

Nollkaemper, Andre, 'Rethinking States' Rights to Promote Extra-Territorial Environmental Values', in: *International Economic Law with a Human Face*, Friedl Weiss, Erik Denters and Paul de Waart (eds.), Kluwer Law International, The Hague etc., 1998, pp. 175-201.

Nowak, Manfred, *U.N. Covenant on Civil and Political Rights: CCPR Commentary,* Engel, Kehl am Rhein, 1993.

Nørgaard, Carl Aage, *The position of the individual in international law*, Munksgaard, Copenhagen, 1962.

O'Connell, D.P., *International Law*, Vol. 1, London, 1965.

O'Reilly, Paddy and Sophia Tickell, 'TNCs and Social Issues in the Developing World', in: *Human Rights Standards and the Responsibility of Transnational Corporations*, Michael K. Addo (ed.), Kluwer Law International, The Hague etc., 1999, pp. 273-285.

OECD/OCDE, Working Party of the Trade Committee, *Codes of Corporate Conduct: An Inventory*, TD/TC/WP(98)74/Final.

Oldenziel, Joris, *The 2000 Review of the OECD Guidelines for Multinational Enterprises: A New Code of Conduct?*, SOMO and Duurzame Wereld NDCO, Amsterdam, September 2000.

Pellet, A., 'A New International Legal Order: What Legal Tools for What Changes?', in: *Transnational Corporations: The International Legal Framework.* The United Nations Library on Transnational Corporations. Vol. 20, A.A. Fatouros, (ed.), Routledge, London, 1994, pp. 318-332.

Pomeroy, Laura Okin, 'The Labor Side Agreement under the NAFTA: Analysis of its failure to include strong enforcement provisions and recommendations for future labor agreements negotiated with developing countries', Note in: *George Washington Journal of International Law and Economics*, Vol. 29, 1996, pp. 769-801.

Prakash Sethi, S. and Oliver F. Williams, *Economic Imperatives and Ethical Values in Global Business. The South African Experience and International Codes Today*, 2000, Kluwer Academic Publishers, Boston etc., 2000.

Preston, Lee E., 'The Evolution of Multinational Public Policy Towards Business: Codes of Conduct', in: *Multinational Culture, Social Impacts of a Global Economy*. Contributions in Economics and Economic History, No. 122, Cheryl R. Lehman and Russell M. Moore (eds.), Greenwood Press, New York, 1992.

Pursey, Stephan, *Multinational Enterprises and the World of Work: Globalisation with a Human Face. Article on the 20th Anniversary of the ILO Declaration on Multinational Enterprises and Social Policy.* Document available at: http://www.icftu.org/english/tncs/tncs98ilo.html (accessed on 2 September 1998).

Qureshi, Asif, 'International Trade and Human Rights from the Perspective of the WTO' in: *International Economic Law with a Human Face*, Friedl Weiss, Erik Denters and Paul de Waart (eds.), Kluwer Law International, The Hague etc., 1998, pp. 159-172.

Raimo, Tyler, 'Winning at the Expense of Law: The Ramifications of Expanding Counterterrorism Law Enforcement Jurisdiction Overseas', in: *American University International Law Review,* Vol. 14, 1999, pp. 1473-1513.

Ramcharan, B.G., 'The Concept and Dimensions of the Right to Life', in: *The Right to Life in International Law*, B.G. Ramcharan (ed.), Martinus Nijhoff Publishers, Dordrecht etc., 1985.

Rankins, Zennith K., 'U.S. Laws in the Rainforest: Can a U.S. Court Find Liability for Extraterritorial Pollution Caused by a U.S. Corporation? An Analysis of *Aguinda* v. *Texaco*', in: *Boston College International and Comparative Law Review*, Vol. 18, No. 1, 1995, pp. 221-263.

Ratner, Steven R. and Jason S. Abrams, *Accountability for Human Rights Atrocities in International Law. Beyond the Nuremberg Legacy*, Clarendon Press, Oxford, 1997.

Remmelink, J., *D.Hazewinkel-Suringa's Inleiding tot de Studie van het Nederlandse Strafrecht [Introduction to Dutch Criminal Law],* 15th edition, Gouda Quint, Deventer, 1996.

Rigaux, Francois, 'Transnational Corporations', in: *International Law: Achievements and Prospects*, M. Bedjaoui (ed.), UNESCO, 1991, p. 129.

Rodley, Nigel S., 'Can Armed Opposition Groups Violate Human Rights', in: *Human Rights in the Twenty-first Century*, K.E. Mahoney and P. Mahoney (eds.), 1993, Kluwer Academic Publishers, The Hague, pp. 297-318.

Röling, B.V.A and Antonio Cassese, *The Tokyo Trial and Beyond, Reflections of a Peacemonger*, Polity Press, Cambridge etc., 1994.

Ross, Alf, *A Textbook of International Law. General Part*, Longman, Green and Co., London, 1947.

Sacharoff, Ariadne K., 'Multinationals in Host Countries: Can They Be Held Liable Under the Alien Tort Claims Act for Human Rights Violations ?', in: *Brooklyn Journal of International Law*, Vol. XXIII, No. 3, 1998, pp. 927-964.

Sampford, Charles, 'The Four Dimensions of Rights', in: *Rethinking Human Rights*, Brian Galligan and Charles Sampford (eds.), The Federation Press, Sydney, 1997, pp. 50-71.

Sanders, P., 'De Naleving van Internationale Gedragscodes voor Multinationale Ondernemingen' [The Compliance with International Codes of Conduct for Multinational Enterprises], in: *Gratia Commercii,* Zwolle, 1981, blz. 263-276.

Sauvant, K.P. and V. Aranda, 'The International Legal Framework for Transnational Corporations', in: *Transnational Corporations: The International Legal Framework.* The United Nations Library on Transnational Corporations. Vol. 20, A.A. Fatouros, (ed.), Routledge, London, 1994, pp. 83-115.

Schachter, Oscar, 'The erosion of state authority and its implications for equitable development', in: *International Economic Law with a Human Face*, Friedl Weiss, Erik Denters and Paul de Waart (eds.), Kluwer Law International, The Hague etc., 1998, pp. 31-43.

Schachter, Oscar, *International Law in Theory and Practice*, Kluwer Law International, The Hague etc., 1995.

Schapers, M., *De OESO-Gedragscode voor Multinationale Ondernemingen: de stand van zaken na twintig jaar*, [The OECD code of conduct: the state of affairs after twenty years], Leiden, 1996.

Scheinkam, Jack, in: *By the Sweat and Toil of Children: the Use of Child labor in American Imports. A Report to the Committees on Appropriations United States Congress*, Bureau of International Labor Affairs. U.S. Department of Labor, July 15 1994.

Schmalenbach, Kirsten, 'Multinationale Unternehmen und Menschenrechte', in: *Archiv des Völkenrecht*, Vol. 39, No. 1, pp. 57-81

Schreuer, Christoph, 'Access to ISCID dispute settlement for locally incorporated companies', in: *International Economic Law with a Human Face*, Friedl Weiss, Erik Denters and Paul de Waart (eds.), Kluwer Law International, The Hague etc., 1998, pp. 497-512.

Schreuer, Christoph, 'The waning of the Sovereign State. Towards a New Paradigm for International law?', *European Journal of International law*, Vol. 4, No. 4, 1993, pp. 447-472.

Scott, Graig, 'Multinational Enterprises and Emergent Jurisprudence on Violations of Economic, Social and Cultural Rights', in: *Economic, Social and Cultural Rights*, 2nd edition, Asbjørn Eide, Catarina Krause and Allan Rosas (eds.), Martinus Nijhoff Publishers,Dordrecht etc., 2001, pp. 563-595.

Scott, Graig (ed.), *Torture as Tort. Comparative Perspectives on the Development of Transnational Human Rights Litigation*, Hart Publishing, Oxford etc., 2001.
Seiderman, Ian D., *Hierarchy in International Law*, Intersentia, Antwerp etc., 2001.
Seidl-Hohenveldern, Ignaz, *Volkerrecht,* 9th edition, Heymann, Cologne, 1997.
Sethi, Prakash and Oliver F. Williams, *Economic Imperatives and Ethical Values in Global Business. The South African Experience and International Codes Today*, Kluwer Academic Publishers, Boston etc., 2000.
Shaw, Malcolm N., *International Law*, 4th edition, Cambridge University Press Cambridge, 1997.
Shelton, Dinah, 'State Responsibility for Covert and Indirect Forms of Violence', in: *Human Rights in the Twenty-First Century: a Global Challenge,* Kathleen E. Mahoney and Paul Mahoney (eds.), Martinus Nijhoff Publishers, Dordrecht etc., 1993, pp. 265-276.
Shepherd Jr., George W., 'Transnational Development of Human Rights: The Third World Crucible', in: *Global Human Rights: Public Policies, Comparative Measures and NGO Strategies*, Ved P. Nanda, James R. Scarritt and George W. Sheperd Jr. (eds.), Westview Press, Boulder etc., 1981, pp. 213-218.
Shue, Henry, 'The Interdependence of Duties', in *The Right to Food*, P. Alston, K. Tomaševski (eds.), International Studies in Human Rights, Netherlands Institute of Human Rights, Martinus Nijhoff Publishers, Utrecht, 1984, pp. 83-95.
Shue, Henry, *Basic Rights. Subsistence, Affluence, and US Foreign Policy,* Princeton University Press, Princeton, New Jersey, 1980.
Sinclair, Ian McTaggart, *Vienna Convention on the Law of Treaties*, 2nd rev. and enlarged edition, Manchester University Press, Manchester, 1984.
Skogly, Sigrun I., *The Human Rights Obligations of the World Bank and the International Monetary Fund*, Cavendish Publishing, London, 2001.
Skogly, Sigrun I., book review of Meyer, William H. *Human Rights and International Political Economy in Third World Nations: Multinational Corporations, Foreign Aid, and Repression*, Westport, Connecticut, Preager, 1998, in : *American Political Science Review,* Vol. 93, No. 3, 1999, p. 761.
Skogly, Sigrun I., 'Economic and Social Human Rights, Private Actors and International Obligations', in: *Human Rights Standards and the Responsibility of Transnational Corporations*, Michael K. Addo (ed.), Kluwer Law International, The Hague etc., 1999, pp. 239-258.
Skogly, Sigrun I., 'Complexities in Human Rights Protection: Actors and Rights Involved in the Ogoni Conflict in Nigeria', in: *Netherlands Quarterly of Human Rights*, Vol. 15, No.1, 1997, pp. 47-60.
Smith, Jackie, Melissa Bolyard and Anna Ippolito, 'Human Rights and the Global Economy: A Response to Meyer', in: *Human Rights Quarterly*, Vol. 21, No. 1, 1999, pp. 207-219.
Smith, Jackie and Ron Pagnucco with George A.Lopez, 'Globalizing Human Rights: The Work of Transnational Human Rights NGOs in the 1990s', in: *Human Rights Quarterly*, Vol. 20, 1998, pp. 379-412.
Sornarajah, M., 'State Responsibility for Harms by Corporate Nationals Abroad', in: *Torture as Tort. Comparative Perspectives on the Development of Transnational Human Rights Litigation*, Graig Scott (ed.), Hart Publishing, Oxford etc., 2001, pp. 491-512.
Steiner, Henry J. and Philip Alston, *International Human Rights in Context. Law, Politics, Morals. Text and Materials*, Clarendon Press, Oxford, 1996.

Stephens, Beth 'Corporate Accountability: International Human Rights Litigation Against Corporations in US Courts', in: *Liability of Multinational Corporations Under International Law*, Menno T. Kamminga and Saman Zia-Zarifi (eds.), Kluwer Law International, The Hague etc., 2000, pp. 209- 231.

Stephens, Beth and Michael Ratner, *International Human Rights Litigation in U.S. Courts*, Transnational Publishers, New York, 1996.

Sunga, Lyal S., *Individual Responsibility in International Law for Serious Human Rights Violations*, Martinus Nijhoff Publishers, Dordrecht, 1992.

Swan, Michael, 'International Human Rights Tort Claims and the Experience of United States Courts: An Introduction to the US Case Law, Key Statutes and Doctrines', in: *Torture as Tort. Comparative Perspectives on the Development of Transnational Human Rights Litigation*, Graig Scott (ed.), Hart Publishing, Oxford, 2001, pp. 65-107.

Thorsen, Sune Skadegard, 'Strategies for the Application of Human Rights to Business', in: *Human Rights Standards and the Responsibility of Transnational Corporations*, Michael K. Addo (ed.), Kluwer Law International, The Hague etc., 1999, pp. 197-200.

Thüsing, Rolf, 'Codes of Conduct -a Growing Concern for Enterprises ?', in: 'Multinational Enterprises and the Social Challenges of the XXIst Century. The ILO Declaration on Fundamental Principles at Work. Public and Private Codes of Conduct', Roger Blanpain (ed.), *Bulletin of Comparative Labour Relations,* Vol. 37, 2000, pp. 95-98.

Toebes, Brigit C.A., *The Right to Health as a Human Right in International Law*, Intersentia, Antwerp etc., 1998.

Tully, Stephen, 'The 2000 Review of the OECD Guidelines for Multinational Enterprises', in: *International and Comparative Law Quarterly*, Vol. 50, April 2001, pp. 394-404.

United Nations Conference on Trade And Development (UNCTAD), *World Investment Report 2001: Promoting Linkages*, United Nations, New York and Geneva, 2001. Available at: http://www.unctad.org/wir/contents/wir01content.en.htm (accessed on 8 January 2002).

United Nations Conference on Trade And Development (UNCTAD), *World Investment Report 2000, Cross-border Mergers and Acquisitions and Development*, United Nations, New York and Geneva, 2000. Available at: http://www.unctad.org/wir/contents/wir00content.en.htm (accessed on 8 January 2002).

United Nations Development Programme (UNDP), *Human Development Report 2000, Human Rights and Human Development,* Oxford University Press, Oxford/New York, 2000.

United Nations Development Programme (UNDP), *Human Development Report 1999, Globalization with a Human Face*, Oxford University Press, Oxford/New York, 1999.

Utting, Peter, 'UN-Business Partnerships. Whose Agenda Counts ?', in: *UNRISD NEWS. The United Nations Research Institute for Social Development Bulletin*, Autumn/Winter 2000, No. 23, pp. 1-4.

Verhey, L.F.M., *Horizontale werking van grondrechten, in het bijzonder van het recht op privacy,[The third party applicability of fundamental rights ('Drittwirkung'), especially the right to privacy*], Tjeenk Willink, Zwolle, 1992.

Verhey, L.F.M., 'De horizontale werking van het EVRM' [the horizontal effect of the ECHR], in: 40 jaar Europees Verdrag voor de Rechten van de Mens, Opstellen over de ontwikkeling in van het EVRM in Straatsburg en Nederland [40 years European Convention on Human Rights, Essays on the development of the ECHR in Strasbourg and the Netherlands], special edition of the NJCM-Bulletin, Leiden, 1990, pp. 19-39.

Vernon, R., 'Codes on Transnationals: Ingredients for an Effective International Regime', in: *Structural Change, Economic Interdependence and World Development*, J.H. Dunning and M.Usui (eds.), Vol.4, Macmillan, Basingstoke, 1978, pp. 227-240.

Verzijl, J.H.W., 'International Law in Historical Perspective', in: *Nova et vetera iuris gentium,* M.Bos (ed.) Series A Modern International Law No. 6., Sijthof, Leyden, 1969.

Vogelaar, Theo W., 'The OECD Guidelines: Their Philosophy, History, Negotiations, Form, Legal Nature, Follow-up Procedures and Review', in: *Legal Problems of Codes of Conduct for Multinational Enterprises,* Norbert Horn (ed.), Studies in Transnational Economic Law, Vol. 1, Kluwer, Deventer, 1980, pp. 127-141.

Volio, Fernando, 'Legal Personality, Privacy, and the Family', in: *The International Bill of Rights: The Covenant on Civil and Political Rights*, Louis Henkin (ed.), Columbia University Press, New York, 1981, pp. 185-208.

Waart, Paul de, 'Quality of life at the mercy of WTO Panels: GATT's Article XX an empty shell', in: *International Economic Law with a Human Face*, Friedl Weiss, Erik Denters and Paul de Waart (eds.), Kluwer Law International, The Hague etc., 1998, pp. 109-130.

Waelde, Thomas W. 'Sustainable Development and the 1994 Energy Charter Treaty: Between Pseudo-Action and the Management of Environmental Investment Risk', in: *International Economic Law with a Human face*, Friedl Weiss, Erik Denters and Paul de Waart (eds.), Kluwer Law International, The Hague, 1998, pp. 223-270.

Wai, Robert, 'The Commercial Activity Exception to Sovereign Immunity and the Boundaries of Contemporary International Legalism', in: *Torture as Tort. Comparative Perspectives on the Development of transnational Human Rights Litigation*, Graig Scott (ed.), Hart Publishing, Oxford etc., 2001, pp.

Wallace, Cynthia Day, *Legal Control of Multinational Enterprises* , Martinus Nijhoff Publishers, The Hague etc., 1983.

Wallace, Don Jr., *International Regulation of Multinational Corporations,* Praeger, New York, 1976.

Warbrick, C. 'The European Convention on Human Rights and the Prevention of Terrorism', *International and Comparative Law Quarterly*, Vol. 32, 1983.

Ward, Halina, 'Governing Multinationals: The Role Of Foreign Direct Liability', *Briefing Paper, New A series* No. 18 February 2001, The Royal Institute of International Affairs. Energy and Environmental Programme.

Webley, Simon, 'The Nature and Value of Internal Codes of Ethics', in: *Human Rights Standards and the Responsibility of Transnational Corporations*, Michael K. Addo (ed.), Kluwer Law International, The Hague etc., 1999, pp. 107-112.

Weiss, Friedl, 'Internationally recognized labour standards and trade', in: *International Economic Law with a Human Face*, Friedl Weiss, Erik Denters and Paul de Waart (eds.), Kluwer Law International, The Hague etc., 1998, pp. 79-106.

Weiss, Friedl, Erik Denters and Paul de Waart (eds.), *International Economic Law with a Human* Face, Kluwer Law International, The Hague etc., 1998, pp. 79-106.

Weissbrodt, David, 'The Beginning of a Sessional Working Group on Transnational Corporations within the UN Sub-Commission on Prevention of Discrimination and Protection of Minorities', in: *Liability of Multinational Corporations Under International Law,* Menno T. Kamminga and Saman Zia-Zarifi Kamminga (eds.), Kluwer law International, The Hague etc., 2000, pp. 119-139.

Weissbrodt, David, 'Non-State Entities and Human Rights within the Context of the Nation-State in the 21st Century', in: *The Role of the Nation-State in the 21st Century: human rights, international organisations and foreign policy: essays in honour of Peter Baehr*, Monique Castermans, Fried van Hoof and Jacqueline Smith (eds.), Kluwer Law International, The Hague, 1998, pp. 175-195.

Wells, Celia, 'Corporate Manslaughter: A Cultural and Legal Form' in: *Criminal Law Forum*, Vol. 6, No.1, 1995, pp. 45-72.

Wells, Celia, *Corporations and Criminal Responsibility,* Clarendon Press, Oxford, 1994.

Wet, Erika de, 'Labor Standards in the Globalized Economy: The Inclusion of a Social Clause in the General Agreement On Tariff and Trade/World Trade Organization', in: *Human Rights Quarterly,* Vol. 17, 1995, pp. 443-462.

Wilson, Andrew and Chris Gribben, *Business Responses to Human Rights*, Ashridge Centre for Business and Society, April 2000.

Winston, Morton E., book reviews of Meyer, William H. *Human Rights and International Political Economy in Third World Nations: Multinational Corporations, Foreign Aid, and Repression*, Westport, Connecticut, Preager, 1998. in: *Human Rights Quarterly*, Vol. 21, 1999, pp. 824-849.

Wise, Edward, 'General Principles of International Law', in: *Model Draft Statute for the International Criminal Court based on the Preparatory Committee's text to the Diplomatic Conference*, L. Sadat Wexler (ed.), Vol. 61m 1998. Cherif Bassiouni (gen. Ed.) 13ter Nouvelles Etudes Penales 1998, pp. 41-44.

Woodroffe, J., 'Regulating Multinational Corporations in a World of Nations States', in: *Human Rights Standards and the Responsibility of Transnational Corporations*, Michael K. Addo (ed.), Kluwer Law International, The Hague etc., 1999, pp. 131-142.

Zadek, Simon, Niels Hojensgard and Peter Raynard (eds.), *Perspectives on the New Economy of Corporate Citizenship*, The Copenhagen Centre, 2001.

Zadek, Simon and Maya Forstater, 'Making Civil Regulation Work', in: *Human Rights Standards and the Responsibility of Transnational Corporations*, Michael K. Addo (ed.), Kluwer Law International, The Hague etc., 1999, pp. 69-74.

Zegveld, Liesbeth, *Armed Opposition Groups in International Law: The Quest for Accountability*, Cambridge University Press, *forthcoming*, dissertation-copy, 2000.

Zia-Zarifi, Saman, 'Suing Multinational Corporations in the U.S. for Violating International Law', in: *UCLA Journal of International Law and Foreign Affairs*, Vol. 81, 1999, pp. 81-147.

TABLE OF CASES

International Criminal Tribunal for Rwanda

United Nations Human Rights Committee (ICCPR)

European System

European Commission and Court of Human Rights

European Committee of Social Rights

Inter-American System

Commission

Court

International Labour Organisation

Other International

Australia

Canada

The Netherlands

United Kingdom

United States of America

Selected United Nations Documents

General Assembly

A/Res/3201 (S-VI), 1 May 1974, *Declaration on the Establishment of a New International Economic Order*.
A/Res/3281 (XXIX), 12 December 1974, *Charter of Economic Rights and Duties of States.*
A/Res/42/115, 7 December 1987, *The Impact of Property on the Enjoyment of Human Rights and Fundamental Freedoms.*
A/Res/48/141, 20 December 1993, *High Commissioner for the Promotion and the Protection of All Human Rights.*
A/Res/53/144, 8 March 1999, *Declaration on the Right and Responsibility of Individuals, Groups and Organs of Society to Promote and Protect Universally Recognized Human Rights and Fundamental Freedoms.*
A/Res/54/165, 24 February 2000, *Globalization and its Impact on the Full Enjoyment of All Human Rights.*
A/55/342, 31 August 2000, *Globalization and its Impact on the Full Enjoyment of All Human Rights*. Preliminary report of the Secretary-General.
A/40/10, *Draft ICC Statute, 1994*. General Assembly Official Records, forty-ninth Session No.10.

Commission on Human Rights

E/CN.4/1426, 19 January 1981, Commission on Human Rights Thirty-Seventh Session.
E/CN.4/1994/85, 9 March 1994, *Situation of Human Rights in Myanmar.*
E/CN.4/1997/110, 31 January 1997, Note by the Secretariat on *the Relationship Between the Enjoyment of Human Rights, in Particular Economic, Social and Cultural Rights and the Development, and the Working Methods and Activities of Transnational Corporations.*
E/CN.4/RES/1999/59, 28 April 1999, *Globalization and its Impact on the Full Enjoyment of All Human Rights.*
E/CN.4/1999/47, 11 January 1999, *Economic, Social and Cultural Rights. Effects on the Full Enjoyment of Human Rights of the Economic Adjustment Policies arising from Foreign Debt and, in particular, on the Implementation of the Declaration on the Right to Development.* Note by the Secretariat.

Secretary-General

S/1993/25704, 3 May 1993, Report of the Secretary-General pursuant to para. 2 of Security Council Resolution 808 (1993), UN doc. S/INF/49 (1994).

Sub-Commission on the Promotion and Protection of Human Rights

E/CN.4/Sub.2/1987/23, 7 July 1987. *The New International Economic Order and the Promotion of Human Rights*. Report on the right to adequate food as a human right submitted by Mr. Asbjorn Eide, Special Rapporteur.

E/CN.4/Sub.2/1990/19, 6 July 1990, *The New International Economic Order and the Promotion of Human Rights*. *Realization of Economic, Social and Cultural Rights*, Progress Report prepared by Mr. Danilo Türk, Special Rapporteur.

E/CN.4/Sub.2/1991/17, 18 July 1991, The *Realization of Economic, Social and Cultural Rights*, Second Progress Report prepared by Mr. Danilo Türk, Special Rapporteur.

E/CN.4/Sub.2/1995/11, 24 July 1995, *The Realization of Economic, Social and Cultural Rights. The Relationship between the Enjoyment of Human Rights, in particular, International Labour and Trade Union Rights, and the Working Methods and Activities of Transnational Corporations*, Background Paper prepared by the Secretary General following resolution 1994/37.

E/CN/Sub.2/1996/12, report on *the Impact of the Activities and Working Methods of Transnational Corporations on the Full Enjoyment of all Human Rights, in particular Economic, Social and Cultural Rights and the Right to Development,* pursuant to resolution 1995/31 of the Sub-Commission.

E/CN.4/Sub.2/1997/8, *The Realization of Economic, Social and Cultural Rights. Final report on the question of the impunity of perpetrators of human rights violations (economic, social and cultural rights)* Prepared by Mr. El Haji Guissé, Special rapporteur, pursuant to Sub-Commission resolution 1996/24.

E/CN.4/Sub.2/1997/9, 30 June 1997, *The Realization of Economic, Social and Cultural Rights. The Relationship Between the Enjoyment of Human Rights, in particular Economic, Social and Cultural Rights and Income Distribution*. Final report prepared by Mr. Jose Bengoa.

E/CN.4/Sub.2/Res/1998/8, 20 August 1998, *The Relationship Between the Enjoyment of Economic, Social and Cultural Rights and the Right to Development, and the Working Methods and Activities of Transnational Corporations.*

E/CN.4/Sub.2/1998/45, 30 September 1998, *Report of the Sub-Commission on Prevention of Discrimination and Protection of Minorities in its Fiftieth Session.*

E/CN.4/Sub.2/1998/6, 10 June 1998, *The Realization of Economic, Social and Cultural Rights: The Question of Transnational Corporations.* Working document on the Impact of the Activities of Transnational Corporations on the Realization of Economic, Social and Cultural Rights, prepared by Mr. El Hadji Guisse, pursuant to Sub-Commission resolution 1997/11.

E/CN.4/Sub.2/1999/9, 12 August 1999, *The Realization of Economic, Social and Cultural Rights: The Question of Transnational Corporations.* Report of the Sessional Working Group on the Working Methods and Activities of Transnational Corporations on its First Session.

E/CN.4/1999/WG.2/1, *Provisional Agenda,* 26 July 1999, Sessional Working Group on the Working Methods and Activities of Transnational Corporations.

E/CN.4/Sub.2/1999/NGO/14,*The Realization of Economic, Social and Cultural Rights. The Question of Transnational Corporations*, Written Statement by the Society for Threatened Peoples, a non-governmental organization in special consultative status, 28 June 1999.

E/CN.4/Sub.2/1999/11, *The Realization of Economic, Social and Cultural Rights: Human Rights as the Primary objective of International Trade, Investment and Finance Policy and Practice.* Working Paper submitted by J. Oloka-Onyango and Deepika Udagama, in accordance with Sub-commission resolution 1998/12, 17 June 1999.

E/CN.4/Sub.2/2000/WG.2/WP.1, 25 May 2001, *Principles Relating to the Human Rights Conduct of Companies.* Working paper prepared by Mr. David Weissbrodt.

E/CN.4/Sub.2/2000/WG.2/WP.1/Add.1, 25 May 2001, *Proposed Draft Human Rights Code of Conduct for Companies.* Working paper prepared by Mr. David Weissbrodt. Addendum. Draft human rights code of conduct for companies with source materials.

E/CN.4/Sub.2/2000/WG.2/WP.1/Add.2, 25 May 2000, *Proposed Draft Human Rights Code of Conduct for Companies.* Working paper prepared by Mr. David Weissbrodt. List of the principal source materials for the draft code of conduct for companies.

E/CN.4/Sub.2/2000/13, 15 June 2000, *The Realization of Economic, Social and Cultural Rights: Globalization and its Impact on the Full Enjoyment of Human Rights.* Preliminary Report submitted by J. Oloka-Onyango and Deepika Udagama in accordance with Sub-Commission resolution 1999/8.

E/CN.4/Sub.2/2001/WG.2/WP.1/Add.1, 31 May 2001, *Draft Human Rights Guidelines for Companies.*

E/CN.4/Sub.2/2001/WG.2/WP.1, 21 May 2001, *Economic, Social and Cultural Rights. Draft Universal Human Rights Guidelines for Companies*. Introduction.

E/CN.4/Sub.2/2001/WG.2/WP.1/Add.1, 21 May 2001, *Economic, Social and Cultural Rights. Addendum 1: Draft Universal Human Rights Guidelines for Companies.*

E/CN.4/Sub.2/2001/WG.2/WP.1/Add.2, 21 May 2001, *Economic, Social and Cultural Rights. Addendum 2: Draft Universal Human Rights Guidelines for Companies with Source Materials.*

E/CN.4/Sub.2/2001/WG.2/WP.1/Add.3, 31 May 2001, *Draft Human Rights Guidelines for Companies. Report of the Seminar to Discuss U.N. Human Rights Guidelines for Companies.*

E/CN.4/Sub.2/2001/10, 2 July 2001, *Economic, Social and Cultural Rights Globalization and its Impact on the Full Enjoyment of Human Rights. Progress* report submitted by J. Oloka-Onyango and Deepika Udagama, in accordance with Sub-Commission resolution 1999/8 and Commission on Human Rights decision 2000/102.

UN Doc.E/CN.4/Sub.2/2001/WG.2/WP.3, *The Realisation of Economic, Social and Cultural Rights and the Question of Transnational* Corporations. Working Paper prepared by Mr. Guissé.

UN Doc. E/CN.4/Sub.2/2001/WG.2/WP.2, *Corporations, States, and Human Rights: A Note on Responsibilities and Procedures for Implementation and Compliance*. Working Paper prepared by Mr. Eide.

E/CN.4/Sub.2/RES/2001/3, 15 August 2001, *The Effects of the Working Methods and Activities of Transnational Corporations on the Enjoyment of Human Rights.*

UN Doc.E/CN.4/Sub.2/2001/9, 14 August 2001, *Economic, Social and Cultural Rights. Report of the Sessional Working Group on the Working Methods and the Activities of Transnational Corporations on its Third Session.*

E/CN.4/Sub.2/2002/X/Add.1, E/CN.4/Sub.2/2002/WG.2/WP.1/Add.1, Draft for Discussion, November 2001, *Economic, Social and Cultural Rights, Addendum 1: Draft Fundamental Human Rights Principles for Business Enterprises.*

UN Doc. E/CN.4/Sub.2/2002/XX, E/CN.4/Sub.2/2002/WG.2/WP.1, Draft for discussion, February 2002, *Human Rights Principles and Responsibilities for Transnational Corporations and Other Business Enterprises.*

Human Rights Committee

A/37/40 (1982) Annex V (pp. 93-94); CCPR/C/21/Rev.1, (pp. 4-6), 27 July 1982, General Comment No. 6 [16], *Right to Life.*
CCPR/C/Rev.1, (pp. 6-7); A/37/40 (1982) Annex V (pp. 94-95), 27 July 1982, General Comment No. 7 [16], *Prohibition of Torture.*
A/37/40 (1982) Annex V (pp. 96-97); CCPR/C/21/Rev.1 (pp.8-9), 28 July 1982, General Comment No. 9 [16], *Prohibition of Humane Treatment of Persons deprived of Liberty.*
A/39/40 (1984) Annex VI (pp. 142-143); CCPR/C/21/Rev.1 (pp. 10-12), 12 April 1984, General Comment 12 [21], *Right to Selfdetermination.*
CCPR/C/21/Rev.1 (pp. 19-21); A/43/40 (1988) Annex (pp.181-183), 23 March 1988, General Comment 16 [32], *Right to Privacy.*
CCPR/C/21/Rev.1/Add.1 (pp. 1-4); A/45/40, Vol. I (1990), Annex VI Sub A (p. 173-175), 9 November 1989, General Comment No. 18 [37], *Non-Discrimination.*
A/45/40 Vol. I (1990) Annex VI sub B (pp. 175-177), 24 July 1990, General Comment 19 [39], *Protection of the Family.*
A/47/40 (1992), Annex VI (pp. 193-195), 3 April 1992, General Comment 20 [44], *Torture.*
CCPR/C/79/Add.14, 28 December 1992, *Concluding Observations of the Human Rights Committee: Bosnia and Herzegovina.*
A/48/40, Part I (1983), Annex VI (p. 208-211); CCPR/C/21/Rev.1/Add.4, 20 July 1993, General Comment 22 [48], *The Right to Freedom of Thought, Conscience and Religion.*
A/49/40, Vol. I (1994), Annex V (p. 107-110); CCPR/C/21/Rev.1/Add.5, 6 April 1994, General Comment 23 [50], *Rights of Persons belonging to Minorities.*
CPR/C/21/Rev.1/Add.6; A/50/40, Vol. I (1995), Annex V (p. 119-125), 2 November 1994, General Comment No. 24 [52], *General Comment on Issues Relating to Reservations made upon Ratification or Accession to the Covenant or the Optional Protocols thereto, or in Relation to Declarations under Article 41 of the Covenant.*
CCPR/C/133, 22 December 1997, *Report on the Informal Meeting on Procedures.* Note by the Secretariat.
CCPR/C/21/Rev.1/Add.9; A/55/40, Vol.I (2000), Annex VI A (pp. 128-132), 18 October 1999, General Comment 27 [67], *Liberty of Movement.*

Committee on Economic, Social and Cultural Rights

E/C.12/1997/4, General Comment 07 (1997), 20 May 1997, *The Right to Adequate Housing.*
E/C.12/1/Add.23, 13 May 1998,*Concluding Observations of the Committee on Economic, Social and Cultural Rights: Nigeria.*
E/C.12/1999/4, General Comment 11 (1999), 10 May 1999, *The Right to Education.*
E/C.12/1999/5, General Comment 12 (1999), 12 May 1999, *The Right to Food.*
UN Doc. E/C.12/1999/9, 26 November 1999, *Substantive Issues Arising in the Implementation of the International Covenant on Economic, Social and Cultural Rights: Statement of the*

United Nations Committee on Economic, Social and Cultural Rights to the Third Ministerial Conference of the World Trade Organisation. Seattle, 30 November to 3 December 1999).
E/C.12/1999/10, General Comment 13 (1999), 8 December 1999, *The Right to Education.*
E/C.12/2000/4, General Comment 14 (2000), 11 May 2000, T*he Right to the Highest Attainable Standard of Health.*

Committee on the Elimination of Discrimination Against Women

A/47/38, 30 January 1992, General recommendation No. 19, eleventh session 1992, *Violence Against Women.*

World Conferences

A/Conf.157/23, 12 July 1993, *Vienna Declaration and Programme of Action.*
A/Conf.166/9, 12 March 1995, *Copenhagen Declaration on Social Development and Programme of Action.*
A/Conf.183/C.1/L.3, 16 June 1998, *Proposal submitted by France to the Committee of the Whole.*
A/Conf.183/2/Add.1, 14 April 1998, *Report of the Preparatory Committee on the Establishment of an International Criminal Court, Addendum.*

Economic and Social Council

Resolution 1982/69, 27 October 1982, *Activities of Transnational Corporations in Southern Africa and their Collaboration with the Racist Minority Regime in that Area.*
Resolution 1983/74, 29 July 1983, *Activities of Transnational Corporations in South Africa and Namibia and their Collaboration with the Racist Minority Regime in South Africa.*
Resolution 1984/53, 25 July 1984, *Activities of Transnational Corporations in South Africa and Namibia and Collaboration of such Corporations with the Racist Minority Regime in South Africa.*

World Health Organisation

WHA/Res/34.22, 21 May 1981, *Adoption of the the International Code of Marketing of Breastmilk Substitutes.*

United Nations Commission/Centre on Transnational Corporations

E/5500/Rev.1/Add 1 (Part 1), 24 May 1974 *The Impact of Multinational Corporations on Development and on International Relations.*
E/C.10/1982/6 of 5 June 1982, *United Nations Draft International Code of Conduct on Transnational Corporations.*
E/1990/94, 12 June 1990, *United Nations Draft International Code of Conduct on Transnational Corporations* (latest version).

International Law Commission

UN Doc. A/CN.4/Ser.A/1975, Add. 1, 'Commentary to article 11, Draft Articles on State Responsibility after the First Reading', *YBILC,* Vol. II, 1975, pp. 70-83.

A/51/10, 6 May-26 July 1996, *Report of the International Law Commission on the Work of its Forty-Eighth Session.* General Assembly Official Records - Fifty-First Session, Supplement No. 10.

A/CN.4/490/Add.5, 22 July 1998, *First Report on State Responsibility, Addendum,* James Crawford, Special Rapporteur, fiftieth session ILC.

A/CN.4/L.602/REV.1, 26 July 2001, *State Responsibility. Titles and Texts of the Draft Articles on Responsibility of States for Internationally Wrongful Acts adopted by the Drafting Committee on Second Reading.*

A/51/10, 23 April – 1 June and 2 July – 10 August 2001, *Report of the International Law Commission on the Work of its Fifty-Third Session.* General Assembly Official Records - Fifty-fifth Session, Supplement No. 10.

INDEX

CURRICULUM VITAE

Nicola Jägers (1971) studied history as well as law at Utrecht University. She obtained a Master's degree in history in 1995, and graduated in international law in 1997. She started working for the Netherlands Institute of Human Rights (SIM), first as a research assistant, later as a PhD-candidate. During her employment at SIM she was involved in various activities, *inter alia*, as the executive secretary of the Foundation Lawyers for Lawyers (*Stichting Advocaten voor Advocaten*), as a member of the Dutch Section of the International Commission of Jurists (NJCM), as a member of the national NGO consultation group on human rights (BMO) and as a member of the board of the *Johannes Wier Foundation,* a human rights organisation for health workers. She has also written and lectured on various topics relating to corporations and human rights. Moreover, she has worked as a lecturer of international law.

School of Human Rights Research Series

The School of Human Rights Research is a joint effort by human rights researchers in the Netherlands. Its central research theme is the nature and meaning of international standards in the field of human rights, their application and promotion in the national legal order, their interplay with national standards, and the international supervision of such application. The School of Human Rights Research Series only includes English titles that contribute to a better understanding of the different aspects of human rights.

Published titles within the Series:

1 Brigit C.A. Toebes, *The Right to Health as a Human Right in International Law*
ISBN 90-5095-057-4

2 Ineke Boerefijn, *The Reporting Procedure under the Covenant on Civil and Political Rights. Practice and Procedures of the Human Rights Committee*
ISBN 90-5095-074-4

3 Kitty Arambulo, *Strengthening the Supervision of the International Covenant on Economic, Social and Cultural Rights. Theoretical and Procedural Aspects*
ISBN 90-5095-058-2

4 Marlies Glasius, *Foreign Policy on Human Rights. Its Influence on Indonesia under Soeharto*
ISBN 90-5095-089-2

5 Cornelis D. de Jong, *The Freedom of Thought, Conscience and Religion or Belief in the United Nations (1946-1992)*
ISBN 90-5095-137-6

6 Heleen Bosma, *Freedom of Expression in England and under the ECHR: in Search of a Common Ground. A Foundation for the Application of the Human Rights Act 1998 in English Law*
ISBN 90-5095-136-8

7 Mielle Bulterman, *Human Rights in the External Relations of the European Union*
ISBN 90-5095-164-3

8 Esther M. van den Berg, *The Influence of Domestic NGOs on Dutch Human Rights Policy. Case Studies on South Africa,Namibia, Indonesia and East Timor*
ISBN 90-5095-159-7

9. Ian Seiderman, *Hierarchy in International Law: the Human Rights Dimension*
ISBN 90-5095-165-1

10. Anna Meijknecht, *Towards International Personality: the Position of Minorities and Indigenous Peoples in International Law*
ISBN 90-5095-166-X

11. Mohamed Eltayeb, *A Human Rights Approach to Combating Religious Persecution. Cases from Pakistan, Saudi Arabia and Sudan*
ISBN 90-5095-170-8

12. Machteld Boot, *Genocide, Crimes Against Humanity, War Crimes: Nullum Crimen Sine Lege and the Subject Matter Jurisdiction of the International Criminal Court*
ISBN 90-5095-216-X

13. Corinne Packer, *Using Human Rights to Change Tradition. Traditional Practices Harmful to Women's Reproductive Health in sub-Saharan Africa*
ISBN 90-5095-226-7

14. Theo R.G. van Banning, *The Human Right to Property*
ISBN 90-5095-203-8

15. Yvonne M. Donders, *Towards a Right to Cultural Identity?*
ISBN 90-5095-238-0

16. Göran K. Sluiter, *International Criminal Adjudication and the Collection of Evidence: Obligations of States*
ISBN 90-5095-227-5

17. Nicola Jägers, *Corporate Human Rights Obligations: in Search of Accountability*
ISBN 90-5095-240-2